THE LIFE AND TIMES OF

Theodore Roosevelt

OTHER BOOKS BY STEFAN LORANT:

I Was Hitler's Prisoner (1935)

Lincoln, His Life in Photographs (1941)

The New World (1946)

F.D.R., A Pictorial Biography (1950)

The Presidency (1951)

Lincoln, A Picture Story of His Life (1952)

The Life of Abraham Lincoln (1954)

THE LIFE AND TIMES OF

THEODORE ROOSEVELT

By

STEFAN LORANT

Doubleday & Company, Inc., Garden City, New York

Library of Congress Catalog Card Number 58–10732
Copyright © 1959 by Stefan Lorant
All Rights Reserved
Printed in the United States of America
First Edition
Designed by Stefan Lorant

For Louise

FOREWORD

Nowadays, if a man has a sharp pair of scissors, a pot of paste, and a wife willing to wade through endless volumes of old pictorial magazines, the obvious thing for him is to do a picture book. A theme is easily found, pictures are quickly collected, and placed on the layout sheets. A few short words serve to identify the subjects, and lo! the volume is finished.

This book was not made in such a way. It took seventeen years to complete it. I began it in the spring of 1942 and finished in the summer of 1959. Nothing in it was left to chance; every item has been thoroughly researched; the arrangements of the pictures followed a carefully thought out pattern.

To map out the chronology of Theodore Roosevelt's life alone took a full year. Collecting pictures and cartoons to illustrate his activities took five years. Sketching out and designing the rough layout took another year. Editing, revising the layout, and researching for additional material took two more years. Work on the first pictorial draft with the illustrations photostated in the size as they were to appear in the volume and pasted in position lasted a year. Another year and a half were spent with revisions and with the first draft of the captions and text.

After the emergence of the first outline, a fresh search was started for items which seemed important to clarify the story. For the next four years, library and private collections were combed, contemporary newspapers and magazines were read. I saw every issue of *Harper's Weekly,* every issue of *Leslie's,* every issue of *Puck, Life,* and *Judge* during Roosevelt's lifetime. Fifty thousand more items were added to the twenty thousand already collected; hundreds of cartoons were reproduced, thousands of photographs acquired. To write the final text and captions took another year and a half.

Problems over problems had to be solved. I attempted to create a certain pictorial style—using pictures as a writer uses words, or as a composer uses notes—and this was no simple matter. At times, the pictures would not fit in the story line; at other times, the story line would not lend itself to illustrations. It was not only a difficult, but often a frustrating undertaking. Here is one example of the vexatious problems: how was I to convey the passing of time? Photographs, in general, do not reveal the time they were taken. A house is a house, a man is a man—whatever year the image is fixed on photographic plates. To indicate the passing of time, I made use of two devices—one was to print full-page photographs of Theodore Roosevelt at frequent intervals, starting out as a baby and following his growth through adolescence, college years, political career, and presidential terms. The changes in his figure, the maturing of his face, show the passing of the years. Another device was to place the portraits of public figures next to that of his—both pictures taken in the same year. Thus, on one page, young Theodore is juxtaposed with Abraham Lincoln; on another page, he is shown as a young assemblyman next to a baby born in the same time—Franklin Delano Roosevelt.

I have attempted to stress the similarities in human existence—the illustration of the dead Civil War soldiers in 1863 is almost identical with the illustration of the dead soldiers on the battlefield of France in 1918. There was much that I could present, but there was still more that I was unable to include. A volume of this kind can never be comprehensive; in it one can only give a feeling, an impression of the times.

In my work, I had a staff of competent helpers, and I was assisted in the most generous way by public institutions and universities. In the research for pictorial material, Fayette Smith-Scheuch, Liljan Espenak, and Eileen Hughes were unsurpassed. They found pictures which I could never have discovered without their diligent work. Mrs. Hughes hunted down and photostated for me thousands of pages from old newspapers. In the text research and the mapping out of the chapters I was helped by Roger Linscott; his expert knowledge of the Roosevelt era saved me from many pitfalls.

Hermann Hagedorn, the moving spirit behind the Roosevelt Memorial Association, answered my many questions with patience; he watched the work's progress during the seventeen years, always encouraging, always a rock of strength. My gratitude to him is everlasting. The late Nora E. Cordingley, for two decades librarian of the Roosevelt Memorial Association sent me materials whenever I have asked for it. How I wish she might have seen the results!

Robert H. Haynes, curator of the Theodore Roosevelt Collection at the Harvard College Library, and his assistant, Audrey Hosford, answered my queries with unfailing courtesy.

During the seventeen years I have often called on Carl E. Stange of the Library of Congress, Josephine Cobb of the National Archives, and Grace Meyer of the Museum of the City of New York for pictures and information; my special thanks to them.

I am deeply indebted to the family of Theodore Roosevelt for their interest and generous help. I saw Mrs. Roosevelt before she died, and she talked frankly about her life and answered my many questions. She also gave me a number of family snapshots, and the Kaiser Wilhelm pictures which are reproduced in the book for the first time. Mrs. Alice Longworth, Roosevelt's eldest daughter, was most kind and helpful whenever I turned to her, as was Mrs. Ethel Derby, the youngest of the President's daughters.

The tremendous job of preparing the pages for the printer was done by Ruth M. Shair of Doubleday. She attended to the many details of the work with superb intelligence; without her this book could never have been done.

Seth M. Agnew, the head of my publisher's production department, and Virginia Muller supervised the cumbersome details of production. George Carnegie of Consolidated Lithographing Corporation kept a sharp eye on the printing. My grateful acknowledgment goes to them.

Mrs. Irene F. Weston, my secretary, typed the manuscript, counted every letter in the captions, and was with the book from the beginning to the end. Her council, advice, and criticism, though not always followed, was always wise.

STEFAN LORANT

Lenox, Massachusetts
August 17, 1959

CONTENTS

Part 4 PRIVATE CITIZEN

PICTURE CREDITS

All illustrations in the book are of contemporary origin; they were made at the time of the events, or shortly thereafter. This applies to cartoons as well. The source of drawings and cartoons from magazines like *Harper's Weekly, Leslie's Illustrated, Puck, Life, Judge* are usually noted in the captions. Photographs and illustrations not otherwise credited are from the author's collection.

The Theodore Roosevelt Memorial Association and the Theodore Roosevelt Collection in the Harvard College Library supplied me with pictures of the Roosevelt family, photographs, cartoons and letters of Roosevelt. T.R.'s childhood diaries and drawings, his picture letters, sporting calendar and war diaries are reproduced by courtesy of the Association.

Mrs. Theodore Roosevelt gave me her portrait as a seven-year-old girl, also snapshots which she had taken and pictures from her scrapbook on the 1896 presidential campaign. The Library of Congress supplied me with the many portraits of politicians and writers of the period, also photographs of the Spanish-American War. The National Archives was the source of the Round Robin telegram, also of photographs from World War I and pictures of Wilson's trip to Europe.

The drawings of early New York are from the contemporary volumes of Valentine's Manual.

The Museum of the City of New York supplied me with pictures of actresses, social figures at the Vanderbilt ball, photographs by Byron of the Mark Twain banquet, and the skyline photograph of New York in 1919. Brown Brothers have given me some of the pictures depicting America in 1905, the Russo-Japanese peace negotiations, Wall Street in 1907, and some of the photographs of Roosevelt in Europe and his homecoming; also the photograph of the Newett libel suit and T.R.'s portrait with Taft. Underwood and Underwood supplied the photographs of Roosevelt's speaking tour in 1902 and 1903 and his photograph on the Mayflower.

Eric Schaal is responsible for the picture of Roosevelt's bedroom in Sagamore Hill; I. S. Seidman for New York City street photographs in 1919; Princeton University for the photographs of Woodrow Wilson. The American Museum of Natural History allowed me to reproduce its diorama of the Bad Lands, the Kansas City Historical Society sent me the portrait of Senator Bristow.

To all individuals and institutions my heartfelt thanks for their courtesies.

Part 1:

YOUTH

CHAPTER 1

A NEW ROOSEVELT IS BORN

The transatlantic cable, at last completed, on August 5, 1858, sputtered its first message. Victoria, then in the twenty-second year of her long reign, sent her congratulations to President Buchanan, who cabled back a greeting. But even these high personages could not ward off the lampoons directed from the start at the cable. A parody of the official exchange found its way into the New York *Evening Post,* evading the eye of its impeccably mannered editor, William Cullen Bryant:

> "Dear Buchanan: I send this by my rope."
> "Dear Victoria: I send this to *Europe.*"

One hundred guns at Battery Park boomed a salute to the miracle, and brilliant plumes of fireworks emblazoned the skies above City Hall, incidentally setting fire to the cupola and roof. The celebration ended ignominiously—and so did the cable. After a few more spurts it went dead, and skeptics declared it a hoax.

In this year of marvels—1858—the young United States of America, with a population of almost thirty million scattered among thirty-two "sovereign" states, signed favorable trade treaties with Japan and China and opened a diplomatic mission in Bulgaria, Napoleon III stood ready to invade Italy, and Alexander II had just added a large slice of Chinese territory to "all the Russias." Frederick William IV was adjudged insane, and his brother William— paunchy and oblivious of the great destiny that Bismarck was forging for him —became regent of Prussia.

The Ottoman Empire, still swayed by Western ideas acquired during the Crimean War, abolished feudal land holdings. Mexico's liberal government, set up by Benito Juárez, was recognized by the United States within a year. The British Government, also undergoing modernization, dissolved the East India Company and transferred to the Crown the administration of India. The intrepid Livingstone was trekking through Africa for the third time. The Suez Canal Company was organized.

In the United States itself, the Missouri Compromise had been declared unconstitutional, the Dred Scott decision had affirmed that a slave was property and thus not eligible for citizenship, and Mrs. Stowe's *Uncle Tom's Cabin,* though published in 1852, was efficiently rousing antislavery feeling. Lincoln had already declared that "a house divided against itself cannot stand . . . this government cannot endure permanently half slave and half free" when, in August, he began his debates with Stephen A. Douglas. At Freeport, Illinois,

13

before 15,000 people, he asked the Little Giant the fateful question: "Can the people of a United States territory, in any lawful way . . . exclude slavery from its limits, prior to the formation of a state constitution?" Although only a senatorial seat was immediately involved, the whole country was listening to the debates, for Douglas aspired to the presidency. Answering honestly, Douglas lost his chance to carry the South: "I answered emphatically . . . that in my opinion the people of a territory can, by lawful means, exclude slavery from their limits prior to the formation of a state constitution. . . ."

On October 25, Senator William H. Seward, speaking at Rochester, declared: "It is an irrepressible conflict between opposing forces and it means that the United States must and will, sooner or later, become entirely a slave-holding nation or entirely a free-labor nation." That speech clarified the position of the four-year-old Republican party and uncovered the fundamental cause of the conflict: free vs. slave labor.

Two days later Theodore Roosevelt was born.

The Roosevelt (pronounced *Rose*-a-velt) family in America goes back to Klaes Martensen van Rosenvelt, who forsook his Dutch rose fields to settle in New Amsterdam in 1644. Theodore Roosevelt later described this ancestor as a " 'settler'—the euphemistic name for an immigrant who came over in the steerage of a sailing ship in the seventeenth century instead of a steerage of a steamer in the nineteenth century." Klaes and his wife landed on Manhattan Island only eighteen years after Peter Minuit had bought it from the Indians for the equivalent of twenty-four dollars. Their son Nicholas was the first Roosevelt born in America, in 1658. When New Amsterdam, on passing to England, became New York, van Rosenvelts gave way to Roosevelts and intermarried with Scotch, Irish, Welsh, Huguenot French, and Germans. T.R. shrewdly exploited this mixed ancestry: "Ah! So you're Scotch!" he would say to a Scotchman. "Well, I have Scotch blood, too!" There is a story that he automatically greeted a Jewish caller at the White House with these words: "Congratulations! I am partly Jewish, too!"

The Roosevelts became merchants, traders, bankers. Great-grandfather James, with others of the clan, served in the Continental Army during the Revolution. When the fighting was over, he opened a hardware store in Maiden Lane, which continued under the name "James Roosevelt and Son" until 1824. The "and Son" referred to Cornelius Van Schaack Roosevelt, who at his father's death inherited both a fortune and the knack of handling money. He invested in many businesses, bought real estate, engaged in importing, and became one of the richest men in New York, right behind Cornelius Vanderbilt, Alexander T. Stewart, and William B. Astor.

When T. R.'s father, the youngest of "the five horrid Roosevelt boys," was nineteen, he was carried off to Georgia by Hilborne West, a young Philadelphia doctor, who was his brother-in-law. West was in love with Susan Elliott, a beautiful Southern girl. Theodore met Susan's fifteen-year-old half sister, Martha Bulloch, and was charmed by her. Three years later—on December 2, 1853, they were married. The wedding was held at Roswell, the Bullochs' estate in Georgia. Ice was hauled from Savannah—more than two hundred miles distant—to make ice cream, served at the wedding reception. Cornelius Van Schaack Roosevelt gave the newlywed couple a brownstone house on East Twentieth Street, and there—a year later—their first child, Anna, was born. And there, at a quarter to eight on the evening of October 27, 1858—while carriages were hurrying New York society to hear Mlle. Piccolomini in Donizetti's opera, *The Daughter of the Regiment*—their second child, Theodore, first saw the light of the world.

New York was the city for shopping. At this time, it had a population of seven hundred and fifty thousand; its sister city, Brooklyn, had two hundred thousand inhabitants. Horse-drawn cars, charging a six-cent fare, ran on Second, Third, Sixth, Eighth, and Ninth avenues. More than four hundred stages—called "omnibuses"—rumbled through the paved streets, and ferries connected upper Manhattan with the city. The Battery and lower Broadway constituted the hub of the metropolis, featuring modish shops, theaters, hotels, and offices. The finest houses lined Union and Madison squares; only a few mansions ventured onto upper Fifth Avenue.

Lumberyards, brick and lime kilns, stables, warehouses, and distilleries crowded Chelsea—the West Twenties. The Thirties reeked with the stench of slaughterhouses, though the immigrant workmen did not seem to mind, judging by the shacks and shanties that sprouted near by. Upper New York City, a rocky wasteland, was overrun with pigs and goats. Hordes of squatters, many of them Irish immigrants, built makeshift hovels here, drank goat's milk, and fed themselves the flesh of their skinny pigs; their huts they heated with coal salvaged from the ashes dropped by the railroad engines. Harlem, a self-contained village, was an hour-and-twenty-minute ride by Third Avenue horsecar from lower Broadway. It was easier to take a boat for a visit to New York than going overland.

"The great characteristic of New York," asserted *Miller's Guide*, "is din and excitement—everything is done in a hurry—all is intense anxiety. It is especially noticeable in the thoroughfare of Broadway, where the noise and confusion caused by the incessant passing and repassing of some eighteen thousand vehicles a day render it a Babel scene of confusion." This already famed thoroughfare was paved as far north as Forty-fourth Street and was adorned with marble and stone buildings of "great architectural elegance."

In the shopping district, Stewart's Marble Palace, the largest dry-goods store in the world, had a stock worth $50,000,000. Brooks Brothers was the fashionable men's shop, and society flocked to Tiffany's for silverware and jewelry. The city's newest building, "a noble structure," five stories tall, housed the offices and presses of the New York *Times*. Among the many hotels, the best publicized were the Astor House, the Metropolitan ("with thirteen thousand yards of carpeting"), the St. Nicholas ("lighted by gas . . . As security against fire the entire establishment can be deluged with water in five minutes"), the Prescott House, the Fifth Avenue Hotel (soon to feature the first passenger elevator), and the Brevoort. Throughout the city, rooming houses catered to the less affluent, their rates ranging from three dollars to twelve and a half cents a week. Guides and guidebooks spoke of the inconveniences and possible perils of the twelve-and-a-half-cent variety.

The largest and most expensive restaurants were Taylor's, Thompson's, and Maillard's. Oysters were the most esteemed delicacy; for them New Yorkers spent $15,000 a day during the season. They were especially featured at Florence's, Kiefe's, and Delmonico's (which was soon to become the ultra-fashionable rendezvous).

New York in 1858 also had—despite three hundred churches—its bad side. Its "odors and . . . malaria might rival those of a medieval town." The Battery, at one time the city's fairest green, had become a noxious waste, and Castle Garden, where Jenny Lind sang in 1850, had been degraded into a brutally managed herding place for most immigrants into the United States. The notorious Five Points, though somewhat tidied up, still spilled its crime over the city. "Its neighbors were miserable tumble-down buildings swarming with squalid men, women, and children of every hue; liquor shops were everywhere, and nearly every house was a brothel." And well they might be: a housing investigation in 1856 had reported that five families—twenty persons—often lived in a room twelve feet square, with only two beds, no table or chair, and no partition or screen.

Newsboys "slept in boxes, alleys, doorways, under stairways, on hay barges, in the coldest weather . . . They were pushed about by the police, and there was not a single door in the city open to . . . them." This hideous state of affairs obtained until a handful of public-spirited citizens, among them Theodore Roosevelt, Senior, took heed of their sufferings, and established a lodging house for them.

Bettering the newsboy's lot was the beginning of a reform wave that in 1858 washed out of office Fernando Wood's corrupt administration, though Wood was shortly to play a return engagement on the Tammany ticket and outdo even himself in civic depravity. Daniel Tiemann, his successor for a term, promised more than he could fulfill. One of the few reforms he managed to carry through was the dispersal—temporarily—of fortunetellers and astrologers. Droves of these "witching beldames" (already, the glamorizing influence of the press was at work) were arrested, but it took a pitched battle at City Hall and the intervention of the Seventh Regiment to calm the resentment of their clients.

In 1858 the year-old Metropolitan Police, successors of the crooked Municipal Police, were striving heroically to enforce law and order in the rapidly expanding city. Central Park was being laid out, and St. Patrick's Cathedral was rising. In line with the general beautifying of the city, Potter's Field was moved to Ward's Island, at the intersection of the East and Harlem rivers. Staten Island was the scene of a riot which ended in the burning of the quarantine station; with the disappearance of this unpleasant spot the island became a fashionable summer resort. Crystal Palace, built to house the World's Fair of 1853, burned to the ground early in October, but not before it had demonstrated the effectiveness of its huge glass windows. And on the day after

Theodore Roosevelt was born, R. H. Macy opened his first store, on Sixth Avenue, one door from Fourteenth Street.

New York women assiduously followed the mode. Crinolines and hoop skirts, introduced by the Empress Eugénie, became the rage. They were not so universally accepted as at the court of Louis Napoléon: the United Brethren resolved that "the wearing of the crinoline is incompatible with a true Christian profession," and Bishop Russell decided that no woman in a hoop skirt could partake of the sacrament. Men, no more notable for their dress than now, were bearded luxuriantly: these were the days when "kissing a man without a mustache was like eating an egg without salt."

New Yorkers read the *Tribune* (Horace Greeley's paper, and the mouthpiece of the Republican party), the *Times,* the *Herald,* the *Sun,* the *World,* and the *Evening Post* for their daily news. If they hungered after sensationalism, they read the *Police Gazette.* The leading magazines were *Harper's Weekly, Frank Leslie's Illustrated Newspaper,* the *Ledger,* and *The Independent.* The poets America called her best were Bryant, Whittier, Longfellow, and Nathaniel P. Willis— all best-sellers. Longfellow's *Courtship of Miles Standish,* published in the very month Theodore Roosevelt was born, sold 25,000 copies the first week. The historians Bancroft, Motley, and Prescott were all at the height of their fame.

Theatrical entertainment—including oratory—was the chief diversion of literate New Yorkers. The drearily polished Edward Everett was accepted everywhere—even in London—as the modern Demosthenes. At the Academy of Music, performances of opera in Italian starred such artists as Patti and Brignoli. The theater cherished memories of Shakespeare readings by Fanny Kemble, and Edwin Booth had magnificently interpreted *Richard III.* Wallack's gave the customers their money's worth with a triple bill, *Marriage Lottery, Dying for Love,* and *Neptune's Defeat,* while Niblo's Garden played Dion Boucicault's *The Pope of Rome.* Laura Keene's Theater played *Our American Cousin* (the perennial that Lincoln was seeing the night of his assassination), with Mrs. Keene and Joseph Jefferson in the leads. New Yorkers also loved minstrel shows, and troupes like Bryant's and Wood's gave regular performances. Barnum's American Museum, though not a theater, presented its own curious fictions. "The Bearded Baby," the infant son of the "Bearded Lady," was Barnum's leading come-on.

"The Bearded Baby" grew up in obscurity, but not so another infant born at this time. Of little "Teedie" his grandmother wrote in a letter: "He is as sweet and pretty a young baby as I have ever seen," and he weighed eight and a half pounds. His mother viewed him in quite a different light. She thought him hideous—"a cross between a terrapin and Dr. Young."

FATHER

"My father was the best man I ever knew," wrote Theodore Roosevelt in his *Autobiography*. "He combined strength and courage with gentleness, tenderness, and great unselfishness." The elder Roosevelt, whose name his son inherited, came from one of the richest New York families. Born in 1831, he married when he was 24 and died at 46. He worked hard, but also had a zest for the lighter side of life, enjoyed dancing and driving a four-in-hand. He seemed to have unbounded energy, which came down to his son, made friends easily, was a warmhearted, affectionate man who loved people. He was one of the founders of the New York Orthopedic Hospital, the Museum of Natural History, the Metropolitan Museum of Art, the Children's Aid Society and the Newsboys' Lodging House. In politics he was a strong Lincoln Republican; in religion, a Presbyterian. "Take care of your morals first," he advised his son, "your health next, and finally your studies." And his son said: "I was fortunate enough in having a father whom I have always been able to regard as an ideal man."

MOTHER

Martha Bulloch, one of the most attractive girls of Savannah, was born in 1834. She came of an aristocratic Southern family. Married at 19, she left "Roswell," her spacious Georgia home, for New York, where she lived till her dying day. "Mittie" was a frail person of delicate health and with a mania for cleanliness. She had the habit of taking two baths in succession, one for cleaning, the other for rinsing. And she spread sheets over chairs so that no stranger should soil the fabrics. "Little Motherling," as her children adoringly called her, lacked money sense and she lacked a sense of time. She never learned to handle the household finances, nor was she able to keep her appointments. Her youngest daughter, Corinne, described her as one of the most beautiful women of New York City, a blue-eyed brunette with hair of a fine texture and a skin of "the purest and most delicate white, more moonlight-white than cream-white, and in the cheeks there was a coral, rather than a rose, tint." She died in her fiftieth year.

THE ROOM WHERE THEODORE ROOSEVELT WAS BORN

It was on the second story of a brownstone house at 33 East 20th Street. The narrow building had four floors. Theodore Roosevelt gave a good description of it in his *Autobiography*. "It was furnished in the canonical taste of the New York which George William Curtis described in the *Potiphar Papers*," he wrote. "The black haircloth furniture in the dining-room scratched the bare legs of the children when they sat on it. The middle room was a library, with tables, chairs, and bookcases of gloomy respectability. It was without windows, and so was available only at night. The front room, the parlor, seemed to us children to be a room of much splendor, but was open for general use only on Sunday evening or on rare occasions."

Theodore, the second child of his parents, was born at quarter of eight in the evening of October 27, 1858, as carriages took operagoers to the nearby Academy of Music, where the celebrated Mlle. Piccolomini was to appear in Donizetti's *The Daughter of the Regiment*. His maternal grandmother, who was present at his birth (as was his paternal grandmother), described the event to her daughter Susan, in Philadelphia: "No chloroform or any such thing was used, no instruments were necessary, consequently the dear little thing has no cuts or bruises about it." She further reported that her newborn grandchild "weighed 8 pounds and a half before it was dressed." Although to Grandmother Bulloch the little Theodore looked "as sweet and pretty a young baby as I have ever seen," to his mother he seemed hideous, "a cross between a terrapin and Dr. Young," a description probably made in jest.

AN AERIAL VIEW OF THE CITY OF NEW YORK IN THE YEAR OF 1858—AT THE

About three quarters of a million people lived in the city, a quarter of a million more than a decade before. Half of them were foreign-born, mainly Irish and German. In the description of *Harper's Weekly*, "the new magazine of civilization," New York was "a huge semi-barbarous metropolis . . . not well governed nor ill governed, but simply not governed at all—with filthy and unlighted streets—no practical or efficient security for either life or property—a police not worthy of the name—and

TIME WHEN THEODORE ROOSEVELT WAS BORN AT 33 EAST 20TH STREET

expenses steadily and enormously increasing." New York's northern boundary was at 51st Street. Above 42nd Street, except for villages like Yorkville, Harlem, Bloomingdale, or Manhattanville, there were mainly farms. Broadway, no longer a residential street, was lined with hotels, stores, theaters, while Fifth Avenue, now a paved thoroughfare, was studded with residences of the wealthy. The palaces of the rich and the shanties of the poor gave a dramatic contrast of life in the rapidly growing metropolis.

21

BROADWAY FROM EXCHANGE PLACE

The heart of the city. Here were the big stores like A. T. Stewart's Marble Palace, the largest dry-goods store in the world, here were the big hotels: the St. Nicholas, lighted by gas; the Astor House, which gave free lunches in its bar; the Metropolitan, advertising thirteen thousand yards of carpeting. Here were the fashionable eating places, the theaters and the dance halls. Here was Barnum's Museum, and here were the houses of ill repute, which lured the men of the city and those who came to New York to enjoy the excitement the budding metropolis had to offer.

CITY HALL

One of the few outstanding buildings of the city, but fallen into neglect. The dazzling pyrotechnics with which New York celebrated the laying of the Atlantic Cable, the very month Theodore Roosevelt was born, set the building on fire, burned up its cupola and half of its roof, and came near destroying the county clerk's office and unsettling the titles to half the property in the city. The contemporary diarist George Templeton Strong observed dryly: "The Hall presents a most bedraggled and crestfallen appearance, all singed and reeky and shorn of its headpiece."

MARKET SLIP with a view of the harbor, one of the busiest in the nation. From here hundreds of Yankee clipper ships set sail to all parts of the world.

JAMES STREET was like all other streets in New York at the time—badly paved, badly lit, with filth and garbage in the gutters, a vile stench in the air.

CUSTOM HOUSE

at the corner of Wall and Nassau streets, an example of the Greek Revival, a solid, firm, and imposing building. The artist pictured a scene of peace and serenity, but for a contemporary chronicler the signs of the times were not so rosy. "Our imminent pressing peril is neither foreign influence nor the slave power, but simple barbarism," said George Templeton Strong. "Life and property grow less and less secure. Law, legislature and judiciary are less respected. . . . Our civilization is decaying. We are in our decadence. An explosion and wrath must be at hand . . ."

BROADWAY FROM CHAPIN'S CHURCH

New York at this time, so one observer remarked, "possessed a large wealthy class whose members did not quite know how to get the most pleasure from their money. With singular poverty of imagination they proceeded on the assumption that to enjoy their wealth they must slavishly imitate the superficial features, and the defects rather than the merits of the life of the wealthy classes of Europe, instead of borrowing only its best traits, and adapting even these to their own surroundings. They put wealth above everything else, and therefore vulgarized their lives."

THE FIVE POINTS, the hide-out of the organized gangs—the Dead Rabbits, the Empire Club, Mike Walsh's Spartan Band—the lowest of the low.

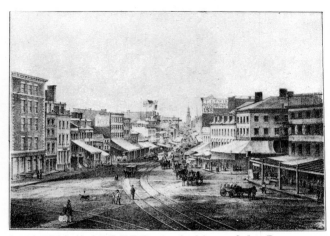

CHATHAM STREET, the habitat of the Bowery Boys, a tough gang of hoodlums. It was unsafe for a well-dressed citizen to venture into this neighborhood.

ONE DAY IN THE SUMMER OF 1860 the Roosevelt carriage took the infant Theodore uptown on Broadway to a photographer's studio. Broadway—according to a contemporary guidebook—was rendered "a Babel scene of confusion" by the incessant passing and repassing of some eighteen thousand vehicles. One surmises that eighteen-month-old Teedie was not disturbed by the din of the traffic—he liked movement and he liked excitement. The result of the trip was the portrait on the right, showing a demure little boy, dressed up in his best Sunday clothes—the first photographic likeness of America's twenty-sixth President.

24

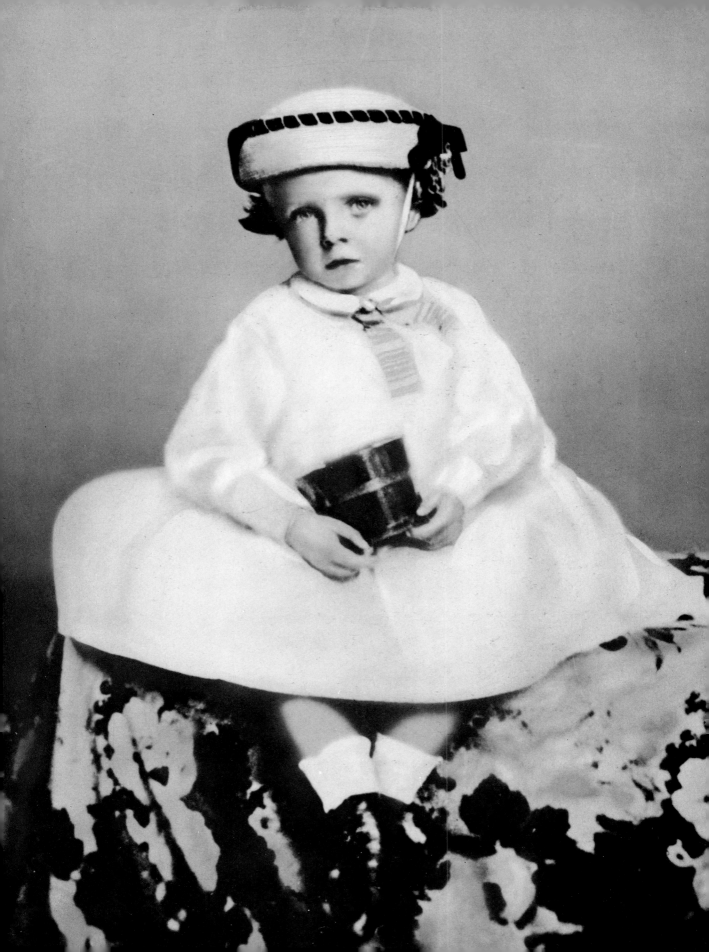

GRANDMOTHER
Martha Stewart Bulloch (1834–1884), second wife of James Stephens Bulloch, was first married to John Elliott, while Elliott's daughter was married to James Stephens Bulloch. When both Elliott and his daughter Hester died, Martha became Mrs. Bulloch.

GRANDFATHER
Cornelius Van Schaack Roosevelt (1794–1871) was one of the wealthiest men of New York. His ancestors, the Roosevelts, came from Holland in the 17th century. He ran the family export business in Maiden Lane, lived on Union Square at Broadway.

GRANDMOTHER
Margaret Barnhill (1799–1861), wife of Cornelius Van Schaack Roosevelt, came from Philadelphia of Irish ancestry. On Sundays her five sons and their families came to her sumptuous home on Broadway. At such times the Roosevelts spoke Dutch.

UNCLE
James Dunwody Bulloch, Theodore Roosevelt's beloved "Uncle Jimmy," was the son of James S. Bulloch by his first wife, Hester Amarintha Elliott. In the Civil War he served as an admiral in the Confederate Navy, and was the builder of the warship *Alabama*.

AUNT
Anna Bulloch lived with the Roosevelts until her marriage in 1866 to James K. Gracie. "She was as devoted to us children as was my mother herself, and we were equally devoted to her in return." She taught the children to read and to enjoy good books.

UNCLE
Irvine Stephens Bulloch, the son of James S. Bulloch by his second wife, Martha Stewart, served in the Confederate Navy as a midshipman on the *Alabama*. After the Civil War he lived in voluntary exile with his wife and children at Liverpool, England.

CHAPTER II

BROTHER FIGHTS BROTHER

Theodore Roosevelt was two and one half years old at the time of the opening of the Civil War. The firing on the flag at Fort Sumter split the nation, driving a wedge into every home and family.

The Roosevelt family was no exception. Theodore's father was an antislavery Republican, while his wife, his mother-in-law, his sister-in-law—all living under the same roof—were praying for the victory of the Southern arms. On one occasion Grandmother Bulloch exclaimed that she would "rather be buried in one common grave than live under the same government again." James and Irvine Bulloch, brother and half brother of Mrs. Roosevelt, fought under the Confederate colors, but the Roosevelt clan was solidly for the North. That there were debates and arguments about the war in the Roosevelt home, one can assume. In a letter to his wife, the father of Theodore Roosevelt wrote: "I wish we sympathized together on this question of so vital moment to our country." What Mittie answered, we do not know, but her son noted that his mother was until her dying day an "unreconstructed" Southerner.

The elder Theodore Roosevelt, a "Lincoln Republican," was wholeheartedly for the Union cause. Though he did not join the forces and—so his granddaughter recalls—even paid for a substitute, he worked assiduously for the success of the North. He joined the Loyal Publication Society, an organization which tried to enlighten the public about the reasons for the war; he was a member of the Union League Club's executive committee, which helped to raise and equip the first colored troops; he lobbied in Washington for the creation of an allotment commission, whose duty would be to induce the recruits to send their families some of their pay. And when the bill instituting the Allotment Commission was passed, and he was named as one of the three commissioners for New York, he traveled from camp to camp and urged the men to support their families with allotments. As the war moved toward its close, he was one of the organizers of the Protective War Claim Association, which collected back pay and pensions for the soldiers, and a founder of the Soldiers' Employment Bureau, which tried to find work for crippled veterans.

Why the elder Theodore failed to join the colors is not known. In 1861, when the war began, he was twenty-nine years old, healthy and able, fit to be a soldier. Why wouldn't he carry arms? It is interesting to speculate whether his son—disappointed in his father's failure—forced himself to make amends, whether this was the underlying reason for his rushing into the Spanish-American War and trying to prove a fearlessness whenever an occasion arose.

Obviously the children of the period took sides in the conflict, even though not old enough to understand it. Little Theodore was no exception. He was against the South, especially when he "had been wronged by maternal discipline during the day." At one such time he prayed "with loud fervor for the success of the Union army," pleading with "divine Providence to grind the Southern troops to powder." He raised his voice, making sure that his Southern mother would hear his prayers. Mittie was amused by it, but Father told his son never to do it again.

Theodore's aunt, Anna Bulloch, who lived with the family, relates an episode from the early months of the war. It is undoubtedly the first character sketch of Theodore Roosevelt. Teedie, as he was called by the family, was to be fitted for a Zouave shirt—it was fashionable for little boys to dress like the warring soldiers. Anna described the scene: "Yesterday Teedie was really excited when I said to him, 'Darling, I must fit this Zouave shirt or Mamma cannot have it made.'" At first Teedie would not have any part of it, but then he said: "Are me a soldier laddie?" And when his aunt assured him that he was, he willingly took his orders from "Captain" Anna.

The war caused little change in the Roosevelt home. The children—Anna, born in 1855, Theodore in 1858, Elliott in 1860, and Corinne in 1861—stayed in their New York home during the winter months, and in the summers they vacationed at Madison, New Jersey. And while North and South fought out their differences on the battlefields, the Roosevelt children lived a serene, peaceful, sheltered life.

Theodore was not a healthy child. He related in his *Autobiography:* "I was a sickly, delicate boy, suffered much from asthma, and frequently had to be taken away on trips to find a place where I could breathe. One of my memories is of my father walking up and down the room with me in his arms at night when I was a very small person, and of sitting up in bed gasping, with my father and mother trying to help me." Many are the family records speaking of his asthma attacks, stomach disorders, and other ailments.

The fighting went on—the year of 1861, the year of Bull Run, was followed by 1862, the year of the Peninsular Campaign, Antietam and Fredericksburg, and 1863, the year of Chancellorsville, Gettysburg, Vicksburg, and yet the end was not in sight.

A West Point cadet wrote after the fall of Sumter to his brother in Georgia: "This war is not going to be the 90 day affair that the papers and politicians are predicting. It is going to be fought to the bitter end. For your cause there is but one result. It must be lost. Your whole population is about eight millions while the North has 20 millions. Of your eight millions, three millions are slaves who may become an element of danger. You have no army, no navy, no treasury, and practically none of the manufactures and machine shops necessary for the support of large armies and for war on a large scale. You are but scattered agricultural communities, and you will be cut off from the rest of the world by blockade. Your cause is foredoomed to failure." What an accurate prophecy this was! But at that time very few in the South would have believed in its correctness.

President Lincoln, vacillating at first, was firm on the basic point—the preservation of the Union. He saw that the bedrock issue in the controversy was the survival of democracy itself. "We must settle this question now," he said, "whether, in a free government, the minority have the right to break up the government whenever they choose. If we fail, it will go far to prove the incapacity of the people to govern themselves."

He was searching for a capable war leader, and his search did not come to an end until General Ulysses S. Grant was made the head of the Army. By then three years had passed, three years of anxiety, of blood, of reverses. General George B. McClellan, who replaced old and infirm General Scott, the hero of the Mexican War, was himself relieved after his failure to pursue the Confederates at Antietam. General Ambrose Burnside had to go after the bloody defeat at Fredericksburg; General Joseph Hooker, who followed him and under whose command the battle of Chancellorsville was lost, had to resign to make way for General George Meade. It was after Gettysburg and Vicksburg that Lincoln turned to the man who was to bring the war to its victorious conclusion—General Grant. The new head of the Army moved with bulldog tenacity after Lee, fought stubbornly in the region called the Wilderness, then shifted strategy and attempted to force his way through the peninsula. He would fight it out before Richmond, he said, even "if it takes all summer." It took all summer and more.

Under Grant and Sherman the war took on a new look. The days of gentlemanliness were gone. "If the people raise a howl against my barbarity and cruelty, I will answer that war is war, and not popularity seeking," declared Sherman. He captured Atlanta, hunted out its citizenry, moved across Georgia to the sea, cutting a swath of devastation sixty miles wide and making the state "an example to rebels." By Christmas 1864 he had taken Savannah.

A few weeks before, Lincoln had been re-elected, defeating his Democratic opponent, who was none other than General McClellan. In his second inaugural the President held out a generous hand to the South; he was ready to forgive and forget. Spring came, the spring of 1865, and the end of the fighting.

On April 9, at Appomattox, General Lee surrendered his army to Grant, and Grant soberly advised his troops: "The rebels are our countrymen again; and the best sign of rejoicing after the victory will be to abstain from all demonstrations in the field."

Less than a week later, on April 14, John Wilkes Booth, the actor, shot Abraham Lincoln while the President was listening to a play at Ford's Theatre.

At that time Theodore Roosevelt was six and a half years old. He already knew how to read, and he enjoyed books, especially those which dealt with adventure. "I felt a great admiration for men who were fearless and who could hold their own in the world, and I had a great desire to be like them."

REPUBLICAN CONTENDERS for the presidential nomination, as pictured in *Harper's Weekly* in 1860. In the center, William H. Seward of New York, the favorite; top left, Edward Bates of Missouri; top right, Nathaniel P. Banks of Massachusetts.

Middle row: William Pennington of New Jersey, Salmon P. Chase and John McLean of Ohio, Simon Cameron of Pennsylvania. Bottom row: John C. Frémont, the party's candidate in 1856, John Bell of Tennessee, and old Cassius M. Clay of Kentucky.

THE CHOSEN CANDIDATE Abraham Lincoln, the little-known Illinois lawyer, became the Republicans' standard-bearer. The delegates in the Chicago convention believed it was better to choose a candidate whose opinions on the slavery issue were not so well known as those of William Seward, who spoke of it as an "irrepressible conflict." During the entire campaign Lincoln remained at his home in Springfield, where he received well-wishers and demonstrators (in the photograph Lincoln is standing at the doorway), but kept a tight lip on political issues.

THE COUNTRY ELECTED LINCOLN. As the Democratic party split into two factions—one supporting slavery, the other opposing it—and as each of these factions named a candidate (the pro-slavery Democrats lining up behind John C. Breckinridge, the anti-slavery faction behind Stephen A. Douglas), Abraham Lincoln, the Republican contender, won the election though his popular vote was less than the combined strength of his opponents. He polled 1,866,452 votes against Douglas's 1,376,957, Breckinridge's 849,781, and John Bell's (the candidate of the Constitutional Union party) 588,879. The electoral vote gave Lincoln 180, Breckinridge 72, Bell 39, and Douglas 12.

The figures showed that the majority of the country was for the preservation of the Union and for keeping the peace. John C. Breckinridge, the only pro-slavery and secession candidate, was supported by less than one fifth of the electorate.

THE SECEDED STATES CHOSE DAVIS. After Lincoln's election seven states seceded from the Union, formed a confederacy, and named Jefferson Davis as its first President. Davis, born in Kentucky, began his education in a Roman Catholic seminary, although he was not a Catholic himself. After studying at Transylvania University, he entered West Point, from where he was graduated in 1828. He fought in the Mexican War under Zachary Taylor, whose daughter became his first wife; then served in Congress both as congressman and senator from Mississippi. In 1853 he became Secretary of War in President Pierce's Cabinet, and in 1857 he re-entered the Senate. Following the admission of California and the failure to extend the Missouri Compromise line, Davis was one of those Southern politicians who believed that secession was the only answer. He desired a Southern nation committed to the preservation of the Southern social order—a nation within the Union.

IN HIS FIRST INAUGURAL ADDRESS before the unfinished Capitol, Abraham Lincoln appealed to the South and pleaded for the preservation of the Union. "A husband and wife may be divorced and go out of the presence and beyond the reach of each other; but the different parts of our country cannot do this," he said on March 4, 1861. "In *your* hands, my dissatisfied fellow countrymen, and not in *mine,* is the momentous issue of the Civil War. The government will not assail you." But the South would no longer listen to sensible arguments. The seceded states were ready to fight with arms for their rights.

THE BEGINNING OF THE CIVIL WAR

At 4:30 in the morning of April 12, 1861, the Confederate batteries in Charleston Harbor opened fire on Fort Sumter. They were the first shots in the Civil War—a war which was to last four years.

Ever since that April day people have debated why North and South could not settle their differences through peaceful means. Ever since then people have argued about the reasons that led America to such frightful bloodletting. The immediate cause for the war was slavery, but that issue alone would not have erupted into armed conflict. There were other important underlying factors. (1) North and South had grown into sections of widely disparate social, economic, and political character. While the South was predominantly agricultural, the North had become urban and industrialized. With industrialization had come high tariffs and centralized banking—each an anathema to the South. (2) The Northern population had outgrown that of the South, as had Northern political representation in Congress.

(3) Southerners were apprehensive that in the future the North would dictate the nation's policies, regardless of Southern interests. (4) Southern men believed the Union was a conglomeration of states; as each state was supreme in its own right, each had the right to secede from the Union. (5) The masses of immigrants coming from Europe gravitated to the cities in the North, avoiding the South and its slaveholding society. They were hesitant to settle in places where the scions of old families ruled in a paternalistic way. Thus progress in the South was retarded. (6) The abolitionist agitation in the North caused a severe financial loss to Southern slaveholders; each fugitive slave meant a loss of investment. Southern extremists not only asked for a strict execution of the Fugitive Slave Law, but demanded the extension of the slavery line. On the other hand, extremists in the North pleaded for the total abolition of slavery.

The discord between the factions was fostered by hotheaded politicians, by emotional fanatics, until there was no way to bring about a peaceful solution.

THE FLOWER OF THE NATION COVERED THE BATTLEFIELDS

This is Hagerstown Pike after the battle of Antietam. It is September 1862, the second year of the war. Thus far, in the main, eastern theater, the North had suffered defeat after defeat. The battle of Bull Run at the opening of the hostilities showed how poorly the North was prepared. Its troops were green, untrained, their number small. Lincoln had asked the states for only 75,000 volunteers. The head of the Army was Winfield Scott, hero of the Mexican War, a man in his seventies. When he resigned his post, young and ambitious George B. McClellan took his place and began in earnest to weld a fighting force. But it took him almost a full year—much to the desperation of Lincoln and the Republican press—before he was ready to move into battle. In the spring of 1862 he took the Army up the peninsula in an effort to capture Richmond. But when his outposts were only five miles from the capital of the Confederacy, he was checked. Compelled to give up his position, he retreated, fighting a series of savage engagements—the Seven Days' Battles. To the failure of the Peninsular campaign was added General John Pope's defeat in the second battle of Manassas. Pope was relieved, and once more Lincoln asked General McClellan to head the troops. Under his leadership the battle of Antietam was fought and won. But when vainglorious McClellan was hesitant to take up the pursuit of Lee, Lincoln dismissed him. The President would no longer keep a general who had "the slows." He wanted a man of action.

THE SUNKEN ROAD AT FREDERICKSBURG AND ITS TOLL

In the first week of November 1862 President Lincoln replaced McClellan with General Ambrose E. Burnside, the man whose side whiskers added a new word to our vocabulary. Burnside attacked Fredericksburg on December 13. It was a mad attempt of a frontal charge. The Confederates, who had had time to entrench themselves in the city, mowed down the attackers as a reaper levels cornstalks. By nightfall Burnside's losses mounted to 12,000 men. In his tent the general buried his head in his hands, crying: "Oh! Oh, those men! Oh, those men!" It was one of the worst reverses the North suffered. Lincoln confided to a friend: "We are on the brink of destruction. It appears to me the Almighty is against us and I can hardly see a ray of hope." Burnside's own officers implored the President not to leave the army under the general's command. At first Lincoln was hesitant, but when Burnside and his officers began to fight among themselves, the President had no choice but to remove him. In his stead he appointed General Joseph Hooker, an aggressive and brave officer, prone to boasting and bragging. "Fighting Joe" Hooker had no more luck with Lee than had Burnside. At the battle of Chancellorsville he suffered a disastrous defeat. Once more Lincoln had to make a change. He removed Hooker from his command on June 28, 1863, and replaced him with General George Gordon Meade, "the old snapping turtle." A week later Meade led the North into the battle of Gettysburg.

ONE FOUGHT FOR THE NORTH, THE OTHER FOR THE SOUTH

Now they lie peacefully on the battlefield of Gettysburg, the little Pennsylvania village where, on the first three days of July 1863, one of the greatest battles of the war was waged. The Union forced Lee to retreat into Virginia; never again could his Army cross the border. At about the same time General Grant captured Vicksburg, sealing off the Confederacy beyond the Mississippi. These two major victories turned the tide of the war for the Union.

A few months later President Lincoln left Washington to dedicate the National Cemetery at Gettysburg. The committee for the ceremonies did not believe that Lincoln would be able to make the main oration, so he was asked only to make some "dedicatory remarks." The President spoke briefly, his speech over almost before it began. But his words have remained alive and will last as long as the English language. "The world will little note, nor long remember what we say here," said Lincoln, "but it can never forget what they did here. It is for us the living, rather, to be dedicated here to the unfinished work which they who fought here have thus far so nobly advanced. It is rather for us to be here dedicated to the great task remaining before us. . . ." And he solemnly declared "that these dead shall not have died in vain—that this nation, under God, shall have a new birth of freedom—and that government of the people, by the people, for the people, shall not perish from the earth."

FIVE-YEAR-OLD

odore Roosevelt as he looked in the
of 1863, about the time President
aham Lincoln spoke at Gettysburg.

Y-TWO-YEAR-OLD

ham Lincoln, photographed in No-
er 1863, a few days before he jour-
to Gettysburg to deliver his address.

GENERAL GRANT AND HIS STAFF at Massaponax Church, Virginia, on May 21, 1864. Sitting on the bench in the center, from left to right, are General Horace Porter reading a newspaper, General Grant, General Rawlins, and Ely S. Parker. On the far end of the left bench is General Meade, under whom the battle of Gettysburg was fought.

It is the last day of "trench warfare" at Spotsylvania. The Union had been struggling for the last two weeks, suffering tremendous casualties. Since the opening of the Wilderness campaign, Grant had lost 55,000 men, almost as many as Lee's entire Army. But with bull-dog tenacity he pushed on. His strategy was rudimentary—to harass and attack Lee until the Confederacy was depleted. President Lincoln approved the general's plans and did not interfere with him. Two months before the above photograph was taken, Congress had revived the rank of Lieutenant General of the Army, a rank held previously only by George Washington, and Lincoln conferred the title upon Grant. In him the President had at last found his general. "He is my man and I am his until the end of the war," he said.

GENERAL SHERMAN AND HIS STAFF. While General Grant was hammering against the Confederate capital, General William Tecumseh Sherman was pushing a Southern army back to Atlanta in Georgia. At the beginning of September he occupied the city, requiring "that all the citizens and families resident in Atlanta should go away. . . . I resolved to make Atlanta a pure military garrison or depot, with no civil population to influence military measures." From Atlanta, Sherman began his march to the sea, leaving a wide swath of destruction as his men moved through the country. Sherman's "bummers" lived on the land, looted, burned and destroyed property as they marched along. "War is hell," Sherman's well-known maxim, was proved to the full. By December 22, 1864, his army was at the shore of the Atlantic Ocean. "I beg to present you as a Christmas gift the city of Savannah," Sherman wired to President Lincoln. And Lincoln thanked him: "Now, the undertaking being a success, the honor is all yours." Sherman's success cut into the last remaining Southern railroad arteries. Time was running out for the Confederate States.

CHARLESTON WAS DESTROYED. Only a rubble of stones and masonry remained of this beautiful city after its evacuation by the troops.

RICHMOND IN RUINS. After the Confederate government left the capital, orders were given to destroy the city's arsenals, warehouses, and bridges.

THE END OF THE WAR. General Robert E. Lee on April 9, 1865, signs the surrender terms at Appomattox. General Grant is sitting at center table.

ENJOYING FREEDOM. Great numbers of former slaves roamed the countryside, going from one place to the other, exhilarated by their new-found life.

WITH MALICE TOWARD NONE . . .

The end of the fighting was in sight. It had been a cruel war, with more than 750,000 casualties. The best of the young men lay in their graves. The Union was saved. Yet when the guns grew silent, new problems arose—puzzling, perplexing, and difficult ones. The foremost of these—one which had to be answered immediately—was how the two antagonistic sections could live in peace. Lincoln told a Southerner: "I love the Southern people more than they love me. My desire is to restore the Union. I do not intend to hurt the hair of the head of a single man in the South if it can possibly be avoided."

On a somber and drizzly day in March 1865, with a cold gusty wind blowing, President Lincoln stood before the now-finished Capitol in Washington and spoke the immortal lines of his second inaugural: "With malice toward none; with charity for all; with firmness in the right, as God gives us to see the right, let us strive on to finish the work we are in; to bind up the nation's wounds; to care for him who shall have borne the battle, and for his widow and his orphan, to do all which may achieve and cherish a just and a lasting peace, among ourselves, and with all nations."

COLN DELIVERS
SECOND INAUGURAL

THE SCENE IN FORD'S THEATRE ON APRIL 14, 1865

The war was over, the Union saved. Richmond had fallen on April 3, the Confederacy surrendered on April 9. A day after Richmond's fall the unguarded President visited the captured Confederate capital. To General Weitzel's question about the treatment of the conquered people, Lincoln answered: "If I were in your place, I'd let 'em up easy, let 'em up easy." On April 14 the President went to Ford's Theatre in Washington. And while he was listening to the comedy, *Our American Cousin,* John Wilkes Booth, a member of the celebrated theatrical family, shot him with a small derringer. Then, jumping from the presidential box to the stage, the assassin shouted melodramatically: "The South is avenged!" At the back door his horse was waiting; Booth mounted it and fled. During the night Lincoln struggled with death; at 7:22 A.M. he breathed his last. Not until April 26 was his murderer discovered hiding in a Virginia barn. There he was cornered by soldiers and shot.

THEODORE ROOSEVELT WATCHES ABRAHAM LINCOLN'S FUNERAL

From the second-story window of his grandfather's house in New York, six-and-a-half-year-old Theodore Roosevelt and his brother Elliott (the father of Eleanor Roosevelt) are looking at the funeral procession as it passes by the house on the corner of Union Square and Broadway. The city was in deep mourning on that April 25, 1865, when the remains of the President—after having lain in state at the City Hall—were taken to the funeral train, which was to carry him over a long and circuitous route to Springfield, Illinois. Edith Carow, Roosevelt's second wife, who was a childhood friend of Theodore, remembered that she, too, went to watch the funeral from Cornelius Van Schaack Roosevelt's residence. But, frightened by all the black draperies on the streets, on the lampposts, and the houses, she began to cry. Whereupon the two boys, annoyed by the childish behavior, locked her up in a back room, and thus little Edith Kermit Carow never did see Lincoln's funeral.

43

CHAPTER III

THE BUDDING METROPOLIS

The New York where young "Teedie" Roosevelt spent his early years was a city in transition. It was part of the rapidly changing America which was moving away from an individualized, largely rural society to an urban and interdependent one. The period after the war was an era of contrasts, and nowhere in the United States were these contrasts more marked than in the crowded streets surrounding the Roosevelt household. New York was a city of extreme wealth and wretched poverty, of high culture and sordid vice, of liberal philanthropy and shocking greed.

For all its showy splendor, New York offered its residents a life of considerable discomfort—and for those in the lower income brackets, great suffering. The main thoroughfares suffered from congestion. At the close of the war New York had about 1,400 hackney coaches, seven omnibus lines with 300 vehicles, and no less than sixteen separate horse railway lines with some 800 cars and 8,000 horses. Traffic moved at a snail's pace; fast and easy transportation was still a dream of the future, as was suburban development.

The state of the streets was abominable. Some of them were paved with stone blocks, which gave carriage and horsecar riders a wretched, bumping ride, as debilitating to the vehicles as it was to the passengers' nerves. Cobblestones, still in use, were equally uncomfortable and, like stone blocks, accumulated an odorous filth in their cracks.

For New York's slum dwellers—and there were more than 100,000 of them at the close of the Civil War—urban living meant little but squalor, disease and poverty. The city's cellar population alone totaled some 20,000 persons; nowhere else in the world did so many people live so closely together. The tenements of the poor had no adequate heating; most of the buildings lacked sewer connections. Epidemics—cholera, malaria, and others—came with great regularity. The death toll from smallpox, typhoid, and scarlet fever reached startling proportions.

For prosperous families, like the Roosevelts, life was not too bad. But their homes were uncomfortable and were tastelessly furnished. Wax flowers and potted plants—particularly rubber plants—were universal in well-appointed parlors, and blue glass windowpanes were considered not only beautiful, but also an antidote for rheumatism. A decorative whim at this time was the tying of huge satin ribbons around piano legs, while the rest of the piano would be smothered with draped scarves of Oriental design.

Young ladies were proud of their plush autograph books, filled with poems and sentiments. The gilt-edged pages were full of good wishes like this:

45

"WHEN JOHNNY COMES MARCHING HOME"

The victorious Union troops parade after the war, in May 1865, on Washington's Pennsylvania Avenue.

> In the tempest of life, when you need an umbrella
> May it be upheld by a handsome young feller.

Or a more daring member of the young set might offer:

> You ask me to write something original
> But I don't know where to begin,
> For there's nothing original in me,
> Excepting original sin.

It became inevitable that the increasing urbanization and industrialization would bring new techniques to cope with the problems of congested living. One of the most striking was the huge increase in the manufacture of ready-made clothing for everyday wear—a revolutionary innovation. Another was the growth of the canned-food business and the establishment of large commercial bakeries. Lives of the housewives were made still easier by the new washing and sewing machines, both of which sold in enormous numbers.

A development of the decade was the apartment house, called the "French flat," marking a radical departure in American urban living. Until then, people with means had lived either in single residences or in rooming houses. The "French flat," like similar apartments in Paris, offered the tenant a private and self-sufficient suite of rooms, with bath and kitchen and elevator service. The monthly rents were high—$100 to $150 was not unusual—thus only the well-to-do could afford the luxury. But New York had many well-to-do. In 1874, four years after the erection of the first apartment building, some 3,000 families were enjoying the new and improved way of life.

The buildings of the city grew higher—thanks to the developments in passenger elevators. While formerly a house with three or four stories was considered a tall one, now ten- and twelve-story buildings were erected—the beginning of Manhattan's sky line.

In dress, as in most other things, the city set the pace, although Paris remained the original source of fashion. The crinoline skirt, popularized by Napoleon III's Empress Eugénie, became standard wear in New York by the close of the Civil War, as did colored stockings, Empire bonnets, and gold dust sprinkled on the hair for formal occasions. Men's clothing remained solemn and restrained, with dark suits universal for both daytime and evening wear. The ungainly stovepipe hat continued to crown men's heads at formal functions; and among the more prosperous, a crease in the trousers was looked down upon as evidence that the suit was ready-made.

Men's furnishings for everyday wear included stiff-fronted shirts that buttoned in the back, "choker" collars, bow ties, and embroidered suspenders. For both men and women, nightgowns were standard bed wear, pajamas being considered the affectation of a small and effete minority. Long underwear was worn in all seasons. In addition to his many other clothing accessories, the well-appointed male carried a handsome gold or silver jeweled toothpick on the end of his watch chain.

For the average citizen, life was often as somber as men's attire. Blue laws

46

were numerous, Sunday was observed strictly, and the virtue of young women was protected by a strict code of proprieties. Among the middle class, even in the urban centers, drinking was often frowned upon. Wine was for ceremonial occasions only; hard liquors were not for consumption in the home, and certainly not in mixed company. Divorces were still out of the ordinary—in 1870 the divorce rate was less than one in 3,000 marriages.

The somberness of middle-class life was by no means all of urban America, for the new rich and the more frivolously fashionable sets saw to it that gaiety was not excluded from the daily round. Though many of the oldest New York families looked on with disdain, the theaters, music halls, and race tracks did a thriving business. During the year following the close of the war, Manhattan's theaters took in gross receipts of more than $2,000,000. The opera drew large, glittering audiences of jeweled and ostentatiously dressed *nouveaux*. Abetted by the heavy influx of German immigrants, beer gardens sprang up all over New York. And the concert saloon—a favorite target of moralists—offered drinking, gay music, and the sight of attractive young ladies at a price which the customers could afford.

The growth of urbanization brought with it the emergence of summer resorts, where prosperous families retreated during the hot weather. At Newport, Rhode Island, New Yorkers who found the hotel occupants too unselective began to build great villas that soon made that resort one of the most extravagant in the world. To the south of New York, Long Branch, New Jersey, staked luxurious claims as a place of seaside recreation for fashionable society.

Naturally, only a small part of the population had the time or the money to enjoy resort life. The average worker had no vacations; even the idea of making Saturday a half holiday was not generally accepted by employers until nearly the close of the century. So most New Yorkers had to enjoy simpler pleasures close to home. In winter there was skating at Central Park, tobogganing on the huge slide at the old Polo Grounds on upper Fifth Avenue, and sleighing for every family that could afford to keep a horse.

At other seasons of the year rowing, archery, and bicycling were popular, while croquet became a tremendous fad at homes with the necessary lawn space. Baseball was still in its infancy, but already it was winning out over cricket as the national game. Among the city's numerous fraternal organizations, rifle teams were highly popular, the sport being pursued at boisterous Sunday outings in the country.

New York, the bustling, fast-growing, hurriedly improving metropolis, was the background for Teedie's growing years. He was a city boy, through and through. As he was not a strong child—still suffering from asthma—he was not able to play and roam around with other children. Thus he turned into a bookish boy. He read incessantly, a habit which he kept throughout his lifetime.

He also had an "instinctive interest in natural history," and began to write a natural history of his own, "written down in blank books in simplified spelling, wholly unpremeditated and unscientific." At the age of eight he was busy collecting animals, birds, insects, and he always had a pet mouse in his room. He had a yearning for nature and its mysteries, a fascination for the outdoors.

THE ROOSEVELT'S HOME ON 20TH STREET. On the first floor of the building were the parlor and the library, both opening from the hall. The library had no windows and, as Theodore Roosevelt remembered it, "was available only at night." All the rooms were furnished in the fashion of the day with ornate, black haircloth furniture.

THE DINING ROOM ran across the full width of the house. Roosevelt recalled later that the chairs scratched his legs when he was a child.

THE PARLOR of the house, with a piano and gilded mirrors, was used only when visitors came or when the family gathered together for Sunday dinner.

EIGHT YEARS OLD, sickly and delicate, precocious, constantly fighting asthma attacks. An avid reader, he became a natural-history fan at an early age. "I remember distinctly the first day that I started on my career as a zoologist," he recalled in his *Autobiography*. "I was walking up Broadway and as I passed the market to which I used sometimes to be sent before breakfast to get strawberries, I suddenly saw a dead seal laid out on a slab of wood. That seal filled me with every possible feeling of romance and adventure. . . . I measured it, and I recall that, not having a tape measure, I had to do my best to get its girth with a folding pocket foot-rule, a difficult undertaking. . . . I had vague aspirations of in some way or another owning and preserving that seal, but they never got beyond the purely formless stage. I think, however, I did get the seal's skull, and with two of my cousins promptly started what we ambitiously called the 'Roosevelt Museum of Natural History.'"

AT FIFTH AVENU

WAITING FOR THE PAWNSHOP TO OPEN. A large mass of poverty-stricken people were living in overcrowded and unhealthy tenement houses. The ships brought three to four hundred thousand immigrants—mostly Irish and Germans—to America each year. Their lot was not an enviable one. Work was hard, hours long, wages low, opportunities not so rosy and abundant as they had seemed from the other side of the ocean. Yet the men came, at times with nothing more than a bundle on their backs and a hope for the future.

AFTER THE MATINEE New York with its steady influx of sight-seers was a "good show town." Wallack's Theatre was a favorite; Augustin Daly, a former journalist, offered glittering productions with stars like Ada Rehan or John Drew. Minstrel and variety shows usually drew large audiences—mostly males. Some fifteen principal theaters competed for public favor. There were excellent stock companies and great stars. Tickets were not expensive. Orchestra stalls sold for one dollar, while fifty cents admitted one to the parquet.

SIXTH AVENUE

THE BROKEN LEG ON BROADWAY. It was estimated that 8,000 horses were daily on the streets of New York, pulling railway cars. Traffic moved at snail's pace. The streets were slippery with filth, the poor pavement was a hazard for the animals. To stop the abuse given these horses, Henry Bergh organized a society for the protection of animals. In 1866 he succeeded in having the first specific law passed against persons who "maliciously kill, maim, wound, injure, torture or cruelly beat any horse, . . . or other animal. . . ."

IN UNION SQUARE
On the streets of New York paraded well-dressed people who imported their clothes from Europe. The fashionable females dressed like their Parisian counterparts, while the male of New York society imitated the upper class of England. The "shoddy aristocracy"—the newly rich who had gained affluence because of the war —played a prominent part in the life of the city, trying by an ostentatious display of luxurious living, expensive clothes and jewels to gain recognition from the city's established social leaders.

TRIAL RUN ON THE NEW YORK "ELEVATED" IN 1867

Charles Harvey, the man in frock coat and silk hat, piloting the first car of his elevated railroad on a trial half-mile section on Greenwich Street, was one of the most remarkable men of his age. Before he provided Manhattan with its chief mode of passenger transportation, he was known as the builder of the Soo Canal. Only twenty-three years old, he conceived the idea of building a canal between Lake Superior and the other lakes. This one-mile canal made a thousand-mile waterway possible—from Lake Superior right through to the Atlantic. Men of great importance believed that such an idea bordered on lunacy. Henry Clay declared that it was a pipe dream, "a project beyond the remotest settlement of the United States if not the moon," but Harvey could not be discouraged. He sold the idea to a few hardheaded Yankee businessmen, and they made him the chief engineer of the company. Digging began in the summer of 1853 and went on during the freezing temperatures of the winter months. The diggers rebelled, epidemics decimated their ranks. Yet Harvey drove them on. In two years the work was completed and the first boat went through the locks. The Soo Canal made the United States the first ironmaking country of the world. Ore from the Menominee, the Marquette, the Gogebic and Mesabi ranges could be transported to Pittsburgh, making iron, then steel, cheaper, which in turn helped to build America in a hurry—a tremendous contribution for which Charles Harvey was greatly responsible. It is strange that, in spite of these achievements, his name is hardly known today.

BROADWAY ON A RAINY DAY. The city was ugly, uncomfortable, and unhealthy, a breeding ground of malaria and other infectious diseases. It was badly paved. The New York *Tribune* lamented that gutters of the streets were "stopped up and were creamy with green stagnant matter that looked like vomit seasoned with giblets of rotten meat."

53

CROSS SECTION OF A TENEMENT. More than half a million New Yorkers lived in 15,000 tenement houses. In one block on Avenue B, near the East River, fifty-two tenement houses were occupied by no less than 2,356 people. On the average, ten families lived in each house, but "some swarmed

with two or three hundred persons." The filth was unbelievable, health conditions frightful, infant mortality enormous. "The dwellers in the tenement adjoining ours," wrote an irate observer, "who had lived there 28 years, had had 11 children born to them, of whom two pale boys were the survivors."

THE FAMILY RELAXES
The middle-class New Yorker usually stayed at home in the evening and played parlor games. The homes of the more well-to-do were large but uncomfortable. Ugly and elaborate pieces of furniture, heavy curtains and draperies made the rooms solemn and pompous. With their bric-a-brac and sentimental groups of Rogers statuary, parlors often resembled cheap china shops rather than gracious rooms designed for family living.

IMMIGRANTS ARRIVE
It was at Castle Garden that the men and women who came to America were processed by immigration authorities. Originally Castle Garden was a fort, built in 1811 to defend New York. At that time its name was Fort Clinton. Conveyed to the federal government in 1824, it became a place where social functions were held. Between 1855 and 1890 the garden was a clearing station for immigrants.

INDIGNATION MEETING
The blue laws against serving alcoholic beverages on Sunday were strictly observed. The Germans and the Irish fought these laws as unfair. The former were especially wrought up as they could not bring their families to the *Biergartens* on Sundays. Indignation meetings were held in bars, and speakers harangued against the rich, who could have liquor in their clubs and spacious homes while the unhappy poor had to get along without it.

A CONCERT IN CENTRAL PARK. It took ten years of toil and almost ten million dollars before the barren and rocky wilderness of more than eight hundred acres between 59th and 125th streets was transformed into a beautiful pleasure park. Designed by Frederick Law Olmstead and Calvert Vaux, and virtually completed at the end of the Civil War, Central Park was the common meeting ground of New Yorkers. Here class barriers were down, here rich and poor alike were welcome. In the winter it was fashionable to skate on the pond, in summer to promenade on the Mall. One could watch the passing of the fast trotting horses drawing buggies, broughams, landaus. And if one's means were moderate, one could still rent an open dray and drive around the paths. In the warm months promenade concerts were given in the pagoda-like music pavilion, to which the wealthy came in carriages and listened from the terrace of the nearby Casino, where they could enjoy a meal at the same time. Others heard the concerts from benches, from rented canopied rustic chairs, or simply by sitting on the grass. On occasion, the attendance at these concerts ran into astonishing figures. It was recorded that as many as forty or fifty thousand people were listening to the music. When this was the case the horsecar lines, which financed the venture, raked in a handsome profit on their musical investment.

THE OPULENT [ ]
of Adah Isaacs Menk[ ]
admired by men of a[ ]
Prodigal in love a[ ]
friendships, she w[ ]
hearts of prominen[ ]
among them Ale[ ]
Dumas the elder a[ ]
poet Swinburne. [ ]
Menken" startled Ne[ ]
when she appeared[ ]
play *Mazeppa* on ho[ ]
clad only in flesh-[ ]
tights. Her scanty c[ ]
was the thrill of th[ ]
Grandfather was still[ ]
about it fifty year[ ]

SEX COMES TO AMERICA

THE LYDIA THOMPSON GIRLS were the sensation of New York in 1868. When *The Black Crook*, a musical extravaganza which exhibited the female form in close-fitting tights, turned into an enormous success, girl shows became the vogue. Audiences filled Niblo's Theatre where *The Black Crook* was played for sixteen consecutive months during 1866 and 1867. The following year the English Lydia Thompson brought some British girls to New York, who were not only shapely but radiantly blond. And this in a city of brunettes. The Lydia Thompson girls showed America that girls from the Old Country had everything the American girls had, and even a little bit more. Overnight they

became the toast of the town. The main topic of conversation in oyster houses, in clubs, and in offices was the dazzling blondes and their curves. The New York *Times* was alarmed. In its opinion the "whole blonde business" was a "licentious exhibition" which could only lead to the demoralization of the theater. "If this style of art is permitted to ride rampant much longer, it must eventually make extinct, as it is now doing, the old school of artists, and apply the torch to the dramatic pile," said the *Times*. The Lydia Thompson troupe were the first real show girls; they brought sex to the American stage—a commodity which has shown its endurance and which has remained with us even to the present day.

ANDREW JOHNSON'S

RECONSTRUCTION,

AND

HOW IT WORKS

CHAPTER IV

THE TRAGIC ERA

The years following the war were uneventful in the life of Theodore Roosevelt. He was too young to be aware of the tremendous political issues which were in ferment and which were fought out between President and Congress.

These dark and tragic years brought new prosperity to the North, but poverty and humiliation to the South. The Radical Republicans in Congress were determined to punish the "conquered provinces." Their Reconstruction Acts caused resentment and bitterness. Though the era of reconstruction was short—not more than a dozen years—its evils and hatreds lingered on in the South for decades to come.

On no man did the weight of Lincoln's passing fall more heavily than on Andrew Johnson, the Tennessee Democrat who had remained loyal to the Union and had been selected as the President's running mate in 1864. Johnson pledged to continue Lincoln's policies, to bind up the nation's wounds without hatred or vindictiveness. But the Radical Republicans, a strong and influential group within the Republican party, wanted to use the South's defeat as a political weapon; they wanted Republican dominance over the Democrats. Headed by Thaddeus Stevens, they had been hostile to Lincoln; and when Lincoln died, they hoped that Johnson would more easily be bent to their will.

But Andrew Johnson's background was not that of a man who would readily yield to pressure. He was born in poverty, and his formal education was negligible. At an early age he moved from North Carolina to Tennessee, where he earned his living as a tailor. Fond of political debates, he sided with the Southern poor whites. He reflected their bitterness at the slaveholding aristocracy and at the Whig organization through which this class exercised political control. A driving ambition enabled him to compensate for his lack of formal schooling; while plying his trade, a hired man read to him for fifty cents a day. Later, when he married, his wife taught him to read.

It was inevitable that Johnson should have been drawn into politics, and it was not long before he became one of the most powerful Democrats in his state. The outbreak of the war found him in the Senate of the United States. Although in 1860 he supported Breckinridge, the secession candidate, he could not countenance the breaking up of the Union. He was now squarely behind Lincoln. He said: "I voted against him; I spoke against him; I spent my money to defeat him. But I still love my country; I love the Constitution; I intend to insist on its guarantees. There and there alone I intend to plant myself, with the confident hope and belief that if the Union remains together, in less than four years the now triumphant party will be overthrown." In four years

61

HOMAS NAST CARTOON LAM-
ONING PRESIDENT JOHNSON
D HIS RECONSTRUCTION POLICIES

the same Andrew Johnson became Abraham Lincoln's Vice-President.

His program of reconstruction differed little from that of his predecessor. It was a liberal plan aimed at bringing the Southern states back into the family quickly and without penalties. It called for appointment of a provisional governor in each of the seceded states, a governor with power to call a constitutional convention. Once the delegates to these conventions had agreed to abolish slavery and invalidate their ordinances of secession, they were to be free to organize their states within the provisions of the federal Constitution. Johnson's plan specifically gave the states the privilege of deciding who could vote and who could not, although he added to this his recommendation that Negroes who were able to read and write or who owned property should be enfranchised along with whites.

These magnanimous terms, gratefully received in the South, aroused the fury of the Radical Republicans. For many Radicals, the first and foremost objective was to ensure Republican supremacy by giving the Negroes the ballot and keeping the "disloyal" Southern Democrats from the polls.

The Radicals argued: "When the government decided that the Negro was fit to carry a gun to shoot rebels down, it thereby pledged itself irrevocably to give him the ballot to vote rebels down." For many rational and humanitarian Northerners the idea of Negro suffrage seemed inseparable from emancipation. The powerful Union League Club of New York, which had been instrumental in helping runaway slaves to find freedom before the war, now devoted itself to the suffrage cause, sending organizers among the Southern Negroes to kindle their hatred of their former masters and to stiffen their determination to win equal rights. The Freedmen's Bureau, with offices throughout the South, tended to work toward the same end as it carried out its prescribed function of aiding the Negroes to adapt themselves to freedom.

The South was alarmed by the demand for Negro suffrage. For more than two centuries the Negro had been a chattel, with a legal status scarcely above that of livestock. To accept him as a political equal—with the implication of social equality as well—was a frightening thought. Southerners knew that the great majority of Negroes were not yet ready for the rights of citizenship. As slaves, most of them had been kept in a state of unlettered ignorance and were scarcely better equipped to vote intelligently than their forefathers who were brought to America from the jungles of Africa.

Taking full advantage of President Johnson's proposals, most of the former Confederate states had organized under the terms of his plan by the end of 1865, sending to Washington their representatives.

In Congress the leader of Johnson's Radical opposition was Thaddeus Stevens, one of the most enigmatic characters in American history. Lame from birth, he was a man of great brilliance and bitterness. He was born in poverty in Vermont, and early formed a deep hatred for aristocracy in all forms, but particularly in the form of the Southern slaveholders. To him the Civil War was an opportunity for crushing the hated class. An inveterate gambler, Stevens made and lost two fortunes in the iron industry. He lived with a mulatto housekeeper and never denied reports that she was his mistress. When the war closed, he was seventy-three years old and so infirm that he often attended sessions of Congress racked with pain. He appeared to have voluminous black hair, but once when an abolitionist woman asked for a lock of it, he smilingly removed his wig and handed it to her. He kept his sardonic humor until the last. When, on his deathbed, a friend expressed concern over his appearance, Stevens coined the *bon mot:* "It is not my appearance but my disappearance that troubles me."

With his own reconstruction plan well along toward fulfillment, Johnson reported his progress to Congress late in 1865. His message, ably written by George Bancroft, the historian, presented the doctrine that the Confederate states had never ceased to exist as states but had been in a condition of legal suspension from which they should now be restored as quickly as possible. This argument ran headlong into Stevens' contention that the Confederate states had lost their legal status by seceding and must be considered for the present as conquered provinces without the protection of the federal Constitution—a contention designed to answer Johnson's claim that he could not enforce Negro suffrage because the Constitution left voting questions up to the states. Speaking in the House of Representatives, Stevens stated frankly: "I think there would always be enough Union men in the South, aided by the blacks, to divide the representation and thus continue Republican ascendancy."

The Radicals created a joint House-Senate Committee on Reconstruction to do away with Johnson's plan and replace it with their own. At first it looked as though the President might be able to stem the tide of the opposition, for when he vetoed a bill to extend and expand the powers of the Freedmen's Bureau, he was sustained by a small margin in the Senate. But his victory was short-lived. His subsequent veto of the Civil Rights Bill, which sought to guarantee equal privileges for Negroes, was not sustained. From then on, the Radicals were in the driver's seat.

As the mid-term elections of 1868 were approaching, Johnson set out on a speaking tour in an effort to convince the country of the soundness of his policies. The trip was a failure. The election repudiated Johnson; it gave the Radicals the vote; they had comfortable majorities in both houses of Congress.

Stevens now was able to force through Congress a new reconstruction plan. Five military districts were set up in the South, each one placed under an Army general, and provision made for constitutional conventions to be conducted under Northern auspices. All Negroes were given the right to vote, but the vote was to be withheld from those whites who had been disloyal to the Union. Federal troops would not be withdrawn from any state until its constitution had been approved by Congress and until the Fourteenth Amendment —forbidding the abridgment of citizenship privileges—had been ratified by the state. And even after these conditions had been met, the state could be represented in Congress only by such representatives as would swear that they had never voluntarily given aid to the Confederate cause. These were harsh terms. When a Republican told Thaddeus Stevens that he was conscience-stricken over such measures, Stevens would have no such nonsense. He replied:

"Conscience! Tell your conscience to go to the devil, and follow the party line."

The Radicals' reconstruction program was passed over Johnson's veto, as was the Tenure of Office Act, which tried to tie the President's hands by making it a criminal offense for him to remove without Senate approval any civil officeholder whom he had appointed.

It was the Tenure of Office Act which became the focal point for the increasingly strong Radical demand for Johnson's impeachment. When Johnson dismissed Edwin Stanton, the Secretary of War and a man who worked closely with the Radicals, Thaddeus Stevens offered the resolution to impeach the President. Eleven counts were drawn up against Johnson, nine of them dealing with the Stanton removal, which, it was charged, violated the Tenure of Office Act. The trial that followed was a political spectacle of first magnitude, with bribes offered and votes canvassed as though in a party caucus. And when it was over, Johnson had escaped impeachment by a single vote.

To keep the freedmen from following the political leadership of their former masters, the Radicals used all kinds of methods to wean the Negroes away from them. Representatives of the Union League promised them "forty acres and a mule." Others offered even more. As the time arrived to register them as voters, the vast majority of former slaves had been convinced that their dreams for a better life could be realized only through the Republican party.

The constitutional conventions in the South were dominated by Negroes (who comprised a majority of the voters in five of the ten states), by "carpetbaggers" and "scalawags." ("Carpetbaggers" was a nickname for Northerners who came to the South in search of political fortunes, with their entire possessions in their carpetbags; "scalawags" was a hated term describing the Southern whites who allied themselves with the Negroes.) They quickly assumed the positions of leadership. When the state constitutions prepared by these conventions were submitted to the voters, many of the whites stayed away from the polls. But the Radicals drew the Negroes in such overwhelming numbers to the ballot box that they were able to get the majority ratification. The seven Southern states which were readmitted to the Union before the 1868 presidential election were all in the Republican column.

In some instances the new constitutions were well-drawn documents, more democratic than the ones before the war. But their potentialities were largely dissipated by the corrupt and incompetent officials who were placed in office by the first elections. The highest elective posts went to carpetbaggers, and the lesser offices were distributed among scalawags and Negroes who were far from the best representatives of the freedmen. The new officialdom, moreover, was in a unique position to pursue policies of political irresponsibility, for most of them were men of little property and even less education. In Louisiana, for example, only ten of the new members of the legislature were taxpayers, and in Georgia the total amount of taxes paid by all representatives in both houses of the legislature amounted to but $100.

Under these circumstances, it was natural enough that the new governments tended toward confiscatory legislation and corrupt administration, producing an orgy of misgovernment. Tax rates rose steeply, at the very time when property owners were trying desperately to get back on their feet.

In such an atmosphere the presidential election of 1868 was held. Leading Republican politicians had decided on General Grant, while the Democrats named Horatio Seymour, the former governor of New York. That Grant would win the election was never in doubt. The electorate cared little that he knew nothing about public affairs, that he had only voted once in his life, that he was a poor speaker and not much of a thinker. And the people cared less that the Democratic candidate had all the qualifications for the high office, that Seymour was a profound student of politics, a polished orator, and an experienced administrator. They wanted Grant and no arguments.

The main issue of the campaign was reconstruction. The Republicans took a strong stand for the Reconstruction Acts, while the Democrats maintained that their opponents had "subjected 10 states, in the time of profound peace, to military despotism and Negro supremacy." On the question of Negro suffrage the Republican platform presented two faces, insisting on suffrage in the South but stating that in the North it was a matter for each state to decide individually. A campaign jingle reflected the feelings of many Southerners:

> To every Southern river shall Negro suffrage come,
> But not to fair New England, for that's too close to home.

As expected, General Grant won the election.

The harsh reconstruction program, continued under Grant's term, produced organized resistance in the South. The Ku Klux Klan—at first a harmless organization with no particular program—became an instrument in the hand of Southerners who desired to discipline the Negroes and the carpetbaggers. By 1869 atrocities against Negroes became frequent. Murders, whippings, and tortures were the order of the day, with gangs of white-robed Klansmen riding the countryside at night to terrorize those whom they felt to be responsible for the South's degradation. In the fall of 1869 the more responsible leaders of the Klan and the several similar organizations that had sprung up attempted to disband the lawless elements, but their efforts were unsuccessful.

The Radical reconstruction policies fomented vigorous resistance in the South. The whites, determined to end military control of their government, began to organize themselves to best political advantage and to place increasing emphasis on nonviolent tactics to restore home rule. In state after state the conservatives, operating through the Democratic party, regained control of the government, driving the carpetbaggers and scalawags into retirement. Their efforts were greatly aided by the split in the Republican ranks and by the fact that Northern leniency became greater as the Civil War hatreds were gradually soothed by time.

When Theodore Roosevelt grew up, he learned what disastrous results the Radicals had reaped for the Republican party. Instead of securing the Southern and Negro vote, they had created a "Solid South," the main Democratic bastion for generations to come.

"'BRING A BALM AND OIL FROM GILEAD.'"

"A BALM THAT IS HEALING IN ITS CHARACTER AND POUR IT INTO THE WOUND?"

(ANDY FORGOT

OUR

WIVES & CHILDREN.)

MAD, ANDY.)

"(JEFF DAVIS.)" "THEN I WOULD ASK YOU WHY NOT HANG STEVENS AND WENDELL PHILLIPS?"

"THERE ARE VERY FEW MEN WHO HAVE BEEN ABANDONED BY THE PEOPLE UNLESS THEY HAVE DESERTED THEM FIRST" (THAT'S SO)

"THIS WAS MY OBJECT IN PRESENTING MYSELF ON THIS OCCASION AND TO TELL YOU"

"HOW DO YOU DO", AND AT THE SAME TIME TO BID YOU "GOOD BY"

"Where is the man or woman who can place his finger upon one single act of mine deviating from any pledge of mine!"

"I hold it a solemn obligation in every one of these States where the rebel armies have been beaten back or expelled, I care not how small the number of Union men, if enough to man the ship of State, I hold it to be a high duty to protect and secure to them a Republican form of government until they again gain strength. They must not be smothered by inches."......"These rebel leaders must feel the power of the Government; treason must be made odious, and traitors must be punished and impoverished."......"You have been deeply pained by some things that come under your observation. We get men in command who, under the influence of flattery, fawning, and caressing, grant protection to rich traitors, while the poor Union man stands out in the cold. Traitors can get lucrative contracts, while the loyal man is pushed aside."......"The power of those persons who made the attempt [at rebellion] has been crushed, and now we want to reconstruct the State Governments, and have the power to do it. The State institutions are prostrated, laid out on the ground, and they must be taken up and adapted to the progress of events: this can not be done in a moment. We are making very rapid progress—so rapid that I sometimes can not realize it. It appears like a dream. We must not be in too much of a hurry. It is better to let them reconstruct themselves than force them to it; for, if they go wrong, the power is in our hands, and we can check them in any stage to the end, and oblige them to correct their errors."......"If I were in Tennessee I should try to introduce Negro Suffrage gradually: first, those who had served in the army; those who could read and write; and perhaps a property qualification for others—say $200 or $250.".....'A fellow who takes the oath merely to save his property, and denies the validity of the oath, is a perjured man, and not to be trusted. Before these repenting rebels can be trusted let them bring forth the fruits of repentance. He who helped to make all these widows and orphans, who draped the streets of Nashville in mourning, should suffer for his great crime."......"If a man who gave his means to destroy the Government should be permitted to participate in the great work of reorganization, then all the precious blood so freely poured out will have been wantonly spilled, and all our victories go for naught."—Extracts from Speeches by ANDREW JOHNSON.

JOHNSON'S "SWING AROUND THE CIRCLE"

President Johnson, in his attempt to continue Lincoln's magnanimous policies toward the South, incurred the enmity of the Radical Republicans, who advocated severe measures against the "conquered provinces." The fateful struggle between the President and Congress reached a peak in the mid-term election of 1866. Johnson set out from Washington in a "swing around the circle," traveling as far as Chicago, trying to convince the electorate of the soundness of his policies. The Radicals organized demonstrations against him, hecklers roused his ire and goaded him into intemperate utterances; newspapers fought him, charging him with drunkenness, cartoonists ridiculed him mercilessly, as the artist Thomas Nast has done in this cartoon. Johnson's trip ended in dismal failure; the election upheld the Radicals, who carried both houses of Congress by great majorities. They now were given the mandate to carry out their harsh reconstruction policies in the South.

MILITARY COMMANDERS IN THE SOUTH

In 1867 the Radical Republicans passed three Reconstruction Acts which divided the area of the ten Southern states (Tennessee had already ratified the Fourteenth Amendment and was restored to its full privileges) into five military districts, with a major general in command of each district. The contemporary drawing from *Harper's Weekly* shows General Daniel E. Sickles, General John Pope, General George H. Thomas, General U. S. Grant, Brevet Major General John M. Schofield, General Philip Sheridan, and Brevet Major General E. O. C. Ord.

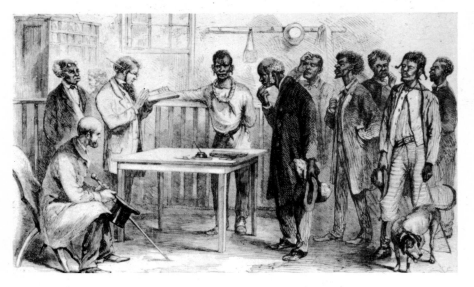

REGISTERING. The Reconstruction Acts of 1867 gave the vote to the former slaves. They now had equal rights with the whites. They flocked to the registration offices, where officials of the military governments read to them their new privileges. Southerners were enraged and humiliated. While the former slaves were given the suffrage, only those whites who were willing to swear that they had not voluntarily joined the Confederate Army were allowed to vote.

THE FIRST VOTE. In the state elections of 1867 the Negroes voted for the first time, outnumbering the whites. The political campaign of the Radical Republicans made it certain that the new voters would cast their ballots for the Republican candidates. The freedmen listened to inflammatory speeches about their former masters, listened to promises of "forty acres and a mule." Not yet mature enough to exercise their political rights, the former slaves voted as they were told. They voted for carpetbaggers (Northern men who came to the South to pursue political careers, most of their possessions in their carpetbags); they voted for "scalawags" (Southern whites who allied themselves with the Republicans); they voted for illiterate Negroes; they voted for men who promised them the stars from heaven. The results of the elections were corrupt governments, enormous state debts, and a hostile white population.

69

CARPETBAG LEGISLATURES IN THE SOUTH

The composite photograph shows the Radical Republican members of the South Carolina Legislature in 1868. That unhappy state, with a legislature made up largely of Negroes unable to read or write, found itself milked dry by graft and extravagance. School funds were stolen; businesses had to make direct payments to public officials for permits and franchises; payrolls were padded. In the State House barroom the average daily consumption for a legislator was a gallon of liquor; some lawmakers staggered into the chamber, wholly drunk.

70

Hang, ours, hang! *
late, to their hanging! * * * * *
Their complexion is perfect gallows. Stand fast, good
If they be not born to be hanged, our case is miserable."

The above cut represents the fate in store for those great pests of Southern society—the carpet-bagger and scallawag—if found in Dixie's Land
after the break of day on the 4th of March next.

The genus carpet-bagger is a man with a lank head of dry hair, a
lank stomach and long legs, club knees and splay feet, dried legs and
lank jaws with eyes like a fish and mouth like a shark. Add to this a
habit of sneaking and dodging about in unknown places—habiting with
negroes in dark dens and back streets—a look like a hound and the smell
of a polecat.

Words are wanting to do full justice to the genus scallawag. He is a
cur with a contracted head, downward look, slinking and uneasy gait;
sleeps in the woods, like old Crossland, at the bare idea of a Ku-Klux
raid.

Our scallawag is the local leper of the community. Unlike the carpet-
bagger, he is native, which is so much the worse. Once he was respected
in his circle; his head was level, and he would look his neighbor in the
face. Now, possessed of the itch of office and the salt rheum of Radicalism, he is a mangy dog, slinking through the alleys, haunting the Governor's office, defiling with tobacco juice the steps of the Capitol, stretching his lazy carcass in the sun on the Square, or the benches of the May-
or's Court.

He waiteth for the troubling of the political waters, to the end that he

THE REACTION TO CARPETBAG RULE.

The Ku Klux Klan, at first a harmless organization, turned into a vicious instrument in the hands of hoodlums who acquired control of many of the Klan's local branches. Atrocities against Negroes, murders, whippings, and tortures became the order of the day.

White-robed Klansmen rode the countryside at night to terrorize those whom they believed to be responsible for the South's degradation. By 1869 the Klan had absorbed "all the horse thieves, cutthroats, bushwhackers and outlaws of every description" and degenerated into a mob of lawless rioters.

THE KLAN AT WORK

The assassination of G. W. Ashburn in Columbus, Georgia, on March 31, 1868, as it seemed to the artist of *Frank Leslie's Illustrated Newspaper*. This and other vile, debasing, and brutal misdeeds kept the Negroes and their allies in constant fear. The attorney who was later to defend the Klan declared that their outrages shocked humanity. In 1868, according to a Southern newspaper, the Klan was being formed for action "wherever the insolent negro, the malignant white traitor to his race, and the infamous squatter" were plotting to make the South "utterly unfit for the residence of the decent white man."

THE IMPEACHMENT COMMITTEE, an official group portrait taken by Mathew B. Brady. Seated, from left to right: Benjamin F. Butler, Thaddeus Stevens, Thomas Williams, and John A. Bingham. Standing: James F. Wilson, George S. Boutwell, and John A. Logan.

THE IMPEACHMENT
OF
ANDREW JOHNSON

The Radical Republicans, angered by President Johnson's mild reconstruction policy and outraged about his independent attitude, passed the Tenure of Office Act, which forbade the President to issue military orders, to remove civil officeholders of the government, or dismiss high military officers without the consent of the Senate. The prime purpose of the act was to keep a check on Johnson and to retain

RACKED IN BODY AND SOUL, Thaddeus Stevens went before the House of Representatives to propose the impeachment of President Johnson.

THE IMPEACHMENT COURT, constituted by the Senate under Chief Justice Chase, deliberated for weeks. It failed to impeach Johnson by a single vote.

PRESIDENT JOHNSON RECEIVES THE SUMMONS. When the President removed Edwin Stanton, the Secretary of War, from office without consulting the Senate, the hostile group of Radical Republicans instituted impeachment proceedings against Johnson.

Edwin Stanton, the Secretary of War and a close friend of the Radicals.

When the President, challenging the constitutionality of the Act, dismissed Stanton, the Radicals charged him with "high crimes and misdemeanors" and voted to impeach him. Nine of the eleven charges against Johnson were based on the Tenure of Office Act. The trial lasted from the middle of March till the middle of May 1868, with the country watching in a high state of excitement. To impeach the President the Radicals needed a two-thirds vote. But their effort failed. In the decisive ballot seven Republican senators sided with the Democrats. Thus, by a single vote, the presidential office as created under the Constitution escaped destruction. Thaddeus Stevens muttered angrily: "The country is going to the devil."

August 15th
Saturday.
All the morning
I Played store and
baby. In the after
noon I wrote, read
and drew. That
afternoon I recieved
a continuence of
Washington's life.

August 16th.
Sunday.
I went to chrvch
After lrench I
did nothing.
August 18 the
Munday.
To day we discover
a little house with
one room, one door
and one window.

Sunday Munday,
and Tuesday Nothing
happened except that
we found a swallow
attentdy and robins nestes.

As I lost My
book I cannot remem-
ber what I have
done, except the
getting of my birds

nests which I will
relate. The robins
and catbirds nest
I pushed from
limbs with sticks.
We knocked down
two pair of birds
nests but did not
take them. All of
a sudden we saw
high in the barn

and with a wasps
nest near it a
swallows nest.
We got it with
a ladder.
Nothing now happene
till the 4th of september
ber.

September 4 th
Friday.
cold and rainy
To day I was called in
from breakfast to a
room. When I went
in there what was
my sur-prise to see
on wall, curtains
and floor about
fourty swallows.
All the morning long

THEODORE'S DIARY, about the time of Johnson's impeachment. The entry dated "Sunday, Munday and Tuesday" is particularly revealing. "As I lost My book I cannot remember what I have done, except the getting of my birds nests which I will relate. The robins and catbirds nest I pushed from limbs with sticks. We knocked down two pair of birds nests but did not take them. All of a sudden we saw high in the barn and with a wasps nest near it a swallows nest. We got it with a ladder. Nothing now happened till the 4th of September." Here we have Theodore Roosevelt, the meticulous reporter, the lover of nature. Almost every day his entries contain some reference to natural history, his lifelong interest. The 4th of September was most exciting. "To day I was called in from breakfast to a room. When I went in there what was my surprise to see on wall, curtains and floor about fourty swallows . . . and about 75 [were] in the house. I caught most of them. The others got out."

74

TROUBLED BY ASTHMA—an entry in Theodore Roosevelt's first childhood diary, dated Monday, August 10, 1868. With characteristic poor spelling Theodore confides: "I had an attack of the Asmer but I did not go to New York." But regardless of his asthma attacks, Teedie exercised, swam, and rode. There are entries in the diary which foretell the vigorous life to which Theodore adhered as a grown man. "Had a ride of six miles before breakfast. I will always have a ride of six miles before breakfast now," he wrote on August 20. Whether he played store and "baby," whether he went to church, whether he "read, wrote or drew," whether he "did nothing," everything was put on paper with systematic care. And while the nation wrestled with the grave problem of reconstruction, while Congress started impeachment proceedings against the President, the Roosevelt children spent an idyllic summer at Barrytown, unaware of the momentous political decisions which faced the country.

THE NEW PRESIDENT AND HIS FAMILY

General Ulysses S. Grant, the hero of the Civil War, became President in 1868. The country looked forward to good times and a decent administration. It attained neither. Under Grant's leadership public morality sank to a new low. Corruption and graft flourished. Though personally honest, the President could not check the misdeeds of his associates. Politicians and speculators abused his trusting nature. Gradually, a disillusioned electorate realized that a successful military man does not necessarily have the makings of a good President.

CHAPTER V

HIS FIRST TRIP TO EUROPE

It was a grand tour that Theodore Roosevelt's father mapped out for his family. They were to go to Europe so the children could see and learn at first hand about the Old World.

The Roosevelts set out from New York on May 12, 1869; nine days later they were in Liverpool, where Uncle Jimmy and Uncle Irving—the brother and half brother of Mrs. Roosevelt—lived in voluntary exile. They had a lovely reunion, and Theodore visited his cousins' school. The only trouble was: "We had a nice time but met Jeff Davises son and some sharp words ensued." From Liverpool the six Roosevelts proceeded to the Lake District, then to Edinburgh, and from there to western Scotland. From Glasgow they traveled via York, Warwick, Oxford to London, where they stayed for three weeks.

Leaving England for Holland, they journeyed to Antwerp, The Hague, and Amsterdam, then to Germany—Frankfort, Heidelberg, and Baden—and from there to Strasbourg and to Basel, in Switzerland. A thorough tourist trip of Switzerland followed, taking in the Jura Mountains, Bern, Lausanne, Montreux, Geneva, Chamonix, the Mont Blanc. Zermatt, Andermatt, Lucerne, Zurich— one gets tired listing the names of the places. The Roosevelts were sight-seers of the first order.

Though there was plenty to watch and plenty to do, Teedie was not too happy. His diary reveals that "I have been homesick all the nights at Luzerne." And in France he "cried for homesickness and a wish to get out of the land where friends (or as I think them enemies) who cannot speak the language are forced on me."

After Switzerland came Italy: Stresa, Lugano, Milan, Venice. Then Austria: Trieste, Vienna, Ischl, Salzburg. Once more Germany: Munich, Nürnberg, Dresden, Berlin, Cologne, then through Belgium to Paris. There they stayed put for a full month, enjoying life in the French capital. But by the end of November they were on the way again: Dijon, Marseilles, the French and Italian Rivieras, and through Genoa and Pisa to Rome. Christmas was spent in Rome, then on to Naples and Sorrento, where they celebrated the New Year.

Back to Rome for six weeks of sight-seeing, then via Florence, Bologna, Turin, to Paris. Six weeks there, a week in London, and a visit to Liverpool to say farewell to the Bullochs rounded out the trip. On May 14 they embarked on the *Russia,* and sailed home.

Theodore closes his diary on an exultant pitch: "This morning we saw land of America and, swiftly coming on, passed Sandy Hook and went in to the bay. New York!!! Hip! Hurrah!"

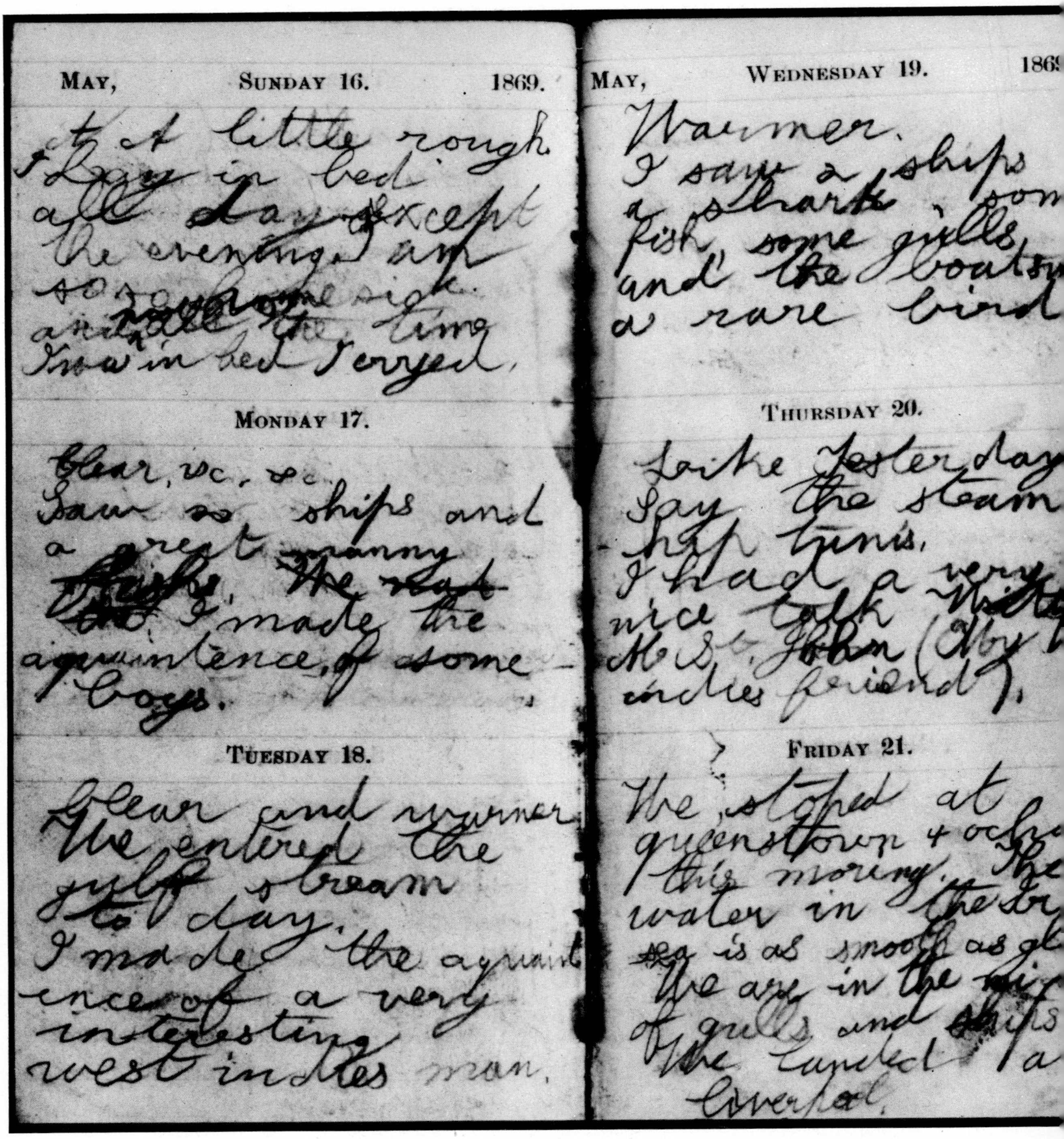

Diary pages

MAY, SUNDAY 16. 1869.

A little rough. I lay in bed all day except the evening. I am so very ... sick and ... all the time. Now in bed. I cryed.

MONDAY 17.

Clear &c. &c. Saw ... ships and a great many fish. The rest ... I made the aquaintence of some boys.

TUESDAY 18.

Clear and warmer. We entered the gulf stream to day. I made the aquaintence of a very interesting west indies man.

MAY, WEDNESDAY 19. 1869

Warmer. I saw a ship, a shark, some fish, some gulls, and the boats ... a rare bird.

THURSDAY 20.

Like yesterday. Spy the steam ship Tunis. I had a very nice talk with Mr St. John (Aby's indies friend).

FRIDAY 21.

We stoped at queenstown & oc... this morning. The water in the ... sea is as smooth as gl... we are in the midst of gulls and ships. We landed a... Liverpool.

THEODORE ROOSEVELT'S CHILDHOOD DIARIES OF HIS FIRST EUROPEAN TRIP

The Roosevelts left New York on May 12, 1869, and after touring England, Holland, Switzerland, Italy, and France, they returned home on May 25, 1870. During the trip Theodore recorded his experiences with methodical exactness. On the voyage to Europe he noted that he was seasick and that he was homesick. He described the fish and birds he saw, remarked about the books he read. When the boat reached its destination the whole ship was in an uproar except Teedie, who "read, entirely oblivious to what was going on." In a letter from Europe his mother confided to her sister that she thought Teedie was a "strange child! I am going to try to wake him up to observe what goes on and *make him observe.*"

78

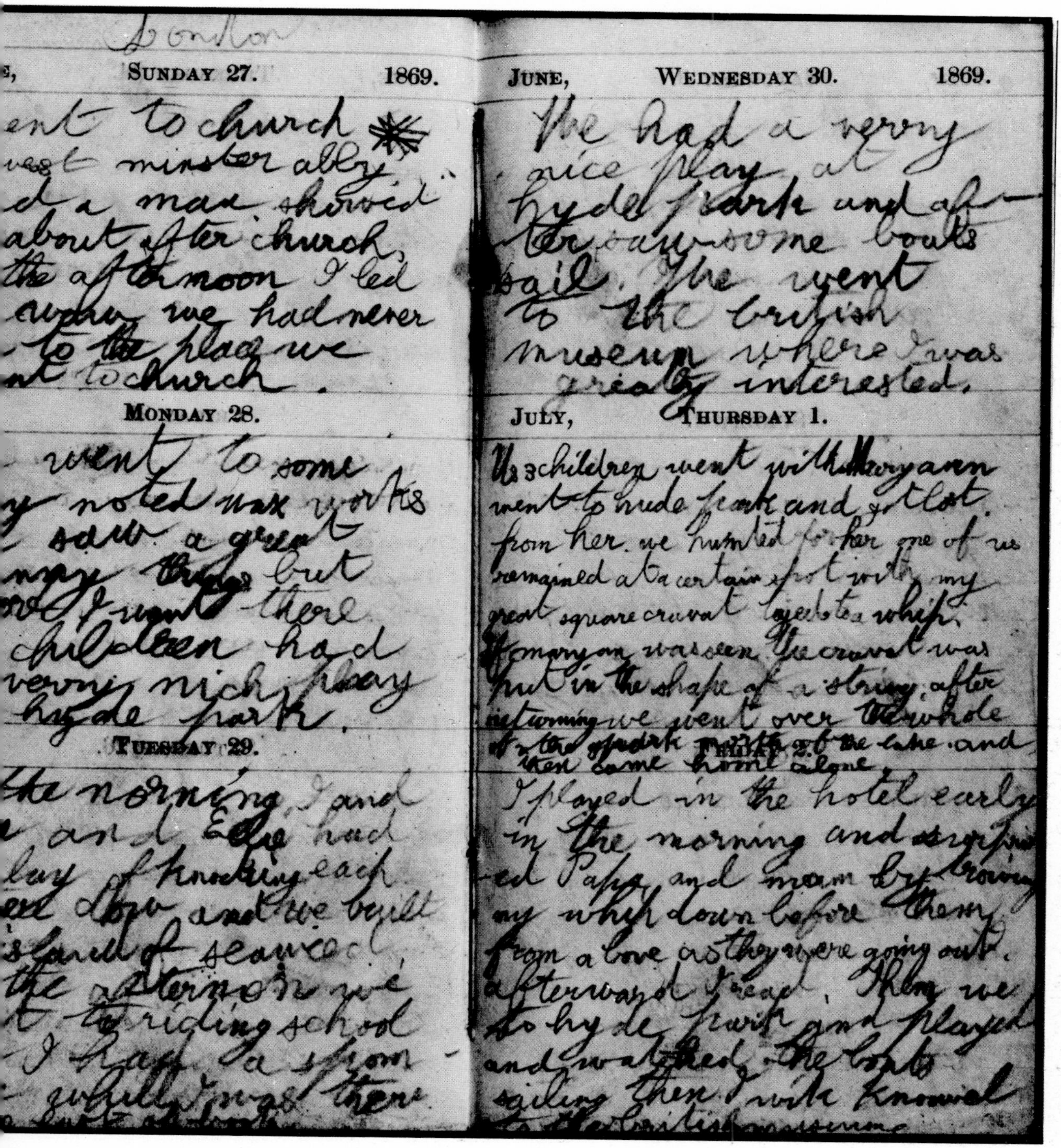

SUNDAY 27. 1869.   JUNE, WEDNESDAY 30. 1869.

[handwritten diary entry, partly illegible]

...ent to church
...west minster abby
...a man showed
...about after church
the afternoon I ed
...away we had never
...to the place we
...at to church .

We had a verry
nice play at
hyde park and af-
ter...saw some boats
sail. We went
to the british
museum where I was
greatly interested.

MONDAY 28.   JULY,   THURSDAY 1.

...went to some
...noted wax works
...saw a great
...many things but
...I want there
...children had
...verry nich play
hyde park .

Us 3 children went with Mary ann
went to hude park and got lot
from her. we hunted for her one of us
remained at a certain spot with my
great square cravat tyed to a whip
if Mary an was seen. the cravat was
put in the shape of a string after
returning we went over the whole
of the park ... the lake and
then came home alone

TUESDAY 29.   FRIDAY 2.

...the morning, I and
...and ... had
...lay of knocking each
...other down and we built
...fand of sea ...
the afternoon we
...to riding school
I had a ... from
...while I was there

I played in the hotel early
in the morning and astonished Papa and mam by throw-
ing my whip down before them
from above as they were going out.
afterward I read. Then we
to hy de park and played
and watched the boats
sailing there I with Knowal
...british museum

THESE WERE HIS FIRST IMPRESSIONS OF THE CITY OF LONDON

The waxworks Theodore speaks about in his diary are Mme. Tussaud's; the hard-to-spell name was conveniently left out. He also records the happy time in London's Hyde Park, his visit to the British Museum and "the Westnubster abby." In London, Teedie suffered severe asthma attacks, and these attacks continued almost throughout the entire jour-ney. There are entries in the diary like "I was verry sick last night," or "I had a miserable night," or "I was rubbed so hard on the chest this morning that the blood came out." Only at a high altitude did he feel better. In Switzerland he went for long walks, sometimes thirteen, sometimes nineteen and sometimes even twenty miles a day to build up his body.

THE YOUNG LOVER

Eleven-year-old Teedie Roosevelt at the time of the European trip. In his diary he noted all the interesting things he saw, all the places he visited. He would have enjoyed the trip more if he had suffered less from recurrent asthma attacks. His elder sister, Bamie, wrote to her aunt: "Poor little Tedie is sick again with the asthma—it was coming on all day yesterday, but in the evening he seemed a little better so Father went out —before his return, however, Tedie had a very bad attack. Mother and I were very much worried about the poor little fellow and at last Mother gave him a strong cup of coffee, which failed as he could not sleep but sat in the parlor to have stories of when Mother was a little girl told him." The boy loved it.

THE OBJECT OF HIS LOVE

Edith Kermit Carow, the seven-year-old daughter of Charles and Gertrude Carow, was an early companion of the Roosevelt children. She lived next door to Grandfather Roosevelt on Fourteenth Street, and her parents were family friends. Theodore was fond of her, though it was his sister Corinne who became Edith's "chum." While the Roosevelts sojourned in Paris, Theodore was shown a portrait of Edith, and the face of the little girl "stired up in me homesickness and longings for the past which will come again never, alack never." Still, Edith was not the only young lady in his life. A few months later in Rome, after the birthday party for his brother Elliott, Theodore confided in his diary: "We then danced and when we had forfeits I was suddenly surprised by being kissed by Elliese Van Schaick as the boy she loved best in the room." Yet it was Edith Carow whom he married after his first wife's death.

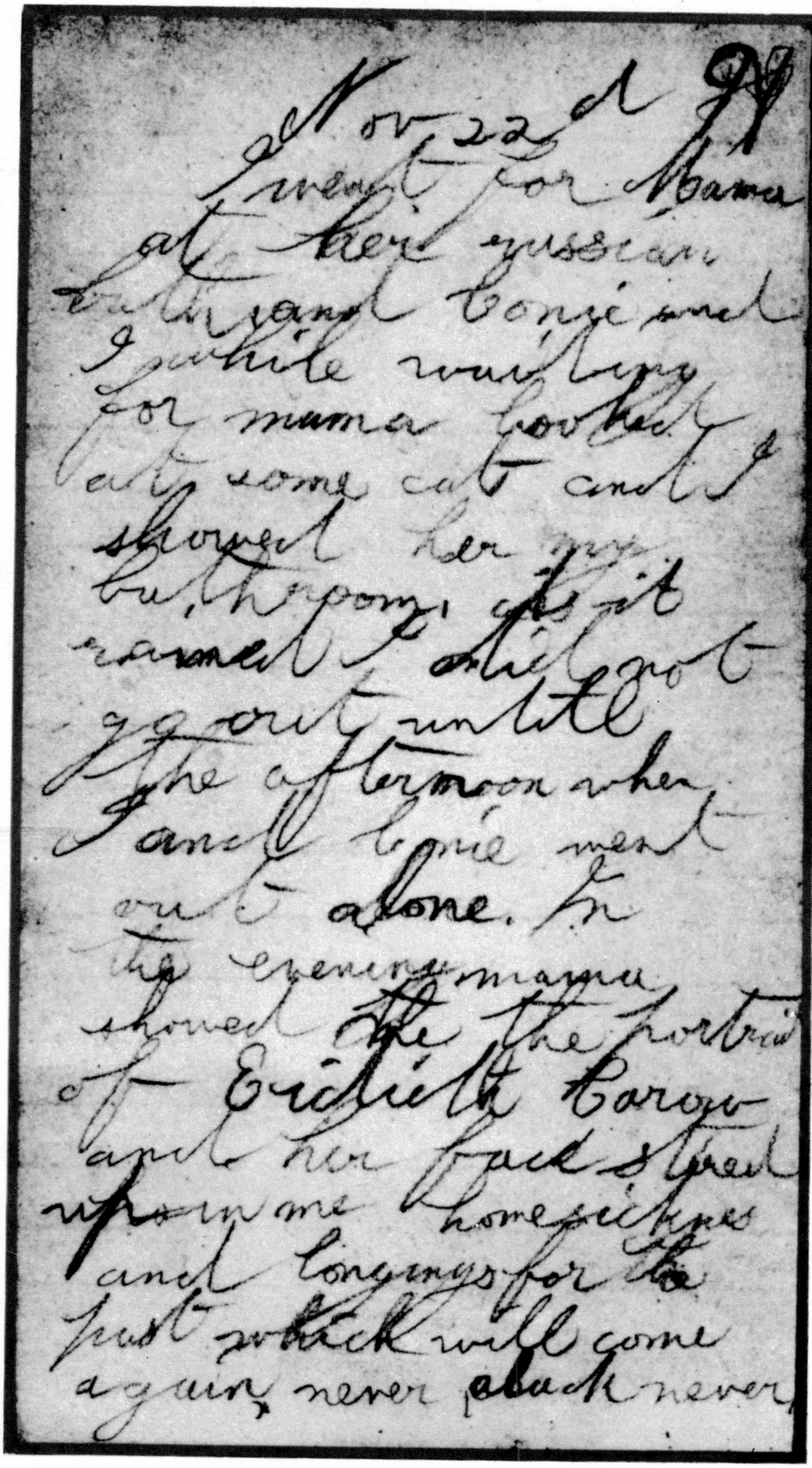

Nov 22d
I went for Mama
at her russian
bath and Conie and
I while waiting
for mama looked
at some cats and I
showed her my
bathroom. As it
rained I did not
go out untill
the afternoon when
I and Conie went
out alone. In
the evening mama
showed the the portrait
of Eidieth Carow
and her face stired
up in me homesickness
and longings for the
past which will come
again never alack never

HE DIARY PAGE of heodore, written in Paris ı November 22, 1869, with e wistful entry about Edith arow. "I went for Mama her russian bath and onie and I while waiting r mama looked at some .ts and I showed her my ıthroom. As it rained I d not go out untill the ternoon when I and Conie ent out alone. In the eveng mama showed me the rtrait of Eidieth Carow d her face stired up in me mesickness and longings r the past which will come ain never, alack never."

PAGES FROM HIS DIARY

The hotel suites in which the family stayed—whether in London, Paris or Venice—are carefully drawn (see below). The times the "big people" went out—that is, father, mother, and his elder sister, Bamie—while Theodore, his brother Elliott, his sister Corinne—"the little people"—were left behind are recorded in minute detail. The entries reveal a methodical, pedantic, orderly mind.

In Paris the young diarist describes how "We annoyed (not really) the chambermaids and waiters and were chased by them." In Trieste: "I am now on the castle and have written my name on the pole there." In San Remo a bit of juvenile jingoism when "We 3" tossed food to a large group of peasant children. "We made the crowds that we gave the cakes to give three cheers for the U.S.A. before we gave them cakes." In Rome: "We saw the Pope and we walked along and he extended his hand to me and I kissed it!! hem!! hem!!"

His keen interest in nature lore found new outlets in Europe, where he visited every natural-history museum he could find, while art exhibits were not to his taste. "If Raphel," he wrote, "had only painted landscapes instead of church things!"

Often a note of unconscious humor found its way into the diary. In Italy the Roosevelts visited "St. John the Baptists chapel where no woman was allowed to enter because Herrodeus had had his head cut off"; in France, "We went to Pere la Chais where we saw severel famous persons interred." Less often there is a note of romantic and world-weary introspection, as when he is told that his Uncle Weir, his father's brother, had died. "It is the third relation that has died in my short life. What will come?" Such morose sentiments might have seemed startling in a child so young, had it not been obvious that he was merely exercising a flair for the dramatic, an art in which he became quite proficient as time passed.

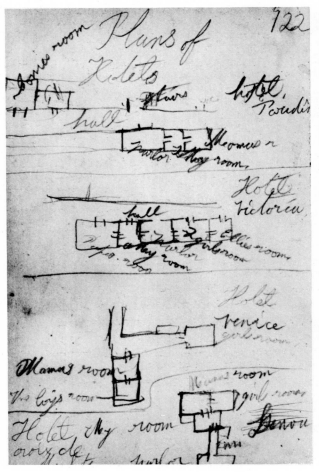
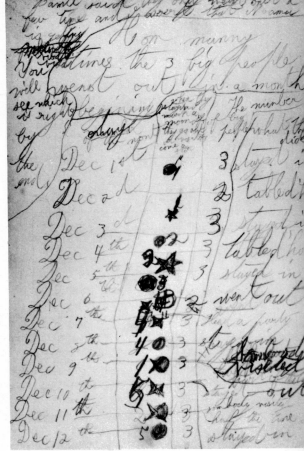

CLASSIFICATIONS AND PROMISES

The countries that the Roosevelts visited received ratings by Theodore. "England not nice at all," said an entry, while "Scotland on the whole verry nice." The four days in "Holand"— with one *l*—and Switzerland must have been the high points of the journey; they were "splendid." For the ten-year-old boy the European countries were either "decent," "nice," "splendid," or "not nice at all." His opinions were clear and firm—he had no doubt about them. In another section of his diary he made careful notation of the promises which were given him on the trip and which had to be fulfilled when the family returned to America. He recorded these promises with great care, so they would not be forgotten. Thus, when Papa said Theodore would get "a verry good bow and arrow," or "a good big geogography," here they were noted in the diary. Similarly, Mama's promise "if possible a room for myself" and Papa's word about letting him know "the names of my forefathers" were put on paper; there could be no argument about the matter later. Theodore would not take any chances.

SCHOOLROOMS WERE OVERCROWDED.
As New York grew too fast, neither housing accommodations nor school facilities could keep pace with the population increase. School classes like the above Grammar School No. 3, photographed in 1873, were large. In 1870 there were 287 schools in the city, with 3,215 teachers (over 3,000 of them women), who taught 251,545 pupils. A contemporary chronicler noted that the best students were the Jews, followed by the Germans, "whilst the Irish, with different traits, have produced from these schools bright specimens of what, with education, they may become."

CHAPTER VI

THE EMERGENCE OF MODERN AMERICA

The forces which Theodore Roosevelt had to master during his presidential years were forged while he was in his short pants, knowing little and caring nothing about them.

The third quarter of the nineteenth century brought a tremendous acceleration to the industrial revolution throughout the Western world, and nowhere did the revolution move more speedily than in the United States.

Statistics cannot fully convey the greatest economic boom the country had ever seen, but they indicate the speed with which industrial expansion drove the nation forward. In 1865 only 1.5 billion dollars were invested in American manufacturing. By 1878 the figure had reached 3 billions. In 1859 there were 140,000 manufacturing plants in the country. Ten years later there were 252,000. Steel production jumped from about 15,000 tons in 1865 to more than 600,000 tons in 1876, while in the eight years following the war the nation's total railroad mileage increased 100 per cent.

Of all the fabulous industrial success stories during the years following Appomattox, none were more remarkable than the growth of two relatively new products: steel and oil. The steel age had been born in England in 1856 through the genius of Henry Bessemer, but it did not get started in America until just after the war. Thereafter, the development of the new product was so fast that steel became as cheap as cast iron. During the early years of the industry, most of the output went into train rails, where its durability made it far superior to iron. If for no other reason than this, steel's influence on American expansion was predominant, since the huge crops of the Middle West and the manufactured goods of the Mississippi Valley could never have been carried without it.

Oil, like steel, was an industry that grew up almost overnight. Before the war, crude oil had been used on a small scale as a lubricant, and on a somewhat larger scale as a "cure-all" medicine to be used either externally or internally for almost any ailment. The boom came, however, with the discovery that a cheap refining process could make the product into a practical source of illumination.

In addition to steel and oil, meat packing emerged as a major business in this postwar period, aided by the growth of cattle ranching, and improvements in rail transportation and refrigeration. The milling industry, superseding the old-fashioned gristmill, the manufacture of ready-made clothing in place of homemade garments yielded quick riches.

The standardization of products was one major characteristic of the industrial boom; another was the rapid expansion of industries in the Middle West, an area which had been almost entirely agricultural a decade earlier. Besides meat packing and milling, foundries sprang up in Iowa and Illinois; breweries in St. Louis and Milwaukee; a thriving watch industry in Elgin, Illinois; stockyards, farm machinery and railroad equipment production boomed in Chicago.

In the exciting drama of taming the Wild West the railroads played a major role. The westward advancement of the frontier settlements during the ten years following Lincoln's death was truly astonishing. Three wartime measures —the Homestead Act, the Morrill Land-Grant Act, and a bill giving huge tracts to the Union Pacific—had thrown extensive public lands open to settlement. Between 1871 and 1876 nearly 40,000 homesteads passed into the possession of settlers. Under the Morrill Act, each state in the Union received 30,000 acres per congressman to sell or rent for endowing colleges of agriculture and mechanics. The railroads—Union Pacific, Santa Fé, and Southern Pacific particularly—were given 20-mile land grants on each side of their tracks in territorial areas, and 10-mile grants in the states. So great was the land distribution that by 1871, when the last of the railroad grants was made, the government had given away nearly 130,000,000 acres—an area three times the size of New England.

The most dramatic—and in many respects ignominious—chapter in the story of the West was the conflict between the new settlers and the Indians. When the Civil War ended, there were about 300,000 "untamed" Indians, of whom the most hostile were the ones living on the Great Plains. Between 1865 and 1870, as the whites moved into the Indian preserves, there was almost constant fighting, and even after that period it continued sporadically for a number of years. The universal attitude on the frontier was cold-blooded and uncompromising: the only good Indian was a dead one—an attitude that led to a great deal of cruelty on both sides.

At the same time that the Indians were being driven back, the buffalo— one of the country's great natural resources—was being systematically annihilated. In the 1860s there were probably about 15,000,000 of these creatures in the West, roaming the plains in great herds. The building of the railroads made these herds accessible, and the demand for buffalo robes and buffalo meat made hunting them profitable, although much of the slaughter was for "sport." Between 1871 and 1874 about 3,700,000 animals were killed in the southwestern herd alone, and the buffalo species was close to extinction.

In the new Middle Western states the two great industries were farming and stock raising. The cattle business contributed stirring chapters in the American legend, and the cowboys who rode the range were in many respects the most colorful and unique characters the nation ever produced. Their lives were rugged, their outlook reckless, and their day-to-day activities were attuned to conflicts with sheep ranchers, Indians, cattle rustlers, and the advancing homesteaders, who fenced off more and more of the best grazing land. It was inevitable that this land should move increasingly into the domain of the farmer, who could use it far more fully and economically than the cattleman.

Farther west, beyond the plains, mining was the great attraction for settlers. The 1849 gold rush to the Pacific coast was followed by the development of the Comstock Lode about 1860 and the Montana gold rush immediately after the war. These sporadic events determined the pattern of settlement in the Southwest, but they did not make for an orderly growth of the region. Over-optimism, hard drinking, and vice of every variety were the characteristics of mining-town life, and at their worst these communities made eastern fleshpots seem very mild indeed.

One notable exception to this pattern was the state of Utah, which had been settled in the 1850s by the persecuted Mormons under Brigham Young. By 1866 Utah had about 120,000 inhabitants, most of them farmers, and was operating under a theocratic government with a remarkable economic system based on barter and tightly controlled by Young himself. This worked as long as Utah could remain Mormon and self-sufficient, but when the Union Pacific brought in swarms of new traders and settlers its doom was sealed. Culturally, Utah scored some remarkable accomplishments, and economically it went far toward abolishing poverty; but it was hamstrung by Young's ironclad administrative system and by the institution of polygamy, which led to internal dissension.

Though the material progress to be seen in the country was breath-taking, it was only part of the story. At the same time that America was striding forward to new economic and geographic frontiers, it was acquiring a new cultural breadth, a new awakening of intellectual national consciousness.

Before the war intellectual pursuits were virtually a monopoly of the eastern seaboard, and particularly of New England; visitors from abroad found the rest of the country little more than a cultural desert. But after the war all this was changed. At Ann Arbor, Michigan, there grew up one of the country's most progressive universities; from the Middle West came such intellectual stimulants as Mark Twain and William Dean Howells; in the Far West the cultural awakening produced Bret Harte, Joaquin Miller, and others.

True, England's Victorian writers continued to set the literary tone. Charles Dickens was still the idol of most culture-conscious Americans; and when he visited this country two years after the war he grossed $140,000 in one tour of the eastern states alone. But native American writers found that they, for the first time, had an audience too. Men like Mark Twain and Bret Harte, who could not have hoped to enjoy wide popularity before the war, were able to capitalize successfully on the new interest in lectures and the rapid increase in readership of current periodicals.

Mark Twain's emergence was an excellent illustration of the thoroughness of the break between prewar and postwar cultural attitudes in America. With few exceptions, the intellectual giants of the ante-bellum years—men like Ralph Waldo Emerson, James Russell Lowell, and Oliver Wendell Holmes—were steeped in cultural tradition and formal education. But Mark Twain conformed to none of the established rules. He came originally from Missouri; his schooling was on river boats and in printing shops rather than in academic halls; his interests ran to plebeian and colorful subject matter rather than to the more refined and elegant subjects that had found the best audiences in the past. Because his work seemed vulgar to many who were influenced by the fastidious tastes of the period, the East was slow to recognize it; but by 1880, even Brahmin Boston was reading and enjoying him.

Mark Twain's first real popular recognition came as a lecturer, and it was in this capacity that many writers of the period found new and eager followers. The lecture bureau was, in fact, one of the great leavening influences in postwar America's cultural development, an admirable medium for disseminating intellectual stimulation.

It was a British-reared journalist, James Redpath, who must be given particular credit for the great growth of interest in lectures, for it was he who put lecturing on a sound, businesslike basis by establishing a central booking office in New York City and routing speakers about the countryside for 10 per cent of their fees. Under the guidance of Redpath and the others who hastened into the business, a steady stream of lecturers circulated through the nation, many of them obtaining fees that seem substantial even by today's standards. Henry Ward Beecher received as much as $1,000 for a single evening; the cartoonist Thomas Nast made $40,000 in a seven-month tour of the East. Soon afterward, the Chatauqua movement—founded in 1874 as a training program for Sunday-school teachers—blossomed into a noncommercial lecture center, sending earnest speakers through the nation, delivering instructive talks in thousands of cities and hamlets.

The revitalized American culture was not reflected in literature alone. Higher education underwent radical changes. The room for progress in this field was almost unlimited at the close of the war, for the nation's colleges were without exception in a deplorable state. Harvard, while perhaps the best of them, was poorly equipped, had virtually no funds for expansion, and offered an ill-organized, backward-looking curriculum that was scarcely above the level of a good high-school education today. Yale was even worse—a quasitheological institution in which free academic inquiry was effectively squelched by a small but dominant group of Congregational clergymen. In almost every college the teaching was uninspired, consisting mostly of dull recitations in which the pupil was taught to memorize and imitate rather than to think for himself.

President Charles Eliot enlarged the Harvard curriculum; he set up a system of "electives," which freed students from the stifling effects of being limited to a rigid and prescribed course; he upped entrance requirements so that Harvard was no longer open to anyone whose only assets were money and social position; he established a program of graduate study in liberal arts; and he raised professional training in law, medicine, and engineering to the postgraduate level.

The most hotly debated of the Eliot reforms was the elective system, which ran directly counter to almost all the accepted notions of the relationship of students to their colleges. Even relatively "liberal" educators felt that Harvard's president had gone too far, but the elective idea rode a ground swell of favorable public sentiment, and soon it was spreading to college after college.

Harvard also led the way in the reform of legal and medical education, both of which were in a particularly sorry state at the time of Eliot's ascendancy. In the law school—aided by the brilliant Dean C. C. Langdell—Eliot changed a haphazard eighteen-month course to a very demanding three-year one, and he changed the technique of teaching to the celebrated "case method." This method, which emphasized learning legal principles through study of actual cases rather than the mere memorizing of statutes, was scoffed at by lawyers until it was found that Harvard's graduates were far better equipped professionally than those from other law schools.

In the field of medical education the need for reform was even more urgent, for the universities had been turning out an astonishing number of dangerously incompetent doctors who were guilty of gross malpractice and, in many instances, killed as many patients as they cured. An indication of the wretched educational background that most medical students possessed was provided in 1870 when the head of the medical school at Harvard objected vigorously to giving examinations on the grounds that "a majority of the students cannot write well enough." But it was at Harvard, nevertheless, that the reforms came, swift and sweeping reforms instituted by Dr. Oliver Wendell Holmes of the medical faculty. A three-year graduate course was instituted, entrance requirements were drastically stiffened, and despite vehement objections from the medical profession, an entirely new concept of professional competence was established.

While these great reforms were going on in the established universities, equally significant strides were being made in the field of women's education. Higher education for women had not been unheard of before the war, but it had been regarded by the average American with profound distrust, as indeed was any concept which seemed to take women out of their traditional role as mothers and homemakers. This distrust, of course, did not disappear in the sixties and seventies, but it was beaten back by reformers to a degree that permitted women's education to move toward a new role in American life. The greatest step was the establishment of three first-rate colleges exclusively for women: Vassar (1865) in New York State, and Smith and Wellesley (both 1875) in Massachusetts. For the first time in its history the nation had women's colleges operating on standards just as high as those of the men's colleges.

The advances in education made scarcely as dramatic a story as the huge economic and social advances represented by the expansion of industry and the opening of the West, but they reflected the cultural changes that made the America of the eighties an incomparably different place from the America of pre-Civil War days. Theodore Roosevelt was one of the first to benefit from these changes.

THE RAILROADS CHANGED AMERICAN LIFE

THE GOLDEN SPIKE CEREMONY on May 10, 1869, in Utah marked the completion of the 3,250-mile transcontinental railroad. From then on, Americans were able to travel from New York to San Francisco in less than a week.

DINING AND SLEEPING CARS made long journeys less tedious and more comfortable. George Pullman first built them in 1864. The air brake, invented by George Westinghouse four years later, and the safety coupler made traveling safe.

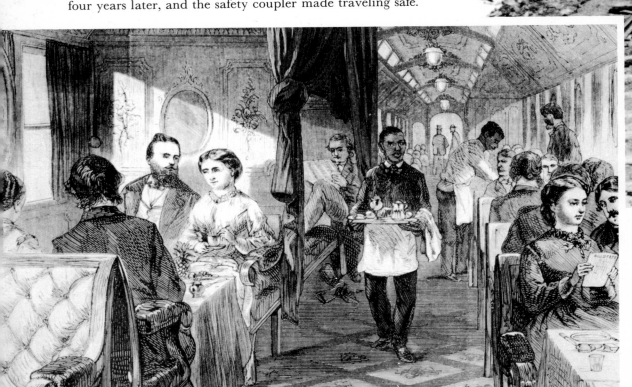

SPANNING THE CONTINENT. The Union Pacific, starting westward from Omaha in 1865, was built in feverish haste. Pushing through the territories of Nebraska and Wyoming and across the Rockies, the rails were laid as far as the Great Salt Basin by 1869. At the same time the Central Pacific, starting eastward from San Francisco, reached Utah. The two rails met at Promontory Point on May 10, 1869. The railroads opened up vast tracts of hitherto inaccessible territory to settlement; they increased commerce a hundredfold; they carried mineral, agricultural and other products from one part of the country to the other.

THE FIRST OIL WELL AND THE FIRST STEEL PLANT

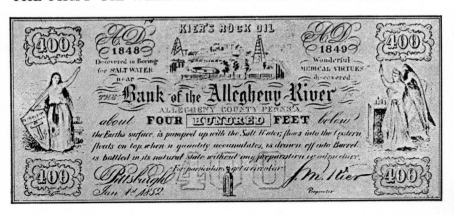

OIL ADVERTISEMENT—one of the earliest on record. Issued by Samuel M. Kier in Pittsburgh in January 1852, four years after oil was "discovered in boring for Salt Water near the Bank of the Allegheny River, Allegheny County, Penna., about Four Hundred Feet below the Earth's surface." This Petroleum, or Rock Oil, as sold by Kier at his Canal Basin store in Pittsburgh, was in the inventor's words "a natural remedy." Another of his advertisements extolled the amazing, all-inclusive healing virtues of the new discovery. "The lame, through its instrumentality, were made to walk —the blind, to see. Those who had suffered for years under the torturing pains of RHEUMATISM, GOUT AND NEURALGIA were restored to health and usefulness," asserted the enthusiastic advertisement.

THE FIRST STEEL PLANT. The Carnegie-owned Edgar Thomson Works made its initial Bessemer blow in August, 1875; shortly thereafter Pittsburgh's first steel rail slid through the rollers. Steel was turned out cheaply and in immense quantities, making huge profits for the mill.

DRAKE'S FOLLY—
In the year 1847 or thereabouts, Samuel M. Kier, the owner of a fleet of canalboats between Pittsburgh and Philadelphia, began bottling and selling petroleum as medicine. He drew this as a by-product of his father's salt wells near Tarentum in Pennsylvania. Although Kier charged a modest fee for his medicine, "the most wonderful remedy ever discovered," he could not sell all

THE FIRST OIL WELL NEAR TITUSVILLE, PA., WAS DRILLED BY EDWIN L. DRAKE

the oil that he produced. In his attempt to find other methods to utilize his oil, he consulted a chemist in Philadelphia for advice, and followed up his conversation with experiments in distilling petroleum. Convinced that if he could eliminate the smoke and odor of the product, petroleum could be used for lighting lamps, he erected a one-barrel still in Pittsburgh—the first oil refinery in the United States. Kier's "carbon oil" was not only cheaper but safer and better than the tallow or whale oil which until then had been used for illumination. At first Kier sold a gallon for 75¢, but when the number of customers increased, he upped the price, first to $1.50, then to $2.00. His chief trouble was that, however hard he tried, he could not increase his supply. This problem was solved when, in the latter days of August 1859, Edwin L. Drake—a former conductor of the New York & New Haven Railroad—struck oil in Titusville, using a six horse-power engine and a "Long John" tubular boiler which was stationary. Time proved he had tapped one of the greatest subterranean deposits of petroleum in America. With Drake's strike, the era of oil began. The photograph shows the Drake well five years later. On the wheelbarrow is "Uncle Billy" Smith, the driller who was paid $2.50 a day and who first perceived the oil floating in the well.

AMERICAN INGENUITY manifested itself in the enormous number of inventions which were patented in the decade after the war. Since the early days of the republic, to invent things has been a great American pastime. In the years before and after the Civil War, American-made sewing machines, American reapers, American revolvers, and American circular saws became popular commodities. With families filling up the country at breakneck speed, the great task before the American inventor was to help the women run their homes with less effort. Labor-saving devices were sorely needed, foremost among them a washing machine. This early contraption was cumbersome, but, to the joy of the housewives, it worked.

TRANSPORTATION PROBLEMS kept many an inventor's mind occupied. The question of how to move from one place to another without much effort waited for solution. Inventors tried feverishly to find a vehicle which would be a substitute for the horse-drawn carriage. They came up with a series of new ideas, one of them the unicycle as pictured on the right. Regular bicycles with rotary cranks were invented in 1865 by Pierre Lallement in Paris. After selling his patent to M. Michaux, Lallement emigrated to America and worked on the same idea. These first machines were extremely heavy and came to be known as "boneshakers" because of their vibration on the rough roads. Some of the models had tremendous front wheels up to 64 inches in diameter, while rear wheels shrank to 12 inches or less.

MAKING CAKES with a cake machine that was invented in the late sixties. New inventions penetrated every industry, every manufacturing establishment, producing goods which for centuries, and sometimes for milleniums—like bread—had been made by hand. Whether it was a machine for making bread or for canning food, every new implement not only increased production, but influenced and changed the habits of the American people. One of the great sights of Washington was the Patent Office. The number of patents granted by the federal government came to 36,000 by 1860. Thirty years later this number had increased over twelvefold. By 1890 half a million patents had been granted to American inventors.

94

THE PORTABLE RANGE, a de-luxe model of 1875. Life for women, not only in the newly broken country, but in the urban areas as well, was harder than that of the men. A woman had to care for her husband and children; she had to tend the chickens and milk the cows. She had to cook for the family, sew the children's clothing, do the laundry, clean the house—and she had to do all this without labor-saving devices. Thus, when inventors lightened her burden with improved stoves or practical sewing machines, such inventions were greeted with enthusiasm. Manufacturers reaped enormous profits on household appliances. A single manufacturer within a year sold 20,000 sewing machines, costing from $50 to $150.

THE TYPEWRITER was first used to help the blind or the paralytic. The early machines were unwieldy and not easy to operate, but by 1867 Christopher Latham Sholes, Carlos Glidden, and Samuel W. Soulé had introduced a practical model. After many experiments, the machine proved a success. With expanding commerce, expanding business, typewriters became an everyday necessity. At first the machines had only capital letters, but when in 1873 the gunmaking firm of Remington and Sons at Ilion, New York, took up manufacturing the Sholes-Glidden machine, the modern typewriter was born. It revolutionized American life; women typists invaded the offices. Theodore Roosevelt was the first President whose letters were almost all typewritten.

MASS PRODUCTION grew to be a burning need as the waves of immigration brought hundreds of thousands of newcomers to America. They needed clothing, they needed shoes, they needed goods. The primitive ways of making apparel at home had to be supplanted by the faster production of machines. Newly developed shoemaking machinery turned out footwear in great quantities, causing distress among the old craftsmen. With the installation of such machines, a master cobbler was not able to earn more than a dollar a day. His job was not steady; for weeks he was without employment. One factory with less than 100 hands produced more footwear in a day than could all the 30,000 bootmakers in Paris during an entire year.

GROWTH. The country expanded rapidly. A year before the Civil War began, the total railroad mileage in the country was 30,000; by the turn of the century it had increased to no less than 193,000.

OVERNIGHT ACCOMMODATIONS could be procured in hotels of the growing towns which mushroomed along the railroad lines. The above is the Grand Island Hotel in Platte, Nebraska.

MAIN STREET of Helena, Montana, in 1863. In 1790 only 5.1 per cent of the population lived in places with more than 2,500 inhabitants; by 1860 this percentage had risen to 19.8; by 1900 to 39.7.

"GIVE ME YOUR TIRED, YOUR POOR, YOUI The land needed men to develop the country and to develop it fast. Men arrived in droves—a quarter of a million in 1865. Eight years later this number had already been doubled. People came, hoping for a better life, hoping for opportunities and work. By

"...HUDDLED MASSES YEARNING TO BREATHE FREE ... SEND THESE, THE HOMELESS..."

...75 about 20 per cent of the nation's population ...s foreign born.

...The greatest number of immigrants came from the ...itish Isles, followed by Germans, Scandinavians ...d Dutch. Some Americans were disturbed by the influx of such a large foreign element; they were critical of the illiteracy of the eastern Europeans; they were worried about the congregation of the Irish in the city slums and the clannishness of the Germans and Scandinavians in the northwest settlements.

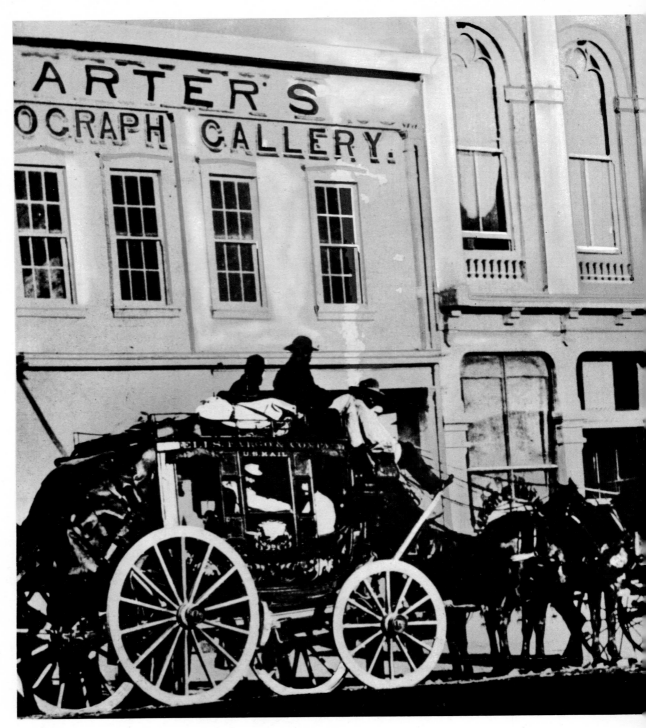

THE STAGE COACH. Not until October 1858—the very month Theodore Roosevelt was born—had an attempt been made to carry mail by means of a regular overland service across the continent to California. Before that, letters from New York were sent by water to San Francisco, taking three to four weeks to arrive. But when in 1860 the Pony Express was established to carry the mail on horseback, changing horses and riders every 50 or 75 miles, the almost 2,000 miles from St. Joseph to San Francisco were made in less than nine days.

The Pony Express appealed to the American imagination. Brave men on brave horses rode at breakneck speed, fighting the elements and the Indians

SHOOTING BUFFALO from the trains of the Kansas Pacific Railroad became an extremely popular sport. Within twenty-five years the great herd, an estimated 13,000,000 animals, had been wiped out.

CATTLE TOWNS like Wichita, Kansas, grew fast. When in 1873 a spur line connected Wichita with the Santa Fé, 350,000 head of cattle were shipped from its yards in that single year alone.

n the way. Unhappily it lasted only a few short months. With the completion of the telegraph line in October 1861, the Pony Express had outlived its usefulness. The overland stages like Holladay's famous line or Wells, Fargo (see above) took mail and passengers. With the expanding railroad lines, the stages, too, were to pass, and with them romance.

PLOWING ON THE PRAIRIES beyond the Mississippi. The newcomer cleared the land, broke the sod, plowed the earth, worked ceaselessly, reaping his reward in the bountiful yield of the virgin soil.

"GO WEST, YOUNG MAN."

In a steady and constant stream, men and women pushed forward to settle and to live on the vast and unexploited land. Conestoga wagons, prairie schooners, drawn by oxen, mules, and horses, two to ten drawing each team, crossed the country, moving slowly, taking people from one frontier to the other. Emigrants traveled together, well armed to protect themselves against the Indians. The journey was perilous. Some of those who were not strong enough to endure the hardships died on the way and were buried in the strange soil. But those who survived pushed on with high hopes. Their faith in the future they painted on the sides of their vehicles in bold letters: "Root Hog or Die," "Pike's Peak or Bust."

This rare photograph taken by Alexander Gardner in October 1867 depicts a bull train crossing the Smoky River near the town of Ellsworth, Kansas. It is the first known picture of such a migration.

"WE CROSS THE PRAIRIE AS OF OLD
The Pilgrims crossed the sea, / To make the West, as they the East, / The homestead of the free!" sang the poet Whittier. This is an early ranch house on a central Kansas homestead. It was photographed, tame elk and all, by Alexander Gardner in 1867. The Homestead Act, passed by Congress in 1862, provided that all present and prospective citizens could receive 160 acres of land free if they would re-side on it for five years. The Act proved a great impetus for many a city dweller and immigrant to move out West. In the year of 1865, no less than 160,000,000 acres were entered under the homestead laws; the following year, 1,892,000 acres; in 1867 the acreage declined slightly to 1,788,000, but in the next year it rose to 2,328,923 acres. After the Civil War, five to seven million acres of land were sold or granted every single year to prospective settlers.

102

CHAPTER VII

A GENERAL IS PRESIDENT

To understand Theodore Roosevelt's actions as President, one has to keep in mind the history of the administrations before him—particularly that of General Grant.

Under Grant's administration public morality reached a new low. There was a tremendous growth in national wealth, but no parallel growth in public sensibilities. Riches were available as never before, and premiums were placed on ruthlessness and avarice. The huge government contracts of the war years had created a new class of coarse and unprincipled men who sought more and more money without regard for the damage that their harsh actions brought to their fellow men.

Because of this, it was unfortunate for America that General Grant, who had served the nation so well in war, should have been elevated to the White House. The same qualities that had contributed to his success as a general tended to make him a bungler in politics, and his ineptitude left him an easy mark for rascals who stood to profit through presidential favors. He inherited from his army life a deep sense of loyalty to friends, and, since his judgment of men was often poor, it placed him constantly in the position of standing by friends who had committed disservices toward both him and the nation. Grant had neither training nor experience for the high political office. His inability to arrive at sound political decisions on his own made him dependent on advisers that he selected with great naïveté. His first Cabinet was the most inept in the nation's history—so impossible, in fact, that all of the men had to be booted out before a year was up.

The general had scarcely been in office six months when he became involved in the first of a number of scandals that were to spatter mud on the administration during his two terms. It was the celebrated "gold conspiracy" carried out in September of 1869 by two of the nation's most notorious speculators, Jay Gould and "Jim" Fisk, who cornered the gold market, created a severe panic on the Stock Exchange and enriched themselves with millions, all within the span of a few days. Both Gould and Fisk maintained an easy friendship with Grant, whom they convinced that it would benefit the country to restrain the Treasury from selling gold. It was a remarkable commentary on the morals of the period that this familiarity was not the subject of widespread condemnation.

Men like Gould and Fisk bought politicians wholesale who favored bills which would further enrich the men who bought them. Their example was followed in almost every state of the Union. In Pennsylvania, Simon Cameron ruled state politics with an iron hand, permitting the Pennsylvania Railroad and the coal companies to abrogate to themselves special privileges that defied any fair estimate of the rights of the general public. In the Kansas Legislature, a fearless and reform-minded representative dramatically laid down on the Speaker's table $7,000 that he was able to prove had been paid to him by the Republican machine in order to assure his voting for the re-election of U. S. Senator Samuel C. Pomeroy. In Illinois, free-spending lobbyists pushed through hundreds of illegal acts of incorporation, and in other Midwestern states the revelation of grafts and scandals was almost daily fare.

If state politics were riddled with scandal, municipal politics were worse; for this was the era in which some of the most flagrant of the corrupt city "machines" rose to power. The grossest performance took place in New York City, where the Democratic "Tweed Ring" operated in an unholy alliance with the upstate Republican machine under an agreement whereby the Republicans pushed favorable legislation through the State House and split the spoils.

The basis of Tweed's political power was significant, for its pattern was followed by other corrupt city machines for many decades to come. It rested primarily on the gratitude and support of the poor, particularly immigrants, who needed help in their daily problems. The machine was ably set up to give this help. Through its ward and precinct organizations it paid poor people's debts, distributed food on holidays, sponsored picnics and social events, squashed court actions against petty offenders, and—most important—found or created jobs for those in need. All it asked in exchange was a vote on election day. At the same time, it staved off opposition from more rich and powerful citizens by selling special privileges on a wholesale basis and by granting fat and corrupt contracts to those from whom it purchased goods and services. Thus the machine had the support of rich and poor alike.

By 1871 it was estimated that the Tweed Ring had stolen a total of about $20,000,000, and all this within a few short months. In one day alone the members of the ring—sitting as a board of special audit—approved expenditures totaling nearly $16,000,000, of which about $14,000,000 was pure graft.

At the national level thievery was not as bald and open as in many of the cities; but it was nevertheless an important characteristic of the postwar years, and its demoralizing effect was all the greater because of the loftier status of its participants. Perhaps the most flagrant among those who sought special favors were the railroad interests, which maintained a corps of well-paid Washington lobbyists with liberal expense accounts. Particularly questionable were the government's relations with the Union Pacific, which received between 1865 and 1869 more than half a million dollars in special subsidies under extraordinarily liberal terms.

The most alarming disclosure of railroad corruption was the affair of the Crédit Mobilier, a company which was formed by a group of Union Pacific stockholders to take over the contract for building the line's transcontinental route. The stockholders awarded themselves contracts for construction and supplies at figures so high that the railroad's profit was drastically reduced, while the holding company—the Crédit Mobilier—paid out large dividends.

To avoid governmental censure, the astute financiers distributed Crédit Mobilier stock to influential congressmen. It was graft of the first order.

Under the influence of booming prosperity and loose political morality, Washington social life blossomed during Grant's terms as it never had before. The dominant note was sounded by the newly rich who had flocked to the capital in pursuit of their business interests. They set a fast, gay pace: epicurean dinners, costly balls, heavy drinking, and much gambling. Older and more staid leaders of Washington society withdrew from the social whirl, disdainfully leaving the field to those with more money and less taste.

It was all but inevitable that the lack of statesmanship in the administration should have produced a rebellion in Republican ranks, particularly in view of the constantly mounting public distaste for the Radicals' stringent reconstruction policies in the South. The rebellion, when it came, was headed by the "Liberal Republicans," a group which numbered among its ranks such distinguished men as Horace Greeley, editor of the New York *Tribune*, Charles Francis Adams, Massachusetts political leader, whose father and grandfather had both been Presidents, and Carl Schurz, German-born newspaper editor who had fled from autocracy abroad and had fought constantly on the side of liberal policies in America.

As the 1872 Republican national convention drew near, it became obvious that the Radical wing of the party wanted Grant for a second term. In the face of this, the Liberals staged a convention in Cincinnati, nominating Greeley for the presidency and B. Gratz Brown of Missouri for the vice-presidency.

The success of the Liberal rebellion hinged on support from the Democrats, and this was obtained at the subsequent Democratic national convention in Baltimore. Greeley, who had once been an abolitionist and who did not favor the other Liberals' opposition to high tariffs, was not particularly pleasing to the Democrats; but they realized that they could not defeat Grant on their own, and so they quickly, if reluctantly, accepted both Greeley and the platform on which he had been nominated. General Sherman, writing to his brother from Paris, remarked: "Grant, who never was a Republican, is your candidate, and Greeley, who never was a Democrat, but quite the reverse, is the Democratic candidate."

In the campaign, personal abuse reached new depths, particularly through the pen of Thomas Nast, whose cartoons lauded Grant and attacked Greeley with unparalleled savagery. Even the campaign songs were vicious, the Republicans singing of Greeley's "free love and free farms," the Liberals singing of Grant "shouting the battle-cry of plunder." Despite the earnestness of their fight, the Liberals' attempt to stop Grant ended in failure. The general won, and Radical Republicanism was in the saddle for another four years.

On the day of General Grant's second inauguration fourteen-year-old Theodore Roosevelt "started out for the Jordan." He had left Jerusalem with his parents three days before, and now they reached the Dead Sea. "Of course we bathed in it," recorded Teedie. "It was a strange bath. You could not sink. You could really sit upright in deep water. The after effects were by no means unpleasant." This could not be said for General Grant's administration.

BLACK FRIDAY, SEPTEMBER 24, 1869. The excitement in the New York Stock Exchange after the Treasury Department placed four millions in gold on the market was immense. With this, the gold conspiracy of the two speculators Jay Gould and Jim Fisk came to a sudden end. The two rascals had taken advantage of President Grant's trusting nature and used him for their own unscrupulous machinations. They cornered the gold market and made a fortune for themselves. Their plan was simple. After persuading the President that farm prices would climb and farmers would be more prosperous if gold became scarce, and that it was poor policy for the Treasury to sell gold and relieve the shortage, they proceeded with their scheme. Not fearing governmental interference, they quickly bought up all the available gold supply, driving the price of gold from 140 to 163½ within four days. As soon as the naïve Grant realized that he had been duped, he ordered the Treasury to put gold on the market. But even before his order could be carried out, the speculators were tipped off by Mrs. Grant's brother. When Abel Corbin informed Gould of the President's decision, the two speculators sold out their holdings in a hurry, making millions of profit on the transaction. But those who had emulated them and who had not received the warning were smashed, their fortunes wiped out. When a congressional committee asked Fisk what had become of the money he made, he replied that "It has gone where the woodbine twineth."

TWO CARTOONS BY THE CELEBRATED THOMAS NAST ON THE *ALABAMA* CLAIMS

Both of them show President Grant with his Secretary of State, Hamilton Fish, and the British lion. During the Civil War, England allowed warships to be built and outfitted for the Confederacy in the British Isles. When these ships were ready, the English Government—in spite of repeated and serious warnings of our Minister—allowed them to leave the shores of England and prey on the commerce of the United States. The most famous Confederate raider was the *Alabama,* which left Liverpool in the summer of 1862, causing an estimated damage of $20,000,000 to the Union's boats and their cargoes. (One of the men responsible for the building of the *Alabama* was Theodore Roosevelt's "Uncle Jimmy" Bulloch.)

When the war ended—and after protracted negotiations between the United States and Great Britain —the two countries finally agreed in 1871 that the damage claims upon the *Alabama* and other warships should be settled by an international arbitration tribunal. This tribunal, meeting shortly thereafter in Geneva, Switzerland, awarded $15,500,000 in damages to the United States. Britain accepted the tribunal's decision with good grace and cordial relations between the two countries were resumed.

GRANT KEEPS THE PRICE OF GOLD DOWN

THE CRÉDIT MOBILIER AFFAIR—one of the great railroad corruptions of the era. The Crédit Mobilier was a construction company of the Union Pacific Railway, formed for the express purpose of taking over the contract for building the transcontinental route. It was a highly lucrative device: as Crédit Mobilier, the Union Pacific stockholders awarded to themselves fatly padded contracts for construction and supplies, thus milking the railroad dry of profits. To avoid governmental interference, the financiers offered influential congressmen Crédit Mobilier stock "at par," far below its real value. It was a clear bribe, and it reflected on the public morality of the time that the legislators were not above accepting such graft. When a congressional committee investigated the sordid business, Massa-

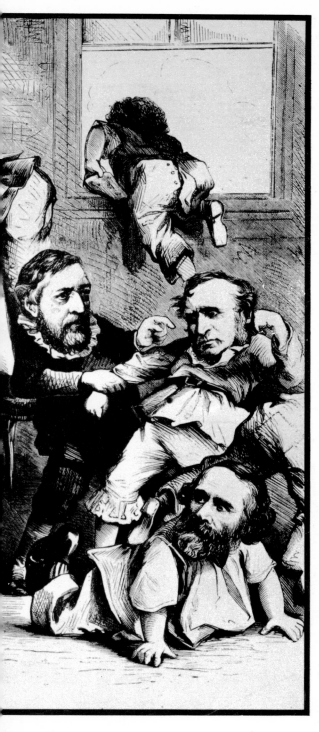

WILLIAM M. TWEED, as chairman of the New York Board of Supervisors and a deputy street commissioner, was in control of expenditures for public works. He concocted a profitable scheme: for every bit of work in the city—be it paving, cleaning of streets, or the purchase of supplies—he asked the contractors for bills which were 60 to 85 per cent higher than the originals. The difference was then distributed between Republican and Democratic legislators—the Tweed Ring—who had originally voted for the improvements. Thus the new county courthouse, which the city was to build for $250,000, cost the taxpayers $8,000,000, out of which $7,000,000 went into the pockets of the politicians. It is said that the Tweed Ring in its short existence stole over $20,-000,000—a large enough sum to have built Brooklyn Bridge.

That Tweed could steal in such grand manner was partly because the poor and ignorant Irish and German immigrants, who were helped by his machine, voted for him and his crooked companions, and partly because rich and powerful citizens received special privileges and were granted fat contracts by the crooks. However, in the end, Boss Tweed was unmasked and put into jail, where he died.

chusetts Representative Oakes Ames—who had distributed the bribes—was singled out as the scapegoat. Ames remarked with dry humor that he felt "like the man in Massachusetts who committed adultery, and the jury brought in a verdict that he was guilty as the devil but that the woman was as innocent as an angel." The above cartoon was drawn by artist Joseph Keppler and appeared in *Puck*.

HORACE GREELEY, the flamboyant editor of the New York *Tribune,* became the presidential candidate of the Liberal Republicans and the Democrats.

THE LIBERAL REPUBLICAN REVOLT

Lack of statesmanship in the administration, the steadily mounting graft and corruption, the Radical Republican stringent reconstruction policies created unrest within the Republican ranks, which gradually grew into an open rebellion against President Grant and his political advisers. Some of the best brains in the party abhorred the low morality of the administration and the malpractices which blossomed out under Grant and were allowed to flourish without punishment. These Republicans—"Liberal Republicans" as they were called—caused a serious split in the party. Determined to block a second term for Grant, they assembled in a separate nominating convention in Cincinnati and issued a platform—a forceful attack on the Grant administration. They pointed out that the President had "openly used the powers and opportunities of his high office for the promotion of personal ends," that he had "kept notoriously corrupt and unworthy men in places of power and responsibility, to the detriment of the public interest," that he had "rewarded with influential and lucrative offices men who had acquired his favor by valuable presents, thus stimulating the demoralization of our political life by his conspicuous example," that he had "shown himself deplorably unequal to the task imposed upon him by the necessities of the country, and culpably careless of the responsibilities of his high office." The Liberal Republicans chose Horace Greeley as their presidential candidate in the belief that the Democrats would also endorse him, which they did.

The scurrilous campaign that followed ended in General Grant's victory. He was still the hero of the people. The defeated Greeley, broken in soul and spirit, died even before the electoral votes were counted.

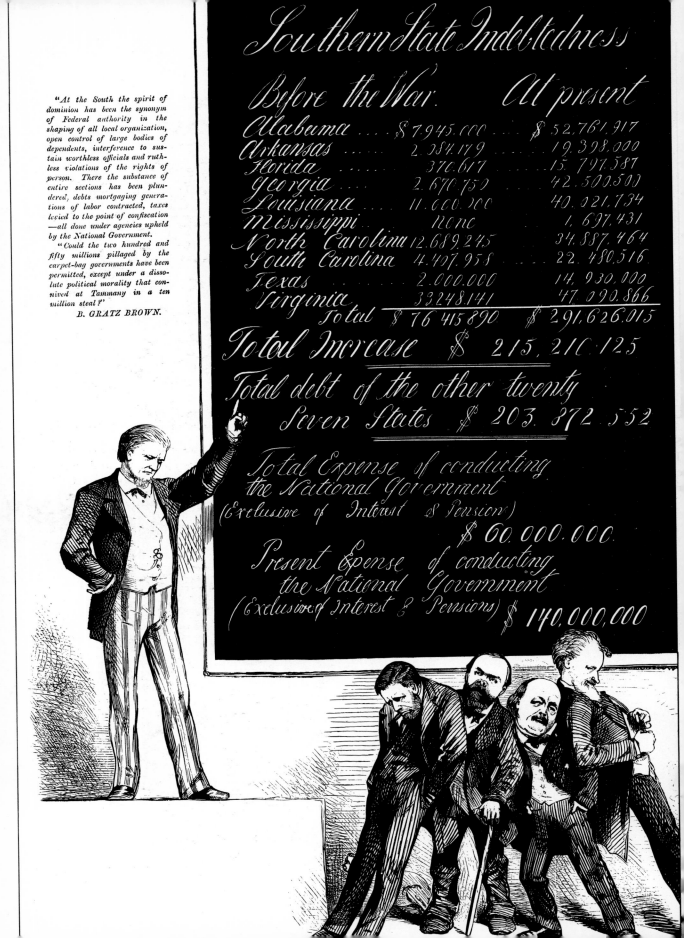

SAVAGE CARTOONS AGAINST GREELEY

Two samples from the pen of Thomas Nast, who ceaselessly assailed Horace Greeley and fought him relentlessly. The harmless sentence which Greeley once used in a speech: "Let us clasp hands over the bloody chasm" was used by Nast over and over again in his text. His drawings repeatedly depicted "Old Horace" as the man "over the bloody chasm."

CHAPTER VIII

"ANOTHER TERRIBLE TRIP TO EUROPE"

In the well-ordered Roosevelt household the postwar clamor of grafters, venal politicians, and the newly rich was scarcely audible. Family life continued to move with grace and serenity.

When Theodore was eleven years old his father had a man-to-man talk with him. "You have the mind, but not the body," the father said, "and without the help of the body the mind cannot go as far as it should. You must *make* your body. It is hard drudgery to make one's body, but I know you will do it."

And the boy responded to his father's advice with characteristic determination. He had embarked on the program of tedious body-building that was to alter his entire outlook on life. The second floor of the 20th Street house had been converted into an outdoor gymnasium with swings, seesaws, and parallel bars. "For many years," his sister Corinne remembered, "one of my most vivid recollections is seeing him between the horizontal bars, widening his chest by regular, monotonous motion."

It was more than a year later that a humiliating incident re-emphasized to Theodore his physical shortcomings. The scene was a stagecoach en route to Moosehead Lake in Maine, where he was being sent to recuperate from a violent attack of asthma. Two boys his own age on the coach began taunting him mercilessly during his coughing fits. Theodore tried to fight them—only to discover that "either one singly could not only handle me with easy contempt, but handle me so as not to hurt me much and yet to prevent my doing any damage whatever in return."

This experience wounded him deeply. "I made up my mind," he later wrote, "that I must never again be put in such a helpless position; and having become quickly and bitterly conscious that I did not have the natural prowess to hold my own, I decided I would try to supply its place by training."

In the fall of 1872 his parents took another trip to Europe. To the children the itinerary was far more exciting than on the first trip, for it included the Holy Land, parts of the Near East, and—best of all—a journey up the Nile River by chartered boat. Elliott noted: "Teedie and I won't mind the Nile very much, now that we have a boat to row in, perhaps it won't be so bad after all what with rowing, boxing, and Christmas and playing, in between lessons and the ruins."

As on the earlier voyage, the boy kept a diary, noting the main events of each day. The first stop was Liverpool, where the Roosevelts visited the Bullochs and where Theodore made the entry that he was "much annoyed by the street boys who immediately knew me for a Yankee and pestered me fearfully." From

GRANT'S RE-ELECTION WAS HAILED BY THOMAS NAST IN THIS BITING CARTOON RIDICULING THE PRESIDENT'S ENEMIES

England the family traveled via Bonn—"an old town and, like all old towns has both advantages and disadvantages"—to Paris, and from there to Brindisi, where they embarked for Alexandria.

The two-month voyage on the Nile was made in a dahabeah, or river boat. The *Aboo Erdan* was comfortable, but old and awkward; when the wind was right, a sail was hoisted, and when sailing was not possible, the craft was towed from the river bank by its native crew. For Teedie the most satisfying part of the journey was the huge variety of strange wild life. Equipped with an ornithological guidebook and a double-barreled shotgun, he began in earnest to collect specimens of birds and animals.

The ornithological book and the shotgun were, in a sense, symbols of a curious conflict that was to take place in the boy's conscience for many years. On the one hand, he had the instincts of an ardent conservationist and lover of wild things. On the other hand, he liked to hunt. To his childhood friend Edith Carow, who later became his wife, he wrote from Egypt that the gun his father gave him at Christmas rendered him "happy and the rest of the family miserable." And he added: "I killed several hundred birds with it, and then went and lost it!"

Along with his new enthusiasm for hunting, Teedie seemed to have acquired a new fund of physical stamina. Asthma attacks occurred, but far less frequently than in the past. For the first time he became the recognized leader of "We Three." His physical energy seemed almost inexhaustible. "He is a most enthusiastic sportsman," his father wrote, "and has infused some of his spirit into me. Yesterday I walked through the bogs with him at the risk of sinking hopelessly and helplessly, for hours, and carried the dragoman's gun, which is a muzzle-loader, with which I only shot several birds quietly resting upon distant limbs and fallen trees; but I felt I must keep up with Teedie." It was the first time that the athletic father had ever found difficulty in matching the pace set by the boy.

When not actually hunting, Teedie was likely to be leading Conie and Ellie on exhaustive explorations through the historic ruins and ancient temples that lined the Nile Valley. On shipboard his principal occupation was skinning and stuffing his specimens, a ritual generally performed on deck before a fascinated audience of native crew men. For the Roosevelt family, however, the boy's taxidermy was not nearly so fascinating. On one occasion there was great consternation when a well-meaning family maid placed in his personal wash kit a toothbrush which, it turned out, he had been using to apply arsenical preservative soap to animal skins. On another occasion Ellie rebelled against sharing hotel rooms with a brother whose luggage included innumerable birds and beasts in varying states of preservation.

In February the family left Egypt for a six-week tour of the Holy Land and Syria, covering most of the route in a series of camping trips. For the children the trip was one of almost continual delight. They tried unsuccessfully to dive in the buoyant water of the Dead Sea; they saw the hill where Jesus was crucified; they talked and traded with Arab sheiks; they crossed the River Jordan and rode caravan to the city of Damascus. From the Middle East the family proceeded to Athens, which Theodore's diary describes as lacking "the magnificent beauty of Baalbek and the gloomy grandeur of Karnak," and a week later to Constantinople.

The parents decided that Theodore, Corinne, and Elliott would be boarded for a few months with a family in Germany so that they might learn to speak German and absorb some Old World culture. The two boys, and ultimately Conie as well, stayed in the household of Dr. Minckwitz in Dresden, where they found a delightful and intellectually profitable atmosphere. They always remembered the kindliness and good cheer of their German hosts. Instruction was ably provided by the three amiable and well-educated Minckwitz daughters; but the two sons, both students at the University of Leipzig, proved more fascinating to the Roosevelt children. Both young men were members of dueling corps, and both had many scars to prove it. One was known as "The Red Duke" because of his scarlet hair, and the other as "Sir Rhinoceros" because a dueling sword had once chopped off the tip of his nose.

In Dresden, Theodore continued his progress in boxing and added specimens to his rapidly growing natural history collection. "Last night," Elliott wrote to his uncle, "in a round of one minute and a half with Teedie, he got a bloody nose and I got a bloody mouth, and in a round with Johnnie I got a bloody mouth again and he a pair of purple eyes. Then Johnnie gave Teedie another bloody nose." In a subsequent letter to his aunt, Theodore happily described himself as "a bully boy with a black eye."

There were other diversions, too. In a letter to his father Teedie remarks that he has been spending much time "translating natural history, wrestling with Richard, a young cousin of the Minckwitz' whom I can throw as often as he throws me, and I also sometimes cook, although my efforts in the culinary art are really confined to grinding coffee, beating eggs, or making hash, and such light labors."

It was in Dresden that the children first saw Shakespeare's *A Midsummer Night's Dream, Twelfth Night,* and *The Taming of the Shrew* on the stage. Plays at the German theaters began at six o'clock in the evening and were over by nine, so the young Roosevelts were able to spend many delightful evenings simultaneously improving their knowledge of German and Shakespeare.

As the summer waned, Teedie recorded the state of his affairs: "Health; good. Lessons; good. Play hours; bad. Appetite; good. Accounts; good. Clothes; greasy. Shoes; holey. Hair; more a-la-Mop than ever." More significant, perhaps, was a report of his brother Elliott about him: "Suddenly an idea has got hold of Teedie that we did not know enough German for the time we have been here, so he has asked Miss Anna to give him larger lessons, and of course I could not be left behind so we are working harder than ever in our lives."

In October, Mrs. Roosevelt arrived in Dresden from Carlsbad, where she had been taking the cure, to pick up her children; and in a few days they, complete with souvenirs and specimens, were bidding fond farewells to the Minckwitz family. The lovely days of Dresden had come to a close.

A DRAWING MADE BY THEODORE on his second voyage to Europe, of various animal skeletons. Shortly before the sailing it had been discovered that he could not see well, and he was taken to a doctor, who prescribed eyeglasses. "I had no idea how beautiful the world was until I got those spectacles," he wrote in his *Autobiography*. "I had been a clumsy and awkward little boy, and while much of my clumsiness and awkwardness was doubtless due to general characteristics, a great deal of it was due to the fact that I could not see and yet was wholly ignorant that I was not seeing."

AN ENTRY IN THE DIARY in Paris, on November 14, 1872: "In the morning I went out and bought some larks and buntings, which I returned home and skinned." Theodore was now in his taxidermist phase. "After dinner I went out and took a little walk, which was abruptly stopped by a rain shower.

"Paris is a good deal changed since 1870. The traces of the Commune are seen everywhere. The Palace of the Tuilleries is a mass of crumbling ruins and the Column Vendome a mere stump. Burnt buildings and pulled down houses are to be seen everywhere. Father and Mother joined us tonight."

For the next week the most important event of the day seemed to be that Teedie had "skinned some birds in the morning," since this sentence is repeated in his diary four times in as many days.

From Paris the Roosevelt family took the train and traveled via Turin and Bologna, where "as usual everybody combines to cheat you," to Brindisi in Italy, where they boarded a ship which was to take them to Alexandria and the wonders of the Nile.

HIS FIRST IMPRESSION OF EGYPT

Theodore wrote lyrically in his diary on November 28, 1872: "At eight o'clock we arrived in sight of Alexandria. How I gazed on it! It was Egypt, the land of my dreams. . . . it was a sight to awaken a thousand thoughts, and it did. . . . The broken remains of numerous old Egyptian Gods were scattered all around. On seeing this stately remain of former glory I *felt* a great deal but I *said* nothing. You can not express yourself on such an occasion."

THE ROOSEVELTS IN EGYPT

In December of 1872 the Roosevelt family and their friends were in Cairo looking for a dahabeah—the houseboat of the land. The *Aboo Erdan* pleased them, "the nicest, coziest, pleasantest little place you ever saw."

Journeying down the Nile, Theodore and his father often left the boat, walking and shooting along the river. The dry air helped Teedie's condition; his asthma attacks subsided. He hunted a great deal, brought animals on board, and stuffed the specimens. Every morning, Anna, the eldest of the children, gave her younger brothers and sister lessons in the French language.

The Roosevelts stopped at Luxor and visited the temple of Karnak. Theodore was overawed. "It was not only beautiful," he wrote in his diary, "it was grand, magnificent and awe-inspiring. It seemed to take me back thousands of years, to the time of the Pharaohs and to inspire thought which can never be spoken, a glimpse of the ineffable, of the unutterable."

The family had a lovely time on the boat, and had a most delightful time sight-seeing and hunting. When the voyage was over and the boat returned to Cairo everyone agreed that it was one of their happiest experiences.

Once, as they were mooring near another dahabeah, they discovered Ralph Waldo Emerson with his daughter, who also were touring Egypt, and they called on him. What Theodore's impression was of Emerson, we do not know; unfortunately, he did not record it. But he recorded that "There has always been something to do, for we could always fall back upon shooting when everything else failed us." And he proudly added up at the end of the voyage his accomplishment: during the journey he had procured no less than "one to two hundred skins."

The group photograph, probably taken during the time the Roosevelts were staying at Shepheard's Hotel in Cairo, shows from left to right (leaning on the chairs): Augustus Jay of New York, Francis Merriam of Boston, and Clift Smith of New York. Sitting: Edith Smith, Mrs. and Mr. Theodore Roosevelt, Mrs. Clift Smith, Elizabeth Clift Smith, and Nathaniel Thayer. The four Roosevelt children on the floor: Anna, Corinne, Theodore, and Elliott.

121

THE DRESDEN LITERARY AMERICAN CLUB: "WE ARE NO ASSES"
The tousle-haired boy on the left, almost fifteen years old, is Theodore Roosevelt; next to
him is his younger brother, Elliott. Standing: Cousin Maude Elliott. On the right: Corinne
Roosevelt and her cousin John Elliott. After their journey in Egypt, Syria, Greece, and
Turkey the Roosevelt children went by boat and train to Dresden, Germany, where they
stayed with a German family. As their mother's sister-in-law, the widow of Stuart Elliott,
was living in Dresden with her four children, she kept an eye on her Roosevelt nephews
and niece—who were studying in the Saxon city the life and language of the German people.

A TRAGEDY is described and drawn by Teedie. "My arsenic was confiscated and my mice thrown out of the window. In cases like this I would approach a refractory female, mouse in hand, corner her, and bang the mouse very near her face until she was . . . convinced of the wickedness of her actions."

THE YOUNG NATURALIST

Animal sketches by Theodore Roosevelt, made in the seventies. He had learned to be more scientific, describing animals with their proper Latin names and where he had observed them. "Elanus coeruleus—I found this handsome little kite common in Egypt in winter. It feeds on insects, which it takes on the wing, and also on lizards, etc. It flies very swiftly and beautifully," reads one of his ornithological observations made in Egypt. Another record from Germany: "Palumbus torquatus—I found it common in summer around Dresden." A French notation: "Podiceps minor—Common in the small pools near Paris."

A PICTURE LETTER BY THEODORE. The last page of one of his letters written in Dresden to his sister Anna, illustrating his idea of the Darwinian theory in reverse as it would affect him, changing his figure into that of a stork, his brother Elliott into a bull, and his cousin Johnny into a monkey.

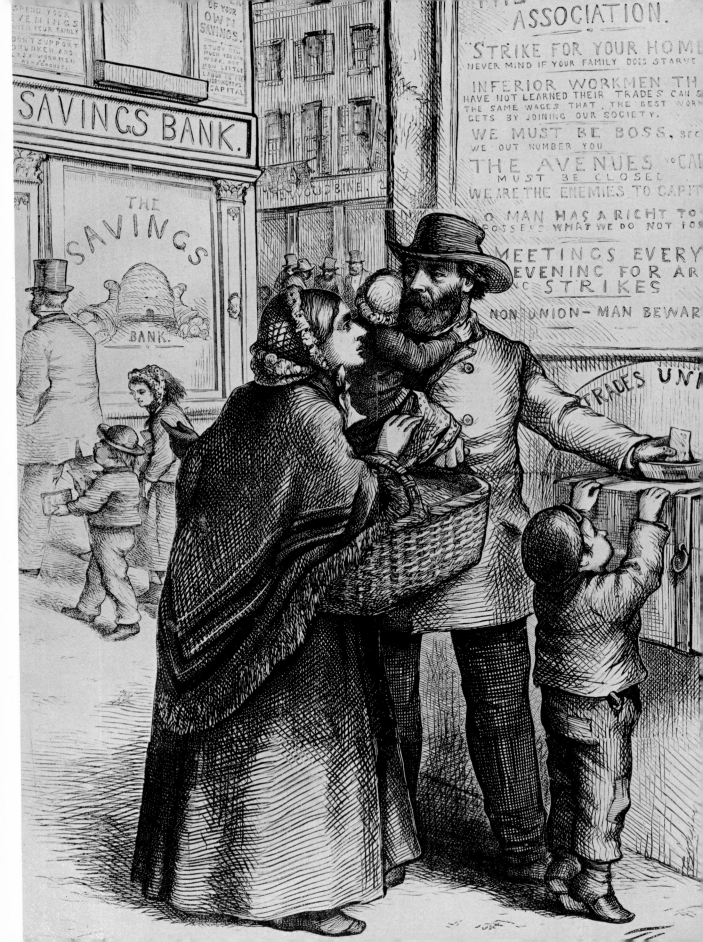

CHAPTER IX

DEPRESSION AND UNREST

On September 18, 1873—about the time the not yet fifteen-year-old Theodore Roosevelt horrified his hosts in Germany "by bringing home a dead bat"—an incredulous American public first heard the news that Jay Cooke and Company, the financial world's Rock of Gibraltar, had gone into bankruptcy. It was the dramatic end to the era of Northern prosperity that followed the Civil War.

The effects of Jay Cooke's disastrous failure were felt all over the land. The New York Stock Exchange suspended operations for ten days. In the economic stagnation that followed, there were 5,830 bankruptcies in 1874; 7,740 in 1875; and 10,478 in the rock-bottom year of 1878. And as the depression spread, half of the iron and steel mills were shut down, and about 500,000 workers were laid off in the railway industry alone.

Augmenting the physical hardship of economic privation was the demoralization brought on by an increasing loss of public faith in the practices of the nation's business community. Almost every business failure revealed some degree of fraud, gross selfishness, or just plain incompetence on the part of private management. When banks closed their doors the small depositors suffered, but the officers and directors usually managed to emerge relatively unscathed. As example after example of financial chicanery was laid bare, Wall Street became the target of an ever-increasing volume of public outcry.

Long before the business panic had struck the industrial East, the farmers of the Middle West were tasting the bitter fruit of economic hardship. As with industry, their basic problem was overexpansion. The amount of flour received in the Chicago market increased tenfold between 1854 and 1868; the amount of wheat more than fivefold. Throughout the Civil War prices remained high. But by 1869 wheat and flour were piling up in the shipping centers, and prices paid to the farmer dropped by 20, 30, and finally as much as 50 per cent.

The American farmer would not accept these conditions without protest. He had gone West in response to the promise of prosperity, and he felt bitter and disillusioned that the promise had been an empty one. For him it was a harsh life, particularly on the Great Plains, where winters were icy, summers parched, and neighbors were few and far between. Many homesteaders had moved to the western country with nothing but a few pieces of furniture, some tools—and hope. When hope failed, there was nowhere to turn but back. A familiar sight during the seventies were the eastward-traveling covered wagons with such inscriptions as "In God We Trusted, In Kansas We Busted."

The bitterness of these hard-pressed farmers was directed at several targets: the railroads, the stock and grain dealers, and the bankers who held farm

EARLY ANTI-UNION CARTOON
BY THOMAS NAST
DRAWN IN MAY, 1871

mortgages. The abuses practiced by railroads were often blatant and open. Freight rates were so high that a bushel of corn might bring the farmer 15¢ in Iowa and yet sell for 70¢ in the East. The railroad men were arrogant, they abused the small farmers in the same way that they abused the government. By issuing free passes, bribing brazenly, and buying legislators, they insured themselves by keeping their special privileges.

If the railroad men were bad, the produce dealers and middlemen were even worse. As they owned storage facilities, they had the power to buy wheat at low prices and sell at high. By 1870 about half the amount paid for a bushel of wheat in the East was going into a middleman's pocket. The banks, meanwhile, were taking advantage of the farmers' poor bargaining position by setting mortgage interest rates as high as 15 or even 20 per cent.

It was not difficult for the farmer to realize that as long as he remained unorganized, the banks, the middlemen, and the railroads would burden him with exorbitant demands. Divided, he was the victim of every businessman with whom he dealt; united, he would exercise tremendous power. Thus, the Patrons of Husbandry—better known as the Grange—the first national farmers' organization, came into being; within a few years it boasted a membership of 1,500,000. Through their organization, farmers were soon learning the advantages of pooling their purchases, of paying cash, and of by-passing middlemen. Typical of the achievements along these lines was the formation, with Grange endorsement, of the great mail-order house of Montgomery Ward. This thriving company saved millions of dollars for farmers simply by forcing local dealers to sell at fair prices.

In many states of the Middle West the farmers formed independent agrarian parties, elected congressmen and legislators to carry out their programs, and requested that private corporations should be regulated by the government in the interests of the public welfare.

Obviously, the lessons of the Grange could not be lost on the urban industrial workers. But unlike agrarian organization, the labor movement—with 3,000,000 unemployed during the depression years—progressed slowly. The leading labor organization was the Knights of Labor, formed in 1869 by the Philadelphia garment cutter Uriah S. Stevens. Dedicated to the aim of "one big union," the Knights aroused little enthusiasm among many trade-unionists who did not wish to join with unskilled workers. Another labor organization was the secret society known as the "Molly Maguires." An outgrowth of the Ancient Order of Hibernians, the Molly Maguire movement was limited to the anthracite coal mining region of Pennsylvania, where it fought bad working conditions by methods of property destruction and even assassination.

Despite the weakness of labor, the first great nationwide strike in the country's history was attempted in the summer of 1877 by the Brotherhood of Locomotive Engineers, an organization that included trainmen, trackmen, and conductors. This powerful union of 50,000 members had long been a thorn in the side of railway management. Determined to break its strength, the railroads ordered flat wage cuts of 10 per cent. In the strike, federal troops and local police fought the battle for management. In Baltimore nine strikers were killed, scores wounded; in Pittsburgh twenty-five were killed, and an enraged mob did millions of dollars' worth of damage to railroad property.

Ultimately the strike failed, but its memory lingered on. Capital learned for the first time that organized workers represented a power that could not be lightly dismissed; and labor, despite its defeat, attained a new sense of solidarity. One direct result of the strike was labor's participation with Western agrarians in the Greenback-Labor movement a year later. On a ticket demanding fiscal and industrial reform, the new party won over a million votes and, to the surprise of everyone, elected fourteen congressmen.

The combination of depression, labor unrest, and agrarian revolt seriously weakened President Grant's popularity. His position was further jeopardized by a series of new political scandals that came to light during his second term, underlining the nepotism and general ineptness of the party in power.

Next to railroad graft, perhaps the most flagrant source of political immorality was the internal revenue system, which presented easy opportunities for unscrupulous corporations that wished to evade taxes. The worst offenders were the liquor distillers. A so-called "Whisky Ring," operating principally in St. Louis and composed of distillers and U.S. revenue agents, had been mulcting the government out of hundreds of thousands of dollars in taxes. Grant's private secretary was implicated, and the President himself, though innocent of any awareness of what had been going on, was found to have accepted gifts from the Whisky Ring that indicated a regrettable lack of sense for the proprieties.

Other revelations proved scarcely more palatable. In the Treasury Department, Secretary William A. Richardson had to send in his resignation after one of his agents had been rewarded with a 50-per-cent commission for collecting $427,000 in overdue revenue. Secretary of War W. W. Belknap also resigned to avoid impeachment when it was discovered that he had been paid a total of $24,450 as a bribe to retain in office an unscrupulous post trader at Fort Sill in the Indian Territory. And Congress did little to purify the Washington atmosphere when in 1873 it callously approved the "Salary-Grab" Act, under which all congressmen were given a 50-per-cent pay increase, retroactive to 1871. This bill met with such vigorous public censure that it had to be repealed in short order.

With so many black marks on its record, there was no surprise when, in the mid-term elections of 1874, the Republican administration suffered a severe setback. Democrats won control of the House of Representatives by a majority of 70—by far their best showing in any national election since the Civil War. Most of the Southern states were in the Democratic column. The Republican dream of using the Negro vote to dominate that area failed.

Thus, while America "went to the dogs," Theodore Roosevelt prepared for the future. It was in September 1873 that he returned from Dresden to the States and, better equipped mentally and stronger physically, took up studies which in three years' time enabled him to become enrolled at Harvard.

THE PANIC OF 1873

The rapid expansion in business and industry turned out goods in greater quantities than the country could absorb. This condition brought on the financial panic of 1873, one of the severest in the nation's history. The cost of living was high, wages were low. In desperation the workers struck back at the employers. There were strikes on the railroads, there were strikes in the mines. The laboring men realized that their demands for higher wages and better working conditions could only be made effective if they acted together as a group and not as individuals. Thus they held congresses in the large cities, in which they asked for the eight-hour working day, for government inspection of mines and factories, for the regulation of railroad rates, the cessation of further land grants to the mammoth railroad corporations, the establishment of an income tax, and the exclusion of cheap Chinese labor. They further demanded free public education for their children and the creation of a Labor Department in Washington. These demands, growing out of hardship and poverty, came as a reaction to the enormous fortunes irresponsible capitalists had amassed by exploiting the men who worked for them. They had to be considered.

UNCLE SAM with his reform stick beats out the corrupt mushrooms of the Grant administration—a cartoon by Joseph Keppler in *Puck,* the outstanding political and satirical weekly.

The country, disgusted with the graft and corrup-

tion of the Grant administration, had turned its back on the Republicans and elected a Democratic House of Representatives. The Senate remained in Republican hands, but by a diminished majority. The reform element in the Republican party—the Liberal Republi-cans—asked for a thorough housecleaning. "Let no guilty man escape," exclaimed President Grant. But these belated and pious words had hardly any mean-ing. Most of the culprits had not only escaped, but had kept the money they had stolen from the public.

GRANT AS CAESAR—a biting cartoon by Matt Morgan in *Frank Leslie's Illustrated Newspaper,* satirizing President Grant as a Roman emperor sitting upon a pile of moneybags, and replying to the pleas of the Boys in Blue: "No! No! I make it a rule only to receive. I never give anything." Toward the end of his second administration the President's popularity was at its lowest ebb. The country which had cheered him so enthusiastically at the commencement of his presidency was sorely disappointed. With the aureole of the military hero dimmed, Grant was seen in his real colors—an inept bungler under whom graft and corruption were rampant. The American people grew bitter that their hero did not measure up to their ideal, they grew bitter when they discovered that he had feet of clay.

SCANDALS UNDER GRANT—the Sanborn contracts. A law of 1872 allowed high fees for collecting bad debts for the government. A man named Sanborn began to collect not bad but good debts to the tune of almost half a million dollars, keeping 50 per cent as commission, a large part of which went to Benjamin F. Butler, a political friend of the President.

SCANDALS UNDER GRANT—the Whisky Ring and the Belknap bribe. (1) A ring of revenue officials in St. Louis accepted large sums of money from distillers for nonpayment of taxes on whisky. (2) Secretary of War William Belknap was allowed by President Grant "with great regret" to resign after taking bribes from an Indian agent at Fort Sill.

TROUBLES UNDER GRANT—the farmers in the West rebelled. Their demands for a better life were attacked and labeled by some papers as Communist and un-American.

A FOREIGN AND POISONOUS WEED.
U. S. "That's right, Mr. GRANGER; I thought you would not have *that* in your *field.*"

THE AMERICAN TWINS.
"United we stand, Divided we fall."

CHAPTER X

THE PLEASURE OF GROWING UP

By the time the Roosevelts were settled in their new house in New York— Mr. Roosevelt had sold the 20th Street property and moved "uptown" to a house near the corner of 57th Street and Fifth Avenue—the depression was at its height.

Bad times had no effect on the Roosevelts, whose economic prosperity rested on a sound and conservative foundation. Least of all did they affect the existence of young Theodore, whose major problem at this time was to prepare himself for admission to Harvard College.

Although his health had greatly improved, his asthma attacks were still too troublesome to permit his being sent away to boarding school. His previous education had been so irregular that there was no school into which he could have fitted readily. In some subjects—history and languages, for example—he was well ahead of most boys his age. In other subjects, most notably Latin and mathematics, he was far behind. Therefore it was thought that the best solution was to place him in the hands of a young tutor, who could also supervise Elliott and Corinne's studies as well. Such a man was found in the person of Arthur W. Cutler, who later founded the Cutler School in New York. His able tutelage —combined with the conscientiousness of the pupil—enabled Theodore to accomplish three years' work in two.

The job of preparing Theodore for college was made somewhat easier by the huge fund of miscellaneous geographic and historical knowledge the boy had acquired in Europe, and by the scientific background that his interest in natural history had given him. Most helpful of all, he had been a voracious reader throughout his young life. "There was," he recalled later, "very little effort made to compel me to read books, my father and mother having the good sense not to try to get me to read anything I did not like, unless it was in the way of study. I was given the chance to read books that they thought I ought to read, but if I did not like them I was then given some other good book that I did like." This wise parental policy made books a joy and encouraged the boy's reading habits; thus, at the age of ten, he was able to record in his diary that he had already devoured some fifty novels.

Concentrated though his college preparatory studies were, they did not curtail Theodore's progress in other fields. He matured rapidly; the small-boy nickname of "Teedie" was applied to him less and less frequently. Friends addressed him now as Teddy (which he disliked throughout his life) or, more

133

THEODORE AND ELLIOTT ROOSEVELT WITH EDITH CAROW (ON THE GROUND) AND THEIR SISTER CORINNE IN THE YEAR OF 1875

often, as Theodore. He became more interested in girls and joined in the well-regulated social life of the young people in his family's milieu. He attended with pleasure a carefully recruited dancing class that his parents had organized in the city; and he became a leader in such group activities as skating parties and picnics in Central Park.

This blossoming social life was given considerable impetus in 1874 when his parents decided to join the summer colony that had been started at Oyster Bay, Long Island, many years earlier by the children's grandfather. The house they rented for the next three summers was named "Tranquillity"—a source of considerable amusement to their friends. "Anything less tranquil than that happy home at Oyster Bay could hardly be imagined," Theodore's sister recalled.

But to the Roosevelt children it seemed enchanted. There were endless horseback rides through open fields and country lanes. There were swimming parties and picnics. And, most enjoyable of all, there were frequent all-day boat trips across the bay, where the children and their friends would spend the afternoon stretched out on the sand, indulging in poetry contests or reading aloud to one another. A favorite companion for Theodore on these excursions was Edith Kermit Carow, who was one day to become his wife—the same "Eidieth" whose portrait had led Teedie to such pangs of homesickness in Paris five years earlier.

Theodore's new social life was not without its minor catastrophes. His sister has described one ridiculous episode that took place when Theodore rowed across Oyster Bay to visit a young lady on the opposite side. "He started at five o'clock in the morning," writes Corinne, "and reached the other shore at eight o'clock. Thinking it too early to pay a call, he lay down on a large rock and went to sleep, waking up to find his boat had drifted far away. When he put on his spectacles he could see the boat at a distance, but, of course, did not wish to swim with his clothes on, and decided to remove them temporarily. Having secured the boat, he forgot that it might be wise to put on his clothes before sleeping again under the dock. To his perfect horror, waking suddenly about an hour later, the boat, clothes, and all had vanished. At the same moment he heard the footsteps of his fair inamorata on the wooden planks of the dock above his head. She had walked down with a friend to greet the admirer whom she expected at about nine o'clock. His description of his feelings as he lay shivering, though not from cold, while above him they calmly discussed his probable arrival and the fact that they thought they would wait there to greet him, can probably be imagined." Eventually he was able to retrieve his clothes, but he was so annoyed at being placed in that embarrassing plight that he rowed back home without paying the proposed visit.

Along with his social and academic activities, Theodore also found time to continue the body-building program he had launched in the gymnasium on 20th Street five years earlier. In Dresden he had stopped keeping his youthful diary; now it was resumed in 1875 as a "sporting calendar," in which he recorded the milestones of his athletic progress. The entries were terse and uniformly favorable to Theodore, who referred to himself in the third person throughout: "Race between Johnny & Theodore. Theodore won." "Theodore & West wrestling and boxing. T. won." "Vaulting. Theodore, Elliott & W. Jacobs. T. won making 5 ft. 8½ in." "Wrestling Theodore beat Elliott."

Boxing lessons under the kindly tutelage of ex-prize fighter John Long continued. On one occasion the instructor, hoping to encourage more vigorous competition among his pupils, staged a tournament in which, to everyone's surprise, Theodore won first prize among the lightweight contenders and was duly awarded a pewter mug to commemorate the triumph—one of his favorite possessions. His increased physical stamina also became evident on the several camping trips that he made during this period in the Adirondack Mountains and in the Maine woods. To his sister Anna he wrote from Maine in 1875: "I have just come back from an eight days trip to Mt. Katahdin with Arthur and Emlen. Rather to my surprise I found that I could carry heavier loads and travel farther and faster than either of them; and could stand rough work better."

Other letters to his elder sister revealed his continuing interest in natural history. From Oyster Bay he wrote in August 1876: "I spent the early part of this week at the Osbornes and had a lovely time, the days being full of 'ornithological enjoyment and reptilian rapture.' I came home with a jar of pickled toads and salamanders." Again from Oyster Bay: "I am writing in a rather smelly room as the fresh skins of eight night herons are reposing on the table beside me." Long Island proved a fertile field for the young ornithologist, and he happily put in long hours at gathering, mounting and classifying his growing collection of specimens. "I worked with greater industry than either intelligence or success," he noted forty years later, "and made very few additions to the sum of human knowledge; but to this day certain obscure ornithological publications may be found in which are recorded such items as, for instance, that on one occasion a fish-crow and on another an Ipswich sparrow, were obtained by one Theodore Roosevelt Jr. at Oyster Bay, on the shore of Long Island Sound."

Theodore was keen to make natural history his profession. During the summers at Oyster Bay and the first year at college, he and his father had many long and serious talks on this subject. The father's advice was tolerant and sensible: if Theodore really wanted to devote his life to nonremunerative scientific work, he was free to do so, and with parental blessing. But he must realize that it would mean a far more modest scale of living than he had been accustomed to; and above all, he must approach any such work, not halfheartedly, but with just as much determination and earnestness as if he were trying to make his own way in the business world. Choosing a naturalist's career must under no circumstances serve as an excuse for a life of mere dilettantism.

In the spring of 1876 he took the entrance examinations for Harvard, passing them with ease. And in September of the same year he left Oyster Bay and the house on 57th Street for Cambridge.

AFTER THE SECOND TRIP TO EUROPE

Theodore was more confident of himself than ever before. He was no longer a weak and sickly boy, no longer an easy prey for bullies. He could take care of himself, he could use his fists and his muscles.

Carleton Putnam in the outstanding study on Roosevelt's formative years gives this perceptive thumbnail sketch: "Young Theodore's rebellion against his personal limitations and the traits this struggle had developed were already beginning to be transferred to other, more objective fields. He was continuing to show an almost ruthless singlemindedness where his interests were aroused. The exhaustive fashion in which he described and classified his collection, the pains he took in skinning, dissecting and stuffing specimens, above all the initiative and sustained effort implicit in his approach, were more and more suggestive of a purposeful, determined personality." He had positive opinions, he had definite judgments, which—though at times wrong—were always firm. Following the footsteps of his father, whom he admired, he lived a clean and moral life. Aware of his social position, he was willing to give a shining example of how to behave toward those who were less fortunate than he himself.

On his return with his family from a long European trip President Roosevelt, then Theodore Roosevelt, Jr., began his preparation for college in October 1873 under the direction of Arthur H. Cutler. It was the family plan from the beginning that young Roosevelt's education should be as practical as the demands of Harvard then allowed, hence he was prepared on the minimum requirement only in Greek, but emphasis was laid on Mathematics, Elementary Science, Latin and History, while modern languages were studied under native teachers. At first the studies were carried on by the method of class work, President Roosevelt being joined by his brother, the late Elliot Roosevelt and by his cousin, the late Dr. West Roosevelt in forming the class, but during the last part of his preparation the work was entirely individual as he alone of the three proposed to enter Harvard. Although this preparation was begun in a tentative way in 1873 it was not until the summer of 1874 that a serious plan of study was undertaken, but from that time the alert, vigorous character of young Roosevelt's mind became evident and he completed in two years the work which had usually required three years. It cannot be said that the future President exhibited proficiency in one line more than another; he did excellently in all lines and while he seemed to enjoy more the study of Modern Languages and History, he did not neglect Mathematics or the dry ancient languages.

It was the family belief that study should continue in summer as well as in winter, and so work was pursued at Oyster Bay during July, August and September as at the town house 6 West 57th Street during the rest of the year. Study was not severe during the summer, recitations and preparation rarely lasting more than three hours daily, from 9 to 12, while the winter work took from six to eight hours daily. There were short recesses too of ten days or a fortnight, one late in June, another in August for a camping excursion to the Adirondacks, a third late in September and a fourth at Christmas, but there were substantially ten months of formal study in each year. How much informal study there was President Roosevelt himself alone can tell for his mind was attracted in many directions then as now. The young man never seemed to know what idleness was and every leisure moment would find the last novel, some English classic or some abstruse book on Natural History in his hand. The study of Natural History was his chief recreation then as it has continued to be. He had an unusually large collection of birds and small animals, shot and mounted by himself, and ranging in habitat from Egypt to the woods of Pennsylvania. In his excursions outside the city, his rifle was always with him, and the outfit of a taxidermist was in use on every camping trip.

What began as a class for the Roosevelt boys has now expanded in the Cutler School of this city, but school life with the ramifications of athletics, societies and school theatricals was unknown at that time, but the future President had much sport if there was no gridiron football field where he could tackle his opponant nor any cinder track where he could sprint. He rode horseback much and well, he boxed well, he shot well (as we have said) and he was the fleetest of his mates in their boy foot races. He seemed to have less interest in sailing than would be expected of one who spent three months of each year at Oyster Bay, but that was probably because so many other things intrested him.more.

REMINISCENCES OF HIS TUTOR. Theodore Roosevelt began serious preparation for Harvard in October 1873. His tutor was Arthur H. Cutler, who left a memorandum as to his pupil's ability. "He completed," wrote Cutler, "in two years the work which had usually required three years." Theodore studied diligently summer and winter, especially enjoying the study of modern languages and history.

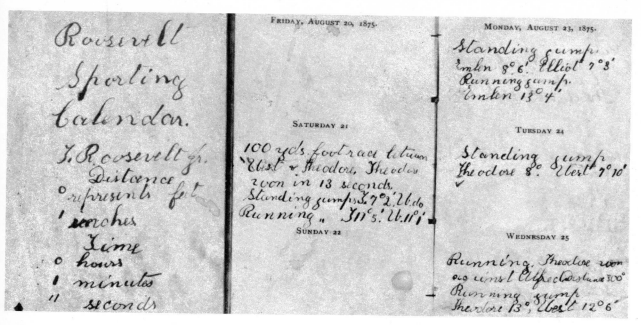

THEODORE'S SPORTING CALENDAR, in which he noted the exact measurements of his chest, waist, thigh, neck, shoulders, and arms on November 1, 1875. Now seventeen, he was still slender; his weight was 124 pounds, his height 5 feet 8 inches. In keeping track of his athletic achievements he jotted down everything that seemed to him important with the same care which had characterized his diaries.

THE NEW SUMMER HOME on Cove Neck Road, at Oyster Bay, Long Island, where the Roosevelts went after their return from abroad in 1874. It was called "Tranquillity" and looked somewhat like Mrs. Roosevelt's paternal home in Georgia. The family stayed there in the summer months, while their winter address was now 6 West 57th Street. The former home on 20th Street had been sold so they could be nearer Central Park and out in the country, which 57th Street was in those days.

CHAPTER XI

THE YEAR OF 1876

In 1876, the year Theodore entered Harvard, the United States celebrated the centennial of the Declaration of Independence. In its first hundred years the country had grown far beyond the wildest dreams of the Founding Fathers. It had grown into a spectacular land, in which good and evil were holding a precarious balance. An unfriendly observer coming to our shores in 1876 might have painted a gloomy picture of American life, showing in dark colors the worst aspects: industrial strife, demoralizing bread lines, political corruption, ugly and decrepit housing conditions of the poor. But a friendly observer, while admitting all the abuses, would have pointed out that beneath the troubled surface the progress of the nation had been greater than that of any other country in all the world's history.

The event that did more than anything else to make Americans appreciate their own achievement was the great Centennial Fair at Philadelphia. The numerous exhibits from abroad were balanced by thousands of American ones. Household wares from England, textiles from France, jewels from India, watches from Switzerland, lacquer from Japan, ivory from Africa, clocks from Germany were more than matched by demonstrations of special skills by Waltham's watchmakers, Trenton's ceramic workers, Lowell's textile weavers. It was perhaps the greatest exhibition of all times. Ten million visitors came— almost a fourth of the country's population—to gasp at the industrial, technical, and cultural wonders.

A few short weeks after the fair closed, the nation went to the polls to select its next President in the most closely contested election of American history. Ever since the Democratic resurgence in the mid-term elections of 1874, it had been apparent that the Republican party was in danger of losing the Presidency. With business failures steadily increasing and with scandal after scandal revealing the ineptitude of the Republican administration, the Democrats were certain that the next Chief Magistrate would be chosen from their ranks.

For the high office, Rutherford B. Hayes, the Republican governor of Ohio, opposed Samuel J. Tilden, the liberal, reform-minded Democratic governor of New York. And when the votes were counted, it seemed that Samuel J. Tilden would be the next President of the United States. On the night of the election, even the most resolutely Republican newspapers conceded his triumph. But in the early hours of the following day, editors of the New York *Times* discovered a ray of hope; they saw a possibility of eking out a Republican victory in the electoral college. At daybreak they sent a message to the party's national chairman, Zachariah Chandler, who was at the time sleeping off the effects of

139

EADY FOR HARVARD.
HEODORE IN 1876

liquor taken the previous night. Republican victory depended on winning three Southern states—South Carolina, Florida, and Louisiana—which had been generally assumed to have gone Democratic but which were still under carpetbag control. If the Republicans could retain their grip in these three states, the victory would be theirs. In the electoral college 185 votes constituted the majority. Thus, if the votes of the three doubtful states could be counted for Hayes, he would be the President, winning the office by a single vote.

Instantly telegrams went out from party headquarters to Republican leaders in the three states. "Hayes is elected if we have carried South Carolina, Florida, and Louisiana. Can you hold your state?" By late afternoon Chandler felt confident enough to issue the statement: "Hayes has 185 electoral votes and is elected."

It was many weeks, however, before this verdict could be reached officially. Congress placed the decision in the hands of an electoral commission, and this commission, by a strict party-line vote, decided in favor of Hayes. Thus the Republicans won the Presidency—but in a larger sense it was a Democratic victory. The federal troops were withdrawn from the South, bringing to an end the Reconstruction era, and from that time on, the South has been a stronghold of the Democratic party.

During the seventies the idealistic energies of social reformers began to take root in American soil. The American people, painfully aware of their short-comings in their moral and social responsibilities, began to correct their faults.

The first municipal health board in New York was given power to close up some of the city's disease-infested slums, ordering tenement owners to improve housing conditions for their more than 100,000 tenants. The "poorhouses," filthy and unsanitary, holding indigent families, were improved. The reformers turned their attention to prisons, rampant with corruption and cruelty, to abuses of animals, and this, in turn, led to the crusade against cruelty to help-less children. That story is a fascinating one and worth telling.

It was in 1874 that a starved and beaten nine-year-old girl was brought be-fore a New York municipal court, and the court was asked that the girl be con-sidered an animal, because as such she would have the protection of the law for mistreated beasts. The reformer Jacob Riis, later a friend of Theodore Roosevelt, described the scene in the courtroom: "I saw the unclothed child laid at the feet of the judge, who turned his face away, and in the stillness of that courtroom I heard a voice raised, claiming for that child the protection man had denied it, in the name of the hopeless cur on the streets." The case of the little girl impressed the people so deeply that it led to the formation of the Society for the Prevention of Cruelty to Children.

One questions why conditions could become so wretched in a free, demo-cratic society. The answer is not hard to give. The seventies and the decades after them were the decades of the laissez-faire philosophy. Let people alone, let them solve their own problems and difficulties; do not interfere with them. Society believed that as there should be no restriction or governmental inter-ference with business, there should likewise be no interference in the relation-ship of parents and their children. But, when freedom of action was abused by irresponsible men, it became necessary to put restrictions on such freedom to protect the weak and the helpless.

Much of the humanitarian endeavor originated in the nation's churches, where men like Dwight L. Moody, the great evangelist, made Americans aware of their obligation to better the lot of their fellow men. One direct outgrowth of this "revivalist" movement was the American branch of the Salvation Army, which achieved early and widespread support for its program of rescuing the souls of society's derelicts. More secular, though also with heavy religious overtones, were the Young Men's and Young Women's Christian Associations, which both scored tremendous gains in membership during the seventies.

But the movement through which religion accomplished its greatest social influence was the crusade against intoxicating liquor. As a natural reaction against the moral laxity of the postwar years, the movement acquired new aggressiveness in the 1870s with a war against "Demon Rum" and the political and social problems that intemperance had created. The Women's Christian Temperance Union, which started in 1874 as a praying crusade to shut down saloons in upstate New York and Ohio, became by the end of the decade a national organization of such strength that it caused serious concern to the liquor interests and practical politicians.

Closely allied with the temperance movement was the women's suffrage crusade, which had its beginnings in pre-Civil War days but emerged with new vigor in these years. The emancipation of the Negro added an effective weapon to the suffrage advocates' arsenal: why, so people asked, were women not entitled to equal rights with ex-slaves? Two indefatigable women, Susan B. Anthony and Elizabeth Cady, led the battle, lecturing, writing, and organizing demonstrations wherever they could obtain a hearing. "We speak in school houses, barns, sawmills, log cabins with boards for seats and lanterns strung around for lights," wrote Miss Anthony during a crusade in Kansas, "but people come twenty miles to hear." Often ridiculed by women as well as by men, they nevertheless added thousands of converts to their banner with each succeeding year. That, in the end, success would crown their endeavor could never be in doubt.

Though many good citizens joined the reform movements, many opposed them, as they interfered in affairs that were said to be none of the reformers' business—a cry which one has heard whenever powerful interests have had to submit to regulations making them respect the rights of their economically inferior brother. But the very fact that such movements could flourish in the America of the seventies and that they could produce results was greatly heartening; it indicated that the country was awakening to its moral and social responsibility. The new interest in humanitarian endeavor, like the accomplishments displayed at the great centennial in Philadelphia, was welcome evidence that the nation was entering its second century of existence in a fundamentally sound condition.

THE CENTENNIAL OF INDEPENDENCE was celebrated by a great world's fair at Philadelphia, the birthplace of the republic. On May 10, 1876, President Ulysses S. Grant opened the Exhibition. It was a great moment in the nation's history. Casting aside the cares and worries of the depression, Americans renewed their faith in themselves. They showed their industrial, scientific, and cultural achievements, and what glorious achievements they were! The Exhibition pointed to a new era of industrial expansion, to an era of abundance and of better and more comfortable living for all those who could afford it.

THE CORLISS ENGINE, one of the industrial wonders of the fair, furnished power to all the machinery in the main exhibition hall. This marvel of the age had 1,500 horsepower and weighed 8,000 tons. Ten million visitors came to see it and the other exhibits that showed the enormous strides that had been made in technology. True, the country was in the midst of a severe depression with hundreds of thousands unemployed and with bread lines miles long, but it was true also that within the last two decades the nation's wealth had increased threefold; the steel output alone had in one decade multiplied almost a hundred times.

142

THE KRUPP GUN EXHIBIT, a proof of German superiority in the construction of murderous weapons, weapons so frightening that they were to stop all wars. The possible havoc of such guns would be so great—so the political oracles said—that it would not pay nations to settle differences on battlefields, a prophecy which, as we learned, was not quite proved by subsequent events. And while the Germans impressed the fair's visitors with guns, America showed exhibits of ores and mining processes, of scientific techniques for soil conservation, of industrial products, and other of its peaceful achievements.

MOST ADMIRED EXHIBIT was the telephone, the invention of Alexander Graham Bell, called by the London *Times* "the latest American humbug." In March 1876—after three years of experiment on a device which could reproduce by means of electricity the tones of the human voice—Bell talked into his machine, and his words, "Mr. Watson, come here; I want you," were heard around the world. At first telephones were rented out in pairs for parties who desired to communicate with each other, but in 1878 the first commercial switchboard was installed in New Haven with a subscriber list of twenty-one.

LIFE IN THE COUNTRY: spelling matches—especially in the West—were popular and drew large audiences. The age of amusements was still in the future—no motor cars, no movies, no gramophones yet—the people had to be content with simple pleasures. They played parlor games, went to lectures, listening to the orations of the great men, read books and magazines, and enjoyed each other's company. Some of their grandchildren in later years said that their grandparents lived a rather boring and dull life, that they had few diversions and not many pleasures. One wonders whether their criticism had validity; one wonders whether grandfather and grandmother did not have a more purposeful and enjoyable existence than their fun-seeking grandsons and granddaughters two generations after them.

TRAVELING BECAME EASY

An artist's impression of the smoking saloon and the parlor car on a train of the Pennsylvania Railroad, which operated between New York and Philadelphia. Americans began to move around the country; they traveled in trains, though the well-to-do still preferred a European voyage to a trip at home. America was not yet fashionable; Europe was still the vogue. The "better classes" still imitated European customs and European manners. Mothers of wealthy girls were still looking for a European prince or count or baron for their offspring.

LIFE IN THE CITY: Christmas shopping in New York. The gulf between rich and poor was vast. On one side were the wealthy, as pictured in the drawing by an artist of *Frank Leslie's Illustrated Newspaper* in 1876, able to buy all the expensive dolls and presents for their children, while on the other side—peeping through the window—was the poor family of immigrants who could only look at the "holiday goods of every description." Though the artist may have overdrawn conditions, generally he was not off the mark. More than 100,000 people in New York alone dwelt in slums; the "poorhouses" were filled with families who could not make the grade; prisons harbored many a young man who had turned in despair to crime. Social consciousness had not yet awakened in the minds of the well-to-do.

THE PRODUCE EXCHANGE of New York. The artist pictured the excitement in the trading room when the news came from Russia that that country had declared war. Wars are always beneficial to prices of foodstuffs. With tremendously increasing crops—in the state of Kansas alone the corn crops had increased within two decades from 6,000,000 to over 100,000,000 bushels—it became lucrative to speculate on the Produce Exchange. Fortunes were made as America was expanding its economy and as the frontier was pushed farther and farther back.

THE HAYES-TILDEN ELECTION

THE ELECTORAL COMMISSION, eight Republicans and seven Democrats, gave the votes of the three disputed Southern carpetbag states to Hayes.

REPUBLICAN APPROVAL. Senator Conkling, a prime mover behind the scenes, tells Zachariah Chandler to disband his "noble army of conspirators."

DEMOCRATIC PROTEST. When the Electoral Commission gave the votes of Louisiana to Hayes, the Democrats in the House promptly signed a protest.

"TILDEN OR BLOOD" says the cartoon. But Tilden, the Democratic candidate, accepted the verdict of the commission, preferring it to Civil War.

ANNOUNCING THE RESULT in the early hours of March 2, when the president of the Senate revealed that Hayes received 185 votes and won the election.

146

MIDNIGHT, MARCH 3, 1877. President Grant and members of his political family, waiting at the Capitol in Washington to sign the last bills of the outgoing administration. Standing in front, the second on the left, is Secretary of State Hamilton Fish, by far the most outstanding man in Grant's Cabinet.

By midnight of election day, Rutherford Hayes, the Republican candidate, went to bed in the belief that he had lost the election. But during the night the chairman of the Republican congressional committee, alerted by the managing editor of the New York *Times,* wired to the party heads in the three carpetbag states of Louisiana, South Carolina, and Florida: "Hayes is elected if we have carried South Carolina, Florida, and Louisiana. Can you hold your state?"

Counting Louisiana and South Carolina for Hayes, the *Times* gave in its morning edition 184 electoral votes for Tilden and 181 for Hayes, leaving the four Florida votes in doubt. With 185 votes constituting the majority, Tilden needed only one more vote to become President. But if the Republicans could secure the four Florida votes, Hayes would have the 185 votes. The struggle for this extra vote kept the country in a state of excitement for weeks to come. Republicans and Democrats fought for it with great vehemence. Not being able to agree, Congress formed a special commission which gave the votes to Hayes. Thus, the Republican Hayes became President.

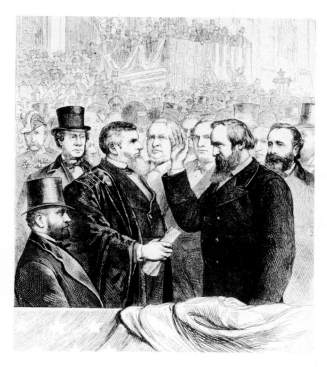

Within the cartoon, on the sign:
STRAYED FROM HIS HOME!
MY DARLING SOUTH!
WAS LAST SEEN IN THE
COMPANY OF AN ELDERLY
PERSON WHO CLAIMED
TO BE HIS GUARDIAN.
A NATION'S GRATITUDE
SHALL REWARD HIM WHO
RESTORES MY SON TO
HIS DISTRESSED
MOTHER.—COLUMBIA.

C. S. REINHART

THE BENEFICIAL RESULT of the disputed Hayes-Tilden election was the withdrawal of federal troops from Louisiana and South Carolina, the last two carpetbag states. Florida, whose returns were disputed as well, was no longer counted as a carpetbag state; eight weeks before the new President's inauguration, that state had installed a Democratic governor and taken its rightful place with the sister states.

It was said that the Democrats accepted the verdict of the Electoral Commission only after they were promised by the Republicans that the troops would be withdrawn from the two remaining Southern states if they would accept Hayes's presidency. Rutherford B. Hayes, whom the opposition press from that day on branded as "Rutherfraud" B. Hayes, denied that he had any part in the bargain, and it is probable that he hadn't even heard of it. Still, the fact remains that not long after assuming office he ordered the withdrawal of the military from the South. With this, the era of Radical Reconstruction—lasting twelve ignominious years—came to an end.

In the above cartoon C. S. Reinhart, a cartoonist for *Harper's Weekly*, indulged in some wishful thinking. He pictures the Democratic party as an old, wailing woman, lamenting the fact that the Republican President had stolen her child—the South. On the right of the drawing, the figure of Columbia thanks Hayes: "Oh, bless you, sir! You've brought us all together again."

In reality the situation turned out to be exactly contrary to this Republican daydream. The Republicans had not captured the South—far from it. The withdrawal of the federal troops resulted in the emergence of the South as the bulwark of the Democratic party from that time on. For decades afterward, up to the present, the "Solid South" was in the Democratic column, sending Democratic senators and Democratic representatives to Washington.

A THOMAS NAST CARTOON ON
THE REPUBLICAN VICTORY

HERE LIES THE DEMOCRATIC TIGER.
GREATLY MOURNED BY THE BEREAVED FILIBUSTERS.

"ANOTHER SUCH VICTORY, AND I AM UNDONE."—Pyrrhus.

CHAPTER XII

COLLEGE DAYS IN CAMBRIDGE

Freshman Theodore Roosevelt was not like other Harvard boys. In the Harvard of the seventies one had to be orthodox in dress, mannerism, and outlook; one had to walk a certain way, one had to speak in a certain manner. Theodore did not conform to such patterns. A classmate of his recalled that at a time when "it was not considered good form to move at more than a walk, Roosevelt was always running." When all others followed the prevailing fashion of marked indifference, he seemed in a perpetual state of excitement. He interrupted professors with questions and critical observations during lectures. He read books, not only for examinations but for knowledge.

He was thought queer, "a good deal of a joke." He did not smoke or drink, and he was proud of the fact that at his dining table "no less than seven do not smoke and four drink nothing stronger than beer." And to top all this nonconformity he taught Sunday school at the Cambridge Episcopal Church. He kept these Sunday-school classes until the rector discovered that he was a Presbyterian. When told that if he wished to retain his post he must join the Episcopal Church, Theodore refused. "I told the clergyman I thought him rather narrow-minded; especially as I had had my class for three years and a half," but the rector was adamant and so the teaching had to be given up.

Harvard in 1876 had 821 students. Classrooms and dormitories were confined to the ivy-walled enclosure—the Yard. The college, though at the same location as today, appeared to be much farther from Boston, accessible by rough-riding and uncomfortable horsecars. And while the area around it was growing up rapidly, Cambridge still retained a stiff and somewhat stultifying moral atmosphere.

Theodore was astonished "how few fellows have come here with any idea of getting an education." He did well in his studies, though he was not outstanding by any means. He had to work hard. His selection of courses was conventional, with science and languages predominant.

His style was not distinguished. Thomas Perry, his instructor, recalled that his "writing was to the point, but did not have the air of cultivation."

Academically, the greatest disappointment was the manner of teaching natural history. During his freshman and sophomore years he had fully intended to make his career as a naturalist, but by the time of his graduation he had abandoned the plan. The reason for this change, as he later explained, was that Harvard, like most other colleges, "utterly ignored the possibilities of the faunal naturalist, the outdoor naturalist and observer of nature. They treated biology as purely a science of the laboratory and the microscope . . ."

151

THEODORE, THE BOXER.
HARVARD PHOTOGRAPH

Before the dream was abandoned, Theodore had added considerably to his field knowledge of eastern American fauna. As a freshman he had found a fellow nature lover in Henry Davis Minot, a classmate who lived just outside Boston in West Roxbury. He and Minot made collecting excursions through the Massachusetts countryside, and in the summer of 1877 they journeyed together to the Adirondacks for further field studies. The result of this trip was the publication (at the young naturalists' expense) of a pamphlet entitled *The Summer Birds of the Adirondacks in Franklin County.*

Before he left Harvard, Theodore was working on a second publication—a very different one, reflecting the marked change in his interests. The War of 1812, he decided, had never been adequately treated by historians, and so he decided to make up the deficiency himself. The book that resulted was later published, but only two chapters were completed before Theodore's graduation. "Those chapters," he later commented, "were so dry that they would have made a dictionary seem light reading by comparison."

If Harvard discouraged his interest in natural history, it did not have a similar effect on his athletic interests. By the middle of his freshman year he was writing his family that he sparred daily with the boxing master at the college gymnasium, and the following year he was entertaining hopes of winning the undergraduate lightweight championship. He entered the competition, but, after an initial victory, was defeated by a superior contestant who, according to a brief item on the sporting page of the New York *Times,* spent most of the match "punishing Roosevelt severely." The same newspaper item described the competition as "sparring bouts"—a designation that brought a prompt and indignant rejoinder from *The Harvard Advocate,* of which young Roosevelt was an editor. The *Times,* complained the student publication, had apparently not understood that the competition consisted solely of "friendly encounters between gentlemen."

Outside of boxing, Theodore was not notably active in Harvard athletics, although he participated occasionally in wrestling matches and track events.

Athletics then as now formed a principal subject of undergraduate conversation, however, and it is interesting to note that Theodore found this overemphasis distasteful, despite his enthusiasm for the strenuous life. Shortly after the start of his sophomore year he wrote to his sister: "My respect for the qualities of my classmates has much increased lately, as they now no longer seem to think it necessary to confine their conversation exclusively to athletic subjects. I was especially struck by this the other night, when, after a couple of hours spent in boxing and wrestling with Arthur Hooper and Ralph Ellis, it was proposed to finish the evening by reading aloud from Tennyson and we became so interested in 'In Memoriam' that it was past one o'clock when we separated."

He was always fond of poetry. His sister later recalled how he had sent her, shortly after the close of his freshman year, Swinburne's poem *The Forsaken Garden,* which he had copied from memory while on a hunting trip in the Maine woods. He enjoyed reciting Swinburne and Edgar Allan Poe, whose poems he was given to chanting "in a strange, rather weird, monotonous tone," although he could never really convert his college friends to love his recitations.

On the whole, the four years at Cambridge were four pleasant years for Theodore. It was a gay and social life with dances and parties, with sleigh rides, and invitations to the best Boston homes. He grew more fastidious in his attire, more fashionable in his likes and dislikes. The lyrics of a song in one of the undergraduate musical shows described him as "awful smart, with waxed moustache and hair in curls."

While he was at Harvard two great personal events stand out: one was his father's death in his sophomore year, the other his engagement to Alice Hathaway Lee in the senior year.

He always loved his family, and he admired his father. Shortly after his arrival at Cambridge he wrote to him: "I do not think there is a fellow in college who has a family that love him as much as you all do me." And in another letter he said that it was "perfectly wonderful, in looking back over my eighteen years of existence, to see how I have literally never spent an unhappy day unless by my own fault, and I am *sure* that there is no one who has a father who is also his best and most intimate friend, as you are mine."

Thus, when his father died in February 1878, Theodore's whole world seemed to crash. He gave himself to grief—as to everything—with great abandon. "It is impossible to tell in words how terribly I miss him," he wrote in his diary. "Every event of my life is bound up with him; he was as pure and unselfish as he was wise and good." A month after the funeral his gloom was no less. "Have been thinking over the many, many lovely memories I have of him; had another square breakdown." Throughout his life he preserved the letters that his father had written to him. They were his "talisman against evil."

Slowly, very slowly, he regained his composure. And only when "Sunshine" came into his life was his recovery complete. "Sunshine" was the nickname of Alice Hathaway Lee, a cousin of his classmate Richard Saltonstall. Theodore fell in love with her almost instantly—it was his first love. Like all lovers, he was convinced that his was the only real emotion in the whole universe. He pursued Alice, he spent every free minute with her, he suffered over her caprices, endured tormenting and sleepless nights; and when she made him happy, he was ecstatic in his happiness. "I have been in love with her for nearly two years now, and have made everything subordinate to winning her . . ." he wrote. At long last Alice accepted his proposal.

It was only a year earlier that he had noted in his diary: "Thank Heaven, I am at least perfectly pure," and he noted with satisfaction that if he ever got engaged, he could tell his fiancée "everything I have ever done." Now he had a fiancée. "Truly these are the golden years of my life," he exclaimed. "My cup of happiness is almost too full." With Alice "to love me, life will always seem laughing and loving."

They were married on his twenty-second birthday. Theodore entered in his diary: "She made an ideally beautiful bride, and it was a lovely wedding. Our intense happiness is too sacred to be written about."

CERTIFICATE OF ADMISSION. On July 3, 1876, Theodore Roosevelt was admitted to Harvard College as one of the 246 members of the incoming freshman class. "I thoroughly enjoyed Harvard," he wrote later, "and I am sure it did me good, but only in the general effect, for there was very little in my actual studies which helped me in after life."

THE EIGHTEEN-YEAR-OLD FRESHMAN sports a fashionable beard. "When I entered college, I was devoted to out-of-doors natural history, and my ambition was to be a scientific man of the Audubon, or Wilson, or Baird, or Coues type," wrote Roosevelt. "My father had from the earliest days instilled into me the knowledge that I was to work."

STUDENT QUARTERS AT HARVARD in the seventies. Theodore's class had many young men who later became prominent in public life. Among them were William Bushnell Hart, the historian, and Robert Bacon, Secretary of State under Roosevelt.

WHERE HE STAYED WHILE IN HARVARD. For four years Theodore's address was 16 Winthrop Street, on the corner of Holyoke Street, only two short blocks from Harvard Square. His room with four windows was on the second floor of the building.

A LETTER TO HIS SISTER soon after he arrived at Harvard. Theodore thanks Bamie for her efforts to fit out his room in such exquisite taste. "Ever since I came here I have been wondering what I should have done, if you had not fitted up my room for me. The curtains, carpet, furniture—in short everything is really beautiful; I have never seen prettier or more tasteful wall paper. When I get my pictures and books, I do not think there will be a room in College more handsome or comfortable."

As time passed, he livened up his quarters with decorations of his own. "It was a veritable museum," remembered a classmate of Theodore, "with stuffed animals and mounted birds perched on desk and table; and here and there a pair of antlers looked down from the wall to tell of their owner's prowess in the Adirondacks or in Maine." On one side of the room stood a homemade cage which housed—despite the landlady's misgivings—a transient population of live snakes and turtles.

His schedule was an arduous one, though he had no complaints about it. He usually rose at 7:15, went to chapel at 7:45, had his breakfast at 8. From 9 to 12 and from 2:30 to 3:30 he attended classes. Between lunch and classes he studied; after classes he exercised, strenuously attempting to improve his health and his muscles: he lifted weights, jumped rope, he boxed, he rowed, he rode, and in the winter months he skated. He took dinner at 6, and after dinner until bedtime, which usually was about eleven o'clock, he studied and read. Another of his schoolmates recalled that he could read in the noisiest room, "oblivious to all that was going on around him."

To the undergraduate Theodore seemed queer, eccentric, "a good deal of a joke," ever in a hurry, rushing from one classroom to the other. Though his father gave him the advice "that, if I was not going to earn money, I must even things up by not spending it," he seemed to have resources enough to drive a dogcart and to indulge in expensive pastimes.

At Harvard, Theodore Roosevelt was somewhat of a snob and somewhat of a prude. "I most sincerely wish I knew something about the antecedents of my friends," he wrote. "On this very account I have avoided being very intimate with the New York fellows." As an example of his righteousness is his entry in his journal after he learned that one of his cousins had married a French actress: "He is a disgrace to the family—the vulgar brute." And the virtuous lad gave praise to the Almighty: "Thank Heaven, I am at least perfectly pure."

THE EDITORS OF *THE ADVOCATE*. Roosevelt was one of the editors of *The Harvard Advocate,* the monthly literary magazine of the undergraduates.

THE "BIG SIX," classmates of Theodore in Harvard. Standing: Richard Saltonstall, whose cousin Roosevelt was to marry, Minot Weld, and Theodore. Seated: John Tebbets, H. B. Chapin, and Harry Shaw.

THE O. K. CLUB was another of Roosevelt's affiliations while at Cambridge. Theodore liked company, he liked good fellowship; he was a great joiner.

HIS AFFILIATIONS AT HARVARD. The Porcellian Club, one of the most exclusive clubs on the campus, offered a membership to Theodore and he accepted. It was a great honor, as the Porcellian took in only eight men from each of the upper classes.

He also belonged to the Institute of 1770 from his

sophomore year on, and was a member of the Hasty Pudding Club. In his senior year he was president of Alpha Delta Phi, treasurer of the O.K. Club, secretary of the Hasty Pudding Club, vice-president of the Natural History Society, an editor of the undergraduate magazine *The Harvard Advocate,* an honorary member of the glee club, and to top all these honors he was chosen by his classmates as a member of the Class Committee. Because of his good marks he belonged to Phi Beta Kappa, which was presided over at Harvard by no less a man than Oliver Wendell Holmes. The early coolness of his classmates had disappeared; before his last term had ended, Theodore was one of the best-liked fellows at Harvard College.

HIS MARKS IN 1876-77. Roosevelt's best subject was German, in which he had 92 per cent, his worst was Greek, with a score of only 58 per cent.

HIS MARKS IN 1877-78. In his sophomore year he received 96 per cent in German, 94 per cent in rhetoric, but, strangely, only 51 per cent in French.

T.R. AS A FRESHMAN

When he entered Harvard in the fall of 1876 he was one of 246 freshmen. His courses for the first year were all prescribed: Latin, Greek, advanced mathematics, chemistry, and physics. Learning did not come easily to him; he had to work hard, particularly in Greek and mathematics. "I do not seem to make headway at all in this," he complained to his father. His freshman year was uneventful; he made acquaintances and friends, he felt his way.

In his sophomore year he found his stride. Now Harvard for him was "home." In that year he chose German, French, comparative anatomy, and elementary botany besides the prescribed rhetoric and history.

It was during his second year in college—on February 10, 1878—that his father died. Theodore, who admired and worshiped him, was stricken with grief. "I have lost the only human being to whom I told *everything,* never failing to get loving advice and sweet sympathy in return." He solemnly vowed that "With the help of my God I will try to lead such a life as he would have wished." He felt it his duty "to study well and live like a brave Christian gentleman," so he could be worthy of his father's memory.

HARVARD COLLEGE

By the regulations of the Faculty I am directed to print, at the end of each Academic Year, the names of all students who have attained seventy-five per cent of the maximum mark in any elective study, or seventy per cent in any prescribed study, and to send copy of this publication to the father or other guardian of each student. A list of the members of the *Junior* Class of 1878-79 who attained these percentages in any study will be found on the following pages.

The studies pursued by *T Roosevelt* in which he did not attain these percentages, will be found among those below with the percentage attained by him in each.

☞ His per cent on the work of the Junior year is *above* seventy. *Average 87+°*

C. J. WHITE,
Registrar of the Faculty.

Sanskrit	English V.	Philosophy I.	Physics (Post-Graduate)
Classics	German I.	Philosophy II.	Chemistry I.
Greek II.	German II.	Philosophy V.	Chemistry II.
Greek IV.	German III.	Philosophy VI.	Chemistry III.
Greek V.	German V.	Philosophy VII. 89	Chemistry IV.
Greek VI.	German VI.	Philosophy (Post-Grad.)	Natural History I. 92
Greek VII.	German VII.	Logic	Natural History II.
Greek VIII.	German VIII. 82	History II.	Natural History III. 97
Greek IX.	French I.	History III.	Natural History IV.
Latin I.	French II.	History IV.	Natural History VI.
Latin II.	French III.	History VI.	Natural History VII.
Latin III.	French IV.	History VII.	Music I.
Latin IV.	French VI.	History (Post-Grad.)	Music II.
Latin V.	Italian I. 82	*Historical Sources*	Music III.
Latin VI.	Italian II.	*Roman Law*	Music IV.
Latin VII.	Spanish I.	Mathematics I.	Fine Arts I.
Latin VIII.	Spanish II.	Mathematics V.	Fine Arts II.
English I.	Themes 76	Mathematics VI.	Fine Arts III.
English II.	Forensics 66	Mathematics VII.	
English III.	Prescribed Logic 84	Physics I.	
English IV.	Presc. Metaphysics 87	Physics II.	

HARVARD COLLEGE.

In accordance with the regulations of the Faculty, I herewith give the names of those students who have attained seventy per cent of the maximum mark in any study in the academic year 1879-80.

The studies pursued by *T Roosevelt* in which he did not attain seventy per cent, will be found among those below with the percentage attained by him in each.

C. J. WHITE,
Registrar of the Faculty.

Hebrew	German III.	Philosophy VIII.	Mathematics VI.
Sanskrit	German IV.	Political Economy I.	Mathematics VII.
Classics I.	German V.	Political Economy II.	Mathematics VIII.
Greek I.	German VI.	Political Economy III. 78	Mathematics IX.
Greek II.	German VII.	Political Economy	Mathematics X.
Greek III.	German VIII.	(Post-Graduate)	Physics I.
Greek IV.	French I.	History I.	Physics II.
Greek V.	French II.	History II.	Physics III.
Greek VI.	French III.	History III.	Physics IV.
Greek VII.	French IV.	History IV.	Physics V.
Greek VIII.	French VI.	History VI.	Physics (Post-Graduate)
Greek IX.	Italian I.	History VII.	*Experiment. Physics*
Greek (Post-Graduate)	Italian II. 70	History VIII.	Chemistry I.
Greek Etymology	Italian III.	History X.	Chemistry II.
Latin I.	Italian (Post-Graduate)	Roman Law	Chemistry III.
Latin II.		History (Post-Grad.)	Chemistry IV.
Latin III.	*Duate, Div. Comm.*	*Historical Sources*	Chemistry V.
Latin IV.	Spanish I.	*International Law*	Chemistry VI.
Latin V.	Spanish II.	Fine Arts I.	Chemistry VII.
Latin VI.	Spanish III.	Fine Arts II.	Natural History I.
Latin VII.	Sophomore Rhetoric	Fine Arts V.	Natural History II.
Latin (Post-Graduate)	Junior Themes	Music I.	Natural History III.
Virgil, Georgica.	Junior Forensics	Music II.	Natural History IV. 91
English I.	Senior Forensics 65	Music III.	Natural History V.
English II.	Philosophy I.	Music IV.	Natural History VII. 89
English III.	Philosophy II.	Mathematics I.	Natural History (Post-Graduate)
English V.	Philosophy III.	Fresh. Adv. Math.	*Vegetable Physiology*
English VI.	Philosophy IV.	Mathematics II.	*Palæontology*
English VII.	Philosophy V.	Mathematics III.	*Hist. Geol. Opinions*
German I.	Philosophy VI.	Mathematics IV.	
German II.	Philosophy VII.	Mathematics V.	

HIS MARKS IN 1878–79. Natural history was his best subject in his junior year, with 97 and 92 per cent. In other subjects he averaged 87 per cent.

HIS MARKS IN 1879–80. Again he excelled in natural history. In political economy he had 78 per cent, in Italian 70 per cent, in forensics 65 per cent.

T.R. AS A SENIOR

His whiskers had been shaved off, making him look "like a dissolute Democrat of the Fourth Ward," with "an expression of grim misery." Anyhow, that is how he felt about it.

The last two years in Harvard were gayer and easier than the first two. Theodore's diaries and letters are full of notations about lovely dinners and theater parties, Sunday drives and dancing classes. "By Jove," he wrote after a hunting trip to Maine, "it sometimes seems as if I were having too happy a time to have it last. I enjoy every moment I live, almost."

On his vacations he either went to Maine or to the Middle West, hunting and enjoying the open air. But while at college he was busy with his studies, his clubs, his natural history specimens, and most of all with his love for Alice Lee.

In his junior year he had, besides English and elementary philosophy, political economy, Italian literature, geography, and zoology. In his senior year he took geology, advanced zoology, Italian, and a course in English composition.

He graduated twenty-first in a class of 161, the same rank as Ulysses S. Grant's at West Point.

THEODORE

For Theodore Roosevelt, girls whom he was fond of were "sweet and pretty." This, too, was his first impression of Alice Lee, a cousin of his Harvard classmate Richard Saltonstall. A day after he met her, he noted in his diary that she was "a very sweet, pretty girl." The date of the entry was October 18, 1878. But a year and some months later—on January 30, 1880—he confessed to the same diary: "I have been pretty nearly crazy over my wayward, wilful darling." Thus Alice had grown from a "pretty girl" to a "wilful darling."

Theodore was in love, in love for the first time in his life. He saw Alice whenever he could. He went to dances with her, played tennis with her, they were at parties together and at outings in the country. He was eagerly, relentlessly, passionately pursuing the "one all absorbing object"—Alice Lee. Pointing to her one day, he said to a friend: "See

LIFE IN MAINE WAS "BULLY." He went there just before his junior year at Harvard, and he fell in love with the simple life of the people and the beauty of the woods. At Island Falls he formed a friendship with Will Sewall, a lumberman and a hunter, a friendship lasting till the end of his life.

> Friday Feb 13th 1880
>
> Dear Hal,
>
> I write to you to announce my engagement to Miss Alice Lee, but do not speak of it till Monday. I have been in love with her for nearly two years now; and have just made everything subordinate to winning her: so you can perhaps understand a change in my ideas as regards science &c.
>
> Your Aff Friend
> Theodore Roosevelt

ANNOUNCING HIS ENGAGEMENT to Alice on February 13, 1880, to his friend Henry Minot, and telling him that he should "not speak of it till Monday."

IN LOVE

that girl? I am going to marry her. She won't have me but I am going to have her."

Tormented by his "sweet love," he told his diary that when he was alone with her he could "hardly stay a moment without holding her in my arms or kissing her; she is such a laughing, pretty little witch." She was "always present" in his mind: "Not an hour has passed that I have not thought of her." The months before Alice Lee accepted his proposal were months of torture. "Night after night I have not even gone to bed," Theodore wrote in his diary. Then at last—it was at the beginning of 1880 —Alice, "my own sweet, pretty darling consented" to become Mrs. Theodore Roosevelt. "How she, so pure and sweet and beautiful can think of marrying me I can not understand, but I praise and thank God it is so." With her to love him, "life will always seem laughing and loving."

A THESIS while Theodore was at Harvard sets forth his view that "in the abstract I think there can be no question that women should have equal rights with men. . . ."

ALICE LEE, the girl with whom Theodore fell in love, was five feet seven inches tall, slender, with a piquant nose and gay temperament. She was the daughter of George Cabot Lee and Caroline Haskel, whose elegant and spacious home was situated on Chestnut Hill next door to the Saltonstalls.

161

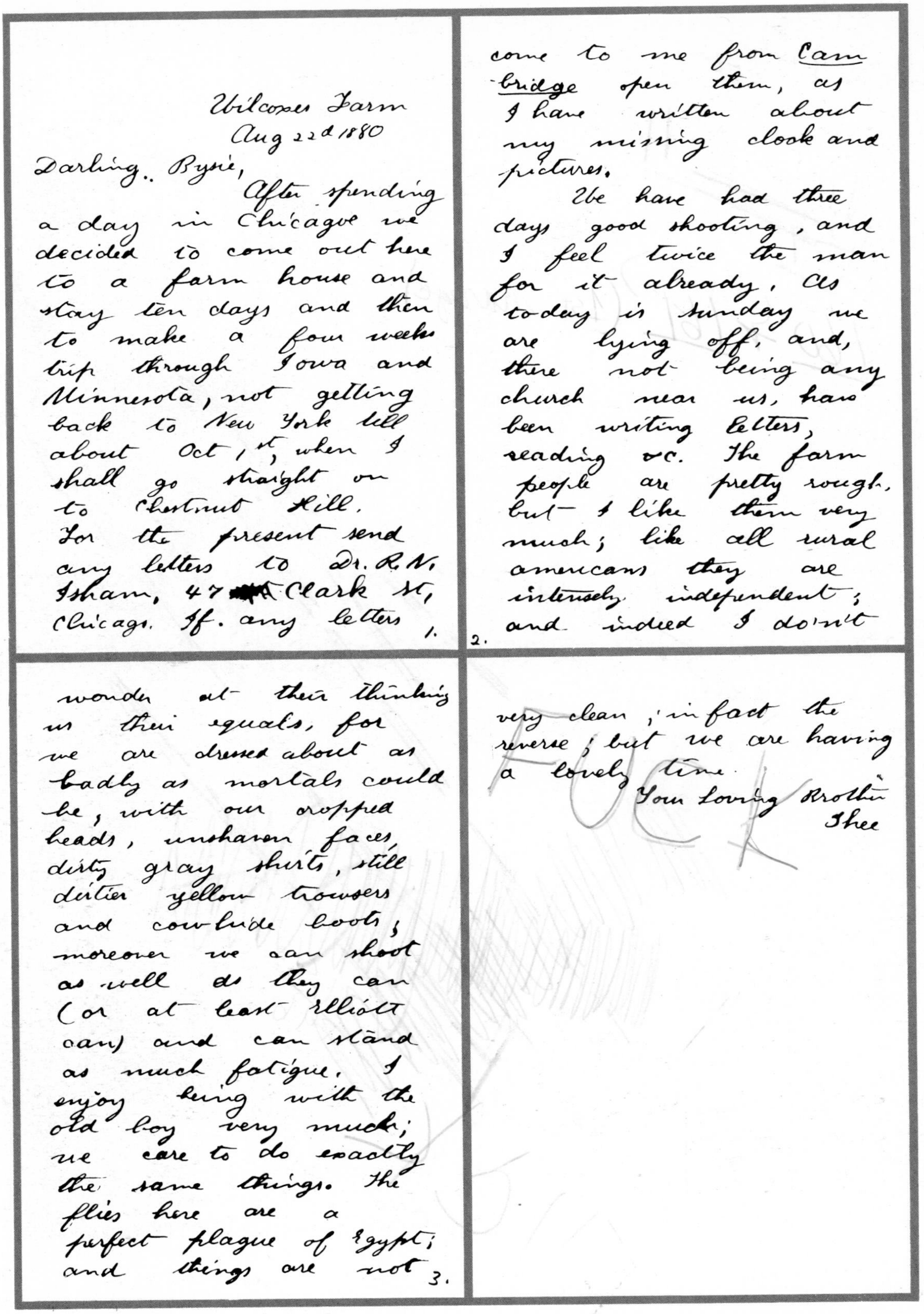

Wilcoxes Farm
Aug 22d 1880

Darling Bysie,

After spending a day in Chicago we decided to come out here to a farm house and stay ten days and then to make a four weeks trip through Iowa and Minnesota, not getting back to New York till about Oct 1st, when I shall go straight on to Chestnut Hill.

For the present send any letters to Dr. R. N. Isham, 47 ~~North~~ Clark St, Chicago. If any letters

1.

come to me from Cambridge open them, as I have written about my missing clock and pictures.

We have had three days good shooting, and I feel twice the man for it already. As to-day is sunday we are lying off, and, there not being any church near us, have been writing letters, reading &c. The farm people are pretty rough. but I like them very much; like all rural americans they are intensely independent; and indeed I don't

2.

wonder at their thinking us their equals, for we are dressed about as badly as mortals could be, with our cropped heads, unshaven faces, dirty gray shirts, still dirtier yellow trowsers and cow hide boots; moreover we can shoot as well as they can (or at least Elliott can) and can stand as much fatigue. I enjoy being with the old boy very much; we care to do exactly the same things. the flies here are a perfect plague of Egypt; and things are not

3.

very clean; in fact the reverse; but we are having a lovely time.

Your Loving Brother
Thee

A CHATTY LETTER TO HIS SISTER ANNA FROM WILCOX'S FARM IN ILLINOIS

ON A HUNTING TRIP in the Middle West with his brother, Elliott. It was not long before his wedding that Theodore went West to hunt. To his mother he wrote that the trip would build him up. It did. He and his brother Elliott were "travelling on our muscle, and don't give a hang for any man." The boys went as far as Minnesota. Theodore's bag on the last trip alone was 203 animals, Elliott's 201.

HIS HARVARD DIPLOMA. On June 30, 1880, Theodore Roosevelt, by grace of Harvard College, became a Bachelor of Arts. In summing up his four years as a college student he wrote: "I have certainly lived like a prince. . . . I have had just as much money as I could spend. . . . I have kept a good horse and cart; I have had half a dozen good and true friends . . . a lovely home; I have had but little work, only enough to give me an occupation, and to crown all infinitely above everything else put together—I have won the sweetest of girls for my wife. No man ever had so pleasant a college course."

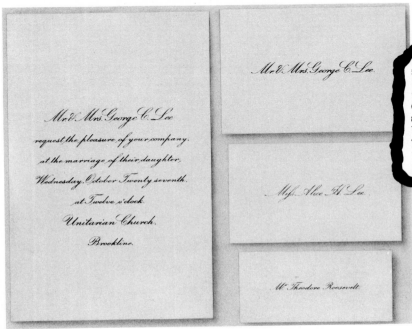

—There was a fashionable wedding at the First Parish Church, on Wednesday of this week, the contracting parties being Miss Alice H., daughter of George C. Lee, Esq., of Chestnut Hill, and Mr. Theodore Roosevelt, of New York. The Rev. J. A. Buckingham performed the ceremony. A reception was held at the residence of the bride's parents in the evening.

HE MARRIED on his twenty-second birthday, October 27, 1880, the nineteen-year-old Alice H. Lee, of a prominent Boston family. According to the local newspaper it was "a fashionable wedding" in the Brookline Unitarian Church with Rev. J. A. Buckingham officiating.

Part 2:

PUBLIC SERVANT

CHAPTER XIII

AMERICA IN THE EIGHTIES

Theodore Roosevelt was graduated from Harvard in the summer of 1880. He married that same fall and with his "devoted little wife" settled down in New York, enrolling as a law student at Columbia University.

In that year the population of Manhattan Island was 1,164,673. New York was a metropolis, with part of Broadway lit with the marvel of the era—electricity. Two more years and Edison's giant dynamos were to supply electric current to the blocks between Nassau, Pearl, Spruce, and Wall streets. Progress was marching. Three more years and Brooklyn Bridge would be ready to use, as would be the new Metropolitan Opera House. And by 1885 all telegraph, telephone, and cable wires and cables had become such a hazard to traffic that they had been ordered to be removed from the streets.

New York was a city of contrasts: the rich—like the Vanderbilts and Astors—lived in palaces with a galaxy of rooms, some of them large enough to hold a gathering of a thousand people, while families on the lower East Side housed in a solitary room ten or more human beings.

The decade of the eighties were years of transition. The forces that had been put in motion by the Civil War and the years after came to a sudden fruition. In this decade rural, pioneering America changed into an urban, industrial colossus. The frontier line was gone; one could no longer push forward into virginal, new lands. The passing of the frontier closed one of the primary escape valves for our national energy; for want of room to grow on, Americans were beckoned toward imperialistic adventures overseas.

The mushrooming railroads brought an increasing number of settlers to the West. Within the eighties the population of Montana, North and South Dakota quadrupled and quintupled. With the cattlemen fencing in their lands, the era of the open range and the cattle kings came to an end. J. F. Glidden's barbwire fenced in the plains at the rate of some six hundred miles a day.

The network of the railroads connected the principal cities; "Empire Builder" James J. Hill, who started on a shoestring, extended his Great Northern system into a vast domain. Americans moved around their country; as they crossed the plains they no longer had to fear the Indian menace.

Men were needed to build, to work, to till the land. The tidal wave of immigrants brought masses of them. During the single decade of the eighties 5,246,613 men and women landed on our shores. Of Wisconsin's population 73 per cent were foreign-born; of Minnesota's, 71 per cent. Agents for the big industries scoured Europe, luring the workers who were sorely needed in the rapidly expanding country.

The eighties were a dividing line in immigration. Before 1880 immigrants had come mostly from northern and western Europe and they usually settled in rural areas. But after the eighties, when cheap land became rare, the newcomers were forced to try their luck in the cities. Though the immigrants from northern and western Europe were still predominant, the number of Italians, Hungarians, Greeks, Poles, Russians, Rumanians—former inhabitants of eastern and southern Europe—increased many times. In the decade before, in the seventies, only 145,000 immigrants arrived from southern and eastern Europe; in the eighties this number jumped to 954,000, only to skyrocket in the nineties to 1,914,000. A decade later this number grew to 6,224,000, while in the same period the number of immigrants from northern and western Europe was only 1,912,000. Many thoughtful citizens worried about the new type of immigrant—they were fearful that the multitudes belonging to the Roman Catholic, Greek Orthodox and Jewish faiths would cause radical changes in the life of America. They questioned whether these immigrants, many of them with scant knowledge of the English language, many of them unable to read and write and with no previous experience with the democratic process, would bring benefits to the United States.

Such rapid changes were bound to bring inequities. For the poor, life was a grim struggle for survival; for hard-pressed homesteaders on the dry and lonely plains, for exploited workers in the overcrowded New York tenements, it was more a chore and a burden than a "pursuit of happiness."

But for the rich it offered unexpected pleasures. With money to spend and leisure to boot, they began to learn how to enjoy their free time and the many luxuries their money could buy. Traveling and visiting foreign countries became a vogue, as did the elaborate homes both in the city and the country, where lavish entertainments were the order of the day.

America grew at a rapid pace and people grew with it. New inventions raised the standard of living and made life comfortable. Burroughs' adding machine, Mergenthaler's linotype machine, McCormick's harvester and threshing machine, DeLaval's steam turbine and other similar inventions brought immense changes in their wake.

The urgent needs of the masses created millionaires almost overnight. Carnegie, Vanderbilt, Rockefeller, Astor, Gould, Fisk—to name only some of the chosen few—amassed enormous fortunes. They made money in a hurry, more often than not caring little what happened to the economically weaker in the process. The wealthy classes had not yet acquired a social conscience—that was to come later. When it was suggested to William K. Vanderbilt that it might have been wise to run his railroad for the benefit of the people, he blurted out: "The public be damned!" And when Jay Gould departed for less lucrative fields, he left $77,000,000 to his children, having raised to the level of a fine art "the methods of acquiring the control and possession of other people's property." It took generations before the cumulated fortunes of the robber barons found their way back to the people in the form of philanthropic grants.

Politically the eighties was a period of small men of small vision, a period of stagnation. Politicians, as usual, were behind the times; they had no comprehension of the great forces which welded the nation. Many of them were bought and dominated by corrupt businessmen, and they sheepishly executed the orders of their masters.

The Republican party turned into the businessmen's party—the idealism of their beginnings no more a driving force. Divided into "Stalwarts" and "Half-Breeds"—one supporting Senator Roscoe Conkling, the other Senator James G. Blaine—the two factions fought each other, not so much on political principles, but on how to divide the spoils.

In the 1884 Republican nominating convention in Chicago, Theodore Roosevelt, after having been elected as assemblyman to the New York Legislature for three consecutive terms, was one of the delegates of his state. There, allying himself with other young Republicans, he fought against Blaine's nomination; but when Blaine won, Theodore would not join the "mugwumps" —those reform-minded Republicans who were to vote for Grover Cleveland, the Democratic candidate.

"I intend to vote the Republican presidential ticket," he said to an interviewer from the Boston *Herald*. "While at Chicago, I told Mr. Lodge that such was my intention; but before announcing it, I wished to have time to think the whole matter over. A man cannot act both without and within the party; he can do either, but he cannot possibly do both. Each course has its advantages, and each has its disadvantages, and one cannot take the advantages or the disadvantages separately. I went in with my eyes open to do what I could do within the party; I did my best and got beaten; and I propose to stand by the result."

This was a clear decision—a decision which created many adverse comments. Newspaper writers called Roosevelt a turncoat, a man without character, and the abuse grew in intensity when he entered the campaign and made speeches on Blaine's behalf.

But when the election was over and Blaine had lost, Theodore gave his reasons to his friend Cabot Lodge. "Every now and then," he wrote, "I meet an Independent who, taking it for granted that you and I were actuated by selfish motives, points out how much better for ourselves we would have done to have bolted. I always surprise him by saying that we have always been very well aware of that fact, and knew perfectly well that we had been effectually killed as soon as Blaine was nominated. If our consciences would have permitted it, I have not the slightest doubt that by bolting we could have done an immense amount for ourselves, and would have won a commanding position—at the cost, perfectly trivial in true mugwump eyes, of black treachery to all our warmest and truest supporters and also at the cost of stultifying ourselves as regards all of our previous declarations in respect to the Democracy."

Thus spoke the man who twenty-eight years later headed the Progressives against William Howard Taft, the official candidate of his party. In that twenty-eight years Roosevelt had learned a great deal, but had also forgotten some of the maxims he knew at the outset of his political career.

THE MARVEL OF THE ERA

ELECTRICITY IN THE HOMES. In 1882 the Edison Electric Company opened the first power plant in New York to supply current for customers.

EDISON IN HIS WORKSHOP. A contemporary drawing by H. Muhrman of the Wizard of Menlo Park—title page of *Harper's Weekly* on August 2, 1879.

THE DURABLE ELECTRIC BULB was born on October 19, 1879, when Thomas Alva Edison successfully demonstrated his incandescent lamp. The inventor discovered a cheap and durable filament for the bulb which allowed the lamp to burn continuously for over forty hours—thus ushering in the electric age.

At the right of the lamp, Edison drives the gas from the filament with electric current. His assistant, Francis Jehl, standing on the bench, fills the Sprengel pump with mercury. The others in the drawing are from left to right, John Kruesi, Martin Force, Ludwig Boehm, Charles Batchelor (the tall man with the beard), and Francis R. Upton.

Edison was a remarkable man. Born in 1847 of Dutch and Scottish ancestry, he went to public school for no more than three months. When he was twelve years old he became a railroad newsboy, selling newspapers on the trains of the Grand Trunk Railway. Conceiving the idea of bulletin boards at the principal stations on his route, he telegraphed ahead the important news; thus, when he arrived with his papers he sold them quickly. In the baggage car of his express train he set and printed the *Grand Trunk Herald*. He also put up a chemical laboratory, which he was forced to discontinue when an explosion set the car afire. About the time he was fifteen he found employment in Cincinnati as a telegraph operator of the Western Union Company. Saving most of his earnings, spending very little on himself, he invested all he had in technical experiments. Time after time his efforts brought fruit, proving his inventive genius. Soon he received a patent for a duplex telegraph machine by which two messages could be transmitted on the same wire simultaneously. Other successes came. In 1872 he worked out a quadruplex system of telegraphy by which four messages could be sent at one time on a single wire. In 1877 he received a patent for his phonograph or speaking machine. By 1880, when he was only thirty-two years old his name was a household word, and his earnings ran as high as $50,000 a year.

LIFE IN NEW YORK

WINTER SCENE on New York's Central Avenue near M'Comb's Dam Bridge at the opening of the sleighing season. Both young and old enjoyed the fun.

THE SECOND AVENUE ELEVATED opened in March, 1880, bringing thousands of New Yorkers to the transfer station at Chatham and Division streets.

IMMIGRANTS LANDING at Castle Gardens. The flux of immigrants was still holding. As many as 4,000 newcomers were received and dispatched in a day.

THE METROPOLITAN MUSEUM OF ART was opened to the public on April 1, 1880. It was one of the great events of the New York social season.

SKATING
"Two dear skates,
  Têtes-à-têtes,
  With them wonders she
    creates,
  And with web and woof
    she'll weave
  Fairy spells you can
    not leave."

STARVING CHILDREN from the tenements are taken by officers of the Society for the Prevention of Cruelty to Children to be given a decent meal.

IN THE ITALIAN QUARTER the Business Men's Society distributed free ice water "for the encouragement of moderation," eagerly taken by all children.

THE TELEPHONE EXCHANGE of 1880. There were about 20,000 subscribers in New York City, paying a monthly rental fee of ten dollars a head.

IRISH DEPOSITORS of the Emigrant Savings Bank lining up at the windows to withdraw money which they will send to suffering relatives at home.

ARCHERY in Central Park. In this decade the American people had more leisure and began to learn how to use it. The craze was still croquet, but other sports like lawn tennis, cycling, and archery had ardent followers.

PROMINENT MEN OF SOCIETY—HALSEY HAIGHT, JOSEPH GRAFTON MINOT, C. STA

KATE STRONG

THE VANDERBILTS' BALL

Cornelius Vanderbilt, the former ferryboat operator, always looked at a penny twice before spending it. Even on his deathbed, when his doctor suggested champagne to relieve his discomfort, the old man groaned: "I can't afford champagne. A bottle every morning! Oh, I guess sody water'll do." Beginning to buy railroads at the age of sixty-eight, he had increased his fortune of ten million dollars to more than a hundred millions before he died.

His son and heir, William Henry, inherited his father's ability to make money. Within nine years he doubled his legacy of ninety million dollars.

With the Commodore's passi William Henry and his son, Willi Kissam, gave up the pretense frugality. Thus the architect Rich Morris Hunt was commissioned build a palace on the corner Fifty-second Street and Fifth A nue, which when completed loo like the Chateau de Blois in Fra and cost three million dollars.

Alva Smith, the Alabama-b wife of William Kissam Vander had set her heart on conquering hitherto impregnable fortress New York society. When their m nificent building was comple she planned a housewarming tume ball on such a lavish scal had never been held before.

RK, JOHN LAWRENCE—AS THEY WENT TO THE VANDERBILT BALL ON MARCH 26, 1883

ALVA SMITH VANDERBILT

ing to the New York *Times*, the me problem "disturbed the and occupied the waking hours cial butterflies, both male and le, for over six weeks."

hen word reached Mrs. Vanilt that young Caroline Astor her friends were rehearsing a quadrille" to be danced at her she let intimates of Mrs. Astor v that she could not invite Miss r or her mother because neither paid her a call. For years Mrs. r, the arbiter of the social set, ignored her; now Alva forced o make a decision. When Mrs. r's soul searching was over, she d for her carriage and, driving e Vanderbilt mansion, sent in

her calling card, signifying acceptance of the Vanderbilts to the rarefied ranks of high society. It must have been the greatest triumph in the life of Alva Vanderbilt. Overjoyed, she sent a footman to the Astor residence with the last of twelve hundred invitations to her ball.

The ball itself surpassed anything in living memory. Costing a quarter of a million dollars, it was the greatest social event of the age. The banker Henry Clews compared it with fetes given by Cleopatra, Louis XIV, and Alexander the Great, and asserted that it was "superior to any of those grand historic displays of festivity."

175

LIFE IN THE EIGHTIES
An after-dinner scene in the executive mansion in Washington, the cares of the day forgotten. President Hayes and family are listening to Carl Schurz's playing; in the background John Sherman, Secretary of the Treasury, tests the knowledge of the President's daughter.

A PARTY IN PHILADELPHIA, given in honor of General Ulysses Grant, who was to depart on his tour around the world. His host was George W. Childs, one of the richest men of the Quaker City.

FAN DRILL of young ladies of the Lake Erie Seminary at Painesville on November 18, 1880. On the right is James A. Garfield, whom the country had elected to the presidency only a few days before.

176

THE BICYCLE was introduced in the United States in 1877 by a young lawyer of Boston, and ever since then that city has been the headquarters of cycle enthusiasts. From Boston the craze for the new vehicle spread to all other large cities except New York, which showed little interest in it at first. But when, on the first day of January 1880, the American Institute Fair opened a bicycle rink, New Yorkers, too, became addicted to the fad.

"THE CINDERELLA OF THE REPUBLICAN PARTY AND HIS HAUGHTY SISTERS"

A much debated cartoon by Joseph Keppler, showing Senator Roscoe Conkling, the head of the Stalwarts (the conservative section of the Republican party), leading ex-President Grant to the ball, while Cinderella Hayes is left at the hearth. The Stalwarts withheld their support from President Hayes; they wanted Grant again. The Half-Breeds (the other faction of the party, opposing the Stalwarts) were led by Senator James G. Blaine, who desired the nomination for himself. In the convention the Stal-warts were solidly behind Grant with their 304 votes, but Blaine's strength was almost as great. For thirty-six times the convention balloted, and though Grant kept ahead in the balloting, he could not clinch the nomination. To break the deadlock the delegates were compelled to settle on a compromise candidate —Senator James A. Garfield from Ohio.

And to please the Stalwart faction, Conkling's hench man, Chester A. Arthur, "the gentleman boss" of the N. Y. Custom House, was given the vice-presidency

REPUBLICAN SEARCH FOR A CANDIDATE

EX-PRESIDENT GRANT after his triumphal tour around the world was ready to enter the political arena, seeking the Republican nomination once more. He had the unswerving support of the loyal Stalwarts, but their enthusiasm and their 304 votes were not enough to secure for him the nomination.

JAMES G. BLAINE, the leader of the Half-Breeds and Grant's chief rival. Though accused of unethical financial conduct, he had strong support among the rank and file. Blaine was a charming man, a good speaker, with a captivating personality. Nast lampooned him as a magnet.

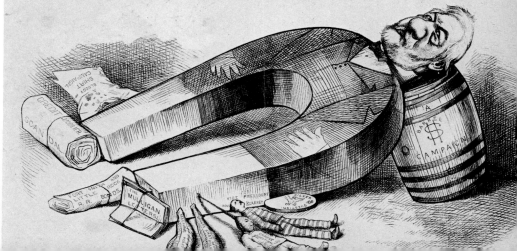

CHAPTER XIV

THE BEGINNING OF HIS POLITICAL CAREER

After their wedding the young couple spent a short honeymoon at "Tranquillity," the Roosevelt's summer place on Long Island. Theodore was in a jubilant mood. He confessed to his diary: "It is impossible to describe the lovely, little teasing ways of my bright, bewitching darling; I can imagine no picture so pretty as her sweet self, seated behind the tea things in the daintiest little pink and gray morning dress, while, in my silk jacket and slippers, I sit at the other end of the table."

The happy fortnight at Tranquillity was all too short. From Oyster Bay the newlyweds moved to the Roosevelt's New York home at 6 West Fifty-seventh Street. Theodore was pondering what he should do. He had some money, but not enough. The $125,000 which he had inherited from his father gave him a yearly income of $8,000. "I had enough to get bread," he recalled later. "What I had to do, if I wanted butter and jam, was to provide the butter and jam but to count their cost as compared with other things. . . . As I had some money I felt my need for more money was to be treated as a secondary need, and that while it was my business to make more money where I legitimately and properly could, yet that it was also my business to treat other kinds of work as more important than money-making." He decided to enroll as a student at Columbia Law School, and he continued to work on his study of *The Naval War of 1812*.

Not long after he settled in New York, he joined the Twenty-first District Republican Club because "a young man of my bringing up and convictions could join only the Republican party." That both his uncle and father-in-law were good Democrats was brushed aside. By the end of the year he was a regular attendant of the monthly meetings in Morton Hall, "a large barn-like room over a saloon" at Fifth Avenue and Fifty-ninth Street. For Theodore a new world opened its doors—a world of spittoons, of cigar smoke, of coarse stories told by florid ward heelers, alien and distasteful, yet fascinating. That the political arena lured him is easy to comprehend. He always tried to fashion himself after his father, follow his example, and accept public service as the elder Roosevelt did. Theodore, with his keen moral sense, looked with contempt on those educated people who "shrink from the struggle and the inevitable contact with rough politicians."

The following summer—the summer of 1881—with his future still clouded in uncertainty, he took his bride to Europe—his third trip abroad and her first. Although Alice suffered miserably from seasickness on the way over, she regained her spirits upon landing, and the couple made an idyllic tour across

THE NEW PRESIDENT:
JAMES A. GARFIELD
WITH HIS DAUGHTER

the British Isles and thence to Paris, Venice, the Alps, the Rhineland, and the Low Countries—"The loveliest trip I have ever had," exclaimed Theodore. It was—like all Roosevelt trips—a strenuous tour, particularly in Switzerland, where the young American, challenged by two English climbers who were staying at the same hotel in Zermatt, made the difficult ascent of the Matterhorn.

When the belated honeymooners returned to New York in September, Theodore expected to resume his law studies, but events at the Twenty-first District headquarters were conspiring to chart his course in another direction. Jacob Hess, an affable German who was Republican boss of the district, was being challenged by a lieutenant named Joseph Murray, an ex-Tammany Irishman who had taken a liking to young Roosevelt. Although he declined when first approached, Theodore finally consented to be Murray's candidate for nomination to the state Assembly. At the nominating caucus, preceded by some adroit politicking on the part of Murray, he prevailed over the incumbent, William Trimble, the choice of Hess and the party regulars.

So Roosevelt, at twenty-three, began a career to which he remained true till the end of his life. His friends were doubtful whether he had made the right decision, while his new political associates were downright amused. There is a story that during the campaign Theodore told an influential German saloon-keeper on Sixth Avenue that, in his opinion, the liquor license should not be lowered but raised. "I don't think you pay enough. I thought it would be at least twice as much," he said with conviction, whereupon the district leaders hustled him away and advised him to confine his campaigning to "the college boys and his friends on Fifth Avenue." They said it would be better if he would stay away from the less fashionable neighborhoods; they themselves would see that these people cast their votes in the proper way—meaning for the Republican candidate. Thus Theodore won the election by the handsome margin of 3,490 votes to 1,989 of his Democratic opponent. The New York *Evening Post* congratulated the district on electing a man of independent means who "doesn't need to trim to suit the bosses."

On the first day of January 1882 Theodore Roosevelt set out for Albany to assume his legislative duties. He wore eyeglasses which dangled on a silk cord, and he sported an enormous overcoat. His colleagues in the legislature thought him a dude—"the way he combed his hair, the way he talked—the whole thing." His high-pitched, squeaky voice seemed out of place in the Assembly chamber; his accent and his manners seemed so different from those of the other lawmakers. But when a few weeks later the young assemblyman boldly introduced a resolution demanding an investigation of Judge Theodore Westbrook of the New York Supreme Court, those who ridiculed him had a rude awakening. Westbrook, so Roosevelt charged, had joined in a conspiracy to give Jay Gould and other "stock-jobbers" control of the Manhattan Elevated Railway Company in a maneuver that ruined many innocent investors. The bluntly worded resolution was greeted by appalled silence and an immediate motion to table. By persistence and parliamentary maneuver, however, Roosevelt brought it to a vote, and the pressure of public opinion forced the

Assembly to approve it. As expected, the Judiciary Committee absolved the judge, but the controversy skyrocketed Roosevelt's reputation as a crusading young "comer" who was not afraid to take on the wealthiest and most powerful citizens of his time.

His Democratic uncle helped him to secure a seat on the Committee on Cities, where his alertness in detecting venal legislation soon prompted the New York *Herald* to call him "a watchdog over New York's treasury."

The bills he introduced during this term were as varied as his interests. The first one—"to reorganize the local government of the City of New York" by changing the methods of the election of aldermen—was passed; others like the bill "to provide for a sufficient supply of pure and wholesome water for the city of New York," the bill proposing the establishment of a public park in the Twenty-fourth Ward, or the bill dealing with "the killing and wounding of pigeons, fowls, birds, and other animals" came to nothing. About his bill to change the method of electing aldermen, the New York *Times* said (Feb. 24, 1882) that it was "a very desirable end, the weakening namely, of the power of the party machine and the protection of the rights of voters." Roosevelt explained, "In New York, where the nominating power is so largely divorced from the mass of the voters of the same party, it is peculiarly necessary to have the machinery of elections easily understood by outsiders, and, moreover, to enable the people who vote to pass as directly as possible upon the candidates proposed by the people who nominate. The present system is so complicated that nine-tenths of the voters do not understand it at all. Out of my six Republican colleagues among the New York Assemblymen, three did not know anything about our Aldermanic representation. I question if one in ten of my constituents is aware of the real working of so called minority representation..."

The regular Republicans were sullen; they had no use for Theodore's independent spirit. "Old Salt" Alvord, an assemblyman from Syracuse, remarked bitterly that his party had sixty and one half members in the Assembly, sixty regular ones and "that damn dude." But the New York *Times* was of other opinion. Said the newspaper: "Mr. Roosevelt has a most refreshing habit of calling men and things by their right names, and in these days of judicial, ecclesiastical, and journalistic subserviency to the robber barons of the Street it needs some little courage in any public man to characterize them and their acts in fitting terms."

And Roosevelt, disregarding the regulars' hostility, poured his venom not on them, but on the opposition. He said that "over half the Democrats, including almost all of the City Irish, are vicious, stupid looking scoundrels." Furthermore—so he went on—"the average Catholic Irishman of the first generation, as represented in this Assembly, is a low, venal, corrupt and unintelligent brute." When he made that speech he was twenty-three years old.

His first-term record was good enough to secure his re-election in the fall of 1882 by a two-to-one majority, a great victory, enhanced by the fact that in that election Grover Cleveland, the Democratic party's gubernatorial candidate, carried the Twenty-first District. Back in Albany at the start of the 1883 session, the "Young Reformer" was his party's nominee for the post of Speaker —a singular distinction, although an empty one in a Democratic-controlled Assembly, which would elect a Democratic Speaker. Nevertheless, the honor placed Roosevelt at the head of his party. He became known, his name was frequently mentioned in newspapers, his efforts in the Assembly for a better government acknowledged. On the very day he made his principal speech of the canvass for re-election (it was a day after his twenty-fourth birthday) Carl Schurz, one of the founders of the Republican party, said of Roosevelt that he was one of the "three almost beardless youths who proved to be the exponents of the power and honesty of the City of New York," and who in the Assembly, almost alone, had "stemmed the tide of corruption in that fearful legislative gathering." Theodore was not less pleased with himself than was Schurz. "I rose like a rocket," he declared.

In the winter of 1882–83, Theodore and Alice moved from the Roosevelt's residence to their own apartment at 55 West Forty-fifth Street. Theodore described his happiness in the new surroundings. "Back again in my own lovely little home," he once wrote, "with the sweetest and prettiest of all little wives— my own sunny darling. I can imagine nothing more happy in life than an evening spent in my cozy little sitting room, before a bright fire of soft coal, my books all around me, and playing backgammon with my own dainty mistress."

His second term started off well. In close co-operation with the Democratic governor of the state and in disregard of the patronage-minded organization men in both parties, he threw himself into the successful fight for a state civil-service bill. Cartoons pictured him and Grover Cleveland as allies, independent critics cited him for his willingness to ally himself with Democrats when he believed the end to be just. He was applauded by his few friends and abused by his many enemies when he showed strength of character in confessing an error and reversing himself openly. The issue was a bill reducing from ten cents to five the fares on Jay Gould's Manhattan Railway. Roosevelt at first supported the bill in response to a popular clamor against Gould, whom he hated. But when Governor Cleveland vetoed it on the grounds that it was an unconstitutional violation of the terms of the railway franchise, Roosevelt took the floor to support him, admitting "with shame" that he had been partly motivated by "a vindictive spirit toward the infernal thieves and conscienceless swindlers who have had the elevated railroad in charge" and partly by "the popular voice of New York." He called Jay Gould and his cohorts "part of that most dangerous of all dangerous classes, the wealthy criminal class." For this courageous admission of error, Roosevelt was labeled a "weakling" by the New York *Sun,* while the *Evening Star* of Boston called him a communist and a "bogus reformer" whose career would soon be over.

The criticism Roosevelt received on this issue became even sharper a week later, when he delivered a bitter speech and resigned from the Committee on Privileges and Elections after the Assembly denied his friend, Representative Sprague, a contested seat. He said in a scathing attack on the Democrats: "You can take the record made by their party now in the House; the shameless partisanship they have displayed; the avidity they have shown for getting control of even the smallest offices; the way they have endeavored to legislate Republicans out of office and put their own members in. . . ." Here was the self-righteous politician to whom everything the opposition attempted was evil, while he regarded the faults of his own party as only unintentional mistakes. The New York *Observer* called him "very silly and sullen and naughty" and said: "When young Mr. Roosevelt finished his affecting oration, the House was in tears—of uncontrollable laughter." Roosevelt himself (writing to his son many years later) admitted: "I came an awful cropper and had to pick myself up after learning by bitter experience the lesson that I was not all-important and that I had to take account of many different elements in life. It took me fully a year before I got back the position I had lost, but I hung steadily at it and achieved my purpose."

Besides his support of the civil-service reform bill in the 1883 session, he introduced a bill to control the liquor traffic by raising the license fees, introduced a bill "to provide for the infliction of corporal punishment upon male persons" (public whipping of any male who "inflicted brutal or unusual pain or violence upon the person of a female or a male under fourteen years of age"), and spoke against an appropriation for a Catholic protectory ("no state funds should be granted to a religious sect").

In September of 1883 he went to the Dakotas on a hunting trip, getting his first taste of buffalo and of the grandeur of the Bad Lands. On his return he campaigned for the third term in the Assembly and was once more re-elected by a thumping majority of 1,200. It was a Republican year, with Republicans recapturing both the House and the Senate. Roosevelt expected to become the Speaker of the Assembly, but in a wild backstage battle the organization Republicans and corporate lobbyists joined forces and blocked his bid. As the New Year dawned—the year of 1884—the New York *Sun* prophesied that "this will not be a happy New Year to the exquisite Mr. Roosevelt."

It was indeed a tragic year—but not because of anything that happened in the Assembly. On Wednesday, February 13, two telegrams reached him in Albany: the first told him that Alice had given birth to a daughter; the second, that his wife's health had taken a turn for the worse. He rushed to New York. A day later both Alice and his mother were dead.

For Roosevelt the double shock was almost too much to bear. An old friend wrote on the day of the funeral that "Theodore is in a dazed, stunned state. He does not know what he says or does."

But four days later he was back in Albany addressing the Assembly on behalf of a bill to strengthen municipal government in Manhattan. In the following month seven of his nine reform bills passed the Assembly. With admirable self-discipline he immersed himself in his work, kept on with his duties. "I have never believed it did any good to flinch or yield to any blow," he wrote to a friend, "nor does it lighten the blow to cease from working." So he kept on with his tasks, pushing himself harder than ever before. "I think I should go mad if I were not employed."

COLUMBIA COLLEGE LAW SCHOOL,

NAMES OF STUDENTS. Write name in full	AGE. Years. Months. Days	COLLEGE OF GRADUATION AND DEGREE	HOME RESIDENCE	CITY RESIDENCE
Charles Converse Tyler	25 3	Dartmouth — B.S.	Yonkers	
Everett Bill Hoover	20 11 17		Hobokasville	322 E. 14 St.
Crawford C. VanPieson	23 8 19	Columbia College A.B.	Montclair N.	34 W 9th St
O. U. Von Schrader	24 —	Washington U. St Louis A.B.	St Louis M.	411 W.
James William McLaughlin	22 — —		Somerville	313 E 3rd St
Alan Douglas Kenyon	23 8 28	College of City of New York A.B.	New York City	331 E 17th St
Laurence Wilkinson	24 0 2	Yale A.B	Greenwich Ct.	215 W 54th St
Stephen G. Williams	21 3	Columbia Ph.B.	20 N. 21 NY City	20 West 21
Marshall R Van Nostrand	31	Princeton A.B.	Elizabeth N.J.	
Douglas Eugene Petit	23 6 17		Syracuse NY	55 W 33
Theodore Roosevelt	22	Harvard A.B	New York	6 W 57 St
Almet F Red Watson	21 0		308 W. 48	New York
Chas R Rudolph	26 1	Boston University B.S.	50 Union Sq	New York
Fred Reynold Dudley	21		Jersey City N.J	
Fielding Lewis Marshall	28 8	Columbia A.B	High Bridge	
Charles D Harrison	34		1. W. 129th	
Eugene Sweeney	27		New York	151 W 129
Frederick Seymour	25	Yale A B	Withers Point N.	123 East 10th St.
George W Seligman	23	Columbia A.M	New York	26 W 34 St
Eugene Seligman	24	Columbia A.M	New York	26 W 34 St

THE COLUMBIA COLLEGE LAW SCHOOL REGISTER OF THE 1881–82 SENIOR CLASS

He gave his age as twenty-two, his college as Harvard, his address as 6 West 57th Street in New York City. In his college years he had pondered what he should become—hesitating at first between natural history and the law. Of the legal profession he thought that it required "less prolonged mental effort than some others and especially fitted for 'the weaker sex.'" But by March 1880, not long after his engagement to Alice, his mind was made up: "I shall study law next year, and must there do my best and work hard for my own little wife."

He enrolled in Columbia Law School, then at 8 Great Jones Street, and he used to make the three-mile distance from his home on 57th Street to the downtown area on foot.

Roosevelt was probably a good and conscientious student, though we have no record of the work he did; he left law school long before his biennial examination. His heart was not in the work. In his *Autobiography* he explained: "If I had been sufficiently fortunate to come under Professor Thayer, of the Harvard Law School, it may well be that I would have realized that the lawyer can do a great work for justice and against legalism. But doubtless chiefly

NEW YORK IN THE EIGHTIES

THE COACHING CLUB DEPARTS

LAWN TENNIS AT THE ARMORY

AN OLD-TIME SLEIGH RIDE

WITH ROOSEVELT'S SIGNATURE ON IT through my own fault, some of the teaching of the law books and of the classroom seemed to me to be against justice."

Theodore felt that the "let the buyer beware" maxim was wrong, because the seller made a profit at the expense of the buyer "instead of by bargain which shall be to the profit of both," and he concluded his observations with this pertinent thought: "If I had been obliged to earn every cent I spent, I should have gone wholeheartedly into the business of making both ends meet, and should have taken up the law or any other respectable occupation."

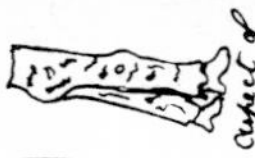

Aspect of Roosevelt's nether limbs in his travelling trousers.

Lucerne
July 19th, 1881

Darling Bysie,

When we reached Munich we were perfectly delighted to receive our letters — two from Oyster Bay and nine from Chestnut Hill. Munich was very hot and we came right on here. The day after we came Alice being tired I walked up and down Mount Pilatus. I took a guide but I tired him out and left him half way. Then I fell in with 1.

two german students and, being for the nonce a bachelor, I fraternised with them and we spent several hours together. It was great fun, and my german held out beautifully until the end, when I was utterly unable to reply when the elder who assured me that meeting me had been to him "an altogether excessive and especially peculiar in no other manner hitherto to be obtained pleasure".

Some how or other we lost a day and both of us waked up on Saturday 2. firmly believing it to be Sunday. We nearly drove the waiter wild asking him ~~about~~ where church was held, until he hit on the happy idea that we were jews. Then, as it was frightfully hot we decided to stay at home, and so did not find out our mistake till the evening. We both felt it was rather a judgment on us for not going to church, so next day we went, very dutifully.

Today we came back from the Rigi Kulm, where we saw a superb sunset and sunrise. You don't know how well I take care of trunks 3.

even when we change cars. I have not had any difficulty yet; though the other day I <u>did</u> mistake a Bavarian cavalry officer for a railway porter, and asked him to wheel my baggage round. The Gorgon's head wasn't a circumstance to the look he gave me.

Best love to darling Muffie & Pussie. ~~Lot~~ Alice and I think Emlen the sweetest old fellow to write to us; we are going to write him long letters.

Your Loving Brother
Thee

4.

LETTER FROM EUROPE WHILE HE WAS ON A BELATED HONEYMOON

AS A MOUNTAIN CLIMBER IN SWITZERLAND IN THE SUMMER OF 1881

CANDIDATE FOR PUBLIC OFFICE. It was a
day after his twenty-fourth birthday that Theodore
Roosevelt entered political life by announcing his
candidacy for the legislature. The New York *Times*
nodded approval. "Every good citizen has cause for
rejoicing that the Republicans of the Twenty-first
Assembly District have united upon so admirable a
candidate for the Assembly as Mr. Theodore Roosevelt," said the first editorial mentioning his name.

★

FIFTH AVENUE IN THE EIGHTIES was studded with comfortable mansions. The northern boundary of the city ran around 59th Street. To the west
New York extended as far as Eighth Avenue, while
on the east, toward the river, the rows of houses were
denser. But even there one could find bucolic scenes
with acres and acres of woodland. On both sides of
Central Park shanty towns grew up as the poor built
crude huts of stolen or discarded material.

Fifth Avenue was Roosevelt's street. He walked it
in summer and winter. He walked to his law school
on Lafayette Place, he walked to the Astor Library
nearby, and he walked to his home on 57th Street.

190

HIS FIRST POLITICAL CAMPAIGN

Young Men's Republican Association,
21st ASSEMBLY DISTRICT.

A special meeting of this Association will be held at Morton Hall, No. 8 East 59th Street, on Thursday Evening, November 3d, 1881, at 8 o'clock, for the purpose of ratifying the nomination of our fellow-member, THEODORE ROOSEVELT, *for member of Assembly. A full attendance is earnestly requested.*

JAMES S. LEHMAIER, *President.*
JOHN R. SANDERSON, *Secretary.*

RATIFICATION MEETING was called by the Young Men's Republican Association, 21st District.

New York, October 31, 1881.
My dear Mr. Roosevelt:
I have been asked how much it is going to cost you to run for the Assembly and who is the treasurer of your Committee. Some of your father's friends think you ought not to be left to bear the whole expense alone, and they would like very much to know how much is needed or how much is unprovided for.
Please see me or drop me a line on the subject as soon as convenient.
Very truly yours
Joseph H. Choate

MEN WITH MONEY offered Theodore campaign contributions. Joseph H. Choate, Harvard alumnus and celebrated lawyer-diplomat, was one of them.

New York, November 1st 1881.

Dear Sir,

Having been nominated as a candidate for member of Assembly for this District, I would esteem it a compliment if you honor me with your vote and personal influence on Election day.

Very respectfully,
Theodore Roosevelt

"I WOULD ESTEEM IT A COMPLIMENT"

Dear Theodore:-
Congratulations my boy, but do write a grammatical circular next time. You see the pedagogue is still critical.
Yours cordially
A. H. Cutler
20 W. 43d St.
Nov. 9/81.

"THE PEDAGOGUE IS STILL CRITICAL"

THE TWENTY-THREE-YEAR-OLD assemblyman from New York's 21st District. Theodore won the election with 3,490 votes against William W. Strew, his Democratic opponent's 1,989, and with this victory his true profession of politics began. At the time this photograph was taken, Roosevelt made his maiden speech in the chamber at Albany, which the New York *Sun* reported with the few lines above. About a week later—on January 30, 1882—in Hyde Park, N.Y., a distant cousin of his was born, a boy of whom the country and the world was to hear more—Franklin Delano Roosevelt.

THE THREE-MONTH-OLD
FRANKLIN D. ROOSEVELT
WITH HIS MOTHER

193

ROOSEVELT'S SURPRISE RESOLUTIONS, demanding an investigation of Judge Westbrook.

A PAT ON THE BACK by the *Evening Post* on June 3, 1883, praising Roosevelt, who had "accomplished more good than any man of his age and experience has accomplished here in recent years."

HIS FIRST BOOK appeared in 1882, when he was only twenty-two years old. He began working on *The Naval War of 1812* while he was at Harvard, but the bulk of the work was done after his marriage to Alice.

THE YEARS IN THE LEGISLATURE

For Theodore Roosevelt the rough-and-tumble of practical politics was a challenge. From the very first day—January 2, 1882—when he arrived in Albany to assume his legislative duties, the old-time political hacks looked at him with amazement and amusement. There was a "perfect dude," complete with Harvard accent, hair parted in the middle, and a pair of eyeglasses suspended from a black silk cord. A newspaperman mused: "What on earth will New York send us next?" But soon, very soon, both the politicians and the newspapermen realized that the young man must be taken seriously. The "damn dude" boldly pressed for the investigation of Judge Theodore Westbrook of the New York Supreme Court, charging the judge with conspiracy to ease the control of the Manhattan Elevated Railway Company into the hands of Jay Gould and his cohorts. Although the judge was absolved of the charges, Roosevelt's reputation as a courageous crusader for clean government had been established.

In the succeeding fall he was re-elected to the Assembly with a walloping two-to-one

New York, _____ 188_

*Election expenses of Theodore Roosevelt
in 1882*

~~Amendment to Association,~~
districts, at ~~10~~ dollars a district
                                        ~~250.00~~

75 00 stamped envelopes
                        168.00

Carriage hire; ~~one back all day~~

posting upwards of 800 bill   *10.00*
~~Billposting~~, *3 cents a bill.*
                                        25.00

*Addressing envelopes, messenger service,
folding ballots*   *42.00*

Printing 90,000 ballots, a large number of *~~10,000~~ cards
for dis distribution, 800 common
posters, 10 muslin posters, and 7500
circulars.*   *·210.00*
                                        ~~310.00~~
(over   ~~700.00~~

*to my share of expenses at polls,
including boxes, district captain,
watches &c, 10 dollars per district,*
                        250
                        _____
                Total 705. dolls

SECOND PAGE of the election expenditures. His share of expenses at polls, including boxes, district captains, watchers, at $10 per district, came to $250.

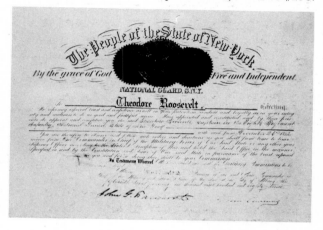

ELECTION EXPENSES as Theodore Roosevelt wrote them out, listing carefully the sums which he paid out during his 1882 campaign, when he ran for re-election to the New York State Assembly.

NATIONAL GUARDSMAN—Roosevelt was commissioned a second lieutenant in B Company of New York's Eighth Regiment on August 1, 1882, and was promoted in the following year to the captaincy.

majority, and such was the respect of his party for him that it named him for the post of Speaker—an honor, though nothing else—in the Democratic-controlled Assembly.

During his second term "the young reformer" fought valiantly for the state Civil Service Bill, allying himself with the Democrats. It was during this term that his attitude toward social legislation underwent a change. Originally Roosevelt had no comprehension of the workingman's lot. He called a bill which was to limit the working day of streetcar employees to twelve hours a "purely socialistic" measure. He fought against wage increases for public employees, and he fought labor leaders who, in his opinion, seemed "the worst foe of the poor man" because they tried to teach him "that he is a victim of conspiracy and injustice." But when the labor leader Samuel Gompers persuaded him to visit the crowded sweatshops in the tenements and see with his own eyes the frightful conditions, he was shocked by the human degradation, and he supported the bill which forbade cigar making in New York tenement houses.

On April 16, 1884, a New York *Times* headline read: "A big day for Roosevelt. Seven of his reform bills passed by the Assembly." It was one of the crowning achievements of his three terms as Assemblyman at the legislature in Albany.

ROOSEVELT.—Suddenly on Thursday, Feb. 14, Alice Lee, wife of Theodore Roosevelt.

Funeral on Saturday morning, Feb. 16, at 10 o'clock, at the Fifth Avenue Presbyterian Church, corner of Fifth avenue and Fifty-fifth street. It is earnestly requested that no flowers be sent.

ROOSEVELT.—Suddenly, on Thursday, Feb. 14, of typhoid fever, Martha Bulloch, widow of Theodore Roosevelt.

Funeral on Saturday morning, Feb. 16, at 10 o'clock, at the Fifth Avenue Presbyterian Church, Fifth avenue and Fifty-fifth street. It is earnestly requested that no flowers be sent.

"THERE IS A CURSE ON THIS HOUSE. Mother is dying and Alice is dying too." Thus spoke Elliott Roosevelt to his brother as Theodore arrived at 6 West 57th Street around midnight February 13, 1884. Theodore rushed to his wife, who on the previous day had given birth to their first child—a girl. By three o'clock in the morning Theodore's mother was dead; Alice, suffering from Bright's disease, died at two o'clock the next afternoon.

ALICE HATHAWAY LEE.

She was born at Chestnut Hill, Massachusetts, on July 29, 1861; I first saw her on October 18, 1878, and loved her as soon as I saw her sweet, fair young face; we were betrothed on January 25, 1880, and married on October 27th, of the same year; we spent three years of happiness such as rarely comes to man or woman; on February 12, 1884, her baby girl was born; she kissed it, and seemed perfectly well; some hours afterward she, not knowing that she was in the slightest danger, but thinking only that she was falling into a sleep, became insensible, and died at two o'clock on Thursday afternoon, February 14, 1884, at 6 West Fifty-seventh Street, in New York; she was buried two days afterward, in Greenwood Cemetery.

She was beautiful in face and form, and lovlier still in spirit; as a flower she grew, and as a fair young flower she died. Her life had

IN MEMORIAM.

been always in the sunshine; there had never come to her a single great sorrow; and none ever knew her who did not love and revere her for her bright, sunny temper and her saintly unselfishness. Fair, pure, and joyous as a maiden; loving, tender, and happy as a young wife; when she had just become a mother, when her life seemed to be but just begun, and when the years seemed so bright before her—then, by a strange and terrible fate, death came to her.

And when my heart's dearest died, the light went from my life for ever.

"AND WHEN MY HEART'S DEAREST DIED, the light went from my life for ever." Thus wrote Theodore in his privately printed memorial about his wife, Alice Hathaway Lee Roosevelt. This sentiment was the last he uttered about her; ever after, he was silent about his "Sunshine." Never again did he mention the name of Alice, not even to their daughter.

*HIS ONLY PHOTOGRAPH
WITH HIS FIRST WIFE
ALICE LEE (ON THE LEFT*

THE FIRST POLITICAL CARTOONS SHOWING ROOSEVELT

The artist Thomas Nast drew the first two Roosevelt cartoons, praising him for his fight for New York's Civil Service bills and for working closely with the state's Democratic governor, Grover Cleveland. Both cartoons appeared in *Harper's Weekly* in the spring of 1884. The first shows Roosevelt as "Our New Watchman," with Cleveland observing from the window; the other is of "Governor Cleveland and Theodore Roosevelt at their good work."

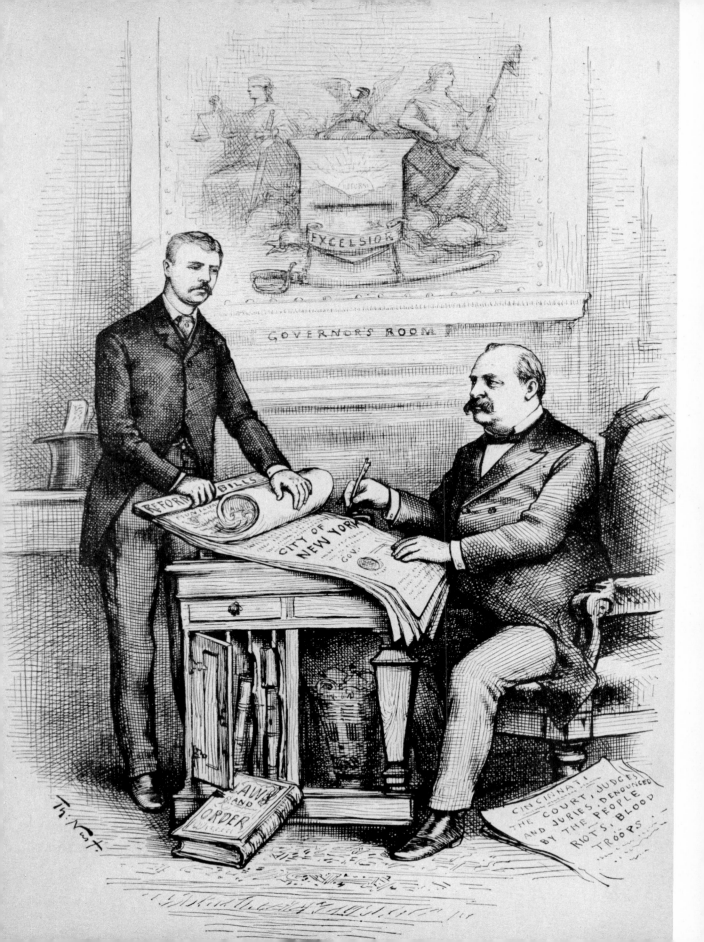

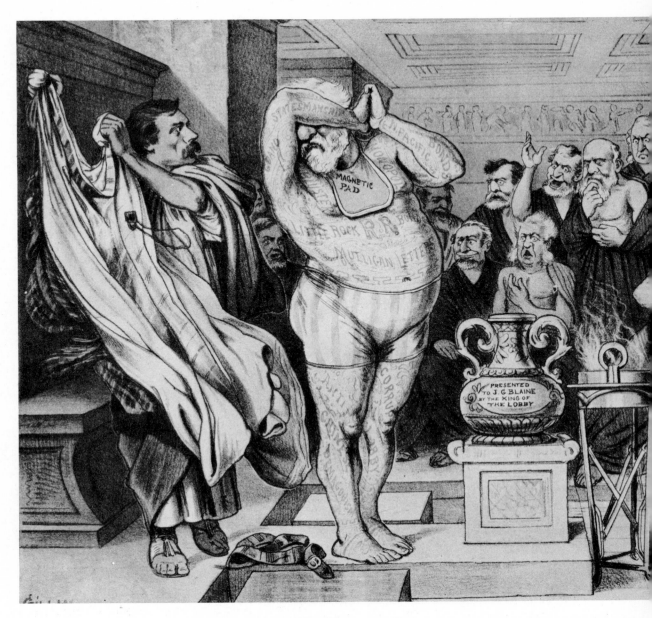

ONE OF THE MOST SAVAGE AMERICAN POLITICAL CARTOONS: GILLAM'S SATIRE ON

James G. Blaine, the Republican candidate, is drawn as Phryne, the Greek hetaera who was charged with impiety and was defended by one of her lovers, securing her acquittal by exhibiting her loveliness.

Blaine's personal honesty was stained by shady deals. The so-called "Mulligan letters" were strong indictment that he had been guilty of accepting gratuities from the Little Rock Railroad of Arkansas.

A prominent candidate in 1876, he had been presented as "an armed warrior" and as "a plumed knight." However, in that convention the nomination went to Rutherford B. Hayes. Four years later Blaine was again in the race, but lost out after

thirty-six ballots to James A. Garfield. And now in 1884 he was once more the foremost candidate.

This time—in spite of all the opposition from the reform and liberal groups—he was nominated amidst cheering that was "fully as deafening as the voice of Niagara." Roosevelt and his young friends fought against Blaine in the convention, but their efforts were doomed to failure.

Blaine was, more than any other politician, typical of the era. A practical wirepuller, personable, opportunistic, and a man of loose ethics, editor Godkin said of him that he "wallowed in spoils like a rhinoceros in an African pool."

200

THE REPUBLICAN CANDIDATE IN 1884

After his nomination the revolt against Blaine spread. Republican newspapers refused their support (the New York *Times* was one which left its close Republican affiliation, never to return again); reform clubs and independent committees "united to rebuke corrupt men and corrupt methods in politics." And when the Democrats named Grover Cleveland, the progressive-minded and reform-conscious candidate, many Republicans—called "mugwumps"—bolted their party and lined up behind him.

The votes of these "mugwumps" helped Cleveland into the presidency—though he won it by only a slight margin.

YOUNG ROOSEVELT SURRENDERS.

He Says He Has No Personal Objections to Blaine and Will Not Bolt.

ST. PAUL, June 9.—The Hon. Theodore Roosevelt of New York spent Sunday in this city, on his way to the Montana ranch. Speaking of the issues of the Chicago Convention, Mr. Roosevelt said:

"The platform is an admirable one, as strong as the party has had since the old war days. It will gain thousands of votes all over the country. Scarcely a Republican or Independent but must endorse it heartily. The Democratic party must follow, in the main, our platform or give up the fight. I did not favor either Blaine or Arthur. My preference was Edmunds. Aside from his own strength of 330 odd votes that would stick to him through thick and thin, the Plumed Knight was the second choice of two-thirds of the remainder of the delegates. As soon as they saw the nomination of their candidate was impossible and Blaine's nomination probable, they flocked to him in a body. This is why no combination against Blaine was possible. Had I not been so positively for Edmunds, I don't know but I would have been carried away myself by the contagion and found myself throwing up my hand for Blaine. Blaine is the choice of two-thirds of the rank and file of the party. I shall bolt the nomination of the Convention by no means. I have no personal objections to Blaine. I think you will find there will be no fatal disaffection. I believe Blaine will be elected. He will sweep the West and Ohio and will carry all New England. I have been called a reformer, but I am a Republican. It is too early to speak of New York. No one to-day can tell how that State will vote. I do not think it impossible for Blaine to carry it. I do not believe there will be an Independent candidate. Those who will not vote a Republican ticket will stay away from the polls. As to the bolt of the *New York Times*, I am inclined to think that it would support either Cleveland or Dorsheimer if nominated by the Democrats."

ROOSEVELT'S INTERVIEW IN ST. PAUL

NEW YORK COMMERCIAL ADVERTISER.

Thursday Afternoon, June 12, 1884.

POSITION OF THEODORE ROOSEVELT.

The *Evening Post* telegraphed to Theodore Roosevelt on Tuesday:

"A St. Paul despatch reports you as saying the Republican platform is admirable; that you will not bolt; that you have no personal objection to Mr. Blaine; that Mr. Blaine will sweep the West and Ohio, carry all New England, and you do not think it impossible to carry New York. Does this represent what you have said?"

To this was received the following answer

"MEDORA, Dak., June 12.

"To my knowledge had no interview for publication; never said anything like what you report. May have said I opposed Blaine for public reasons not personal to myself.

"THEODORE ROOSEVELT."

ROOSEVELT'S ELABORATION of his interview did little to change the impression his original words had created. He would not turn into a "mugwump."

THE REPUBLICAN INDEPENDENTS. A biting comment in *The Judge*. "This is the third time," reads the caption, "they have marched around. There are about nine of them, not ninety thousand." This was untrue. There were enough Independents who were to vote for the Democratic Grover Cleveland to make him President. Theodore Roosevelt (the second on the right) is behind the banner of the New York *Times* and is followed by Carl Schurz, Henry Ward Beecher, and George W. Curtis, editor of *Harper's Weekly*. As one of the leaders of the Independents, Roosevelt worked against Blaine's nomination in the 1884 convention; but when the nomination became a reality he did not bolt the party and support Cleveland. "I intend to vote the Republican presidential ticket," said Roosevelt to a reporter of the Boston *Herald*. "A man cannot act both without and within the party; he can do either, but he cannot possibly do both." He left the Chicago convention "full of heat and bitterness." (*The World*, June 27, 1884.) But when he reached St. Paul he told a newspaperman that he would support Blaine. To his incredulous friends Roosevelt explained that he was a Republican and would not vote otherwise. He even spoke for Blaine in the campaign, saying "The man is not everything; the party is most of all."

However, the country elected Grover Cleveland, though the change of a mere 600 New York votes would have given the election to Blaine. The victory left Roosevelt in a political no man's land. He was distrusted by Republicans and Democrats alike; his future looked bleak.

CHAPTER XV

IN THE BAD LANDS

The first time Roosevelt went to the Bad Lands it was to test his hunting prowess against the vanishing buffalo herd. Traveling the newly completed Northern Pacific Railroad to Little Missouri, a small frontier town named after the bordering river, he took on a guide and set up headquarters at the outpost cabin of Gregor Lang, manager for an absentee owner of a large cattle herd. Joe Ferris, his guide, at first took a condescending attitude toward the non-smoking, non-drinking "four-eyed" Eastern tenderfoot, who was given to exclaiming "By Godfrey!" But when Roosevelt was up every day at the crack of dawn ready to start the day's hunting, Ferris's attitude toward him changed to respect. In the evenings, when the hunters returned to the cabin, instead of piling into his bunk as Ferris did, Roosevelt would stay up into the early hours talking with the Langs about the wonders of the western country. And before forty-eight hours had passed, Roosevelt had decided to become a cattle rancher in the Bad Lands.

The buffalo hunt was successful. Roosevelt—conservationist instincts apparently undisturbed by the bisons' near extinction—finally managed to bring down a handsome bull, an event which he exuberantly celebrated by doing an Indian war dance and presenting a hundred dollars to his guide. Shortly thereafter he headed East. But before he boarded his train, he committed himself to becoming a partner with William Merrifield and Sylvane Ferris in the Maltese Cross ranch on the Little Missouri.

A year later—in 1884—when he returned to the Bad Lands in the wake of personal tragedy and political disappointment—his wife had died in February, his fight against Blaine's nomination in the Chicago convention unsuccessful— he found Little Missouri overshadowed by Medora, a bustling outpost across the river. Medora, which had grown from four buildings to eighty-four during his absence, was the handiwork of the Marquis de Mores, a colorful French adventurer who had married Medora von Hoffman, the daughter of a rich New York banker, and named the settlement after her. De Mores, who hoped to expand his fortune by cattle raising, attempted to lord it over the country-side, picking fights with everyone in sight. His Gallic temperament even threatened to involve him with Roosevelt in a duel. Fortunately for Theodore, who was de Mores' inferior in marksmanship, the combat never took place.

Roosevelt now invested an additional $26,000 in cattle, besides the $14,000 to which he had committed himself before, and selected the site for a second ranch—the Elkhorn—in a more remote location. To build and manage it he brought West the two guides, Bill Sewall and his nephew, Will Dow, of whom he had grown so fond when he hunted in Maine as a Harvard student. "The Elkhorn ranch house," he recalled, "was mainly built by Sewall and Dow who, like most men from the Maine woods, were mighty with the axe. I could chop fairly well for an amateur, but I could not do one-third the work they could. One day when we were cutting down the cottonwood trees, to begin our building operations, I heard some one ask Dow what the total cut had been, and Dow, not realizing that I was within hearing, answered: 'Well, Bill cut down 53, I cut 49, and the boss he beavered down 17.' Those who have seen the stump of a tree which has been gnawed down by a beaver will understand the exact force of the comparison."

During the summer, ranching at Maltese Cross and lumbering at Elkhorn was interrupted with hunting trips, of which the most ambitious was a seven-week expedition to the Big Horn Mountains. The round trip covered nearly a thousand miles, and before the hunt was over, Roosevelt had shot three grizzly bears and six elk. By now he was a toughened Westerner, regarded with respect by the same hard-bitten cowhands who had scoffed at his dudish manners a year earlier. Once, participating in his first roundup, he had caused delighted guffaws among the cowhands by crying out to one of them, "Hasten forward quickly there!"—a remark that became a standing joke in the Bad Lands. But none questioned his endurance or his willingness to carry a full share of the load. The respect for Roosevelt even approached awe when, badgered by a gun-wielding tough who addressed him as "Four-eyes" in the lobby of a hotel outside Medora, he caught the bully off balance and, with three well-placed punches, deposited him unconscious on the floor. That Roosevelt took deep pride in his westernization was evidenced in his remarks that "some of our gilded youth" would be much improved if they were subjected to "a short course of riding bucking ponies and assisting at the branding of a lot of Texas steers."

Despite the intense attraction the Bad Lands held for him, he could not shake off the competing attraction of the East. After completing his role in the unsuccessful Blaine campaign in 1884, he returned to Medora, where he helped organize the Little Missouri Stock Association to help maintain law and order in the area and to protect ranchers' land rights. But by Christmas he was back in New York to spend the holidays with his baby daughter and his sister Bamie. He remained in the city almost three months, writing his *Hunting Trips of a Ranchman* and traveling frequently to Albany to work for a former legislative colleague, Walter Hubbell, in his campaign for speakership of the Assembly and to help William M. Evarts win election to the U. S. Senate.

In April 1885 Roosevelt was back again in the Bad Lands, and within a few weeks the Elkhorn ranch house was finished and occupied. Describing it later in his *Autobiography,* Roosevelt said: "After the first year I built on the Elkhorn ranch a long, low ranch house of hewn logs, with a veranda and with, in addition to the other rooms, a bedroom for myself, and a sitting-room with a big fireplace. I got out a rocking chair—I am very fond of rocking chairs—and enough books to fill two or three shelves, and a rubber bathtub so that I could get a bath. And then I do not see how any one could have lived more comfortably. We had buffalo robes and bearskins of our own killing. We always kept the house clean—using the word in a rather large sense. There were at least two rooms that were always warm, even in the bitterest weather; and we had plenty to eat." The ranch house overlooked the Little Missouri, and the nearest neighbor was a dozen miles away. One could not have asked for a more ideal spot in which to combine the outdoor life with the quiet and solitude Roosevelt wished for writing.

In June 1885, after a strenuous spring on the ranch, he was in New York again, working on details relating to the publication of his book *Hunting Trips of a Ranchman* (which received uniformly enthusiastic notices) and inspecting the progress of his house, Sagamore Hill, on Long Island, which was completed in the fall. He marched in the funeral of General Grant on July 23 and visited his friend Henry Cabot Lodge in Massachusetts—but by the end of August he was back at Medora, attending to his duties as president of the Little Missouri Stockmen's Association and hunting the country north of Elkhorn. Then, early in September, he headed once more for New York to take a prominent part in the Republican state convention at Saratoga. Most of the rest of the year was spent on Long Island, where his social life was far removed from the rough-and-ready existence in the West. He did, however, find an outlet for his physical energies in riding with the Meadowbrook hounds, on one occasion suffering a broken arm and other injuries when his horse missed a jump and rolled over on top of him. Characteristically, he immediately remounted and resumed the hunt after dismissing the injury as "a mere trifle," and that night he went out to dinner in as buoyant spirits as ever.

The following March—March 1886—Roosevelt was back on his ranch and added another chapter to his western exploits by capturing Mike Finnigan and his two cohorts, who had stolen his boat and made off with it down the river. But his story in the Bad Lands was nearing its end. Most of 1886 he stayed in the East, preoccupied with other matters, political and romantic. In the fall of the previous year he had again met his childhood friend Edith Carow, and he married her in London on December 2, 1886. And while he was enjoying a European honeymoon, blizzards and bitter freeze-ups destroyed most of his cattle and helped seal Medora's fate as a cattleman's ghost town. When he returned to the Bad Lands in the spring of 1887 he went there to liquidate his holdings. His subsequent visits to the Elkhorn ranch were only as a hunter and when the last of his remaining cattle were sold off more than a decade later, the books showed a net loss of some $20,000 for his ranching venture.

The extent to which the West shaped Roosevelt's outlook on life is hard to overstate. It had vast influence on his development. It brought the successful culmination of his quest for extraordinary physical stamina. It gave him a profound appreciation of the importance of frontier life and frontier philosophy in the American character. But the most important lesson was summed up by Roosevelt himself at the turn of the century when he addressed a trainside audience in Bismarck while campaigning for the vice-presidency. "I had studied a lot about men and things before I saw you fellows," he said, "but it was only when I came here that I began to know anything or measure men rightly."

THE BAD LANDS
OF
NORTH DAKOTA

THIS WAS MEDORA at the height of its prosperity. The disastrous winter of 1886 made it a ghost village.

MIDDAY MEAL. A Frederic Remington illustration for Roosevelt's book *Ranch Life and the Hunting Trail.*

PLAYING CARDS in the Hotel de Mores. At left: Sylvane Ferris, one of Roosevelt's ranch managers.

THE LITTLE MISSOURI ABOVE ELKHORN

"I first reached the Little Missouri on a Northern Pacific train about three in the morning of a cool September day in 1883," noted Theodore Roosevelt in his *Autobiography.* His main reason for going to the Bad Lands was to hunt buffalo. He planned on a short hunting trip, but within a few days he had fallen deeply in love with the country, and, ready to settle there, he invested a large sum in a cattle ranch.

The wide-open spaces of the Bad Lands became his refuge—he returned there time and time again. He went there to hunt, to write, and to contemplate. There he "felt as absolutely free as a man could feel." He enjoyed the feeling of freedom and the feeling of loneliness. "Nowhere, not even at sea, does a man feel more lonely than when riding over the far-

NEAR THE SITE OF THEODORE ROOSEVELT'S CATTLE RANCH IN THE BAD LANDS

reaching, seemingly never-ending plains; and after a man has lived a little while on or near them, their very vastness and loneliness and their melancholy monotony have a strong fascination for him."

The beauty of the country inspired him to his best literary efforts. "It was a land of vast silent spaces," he wrote, "of lonely rivers, and of plains where the wild game stared at the passing horseman. It was a land of scattered ranches, of herds of long-horned cattle, and of reckless riders who unmoved looked in the eyes of life or death. In that land we led a free and hardy life, with horse and with rifle. We worked under the scorching midsummer sun, when the wide plains shimmered and wavered in the heat; and we knew the freezing misery of riding night guard round the cattle in the late fall round-up. In the soft springtime the stars were glorious in our eyes each night before we fell asleep; and in the winter we rode through blinding blizzards, when the driven snow-dust burnt our faces. There were monotonous days, as we guided the trail cattle or the beef herds, hour after hour, at the slowest of walks; and minutes of hours teeming with excitement as we stopped stampedes or swam the herds across rivers treacherous with quicksands or brimmed with running ice. We knew toil and hardship and hunger and thirst; and we saw men die violent deaths as they worked among the horses and cattle, or fought in evil feuds with one another; but we felt the beat of hardy life in our veins, and ours was the glory of work and the joy of living."

THE BUFFALO HUNT

When Roosevelt came to the Bad Lands in 1883 he had no other reason but to hunt buffalo. As soon as he arrived he hired the Canadian Joe Ferris as a guide and could hardly wait to begin the hunt. The two set out in a buckboard up the Little Missouri, traveling forty-five miles to the cabin of Gregor Lang, which Ferris recommended as a base for their expedition. Making the journey in a single day, they reached the cabin before nightfall. The exhausted Ferris fell into bed, but Roosevelt was full of vigor and talked to his newly met hosts until the early hours of the morning.

The next day it rained, "an impossible day for hunting," but Roosevelt could not be kept indoors. Reluctantly, Ferris went out with him. They were out the entire day looking for buffalo, but had no luck. This went on for days. Each morning they left the cabin in the rain; each evening they returned to the cabin empty-handed.

At night Roosevelt sat up with the Langs, father and son, talking with them on a wide variety of topics. Young Lang remembered these talks as long as he lived. "I learned, for example," he recalled, "that while the world was a good place to live in, just as I had been thinking, there were—to shear the frills —a whole lot of rooting hogs loose in it."

After exhausting days of plodding over the rough terrain, the hunters came at last upon the tracks of a buffalo. They followed the animal, but before Roosevelt could take aim, the buffalo had disappeared.

In the late afternoon of that day the hunters perceived three dark specks on an open plain and stalked them on foot. The last half mile they made on hands and knees, Roosevelt's hands getting filled with cactus spines. Then—hardly more than a hundred yards away—there stood the buffalo. Roosevelt raised his rifle, fired at a bull. Dust flew from the animal's hide, but he dashed off. The hunters raced back to their horses and in the twilight began their pursuit. The full moon was rising above the horizon as they closed in on the wounded animal. "The ground over which we were running was fearful," Roosevelt described the scene later, "being broken into holes and ditches, separated by hillocks; in the dull light, and at the speed we were going, no attempt could be made to guide the horses, and the latter, fagged out by their exertions, floundered and pitched forward at every stride, hardly keeping their legs. When up within twenty feet I fired my rifle, but the darkness, and especially the violent labored motion of my pony, made me miss; I tried to get in closer, when suddenly up went the bull's tail, and, wheeling, he

charged me with lowered horns. My pony, frightened into momentary activity, spun round and tossed up his head; I was holding the rifle in both hands, and the pony's head, striking it, knocked it violently against my forehead, cutting quite a gash, from which, heated as I was, the blood poured into my eyes. Meanwhile the buffalo, passing me, charged my companion, and followed him as he made off, and, as the ground was very bad, for some little distance his lowered head was unpleasantly near the tired pony's tail. I tried to run in on him again, but my pony stopped short, dead beat; and by no spurring could I force him out of a slow trot. My companion jumped off and took a couple of shots at the buffalo, which missed in the dim moonlight; and to our unutterable chagrin the wounded bull labored off and vanished in the darkness. I made after him on foot, in hopeless and helpless wrath, until he got out of sight."

Thoroughly worn out, the hunters lay down on the ground, using their saddles as pillows. At midnight a wolf frightened their horses and they ran off, so the men had to chase them and bring them back. To make life more miserable, it began to rain; the rest of the night was spent shivering under wet blankets. Ferris felt in low spirits, but Roosevelt was elated. "By Godfrey but this is fun!" he repeated over and over again.

As dawn broke, Roosevelt saw a buffalo cow in the driving rain, shot at her, but missed. Later he was thrown by his pony and slightly hurt. Exhausted and disappointed, the two hunters returned to the Lang camp.

By then Roosevelt was under the spell of the Bad Lands. He wanted to become a ranchman. Lang recommended two men as managers of the ranch, and Roosevelt asked him to bring them to the cabin so he could talk to them.

Next morning they hunted west of the river and found a perfect specimen of a bison bull. "His glossy fall coat was in fine trim and shone in the rays of the sun." Roosevelt, with bated breath, moved close to the animal; and when he came within fifty yards of it he fired. The buffalo disappeared over the crest of a hill, leaving a blood trail; Roosevelt found his lifeless body at the bottom of a coulee a short distance away.

It was a triumphant moment; he had bagged his buffalo. So elated was he that he burst out in an Indian war dance, then embraced Ferris and presented him with a hundred dollars.

Well satisfied and pleased, Roosevelt took a train back East, traveling to New York, where his "darling little wife" was waiting for him.

THE "FOUR-EYED" EASTERN TENDERFOOT on his favorite horse, Manitou. "You would be amused to see me," wrote Roosevelt from the Bad Lands to his friend Henry Cabot Lodge back East, "in my broad sombrero hat, fringed and beaded buckskin shirt, horse hide chapajaros or riding trousers, and cowhide boots, with braided bridle and silver spurs." And in a descriptive letter to his sister he speaks of himself as looking "like a regular cowboy dandy, with all my equipments finished in the most expensive style."

COWBOYS IN THE BAD LANDS WHO KNEW THEODORE ROOSEVELT WHEN HE WAS

A photograph taken in 1888 at the H.T. Ranch on Deep Creek in Slope County, showing the owner with the hands of the Little Missouri Horse Company in Dakota Territory. These tough, hard-riding, fun-loving men ran about five thousand horses yearly in the Bad Lands and then sold them to streetcar lines,

breweries, and ice companies in the East. Seated, from left to right: ranch foreman Thomas Franklin Roberts; Norman Lebo, who cooked and was teamster for Roosevelt on the Big Horn hunting trip; A. C. Huidekoper, owner of the ranch; "Hell Roaring" Bill Jones, who drove for Roosevelt; George Wood-

A RANCHMAN AT THE LITTLE MISSOURI

man, later manager of Huidekoper's ranch; Old Mc-Quillen, who "could ketch a horse with his own beard."

Standing is Goose, a Crow Indian, next to Charley Mason; Charles Vansickle; Herman Holst, the cook; Jim Harmon; Dan Fowler; Fred McClain; James Reynolds, and Schuyler N. Lebo, the son of Norman.

"I HAVE NEVER BEEN IN BETTER HEALTH"
A letter from Little Missouri, written to his elder sister on his second trip to the Bad Lands, dated June 17, 1884. Four months earlier Roosevelt had buried his wife and his mother. Only two weeks before, his ambition to check James G. Blaine's candidacy in the Chicago Republican convention had been frustrated. Disappointed, he retired to his ranch, telling his sister that he is having "a glorious time" and that he is "well hardened."

"I have never been in better health," he continues, "than on this trip. I am in the saddle all day long either taking part in the round-up of the cattle, or else hunting antelope. I got one the other day; another good head for our famous hall at Leeholm. I am really attached to my two 'factors,' Ferris and Merrifield; they are very fine men.

"The country is growing on me, more and more; it has a curious fantastic beauty of its own; and as I own six or eight horses I have a fresh one every day, and ride on a lope all day long. How sound I do sleep at night now! There is not much game however; the cattle men have crowded it out and only a few antelope and deer remain. I have shot a few jackrabbits and curlews, with the rifle; and I also killed eight rattlesnakes."

211

We the undersigned, Theodore Roosevelt, party of the first part, and William Merrifield and Sylvanus Ferris, parties of the second part, do agree and contract as follows:

1) The party of the first part hereby agrees and contracts to put on the ranche of the parties of the second part situate on the Little Missouri, in addition to the stock he now has thereon, one thousand head of cattle or thereabouts, the cost not to exceed twelve twenty six thousand dollars (26,000.00).

2) The parties of the second part hereby agree and contract to take charge of said one thousand additional head of cattle on the same terms as they now take charge of the cattle of said party of the first part now on their ranche, pursuant to the contract entered into between said party of the first part and said parties of the second part on the twenty seventh day of September eighteen hundred and eighty three; and all the provisions of said contract are to be held to affect the care, sale and accounting for the said one thousand head of cattle or thereabouts, precisely as if they were part of the herd of cattle now on the ranche of said parties of the second part belonging to said parties of the first part.

signed

Theodore Roosevelt
(party of the first part)

Wm: Merrifield
Sylvanus Ferris
(Parties of the second part)

Witness
J J Macaulay
W. Anyer
Engr Chief

Little Missouri
Dakotah
June 12 1884

HE INCREASES HIS HOLDINGS in the Bad Lands. The second contract that Theodore Roosevelt made with William Merrifield and Sylvanus Ferris, on June 12, 1884, stipulated that Roosevelt would invest $26,000 to buy an additional thousand head of cattle. This raised his investment to $40,000, as in a similar agreement the previous autumn he had already given Merrifield and Ferris $14,000. This ranching venture was financially not rewarding. When the business was finally wound up his books showed a net loss of $20,292.63.

THE LAND. "This broken country extends back from the river for many miles, and has been called always . . . the 'Bad Lands,' partly from its dreary and forbidding aspect and partly from the difficulty experienced in traveling through it. . . . In spite of their look of savage desolation, the Bad Lands make good cattle country, for there is plenty of nourishing grass and excellent shelter. . . . The cattle keep close to them in the cold months, while in the summertime they wander out on the broad prairies stretching back of them."

ROUNDUP IN BAD LANDS—a snapshot taken by Theodore Roosevelt, showing Sylvane Ferris, one of his managers at the Maltese Cross Ranch in the early eighties. Roosevelt in describing the cowboys of the western plains said they were all similar to each other: "Sinewy, hardy, self-reliant, their life forces them to be both daring and adventurous, and the passing over their heads of a few years leaves printed on their faces certain lines which tell of dangers quietly fronted and hardship uncomplainingly endured."

THE CABIN at the Chimney Butte ranch. Of his brand he said that it was "always known as 'maltee cross' . . . as the general impression along the Little Missouri was that 'maltese' must be plural." And of ranch life: "I do not believe there ever was any life more attractive to a vigorous young fellow than life on a cattle ranch in those days. It was a fine, healthy life, too; it taught a man self-reliance, hardihood, and the value of instant decision—in short, the virtues that ought to come from life in the open country."

Little Missouri
June 23d 84,

Darling Bysie,
You have been a perfect trump to have written me so much and so has dear old Douglass.

For the last week I have been fulfilling a boyish ambition of mine — that is I have been playing at frontier hunter in good earnest, having been off entirely alone, with my horse and rifle, on the prairie. I wanted to see if I could not do perfectly well without a guide, and I succeeded beyond my expectations. I shot a couple of antelope and a deer — and missed a great many more. I felt as absolutely free as a man could feel; as you know I do not mind loneliness; and I enjoyed the trip to the utmost. The only disagreeable incident was one day when it rained. Otherwise the weather was lovely, and every night I would lie wrapped up in my blanket looking at the stars till I fell asleep, in the cool air. The country has widely different aspects in different places; one day I would canter hour after hour over the level green grass, or through miles of wild rose thickets, all in bloom; on the next I would be amidst the savage desolation of the Bad Lands, with their dreary plateaus, fantastically shaped buttes and deep, winding canyons. I enjoyed the trip greatly, and have never been in better health.

I shall be back about July 1st or 3d, and will go at once out to Orange, and thence to Chestnut Hill. I will telegraph you.

Your's loving brother
Thee

"A BOYISH AMBITION OF MINE," wrote Roosevelt from Little Missouri to his sister Anna on June 23, 1884, was fulfilled when he went on the prairie with horse and rifle entirely alone. "I wanted to see if I could not do perfectly well without a guide, and I succeeded beyond my expectations. I shot a couple of antelope and a deer, and missed a great many more . . . the weather was lovely, and every night I would lie wrapped up in my blanket looking at the stars till I fell asleep, in the cool air."

THE BAD LANDS IN ALL ITS GLORY

214

THE ELKHORN RANCH SITE, as shown in the diorama at the American Museum of Natural History. The antelopes in the Bad Lands, so Roosevelt wrote, were "always very conspicuous figures in the landscape, for, far from attempting to conceal itself, an antelope really seems anxious to take up a prominent position, caring only to be able itself to see its foes."

★

HIS ARRIVAL in Bad Lands in 1884 was announced in a small item in the *Bad Lands Cowboy*. "Theodore Roosevelt, the young New York reformer," said the paper, "made us a very pleasant call Monday, in full cowboy regalia. New York will certainly lose him for a time at least, as he is perfectly charmed with our free western life and is now figuring on a trip into the Big Horn country. He is perfectly non-committal on politics and the alleged interview with him, published in the St. Paul Pioneer-Press, speaks more for the reporter's assininity than for his perspicacity."

Chimney Butte Ranch
Aug 17th 1884

Darling Bysie,

We have been delayed nearly a week by being forced to get some extra ponies; however I was rather glad of it, as I wished to look thoroughly through the cattle before going. Tomorrow morning early we start out. Merrifield and I go on horseback, each taking a spare pony, which will be lead behind the wagon, a light "prairie schooner" drawn by two stout horses, and driven by an old french halfbreed. I wear a sombrero, silk neckerchief, fringed buckskin 1.

shirt, sealskin chaparejos or riding trousers, & alligator hide boots; and with my pearl hilted revolver and beautifully finished winchester rifle, I shall feel able to face anything. How long I will be gone I can not say; we will go in all nearly a thousand miles. If game is plenty and my success is good, I may return in six weeks; more probably I shall be out a couple of months; and if game is so scarce that we have to travel very far to get to 2.

it, or if our horses give out or run away, or we get caught by the snow, we may be out very much longer — till towards Xmas; though I will try to be back to vote. By the way, Cleveland is by no means such an angel as the Reformers have tried to make out, it seems.

Yesterday I rode 72 miles between dawn and darkness; I have a superb roan pony, or rather horse; he looks well, with his beautifully carved saddle, plaited bridle, and silver inlaid bit, and seems to be absolutely tireless. I grow very fond of this place, and it certainly has 3. a desolate, grim beauty of

its own, that has a curious fascination for me. The grassy scantily wooded bottoms through which the winding river flows are bounded by bare, jagged buttes; their fantastic shapes and sharp, steep edges throw the most curious shadows, under the cloudless, glaring sky; and at evening I love to sit out in front of the hut and see their hard, gray outlines gradually grow soft and purple as the flaming sunset by degrees softens and dies away; while my days I spend generally alone, riding through the lonely rolling prairie and broken lands. I am afraid that it may not be possible for me to get what 4.

"TOMORROW MORNING EARLY WE START OUT," he wrote to his sister Anna on August 17, 1884, a day before he set out to hunt on the Big Horns. "How long I will be gone I can not say; we will go in all nearly a thousand miles. If game is plenty and my success is good, I may return in six weeks; more probably I shall be out a couple of months; and if game is so scarce that we have to travel very far to get it, or if our horses give out or run away, or we get caught by the snow, we may be out very much longer—till towards Xmas; though I will try to be back to vote."

216

HUNTING ON THE BIG HORN

On his third journey to the Bad Lands, Roosevelt hunted in the Big Horn Mountains with William Merrifield as his guide and old Norman Lebo as his teamster. ("He is a weazened, wiry old fellow, very garrulous, brought up on the frontier, and a man who is never put out or disconcerted by any possible combination of accidents.")

One day they rode through a driving rainstorm which developed into a regular hurricane of hail and wind. Roosevelt noted: "The rain lasted all night and we slept in the wagon, pretty wet and not very comfortable. Another time a sharp gale of wind and rain struck us in the middle of the night, as we were lying out in the open (we have no tent) and we shivered under our wet blankets till morning."

He shot a number of prairie chickens, sage hens, and ducks, and a couple of fine bucks, "besides missing several of the latter that I ought to have killed." But when he shot two bucks with one bullet

from four hundred yards, he hailed his achievement as "much the best shot I ever made."

"From morning till night I was on foot, in cool, bracing air, now moving silently through the vast, melancholy pine forests, now treading the brink of high, rocky precipices, always amid the most grand and beautiful scenery; and always after as noble and lordly game as is to be found in the Western World."

Then came the great day when he found himself face to face with a huge creature, nine feet in height, weighing over twelve hundred pounds—"slowly rising from his bed among the young spruces"—a grizzly bear.

"As he sank down to his forefeet I had raised the rifle; his head was slightly down, and when I saw the top of the white bead fairly between his small, glittering, evil eyes, I pulled the trigger. Half rising up, the huge beast fell over on his side in the death throes, the ball having gone into his brain, striking as fairly between the eyes as if the distance had been measured by a carpenter's rule."

PUBLICITY PHOTOGRAPHS

for *Hunting Trips of a Ranchman,* Roosevelt's second book, published by Putnam in 1885. They were posed in a New York studio. The young author, standing on imitation grass, is dressed in a buckskin suit made for

HIS BELOVED RANCH

Roosevelt's Elkhorn Ranch derived its name "from the fact that on the ground where we built it were found the skulls and interlocked antlers of two wapiti bulls who had perished from getting their antlers fastened in battle." He described the place in vivid colors. "The ranch-house stood on the brink of a low bluff overlooking the broad, shallow bed of the Little Missouri, through which at most seasons there ran only a trickle of water, while in times of freshet it was filled brimful with the boiling, foam-

him in the Bad Lands by a Mrs. Maddox, who lived over on the Deadwood Trail some twenty-five miles east of Sage Bottom. Keen to get the suit, Roosevelt rode to her place, making the trip of fifty miles in a single day and shooting his first antelope on the way back.

E LITTLE MISSOURI

ing muddy torrent. There was no neighbor for ten or fifteen miles on either side of me. The river twisted down in long curves between narrow bottoms bordered by sheer cliff walls, for the Bad Lands, a chaos of peaks, plateaus, and ridges, rose abruptly from the edges of the level, tree-clad, or grassy, alluvial meadows. In front of the ranch-house veranda was a row of cottonwood trees," from which "came the far-away, melancholy cooing of mourning doves, and little owls perched in them . . . at night."

422 Madison av.
New York
July 6th 84.

Dear Will,

I enclose you the check of three thousand, for yourself and Will Dow, to pay off the mortgage &c &c.

I have arranged matters in the west, have found a good place for a ranche, and have purchased a hundred head of cattle, for you to start with.

Now, a little plain talk, though I do not think it necessary, for I know you too well.

If you are afraid of hard work and privation do not come west. If you expect to make a fortune in a year or two, do not come west. If you will give up under temporary discouragements, do not come west.

If on the other hand you are willing to work hard, especially the first year, if you realize that for a couple of years you can not expect to make much more than you are now making; and if you also know that at the end of that time you will be in the receipt of about a thousand dollars for the third year, with an unlimited rise ahead of you and a future as bright as you yourself choose to make it; then come.

Now I take it for granted you will not hesitate at this time. So fix up your affairs <u>at once</u>, and be ready to start before the end of this month. We must be on the ranche by August 1st, as I can not hold it longer. So write me as soon as you receive this letter, telling me the earliest possible day at which you can be ready —and make it as early as possible. I will then write you telling the day and to with you to meet me in New York. Address your letter to Theodore Roosevelt care George C. Lee Chestnut Hill Mass and write <u>at once</u>.

Your friend
Theodore Roosevelt

ASKING BILL SEWALL AND WILMOT DOW to come from Maine to the Bad Lands as managers of his cattle ranch. But he warns them: "If you are afraid of hard work and privation, do not come west . . . If on the other hand you are willing to work hard . . . you will be in the receipt of about a thousand dollars for the third year, . . . and a future as bright as you yourself choose to make it, then come."

THREE OLD FRIENDS. Roosevelt induced his two friends from Maine, Will Dow and Bill Sewall, to follow him to Bad Lands "to start the Elkhorn Ranch lower down the river."

THE BRAND OF ELKHORN

Roosevelt's two friends from Maine were not doing too well with their cattle ranch in the Bad Lands. By the beginning of 1885 Sewall was yearning to return to Maine. He wrote to his brother: "I don't like so free a country. Where one man has as good a right as another, nobody really has any right. . . . When feed gets scarce in one place, they drive their cattle where it is good without regard to whose range they eat out. . . . I don't like it and never did. I want to control and manage my own affairs and have a right to what I do have." Things got worse. When, in the fall, the cattle had to be sold for less than the cost of raising, Sewall and Dow asked Roosevelt to release them and let them go home. Roosevelt acceded, turning the management of Elkhorn over to William Merrifield.

It proved the right time to pull out. That winter terrific storms laid sheets of ice over the range, and —foodless—cattle starved and froze to death. Spring found the Little Missouri Valley a scene of desolation.

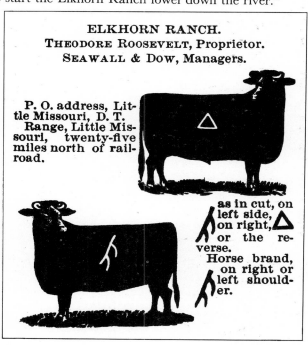

ELKHORN RANCH.
THEODORE ROOSEVELT, Proprietor.
SEAWALL & DOW, Managers.

P. O. address, Little Missouri, D. T. Range, Little Missouri, twenty-five miles north of railroad.

as in cut, on left side, on right, or the reverse. Horse brand, on right or left shoulder.

ONE OF THE MOST GLAMOROUS COUPLES IN THE BAD LANDS
Antoine-Amédée-Marie-Vincent Manca de Vallombrosa, Marquis de Mores (standing in the center, and the portrait on the left), and his wife, Medora von Hoffman (on horseback), the wealthy daughter of a Wall Street banker. They came to the Little Missouri in 1883 with dreams of a cattle empire. The twenty-four-year-old marquis founded a settlement and named it "Medora" after his wife. Behind his back he was called "the crazy Frenchman."

THE HOME OF THE MARQUIS, built on a hill with a magnificent view. A mansion of thirty rooms staffed by twenty servants, it seemed out of place in an area where most people lived in simple cabins. Marquis de Mores and his wife flaunted every tradition of the old West, living as if their château were not in the Bad Lands but in Imperial France. If guests came, "big goblets of champagne" were served, visiting Russian dukes were taken to hunt in fine coaches, and for traveling the marquis used his own railroad car.

Northern Pacific Refrigerator Car Company.

Bismarck
~~Medora~~, Dak., Sept 3 1885

My dear Roosevelt

My principle is to take the bull by the horns. Joe Ferris is very active against me and has been instrumental in getting me indicted by furnishing money to witnesses and hunting them up. The papers also publish very stupid accounts of our quarrelling — I sent you the paper to N.Y. Is this done by your orders. I thought you my friend. If you are my enemy I want to know it. ~~And~~ I am always on hand as you know.

Northern Pacific Refrigerator Car Company.

—

Medora, Dak., 188

and between gentlemen it is easy to settle matters of that sort directly.

Yours very truly

Mores

I hear the people want to organize the county. I am opposed to it for one year more at least

THE MARQUIS' NOTE TO ROOSEVELT

He wrote: "If you are my enemy I want to know it. I am always on hand as you know and between gentlemen it is easy to settle matters of that sort directly." De Mores was upset because he thought that Joe Ferris, Roosevelt's friend, "has been instrumental in getting me indicted by furnishing money to witnesses and hunting them up." Only a week earlier the marquis had been indicted by a grand jury for the murder of Reiley Luffsey and was even put in jail. Bitter about his experience, he wrote this note a few days after his imprisonment. And Roosevelt answered: "Most emphatically I am not your enemy; if I were you would know it, for I would be an open one, and would not have asked you to my house nor gone to yours. As your final words, however, seem to imply a threat it is due to myself to say that the statement is not made through any fear of possible consequences to me; I too, as you know, am always on hand, and ever ready to hold myself accountable in any way for anything I have said or done."

Most emphatically I am not your enemy; if I were you would know it, for I would be an open one, and would not have asked you to my house nor gone to yours. As your final words however seem to imply a threat it is due to myself to say that this statement is not made through any fear of possible consequences to me; I too, as you know, am always on hand, and ever ready to hold myself accountable in any way for anything I have said or done.

Yours very truly

Theodore Roosevelt

ROOSEVELT CAPTURES THREE THIEVES

One day in the spring of 1886 Roosevelt's men on the ranch found that their boat had been stolen. They suspected that the thief was Mike Finnigan, a character who lived up the river with his two cronies—the German Pfaffenbach and the half-breed Burnsted.

Roosevelt had strong convictions about thefts. He wrote: "In any wild country where the power of the law is little felt or heeded and where everyone has to rely upon himself for protection, men soon get to feel that it is in the highest degree unwise to submit to any wrong without making an immediate and resolute effort to avenge it upon the wrongdoers, at no matter what cost of risk or trouble."

Determined to regain his boat, he told Sewall to build a flat-bottomed scow, and on it he, with his two managers, poled and drifted down the river between walls of ice, their faces nipped by the biting wind. On the third morning they spied the stolen boat moored against the bank. And not far away

they found Mike Finnigan and his two cohorts; they were subdued without a fight. "We simply crept noiselessly up," wrote Roosevelt to his friend Cabot Lodge in Boston, "and rising when only a few yards distant covered them with the cocked rifles."

With temperatures below zero, with ice cakes blocking their way, the return journey turned out to be more perilous. Roosevelt did not dare to tie his prisoners because of the danger that their hands might be frozen. It took six full days to reach one of the Diamond Ranch camps. Curiously enough, during these days he read Tolstoi's *Anna Karenina* "with more interest than I have any other novel for I do not know how long."

From the camp the three captives were transported to Dickinson. When Roosevelt reached his destination after two sleepless nights he was exhausted. The local doctor commented: "The average westerner, of course, would have hanged the thieves out of hand. But evidently that did not occur to Roosevelt."

CHAPTER XVI

THE RETURN OF THE DEMOCRATS

While Theodore Roosevelt was busy in New York writing his *Hunting Trips of a Ranchman*, the political picture of the nation underwent a radical change.

March 4, 1885, marked the advent of the Promised Land for the Democrats, who had waited nearly three decades for a presidential victory. To many of the party faithful, the new President appeared as a sort of political messiah who would mercilessly expose the skulduggery of his Republican predecessors and would quickly install good Democrats in every federal office. Grover Cleveland did neither.

To the intense disappointment of Democratic spoilsmen who had hoped for a clean sweep of federal jobs, Cleveland promptly reaffirmed his promise that "merit and competency shall be recognized instead of party subserviency." When one senator complained that the administration should move faster to advance "the principles of Democracy," the President merely replied: "I suppose you mean that I should appoint two horse thieves a day instead of one."

For all his dislike of the patronage system, the President was continually beset by what he termed "the damned everlasting clatter for office," and before his term was over he alienated many former mugwump supporters by letting the Democrats take over most of the best federal jobs—notably in the Post Office Department, where the first assistant postmaster-general, Adlai E. Stevenson, removed so many postmasters that "Adlai's ax" became a byword.

To keep politics and economics as separate entities—the custom of Presidents since the beginning of the Republic—was becoming increasingly difficult, as the rise of trusts and monopolies produced mounting social unrest everywhere. Labor felt that the workingman was gaining nothing from the new industrialism. New machines had made factory work not only monotonous but insecure, without shortening the working day. New sources of wealth had not improved the distribution of money or prevented the cancerous growth of dismal slums. In most cities a workman's average wage was two dollars to three dollars for a twelve- to fourteen-hour day. In filthy tenement sweatshops women and small children worked sixteen hours a day and more. Unemployment was a constant problem.

Workers began to band together in labor organizations. By the mid-eighties the Knights of Labor had three quarters of a million members. The American Federation of Labor, founded in 1886 under the leadership of Samuel Gompers, was composed of craft unions, more exclusive than democratic, more concerned with immediate objectives than with long-range political and social reforms.

Halfway through Cleveland's first term these forces of unrest came to a boil, producing twice as many strikes as in any previous years. On the Gould railroad system of the Southwest, six thousand miles of track were tied up for many weeks, with steady fighting between strikers and troops. In Chicago a series of strikes for an eight-hour day led to a riot in which workers were shot by the police. A day later, at a Haymarket Square mass meeting, a bomb was thrown into the midst of police squads trying to break up the gathering, killing and injuring not only policemen but bystanders. Public indignation ran high, and even though the bomb thrower was never apprehended, eight anarchists were tried and found guilty of murder. The opinion of the country turned violently against "bomb-throwing" labor organizations, and though the Knights of Labor had no hand in the Haymarket tragedy, it brought about the end of that union's influence.

The unrest on the farms found less violent forms of expression, but it was no less deep-seated. Farm prices dropped steadily. Wheat, which sold for $1.45 a bushel in 1866, was down to 69 cents by 1889.

There were many reasons for the unrest. Machinery and new growing methods resulted in overproduction and exhaustion of the soil; specialization destroyed the farmers' old-time self-sufficiency; high tariffs, established by a government that gave its primary allegiance to manufacturers, kept prices high; farmers were forced to buy dear but had to sell their products cheap; as the cost of money went up, they paid as high as 10 and even 20 per cent on mortgages that were generally held by banks and insurance companies in the East. Between the rising cost of money and falling price of farm produce, it took twice as much wheat or corn to pay off a mortgage as it had two decades earlier.

Out of these miseries came the Grange, which had been started as a primarily social organization in 1867, and the Farmers' Alliances, which crusaded for farmers in the 1880s and became the Populist party of the 1890s. Out of these miseries, too, came innumerable devices for bypassing the middleman, from farmers' co-operatives (which often were frustrated by hostile banking interests) to flourishing mail-order enterprises like the one started in 1872 by Aaron Montgomery Ward. Also out of these farm miseries came the Interstate Commerce Act of 1887, perhaps the most important piece of legislation during President Cleveland's first term.

Behind this legislation was a long record of discrimination and mismanagement on the part of the booming railroad industry. In most areas the railroads enjoyed a complete monopoly, which they abused by charging exorbitant rates to farmers and other small shippers while giving secret rebates to favored shippers. In the East a system of secret rebates had given Rockefeller domination over the oil-refining industry, squeezing out and ruining refiners who would not sell out on his terms. In the Middle West and West the principal victims of discriminatory railroad rates were the small farmers, who had no bargaining power as individuals and no alternative means of transportation. With a few notable exceptions like James J. Hill, the "empire builder," railroad magnates tended to regard the farmer as an ignorant peasant who had no business objecting to whatever rates they chose to charge.

But public regulation came, in spite of the enormous political power exercised by the railroads through such devices as outright bribery, political campaign funds, and the distribution of free passes to the families of politicians, editors, and even judges. It came first, in the depression of the 1870s, in the form of state legislation (the so-called Granger Laws) designed to police railroad rate-making. And when these laws were thrown out by the courts on the grounds that states have no right to regulate interstate commerce, it came in the form of the Interstate Commerce Act, which prohibited discriminatory rates, forbade "pooling" arrangements by which competing railroad lines agreed to avoid competition by keeping their rates high and dividing the profits among themselves, and required all lines to file their rate schedules with an Interstate Commerce Commission. In practice the commission found its directives evaded by slippery railroaders and its powers sniped at by a conservative judiciary, but the principle of the public's right to regulate was nonetheless firmly established.

Although this was the most significant legislation of the first Cleveland administration, it was not as controversial as either the pension issue or the tariff question. Since the Civil War, veterans' pensions had been dispensed with increasing prodigality so that by 1885 more than 65 million dollars a year was being paid out. President Cleveland began to scrutinize and veto the hundreds of special pension bills that were passed by Congress each year.

The tariff question had its origin in the Civil War period, when the average duties rose up to 40 per cent. To Cleveland this seemed evil in that it pushed up prices, aided the formation of trusts, and contributed to a mounting treasury surplus which encouraged pension grabs and other governmental extravagances. Thus, the President took the unprecedented step of making tariff reduction the sole subject of his annual message to Congress in December 1887. The message created a sensation. Godkin, of the *Nation,* spoke for reformers generally in calling it "the most courageous document that has been sent from the White House since the Civil War." Republicans of more orthodox stripe, like Congressman William McKinley of Ohio, grimly pictured it as a body blow to every American manufacturer. "Let England take care of herself," said McKinley, "let France look after her interests, let Germany take care of her own people, but in God's name let Americans look after America." Following the Cleveland message, a bill reducing tariffs by about 7 per cent was passed by the Democratic House but blocked in the Republican Senate—thus the electorate was to decide in the shortly forthcoming presidential election whether it was to support Cleveland and tariff reduction or Benjamin Harrison and high protection.

In a base and corrupt campaign, the Republican candidate won, though Cleveland's popular vote was 100,000 larger than that of Harrison. Matt Quay, Pennsylvania's Republican boss, remarked that Harrison would "never know how close a number of men were compelled to approach the gates of the penitentiary to make him president"—an appropriate introduction to an administration that was to set a new record of subservience to special interests.

PROBLEMS UNDER CLEVELAND

WHAT TO DO WITH THE PENSIONS? This cartoon in *Puck* illustrated the pension situation. A year after the Civil War only $15,000,000 was expended on veterans' pensions, but by 1887—because of the powerful pressure brought by the Grand Army of the Republic—this sum had grown to $75,000,000 annually. Many of these pensions were based on fraudulent claims by men who had never seen actual service. Medical examiners approved pension petitions giving such amazing reasons, as that the applicant had a "normal heart" or a "normal liver," and there was a case where the physician supported the applicant's petition because he had "a protuberant abdomen." Congress passed personal pension bills one after the other. As the country had already given $800,000,000 to veterans, President Cleveland made up his mind to halt this unjustifiable drain on the public coffers. In his first term he vetoed 233 pension bills out of 747 passed by Congress.

WHAT TO DO WITH THE SURPLUS? This was one of the crucial questions under the Cleveland administration. The country was prosperous, and the federal income was far greater than the sum needed for running expenses. From $100,000,000 in 1870 the surplus rose to $300,000,000 by 1884.

A simple answer was for the government to repay its debts, redeem its bonds. But this was easier said than done. Such a move would have deprived the public of its best investment, besides reducing the circulation of bank notes for which the bonds were

security. Another way would have been to spend the money on internal improvements—on better harbors, dams, coastal defenses. But this countered the beliefs of the Democrats—the party in power. "The people must support the government," said Cleveland, "but the government must not support the people."

In Cleveland's opinion, the simplest way out of the dilemma was to reduce the tariff, which would not only relieve the people of undue taxation, but would also halt congressional largesse. Thus he devoted his entire 1887 message to Congress to the argument for

tariff reduction, pointing out that for the past eleven months the excess of revenue over expenditure had been $55,000,000 and that by June 30, 1888, the Treasury surplus would be $140,000,000—idly held money, "uselessly subtracted from channels of trade."

The Senate, disregarding the President's plea, would not pass the House-approved tariff reduction bill. Thus the issue was put up to the electorate, which in the following presidential election repudiated Cleveland and his plan and elected Benjamin Harrison, the Republican advocate of high protection.

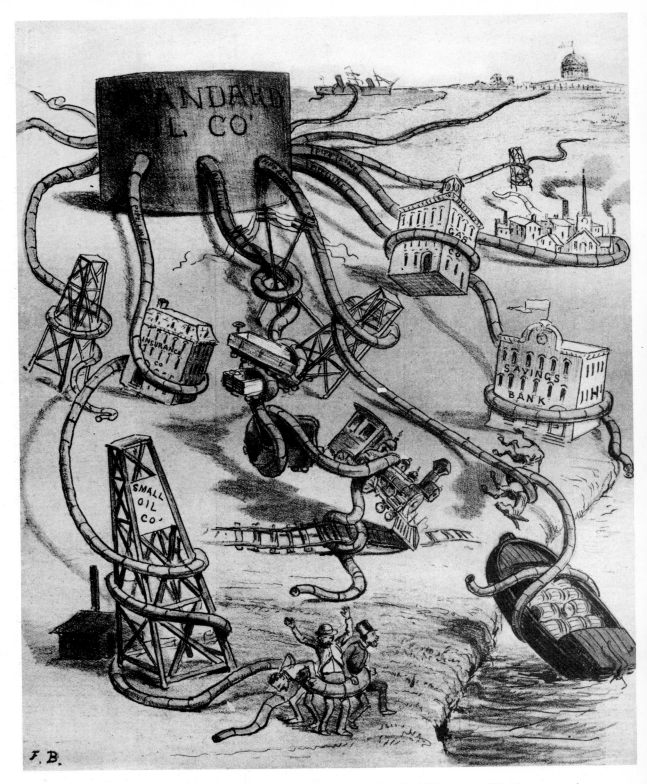

THE MONSTER MONOPOLY, a cartoon on Standard Oil in *Judge.* The late seventies and early eighties saw the birth of large corporations, commonly called "trusts." Oil and lead producers, sugar refiners, lumbermen, whiskey distillers, and other big businessmen turned their holdings into great trusts, wielding enormous political and economic power.

LABOR LEADERS. As capital consolidated itself in trusts, so labor organized into unions, demanding equitable wages, fair working hours, protection against unwarranted discharge, and a minimum security in cases of sickness and disability.

These six men were founders of the Noble Order of the Knights of Labor, a workers' organization which had three quarters of a million members by 1886. It advocated union of all trades, co-operative ownership of means of production, education, and secrecy of rituals. The empty chair is that of the movement's deceased leader, Uriah S. Stephens.

★

VIOLENT STRIKES became marked under Cleveland's administration. In 1884, the year Cleveland was elected, there were 485 strikes; in 1885 the figure rose to 695, and in 1886 to 1,505. The President, deeply concerned about the labor disputes, sent a special message to Congress in the spring of 1886—the first presidential message on labor.

THE HAYMARKET RIOT IN CHICAGO

On May Day 1886 labor struck for an eight-hour day. All over the country, workers demonstrated. Two days later, in a clash between police and pickets at the McCormick Reaper Works, one worker was killed and others wounded.

Next night, in a mass protest meeting on Chicago's Haymarket Square, anarchists addressed the demonstrators; and when the speeches became too inflammatory, the police ordered the crowd to disperse. At that instant a bomb was thrown into the squad, killing eight men instantly and wounding sixty more. The enraged policemen charged into the crowd, the demonstrators returned their fire; there were more

A BOMB EXPLODES IN CHICAGO

ROOSEVELT'S INTEMPERATE REACTION to the Haymarket riots is contained in a letter to his sister Bamie from the Bad Lands. For this note, written in hot anger, he was later severely criticized. "My men here are hard-working, labouring men," wrote Roosevelt, "who work longer hours for no greater wages than many of the strikers; but they are Americans through and through. I believe nothing would give them greater pleasure than a chance with their rifles at one of the mobs. When we get the papers, especially in relation to the dynamite business, they become more furiously angry and excited than I do. I wish I had them with me and a fair show at ten times our number of rioters; my men shoot well and fear very little."

Roosevelt's emotional outburst about the Haymarket riots differed little from those of other propertied men in the country. They were not only outraged because labor broke the law, but because it wanted to strengthen itself by becoming organized. And after the unhappy bomb-throwing affair, labor leaders became confused in their minds with cut-throats and murderers, and labor's demand for better working conditions and job security seemed to them anarchist villainy.

dead and wounded.

Though the person who threw the bomb was never found, eight anarchists were arrested. Four of them were hanged on the charge of inciting people to riot, the others sentenced to life imprisonment.

After the Haymarket incident the mood of the country turned against labor and its organizations.

HIS LETTER ON THE HAYMARKET RIOT

233

THE NEW REPUBLICAN PRESIDENT. Benjamin Harrison, a colorless Indiana lawyer, the grandson of President William Henry Harrison, was an easy butt for cartoonists. Joseph Opper called this caricature which appeared in *Puck:* "Truth is stranger than fiction," and in it the nursery-tale midgets sing: "Great Lilliput! He's smaller than any of us!"

CHAPTER XVII

STARTING ALL OVER AGAIN

After Alice's death, Roosevelt shuttled restlessly between the Bad Lands and the East. By the end of 1884 his term in the legislature was over and, as he was not running for a fourth time, he was ready to turn his back on politics. His future plans were to attend to his ranch, to hunt, to lead the life of a private citizen. And in his spare time he would write. He would be no longer a politician but "a literary feller."

The editor of the *American Statesmen* series asked him to contribute a biography of Senator Thomas Hart Benton. He went at it like a house on fire. Within a few weeks the book was completed. It was a superficial, poorly conceived study, in which Benton was mainly evolved "from my inner consciousness." In fact, Roosevelt had so little knowledge of his subject's life that he asked his friend Cabot Lodge, in Boston, to hire someone in the East to find out for him what Benton did after he left the Senate in 1850. The book is, nonetheless, significant as a statement of Roosevelt's views on the American character and the destiny of the United States. In praising Benton's anti-British stand in the Oregon dispute, the author gave vent to his own nationalistic philosophy. He wrote: "By right we should have given ourselves the benefit of every doubt in all territorial questions and have shown ourselves ready to make prompt appeal to the sword whenever it became necessary as a last resort." No wonder that the reviewer of the *Nation* found Roosevelt's philosophy "too much muscular Christianity, minus the Christian part."

The *Benton* was followed by six articles for the *Century Magazine*, describing life in the cattle country of the Far West. These pieces—completed in Italy a year later—made up the volume *Ranch Life and the Hunting Trail,* a moderate success with three thousand copies sold of the first edition.

Though he went through the motions of feverish activity, this was a bleak period for Roosevelt, a period when he viewed his future with jaundiced eye. His personal life in a shambles, his political life at a dead end, he tried to keep himself frantically busy with his ranch and with his writing. "My chance of doing anything in the future worth doing seems to grow continually smaller," he wrote to his friend Lodge.

Then—all of a sudden—everything had changed; all of a sudden the future looked bright. To pinpoint the turn of his fortunes is hard, but a fair guess is that it came in the fall of 1885 when he met his childhood sweetheart, Edith Carow, again. For the next few months, until Edith moved to Europe with her mother and her sister, they saw each other frequently. Theodore promised to follow her to London in the fall and marry her. Why he needed more time, one can only surmise. Social conventions demanded a restraint; Alice had been dead only two years. Thus, in March 1886 he and Edith parted; Edith sailed for Europe while Roosevelt returned to his ranch in the Bad Lands.

By the first week in October he was back in New York, ready to go after Edith. While in the city he was persuaded by Republican politicians to become the party's candidate for mayor and run against Henry George, the self-educated printer from San Francisco and the author of *Progress and Poverty*, who was the candidate of Labor. The Democrats put up Abram S. Hewitt, the son-in-law of Peter Cooper and a wealthy ironmonger with strong conviction for social reforms. At first it looked as if the Republicans would line up behind Hewitt to ensure George's defeat, but then they settled on Roosevelt, and in the Republican county convention at New York's Grand Opera House, Chauncey M. Depew put his name into nomination.

As Depew was making his speech—according to the New York *Times* report—Assemblyman Isaac Dayton moved to the rostrum in agitation, crying that the man whom they were to nominate was no better than George. "He is a free trader!" asserted Dayton, to which Depew retorted, "I say he is not!" And he added, "He told me so last night." Then Depew went on, praising Roosevelt for "the rare courage to acknowledge that he has recovered from the errors of his youth." It may have been, Depew continued, that Roosevelt when at Harvard "believed in the strange and extraordinary theories of Henry George; he may even have had doubts of orthodox religion." But all this belonged to the past; "today he stands cured."

The delegates accepted Roosevelt's candidacy by acclamation, though many Republicans doubted the wisdom of putting up a candidate who would take votes away from Hewitt and thus make certain the victory for George—a possibility abhorrent to all conservatives. However, the New York *Times* was squarely behind Roosevelt. In a long editorial it asked the citizens of New York to support the Republican candidate, as he "excites more confidence and enthusiasm than has been inspired by any candidate in a mayoralty contest within the memory of this generation of voters."

Roosevelt was not too confident of his chances. Shortly after his nomination he wrote to Lodge: "If at this time the decent so-called Republicans would stand by me I would have a good chance of winning; as it is, if the Hewitt stampede grows strong I will be most disastrously defeated." His premonition proved to be right. The conservative Republicans, "the world that owned houses and lands and stocks," was trembling. Panic-stricken, they gave their support to the Democratic candidate rather than take a chance and vote for Roosevelt. With their votes Hewitt won the election.

Roosevelt was badly beaten; his defeat was worse than he expected. But he had no time to be downhearted; within a fortnight he was on the boat to England, where Edith was waiting for him. On December 2 they were married in London at St. George's Church. Best man was Cecil Spring-Rice, the young

English diplomat whom Roosevelt had met on the voyage to Europe and with whom he struck up a friendship that lasted a lifetime.

After the wedding the young couple traveled in Italy. Roosevelt was not anxious to return to America—not for a while anyhow.

Bad news came from his ranch. There was a disastrous winter in the West; the blizzards left sheets of ice over the ground, leaving the cattle without subsistence. When spring came, the valleys of the Bad Lands were covered with the bodies of dead animals. Roosevelt knew that his cattle venture had ended in a fiasco. Again the future looked bleak. He considered selling Sagamore Hill, his newly built house at Oyster Bay, but he "did not have the heart" to do it. He was pondering what to do. Politics? From Florence he wrote to his sister: "I have not the slightest belief in my having any political future."

Thus, he journeyed from place to place, from Florence to Rome, from there to Milan, and finally "we ended up in Venice by having a real snow storm." Then to London and to the English countryside, visiting Lord North, "a dear old gentleman, a regular old foxhunter, who wears a red dress coat," or having lunch "at the castle of Lord Saye and Seale, a great moated place, built in 1301, and looking as if it came out of an old world romance." But though he enjoyed social life, liked to meet people and to make new acquaintances, "after all I shall be glad to get home; I am an American through to the backbone."

On March 19 he and Edith returned home. A short trip to the Bad Lands— to count his losses and wind up his cattle enterprise—then settling down at Sagamore Hill, working on a biography of Gouverneur Morris and on his most ambitious project, *The Winning of the West*.

The summer of 1887 passed quietly but happily. If there was relatively little entertaining, that was no cause for regret to Edith, who was somewhat bookish and retiring by nature and, moreover, was expecting a child in the fall. There were picnics and rowboat rides and much reading aloud from the works of Browning and Thackeray and Matthew Arnold. And there was little Alice, whom Theodore found a delightful companion for his leisure hours, whether building castles of blocks in the nursery or "cavorting and prancing with that young lady on my back." When Edith's baby, a boy, arrived in mid-September, he was of course named Theodore. His father found him a "very merry lovable little fellow," and not long afterward gave what, by his strenuous standards, must have been the ultimate seal of approval: "He plays more vigorously than anyone I ever saw."

Politically, Roosevelt was in the desert. Editor Godkin, annoyed by his assaults on the mugwumps, deemed them "chatter-box abuse," and declared that he wasn't worth taking seriously as a politician and never had been.

But as time passed and, in the fall of 1888, Benjamin Harrison was nominated as the Republican contender for the presidency, Roosevelt was once more back in the fray, speaking on behalf of the Republican ticket, pleading for Harrison and for high protection. And when Harrison was elected Theodore Roosevelt was on his way to becoming a public figure again.

J. KEPPLER

THE REPUBLICANS SEND THEIR YOUNG AND BRAVE KNIGHT INTO THE BATTLE OF

In 1886 when Henry George became the Labor candidate for the chief city office, both Democrats and Republicans were panic-stricken. George was branded as a dangerous fanatic; his thesis "that with the growth in population land grows in value, and the men who work for it must pay more for the privilege" and his suggested remedy—a juster distribution of wealth through taxation—were anathema to men of property.

To oppose George, Tammany and the Democrats nominated Abram S. Hewitt, a wealthy businessman.

At first the Republicans considered supporting Hewitt to ensure the defeat of George, but then, for the sake of improving their bargaining position, they decided to run their own candidate. They approached Elihu Root and Levi P. Morton, and when both had declined, their choice became Theodore Roosevelt.

As to his chances, Roosevelt had no rosy dreams. On October 17 he wrote to Cabot Lodge that after being entreated by a number of influential Republicans to take the nomination, "with the most genuine

HENRY GEORGE

The candidate of Labor and the liberal element for the mayoralty came from San Francisco to live in New York. Conservative Republicans, fearing George's victory, turned to the Democratic candidate rather than support their own.

ABRAM S. HEWITT

The candidate of the Democrats, a respected ironmonger and philanthropist, won the mayoralty in one of the city's most exciting contests. Hewitt was an ardent advocate of social reforms; he fought corruption in government.

THE NEW YORK MAYORALTY CAMPAIGN

reluctance I finally accepted. It is of course a perfectly hopeless contest." And three days later: ". . . if the Hewitt stampede grows strong I will be most disastrously defeated."

Of the contest—which Hewitt won—Jacob Riis remarked: "And in the wild dread of the disaster that was coming, men forsook party, principles, everything, and threw themselves into the arms of Tammany."

Roosevelt's wire to his friend Lodge was terse: "Am badly defeated. Worse even than I feared."

DEFEATED. Abram Hewitt won the hotly contested election with 90,522 votes. Henry George had 68,110, while Roosevelt ran third with 60,435. *Puck*, the satirical political weekly, wrote in derision: "Be happy, Mr. Roosevelt, be happy while you may . . . Bright visions float before your eyes of what the Party can and may do for you. We wish you a gradual and gentle awakening. We fear the Party cannot do much for you."

239

MARRIED AGAIN

The first girl in Theodore's life was Edith Carow, whom he had known since early childhood. It was her picture which, showed to the eleven-year-old Theodore while he was in Europe, "stired up in me homesickness and longing for the past which will come again never, alack never." Then—while at Harvard —he met Alice Lee, fell in love with her, and married his "wilful darling." Edith Carow remained a friend, but the two saw little of each other. After Alice's death, Theodore deliberately avoided Edith. He had strong moral convictions; with all his dash and bravado, he was heart and soul a Victorian. But then—by one of those coincidences—they met in the fall of 1885. Intending to visit his sister at her Madison Avenue home, Theodore met Edith in the hallway just as she was leaving after a call on Bamie. From then on—for the next five months—they became constant companions. (For days his diary contained no entry but the letter "E.") In the spring of 1886 Edith went to London with her mother and sister; in the fall of the same year—after his defeat in the New York mayoralty contest—Theodore followed her. On December 2, 1886, they were married.

★

EDITH KERMIT CAROW, the "Eidieth" of his childhood, became Roosevelt's second wife. On the marriage certificate (see the facsimile below) the bridegroom gave his profession as "ranchman."

240

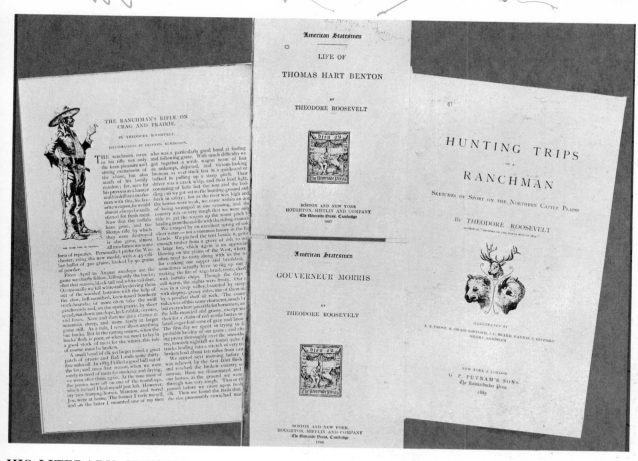

HIS LITERARY OUTPUT

"Writing is to me intensely irksome work," confessed Roosevelt to his sister, yet he kept on writing books in quick succession. In 1885 he published *Hunting Trips of a Ranchman;* a year later he completed the biography of Missouri Senator *Thomas Hart Benton;* 1888 saw the publication of his biography on *Gouverneur Morris,* also his articles on "Ranch Life and the Hunting Trail." During these years he was also working on his major literary opus, a carefully researched study of *The Winning of the West* (published in three volumes) and on his history of the *City of New York.*

SAGAMORE HILL, his home at Oyster Bay, designed by Rich and Lorenzo, with twenty-three spacious rooms was large enough to accommodate a growing family. Completed in the spring of 1885, it cost $17,000. It was not a thing of exterior beauty. "I did not know enough to be sure what I wished in outside matters," Roosevelt said, "but I had perfectly definite views what I wished in inside matters . . . I had to live inside and not outside the house." The result was a solid, immensely livable home with eight big fireplaces, a spacious piazza for viewing the sunset, and an atmosphere of serene permanence.

STREET SCENE IN WASHINGTON in the Spring of 1889, when Theodore Roosevelt moved to the city to take office as U. S. Civil Service Commissioner. The post was an impecunious one, paying only $3,500 a year. But Roosevelt accepted it with alacrity. He desired "to go into politics," and he considered the appointment a good step in that direction.

CHAPTER XVIII

CIVIL SERVICE COMMISSIONER

With Benjamin Harrison in the White House, Roosevelt's hopes soared for a return to public life. Weary of being a private citizen, he sought for a political job. When Cabot Lodge approached the new Secretary of State, James G. Blaine, on his friend's behalf, and Blaine—the same man whom Roosevelt and Lodge had so ardently fought in the 1884 convention—spoke to the President about an appointment, Roosevelt wrote Lodge: "I hope you will tell Blaine how much I appreciate his kind expressions." The post he desired was that of Assistant Secretary of State, but nothing came of it. Roosevelt had to content himself with a much smaller job. He was offered the post of a civil service commissioner at a salary of $3,500 a year, and he accepted it.

Roosevelt had strong feelings about corruption in government and the spoils system. He was an ardent fighter for civil-service reforms. "No republic can permanently endure when its politics are corrupt and base; and the spoils system, the application in politics of the degrading doctrine that to the victor belong the spoils, produces corruption and degradation. The man who is in politics for the offices might just as well be in politics for the money he can get for his vote, so far as the general good is concerned," he wrote for *Scribner's Magazine* in August 1895. And he said: "The spoils-monger and spoils-seeker invariably breed the bribe-taker and bribe-giver, the embezzler of public funds, and the corrupter of voters. Civil-service reform is not merely a movement to better the public service. It achieves this end, too; but its main purpose is to raise the tone of public life, and it is in this direction that its effects have been of incalculable good to the whole community."

As he headed to Washington he told the press: "You can guarantee that I intend to hew to the line and let the chips fall where they will." And to nobody's surprise the chips flew thick and fast. From the day of May 13, 1889, when he took office, until the day of May 5, 1895, when he left his post, the quarters of the Civil Service Commission were in a veritable turmoil. When politicians attacked the commission, Roosevelt returned the attack; when they cut off appropriations, he retaliated by cutting off civil service examinations in their district. Within a few weeks the hitherto obscure commission began making headlines. "No longer," said Roosevelt later in recalling these times, "was there an apology; blow was given for blow." Although the commission never had the desired powers, it made "a resolute fight, and gave the widest publicity to the wrong doing." One of his fellow commissioners recalled: "Every day I went to the office it was as to an entertainment. I knew something was sure to turn up to make our work worthwhile, with him there."

In Washington he took a small house near Connecticut Avenue, and before long it was a gathering place for personalities from both the political and cultural worlds. Henry Cabot Lodge and Cecil Spring-Rice, now attached to the British Embassy, were constant companions; John Hay and William Howard Taft, their fame yet to come, were frequent visitors, along with Henry Adams, whose aloof intellectualism contrasted sharply with Roosevelt's brashness. During this period, also, he came to know Rudyard Kipling and Richard Harding Davis, as well as James Bryce, later British ambassador, who was already embarked on the writing of his monumental *The American Commonwealth*. Kipling used to go with Roosevelt to the Cosmos Club. "I curled up on the seat opposite," he said, "and listened and wondered until the universe seemed to be spinning around and Theodore was the spinner." And in the hours spared from civil service work and Washington social currents Roosevelt continued to work on the third and final volume of *The Winning of the West*, to be published in the fall of 1894. In a chatty letter to his sister he described his life in the capital:

"Washington is just a big village, but it is a very pleasant big village. Edith and I meet just the people we like to see. This winter we have had a most pleasant time, socially and officially. All I have minded is that, though my work is pleasant, I have had to keep at it so closely that I never get any exercise save an occasional ride with Cabot. We dine out three or four times a week, and have people to dinner once or twice; so that we hail the two or three evenings when we are alone at home, and can talk and read, or Edith sews while I make ineffective bolts at my third volume. The people we meet are mostly those who stand high in the political world, and who are therefore interested in the same subjects that interest us; while there are enough who are men of letters or of science to give a pleasant and needed variety. Then besides our formal dinners, we are on terms of informal intimacy in houses like the Cabots, the Storers, the Wolcotts and Henry Adams. It is pleasant to meet people from whom one really gets something; people from all over the Union, with different pasts and varying interests, trained, able, powerful men, though often narrow minded enough."

It was not long before he was entangled in a fight with John Wanamaker, the New York store owner, who, in return for his generous contribution to the Republican chest, had been appointed Postmaster General. Wanamaker insisted that the President "give full weight to the congressional claims of patronage." And Harrison, respectful of Wanamaker's munificence, was inclined to defer. But Roosevelt, shocked by the fact that in the first year of Wanamaker's term no less than thirty thousand postmasters had been dismissed and replaced with "deserving" Republicans, undertook an investigation of corruption in the Baltimore Post Office and recommended dismissing twenty-five of the Wanamaker appointees. "Damn Wanamaker!" Roosevelt shouted when no newspaperman was within earshot. Eventually the charges were investigated and affirmed by the House Civil Service Committee. The incident dismayed President Harrison; he felt Roosevelt had gone too far.

Roosevelt despised Harrison's attitude toward civil-service reform. After a talk with the President, he exclaimed: "Heavens, how I like positive men!" At another time he complained that the President "actually refuses to consider the changes in the rules which are necessary to enable us to do our work effectively. He has never given us one ounce of real backing. He won't see us, or consider any method for improving the service, even when it in no way touches a politician. It is horribly disheartening to work under such a Chief." But when Harrison was asked about Roosevelt, he said: "The only trouble I ever had managing him" was that "he wanted to put an end to all the evil in the world between sunrise and sunset."

Not only the President incurred Roosevelt's displeasure. His temper rose sharply whenever he crossed swords with men whom he thought dishonest. "He is a liar and a coward, and as soon as I get back I shall write him an open letter telling him so," he wrote about one (Grosvenor), and about another (Carlisle): "He is dishonest, untruthful and cowardly."

In the evenings Roosevelt read voraciously—books, magazines, everything. And if he disliked what he read, he let out a yell that reverberated in the ears of his friends and his family. Thus, after reading a story by Henry James in the London *Yellow Book,* he wrote his sister: "I think it represents the last stage of degradation. What a miserable little snob Henry James is. His polished, pointless, uninteresting stories about the upper social classes of England make one blush to think that he was once an American. The rest of the book is simply diseased. I turned to a story of Kipling's with the feeling of getting into fresh, healthy, out-of-doors life."

He thought that Hamlin Garland was faulty in his reasoning about the great literary figures of the past. "He is entirely wrong in thinking that Shakespeare, Homer and Milton are not permanent. Of course they are!" But in his main thesis Garland was right, wrote Roosevelt to his friend Brander Matthews. "We must strike out for ourselves; we must work according to our own ideas, and must free ourselves from the shackles of conventionality, before we can do anything."

In the presidential election of 1892, Grover Cleveland won over Harrison. Roosevelt, who had assailed Cleveland as an enemy of civil service reforms, must have been wondering whether the Democratic President would hold that against him. "I had thought of trying to see Mr. Cleveland but came to the conclusion that this would be an unwarrantable intrusion on my part as he must now be overwhelmed with visitors," he wrote to Carl Schurz, "but I should like to see you who stand so close to him and to tell you exactly how the civil service question appears to me here."

But when Carl Schurz saw the President on Roosevelt's behalf, Cleveland was most cordial. So Roosevelt went to see him "and had a very pleasant half hour's chat with him." Soon Cleveland asked Roosevelt "to stay for a year or two longer," and Roosevelt consented happily. For another three years he remained on the job. Not until the spring of 1895 did he leave Washington.

THE PRESIDENT'S JOB-SEEKING RELATIVES

THE PRESIDENT MUZZLES THE PRESS

PRESIDENT
HARRISON
AS GRINDER
OF THE
ADMINISTRAT
PATRONAGE M

THE ERA OF BENJAMIN HARRISON—AS SEEN THROUGH THE CARTOONISTS' EYES

"Bosses of the Senate," Joseph Keppler's famous cartoon in *Puck,* shows a row of huge human-headed money bags as the real powers behind the Upper House. "This is the Senate of the monopolists, by the monopolists and for the monopolists" reads the sign on the wall—hardly an exaggeration. All the big trusts had their subservient agents. The oil trust had its senators, as had the railroads, the manufacturing and the lumber interests, the insurance and utility companies. Thus, for instance, J. Donald Cameron, of Pennsylvania, looked after the welfare of the Pennsylvania Railroad; Arthur Pue Gorman, of Maryland, after the Central Maryland Railroad; William B. Allison, of Iowa, after the railroads which ran through his state; while Nelson W. Aldrich, of Rhode Island, was a mouthpiece of large manufacturing companies.

The public regarded the Senate as a club of rich men—and rightly so. In that august body sat a number of millionaires—men like Leland Stanford of California, John P. Jones of Nevada, Johnson N. Camden of West Virginia—who were not hesitant to vote upon issues in which they had a personal financial interest. If a man had enough money he could buy a Senate seat. Senators were not yet elected by popular vote; they were named by the state legislatures, and legislators could be bought wholesale. Thus, as the cartoonist points out, all the monopolies had their representatives, while the people's entrance (on the left) was tightly closed.

THE BRAVE LITTLE GIANT-KILLER.

SPOILS SYSTEM GIANT.— Calm yourself, Theodore — if you go too far, you 'll find yourself jerked back mighty sudden!

SIX WEEKS AFTER HIS APPOINTMENT to the Civil Service Commission, Theodore Roosevelt said: "I have made this commission a living force." To political opponents he replied "that as long as I am responsible the law should be enforced up to the handle *everywhere,* fearlessly, and honestly."

As a civil service commissioner, Roosevelt kept himself in the public eye. His name was constantly in the newspapers, and the press reported his pronouncements and quarrels with great glee. Roosevelt knew how to put across his ideas so that everyone could understand them. And despite the coolness of President Harrison (seen in this amusing Dalrymple cartoon holding "the brave little giant killer" on a leash) and the regular politicians toward him, both press and public relished what one observer termed "the spectacle of a man holding a minor and rather nondescript office, politically unimportant, taking a cabinet officer by the neck and exposing him to the amused contempt of all honest Americans."

In the year of 1889 when he became a civil service commissioner, there were only 21,000 federal employees under the commissioners' jurisdiction, but Roosevelt tackled his work as if it were the most important in the whole federal government. He took a forthright stand on the issues, attacking anyone who was in his way, speaking and writing articles publicizing the need for civil service reform.

248

HIRTY-TWO-YEAR-OLD

heodore Roosevelt at the
he served as civil serv-
commissioner. With him
his eldest son, Theodore,
who was born in 1887.

E-YEAR-OLD

photograph of this baby
taken by J. F. Klinger in
unau, Austria, roughly
ut the same period as the
one of Roosevelt with
son. It is the first por-
t of a child—born on
il 20, 1889—who caused a
t deal of upheaval in the
century—Adolf Hitler.

THE ENEMIES OF CIVIL SERVICE REFORM

"When Stanley carried the first steamboat up the Congo," reads the caption under this Louis Dalrymple cartoon in *Puck*, "the natives ran along the banks, yelling with rage, and striving to check his progress by throwing stones and other missiles. Mr. Stanley got there, just the same."

In the cartoon Roosevelt plays the role of explorer Stanley, while the natives are public men who are trying to check his progress. In the background, from left to right: Senator William Mahone, who controlled the patronage of Virginia; "Corporal" James Tanner, the Commissioner of Pensions, in whose opinion "nothing was too good for an old soldier"; Vice-President Levi P. Morton; Secretary of War Redfield Proctor; Colonel Dudley, the treasurer of the Republican National Committee; Senator Matthew Quay of Pennsylvania, the boss of his state's political machine.

In the foreground: Secretary of State James G. Blaine; President Benjamin Harrison; Charles Anderson Dana, the eccentric editor of the New York *Sun,* who said that civil service was "a German bureaucratic system"; Postmaster General John Wanamaker and First Assistant Postmaster General James S. Clarkson, under whom in a single year thirty thousand Democratic fourth-class postmasters were replaced by Republicans; and, finally, Thomas Platt, head of New York's political machine.

Roosevelt as a civil service commissioner was both lauded and criticized. Some of his admirers said that after he took the post, "order began to appear out of chaos" and that members of Congress "went staggering from a contact with the Commission," while his critics held that he talked big but accomplished little. It is true that Roosevelt kept himself steadily in the limelight, but his speeches, his quarrels and his articles were to publicize the weaknesses of the civil service laws. Roosevelt and his fellow commissioners took effective action on many occasions to improve bad situations, and the office was administered impartially, honestly, and with unselfish devotion. Roosevelt's work focused the interest of the people on a much needed civil service reform; if he did nothing more, this was an important contribution.

THE BILLION-DOLLAR COUNTRY

The expenditures of the Fifty-first Congress—from December 2, 1889, to March 3, 1891—ran to more than a billion dollars. When Democrats called it the "Billion-dollar Congress," House Speaker Thomas B. Reed replied brusquely, "Yes, but this is a billion-dollar country."

President Harrison allowed his administration to become subservient to special interests. Under him pension and tariff legislation cut deep into the surplus. The Disability Pension Act of 1890 authorized pensions to any veterans deemed unable to perform manual labor, whether or not the disability was the result of military service. The Grand Army of the Republic, which pressured the law into existence, acknowledged that it was "the most liberal pension measure ever passed by any legislative body in the world."

As to the tariff, Congressman William McKinley of Ohio, the chairman of the House Ways and Means Committee, introduced a bill that demonstrated conclusively the businessmen's domination over government. Duties were increased on almost all articles of household consumption. "Cheap merchandise," said McKinley, "means cheap men, and cheap men means cheap country; and that is not the kind of government our fathers followed, and it is not the kind their sons mean to follow." And while the American people were forced to pay high prices for

PUBLIC OPINION POINTS A FINGER AT TH

Senator John James Ingalls was the President pro tempore of the Senate; Congressman William McKinley, who introduced a highly protective tariff act;

consumer goods, the earning power of the workers and farmers remained the same as before.

As the mid-term election of 1890 approached, the Democrats had three telling campaign issues: 1. They charged the Republicans with extravagant spending (annual appropriations for pensions had increased

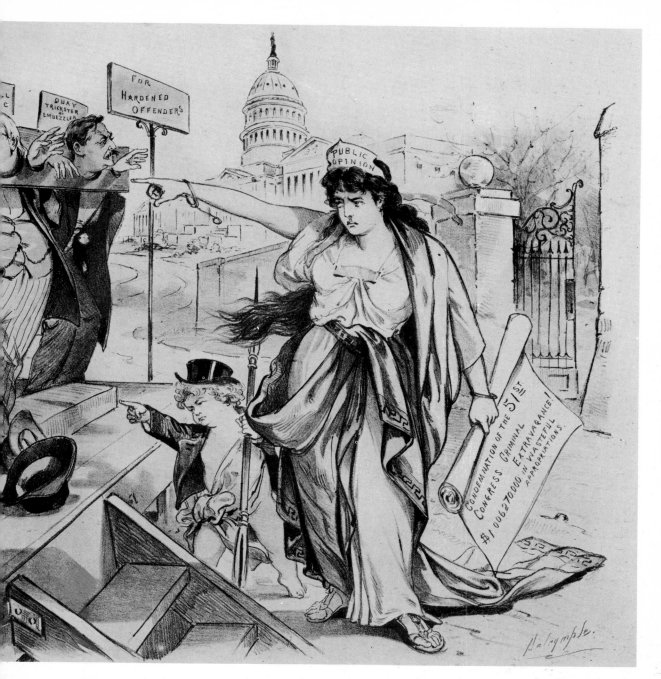

LEADING POLITICIANS OF THE REPUBLICAN-DOMINATED FIFTY-FIRST CONGRESS

Senator George F. Hoar, whose "Force Bill" was to provide supervision of federal elections in the South; Senator Matthew Quay, from Pennsylvania, the ruthless machine politician, and Thomas B. Reed, Speaker of the House of Representatives, who ruled that body with an iron hand and was referred to as the "Czar."

during Harrison's term by leaps and bounds); 2. fomenting sectionalism (the Republican "Force Bill," which passed the House but failed in the Senate, provided for supervision of elections in the South so that the Negroes should not be deprived of the vote); 3. surrender to the trusts (citing the high provisions of the McKinley Tariff Act).

The country agreed with such arguments. The Republicans suffered a disastrous defeat; they lost control in the House and barely kept their majority in the Senate. The Fifty-second Congress was composed of 235 Democrats but only 88 Republicans.

ECONOMIC DISCONTENT. In the beginning of July 1892 resentment between labor and management culminated in pitched battles between striking steelworkers at Carnegie's Homestead Plant in Pennsylvania and those who were engaged by the company to subdue the strike. Henry Clay Frick, the company's general manager, in an effort to wipe out the Amalgamated Association of Iron and Steel Workers, ordered a wage cut. When the workers called a strike, Frick hired three hundred Pinkerton men to break it. As these men descended the Mo-

nongahela in barges, they were spotted by the strikers, who opened fire on them. For the next days the plant and its environs were scenes of violence, with many dead and wounded. With the calling of eight thousand National Guardsmen, the strike was broken. Public indignation against Carnegie and Frick (who had been wounded by an anarchist bullet) ran high and reacted against the Republican party; in the forthcoming presidential election the Republican Benjamin Harrison lost out to Grover Cleveland, once more the candidate of the Democratic party.

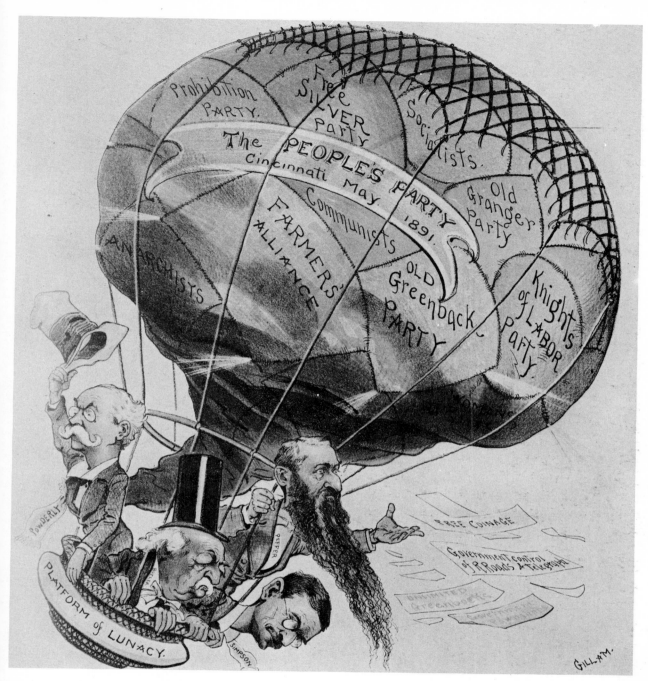

POLITICAL DISCONTENT. The beginning of the nineties saw the birth of a colorful third party—the Populists. Born of bitter poverty on the Midwestern and Southern farms, the People's party (the official name of the Populists) represented a protest against a government which stood aside while the agricultural depression hit the farms and which did little to curb the abuses of the trusts.

The Populists held out a promise to all those who cried for reforms; farmer and labor organizations were brought under the same banner to fight united for their rights. In the ranks of the new party were members of the Farmers' Alliance, of the Knights of Labor; Greenbackers, single-tax men, socialists, suffragettes, free silverites. Gillam called his hostile cartoon "The Party of Patches." Its leaders, driven by an almost religious fanaticism, ranged from Mary Ellen Lease, who urged farmers to "raise less corn and more hell," and Ignatius Donnelly, who agitated for the rights of man, to William Jennings Bryan, the silver-tongued orator from Nebraska, who was to lead the movement to its greatest heights a few years later.

CLEVELAND IS PRESIDENT AGAIN. He was re-elected with 277 electoral votes against Benjamin Harrison's 145. Such was the dissatisfaction with the policies of Harrison that the Populists' candidate, James B. Weaver, received over a million votes. In this superb photograph of the March 4, 1893, inaugural, the outgoing President Harrison (on the right of Cleveland) protects his ears from the chilly winds.

CHAPTER XIX

THE BATTLE OF THE STANDARDS

Cleveland's second administration started off poorly. Weeks before his inauguration, a wildly fluctuating securities market hoisted economic storm signals. Late in February the Philadelphia and Reading Railroad had to declare bankruptcy. With the collapse of the National Cordage Company, a great trust so irresponsibly managed that it announced a large cash dividend in the very month in which it went under, the stage for the panic was set. Within six months the Erie, Northern Pacific, Union Pacific, and Santa Fe railroads were in the hands of receivers, and a wave of bank failures had swept the South and West. By the end of the year there had been some 15,000 bankruptcies involving liabilities of more than one third of a billion dollars, while in the cities and mill towns four million people were out of work. It was a financial depression of great magnitude.

Why should a country so prosperous slide into the doldrums of economic distress? One underlying cause of the trouble was the money question, an issue which had been simmering for a quarter of a century and was now ready to boil over. There were two contrasting views: on the one side were those who demanded the free coinage of silver so that the money in circulation could be increased, on the other side those who desired to hold on to the single gold standard. In reality "the battle of standards," as this struggle became known, was the contest for power between the agrarian South and West against the industrial East—the final chapter in the historic tug-of-war between the Jeffersonian and Hamiltonian concepts of government.

Roosevelt—as his letters of this period show—seemed unconcerned with the economic problems of the day. He directed his attention to the work of the Civil Service Commission, improving the laws and investigating the inequities and irregularities. His life in Washington ran on an even keel. He went to parties, saw his friends, found enjoyment in his growing family. And he kept on working on his historical study of *The Winning of the West*.

And while he immersed himself in his work, the debate in the country on the issue of inflation or deflation—hard money or soft money—proceeded. That the argument turned into gold versus silver was simply because the amount of currency was limited by the amount of gold available to redeem the paper money. The United States was under the gold standard, and while between 1860 and 1890 world gold production had remained static, at the same time America's population had doubled. This caused great hardship to all those who worked for their living, to all those who were compelled to borrow money, to all those who had to take mortgages. As farm prices and prices of goods were down, the debtor class had to work harder and longer to repay their obligations. Thus, a Western farmer who took a $5000 mortgage on his farm after the Civil War—the equivalent of 2500 bushels of wheat—had to produce 5000 bushels of wheat to repay the loan twenty years later.

From the West came the cry that there was not enough money in circulation, therefore it was suggested that the government should allow the free, unlimited coinage of silver, as this would increase the supply of money without a large-scale inflation—a certain result if the government were to print greenbacks unsecured by bullion of any kind. In their demand for free silver the farmers were supported by the silver mine operators, who were producing a steadily increasing supply of the metal and were eager to sell it to the government.

President Cleveland held that the Sherman Silver Purchase Act of 1890 was one of the main causes for the depression, as that law had shaken the confidence of the business interests, thus he pleaded for its repeal. A special session of Congress granted the request, but it turned out to be a Pyrrhic victory for the President. It split the ranks of the Democrats, the silver wing of the party opposing Cleveland's policies and denouncing him as a tool of Wall Street.

However, the repeal of the Sherman Silver Purchase Act had no effect on the depression. The drain on the nation's gold reserves became alarming; the federal surplus which had caused concern four years earlier had disappeared like the snows of yesterday. Because of the high tariff rates, the income of the government dwindled; where for years there had been a surplus, there was now a deficit. And when Cleveland tried to remedy the tariff schedules, protectionist Democrats in the Senate joined the Republicans in so many crippling amendments that the President termed the resultant Wilson-Gorman Act a product of "party perfidy." He sought to bolster federal revenues with a two per cent tax on incomes above $4000, but the tax was declared unconstitutional by a 5–4 decision of the Supreme Court. The Republicans who were against the income tax measure were well pleased with themselves. Senator John Sherman of Ohio declared that the High Court had saved the nation from "socialism, communism, devilism."

"The year of 1894, the year of the Wilson tariff and the income tax decision, was the darkest that Americans had known for thirty years," say Morison and Commager in their *The Growth of the American Republic*. Unemployment reached a new high, bread lines lengthened, farm prices continued a downward spiral. "Everything seemed to conspire to convince the people that democracy was a failure. Prices and wages hit rock bottom, and there seemed to be no market for anything. Half a million laborers struck against conditions which they thought intolerable, and most of the strikes were dismal failures. Ragged and hungry bands of unemployed swarmed over the countryside, the fires from their hobo camps flickering a message of warning and despair to affrighted townsfolk. Coxey's army, consisting of broken veterans of the armies of industry, inspired by the pathetic delusion that a 'petition on boots' might bring relief, marched on Washington where they were arrested for trespassing on the Capitol grounds—a charge which somehow was never preferred against the silk-hatted lobbyists who presented their petitions for higher tariffs. The corn crop was a failure; wheat fell below fifty cents a bushel, cotton to six cents a pound, and bitterness swept over the West like a prairie fire. Never did the government seem more unfriendly, or democratic processes more futile. The Pullman workers struck for a living wage, and every agency of the government was enlisted to smash the strike. Representatives of the people in the lower House tried to reduce tariff duties, and representatives of privilege in the Senate made a farce of the effort. Congress passed an anti-trust law and it was enforced not against the trusts but against labor unions; when the great Sugar Trust was finally called into court, the Attorney-General of the United States sabotaged the prosecution. Congress enacted an income tax and it was voided in the highest court. And the President sold bonds to Wall Street, while silver, the poor man's friend, was disinherited and disgraced!"

The distressing economic conditions brought a devastating Republican sweep in the midterm election, a hopeful augury for winning the Presidency in 1896.

Roosevelt seemed strangely aloof from all the turmoil. He seemed—apart from his civil service job—more interested in personal than in public matters. The behavior of his brother Elliott, who could not resist the bottle, disturbed him. "He can't be helped," he wrote to his sister Anna, "and he must simply be let go his own gait. He is now laid up from a serious fall; while drunk he drove into a lamp post and went out on his head. Poor fellow! if only he could have died instead of Anna." (Anna was Elliott's wife—Eleanor Roosevelt's mother.) And he told Corinne, his younger sister: "It is very sad about Elliott, but there is literally nothing to do. After a certain number of years and trials no one can help another." His attitude seemed callous and showed little understanding of his brother's problems. But when Elliott died in August, he wrote to Corinne: "There is one great comfort I already feel; I only need to have pleasant thoughts of Elliott now. He is just the gallant, generous, manly boy and young man whom everyone loved. I can think of him when you and I and he used to go round 'exploring' the hotels, the time we were first in Europe; do you remember how we used to do it? and then in the days of the dancing class, when he was distinctly the polished man-of-the-world from outside. . . . Or when we were off on his little sailing boat for a two or three days trip on the Sound; or when he first hunted; and when he visited me at Harvard."

In his post on the Civil Service Commission Roosevelt ardently fought for his beliefs. "I don't know that anyone will be fool enough to do as much fighting as I have done," he wrote to a friend. He felt that the entire Cabinet was down on him, though "I have purposely refrained under the present administration from making fights which I should have made under the last, because there continually come up cases which I would be willing to take up with ferocity were the offenders of my own party, but where I fear I can do no good as they are not."

Still, his heart was no longer in his job. He was looking for new horizons.

JOHN BULL AFTER US AGAIN.

UNCLE SAM.—I swan! That feller can't seem to let me alone——I'll hev to fire him out ag'in!

AMERICA—A DEBTOR NATION

Americans are sensitive about foreign influence and foreign criticism. During the nineteenth century, and until the end of World War I, the United States was a debtor nation, with its bonds sold in Europe and held by English, German, and other foreign financiers. Many Americans held that the bankers of England bled white free enterprise in the United States. The above cartoon in *Puck* gives vent to these feelings.

If a foreigner was critical, it was resented. When Theodore Roosevelt entertained the English writer Rudyard Kipling at dinner and Kipling used critical language, Roosevelt would have none of it. "Kipling is an underbred little fellow," he wrote to his sister Anna after the incident, "with a tendency to criticize America to which I put a stop by giving him a very rough handling . . ." The nation was young and needed approval, not criticism.

260

TROUBLES WITH GOLD

At the beginning of President Cleveland's administration in 1893, the gold reserve had dwindled below the dangerous $100,000,000 mark; by the end of the year it was down to $75,000,000. To remedy the situation the Treasury issued $50,000,000 in bonds payable in gold.

When the date of payment for the first installment arrived, the bond buyers withdrew gold from the banks, and the banks—depleted of their gold resources—sent their notes to the Treasury, asking for replenishment of their gold supplies. Thus in an "endless chain" financial institutions took gold from the Treasury, gave it to their customers, who then returned it to the Treasury. This vicious circle was not halted until late in 1896 when the election of the Republican William McKinley to the presidency restored the confidence of the financial community.

In this cartoon President Cleveland heats the gold reserve thermometer with bonds, hoping it will rise.

TROUBLES WITH SILVER

The Sherman Silver Purchase Act of 1890 became law when eastern Republicans traded their votes for western support of the McKinley tariff bill. The deal consummated, the Treasury was compelled to buy 4,500,000 ounces of silver each month to make into coin. But when the depression of 1893 hit the country, President Cleveland pointed to the Sherman Silver Purchase Act as one of the main causes for the nation's economic distress. Calling Congress into a special session, he demanded the Act's unconditional repeal. By adroit use of his patronage powers, he succeeded. The New York *Times* commended him for his "iron firmness" and for saving the country from fiscal ruin.

This cartoon, by Louis Dalrymple, appeared in *Puck* in September 1893.

COXEY'S ARMY MARCHES TO WASHINGTON

The depression of 1893 brought unemployment, lockouts, wage cuts. Jobless men formed into "armies" with "generals" as their leaders.

In April 1894, "General" Jacob S. Coxey, a wealthy quarry owner from Massillon, Ohio (sitting in the carriage), led such a band of unemployed to

Washington, where he demanded that Congress issue five hundred million dollars of legal tender notes for the building of roads as a remedy for unemployment (used four decades later by Franklin D. Roosevelt). Coxey's march ended in ridicule when police arrested him for trespassing on the Capitol lawn.

THE PULLMAN STRIKE IN CHICAGO

came about when the Pullman Palace Car Company, using the depression as an excuse, reduced workers' wages to a minimum. The American Railway Union, headed by energetic Eugene V. Debs, demanded arbitration of the wage issue; when the request was refused, the union forbade its members to handle Pullman cars. By the end of June 1894 from Ohio to California trains lay idle; strikers and federal troops fought all along the railroad lines.

FEDERAL TROOPS were protecting the mails in Chicago. Illinois Governor Peter Altgeld protested their presence, but President Cleveland exclaimed: "If it takes the entire army and navy of the United States to deliver a postal card in Chicago, that card will be delivered."

Though their union urged the strikers to refrain from violence, trains were ditched, buildings burned, property destroyed. A federal court issued a blanket injunction against the labor leaders for obstructing the mails. With the arrest of Debs, and other union leaders, the strike was broken.

ROOSEVELT PLAYING B.
AT SAGAMORE HILL IN
A snapshot taken by Mrs. Roosevel

THE VENEZUELA AFFAIR

ROOSEVELT THREATENS ENGLAND
In a statement on the Venezuela dispute, he said that if England dared to attack the United States, America would march into Canada and occupy it.

J.S.Pughe.

THE VENEZUELAN BOUNDARY DISPUTE
When, in 1886, Great Britain declared that some 23,000 square miles of territory containing valuable mineral deposits belonged to the British colony of Guiana and not the South American republic of Venezuela, war between England and Venezuela seemed to be in the making. As the Monroe Doctrine of 1823 had guaranteed the integrity of the Latin-American republics, the United States was not willing to allow Great Britain to use armed intervention in the Western Hemisphere.

At the request of Venezuela, America offered to arbitrate, but Lord Salisbury, the head of the English government, rejected the offer.

In July 1895 Secretary of State Richard Olney sent a sharply worded note to the English government, telling Salisbury that the United States "is practically a sovereign on this continent, and its fiat is law upon the subjects to which it confines its interposition," so it would "resist any sequestration of Venezuelan soil by Great Britain." As Lord Salisbury was unbending, President Cleveland sent another message to Congress suggesting an American commission which should hand down a decision on the boundary issue. Congress followed Cleveland's proposal and appropriated $100,000 for the expenses of such commission. Lord Salisbury, realizing that the United States would not soften its attitude, changed the tune and declared his willingness to submit the boundary claim to arbitration. On October 3, 1899, a tribunal which assembled at Paris settled the dispute, on the whole favorably for Great Britain.

THE NEW YORK POLICE BOARD

The board had four members—two of them, Avery D. Andrews and Andrew D. Parker, were Democrats; the other two, Theodore Roosevelt and Frederick D. Grant, the son of President Grant, were Republicans.

Roosevelt took office the first week in May 1895; a few days later he wrote to his sister: "I have never worked harder than in these last six days; and it is very worrying and harassing, for I have to deal with three colleagues, solve terribly difficult problems, and do my work under hampering laws. If the Legislature will only give us power to remove our subordinates without appeal to the courts I *know* we can make a thorough and radical reform; without such power we can improve matters a great deal, but we cannot do what we ought to do. But I am absorbed in the work and am very glad I came on. It is well worth doing. So far I get on well with my three colleagues. I have rarely left the office until six in the evenings."

Soon it seemed to the public that the police board had only one member—picturesque, flamboyant, energetic, never-resting, thirty-six-year-old Theodore Roosevelt, battling with police corruption.

CHAPTER XX

POLICE COMMISSIONER

In April 1895, after William L. Strong, a reform-minded businessman, became mayor of New York, Roosevelt was named president of the city's four-man Police Board, or Police Commissioner, as the post was popularly called.

The job was no easy one. "It is absolutely impossible to do what is expected of me," he confided to his sister. "The conditions will not allow it. I must make up my mind to much criticism and disappointment." There was no denying that corruption under Tammany's auspices was rampant and that much of it centered in the Police Department. Appointments to the force, and promotions as well, were paid for in cash. Gambling houses and bordellos had virtual immunity as long as the police captain of the district received his weekly bribe.

Roosevelt's tour of duty started off hopefully. Within weeks Tom Byrnes, the superintendent of police who admitted to a personal fortune of $300,000, was ousted despite thirty-two years of service. "We have a real police commissioner," wrote Arthur Brisbane in the New York *World*. "He makes our policemen feel as the little froggies did when the stork came to rule over them."

As always, one of Roosevelt's most potent weapons for reform was publicity, and he used it adroitly. Not content to sit at Police Headquarters on Mulberry Street, he spent much of his time making the rounds of the outlying beats to check up on his force in action. Most celebrated of all were his nighttime excursions, which were often made in evening clothes after attending a dinner party and in which he was usually accompanied by Jacob Riis, the reform-bent newspaper reporter whose book *How the Other Half Lives* had first awakened Roosevelt to the New York tenement problem some years earlier. Often they would prowl the streets till dawn, alert for policemen who had strayed off their beats, had fallen asleep on duty, or had committed some even greater offense; and often they watched a policeman's truculence suddenly transformed into stammering apologies when the victim realized that he was talking to the police commissioner rather than to an over-inquisitive private citizen. On one occasion, the newspapers related, Roosevelt came upon a thirsty policeman quaffing a glass of beer at the door of a saloon and immediately gave chase, catching the miscreant by the scruff of the neck half a block away and ordering him to stand trial the following day. The work, he told his sister happily, was "eminently practical; it has not a touch of the academic."

The analogy between these nocturnal exploits and the legends of the prowling caliph of Baghdad quickly earned the commissioner the nickname of Haroun al Roosevelt among reporters. It also earned him high praise from their newspapers, and, indeed, from newspapers throughout the nation. Although his wide-brimmed hat and prominent molars were commonly pictured by cartoonists as the most dreaded of sights for any pavement-pounding policeman in New York, he commanded the respect of many if not most of the abler and more honest men on the force. "Hardihood and courage," he later recalled, "were the qualities upon which we insisted and which we rewarded." Patrolmen who distinguished themselves were repaid with promotion, and others whose long and honorable service had gone unrewarded for want of political connections found their path to advancement no longer blocked. Roosevelt was bringing the first glimmerings of a merit system to the New York police.

Despite the initial and substantial victories, however, the new commissioner's popularity began to fade within a year of his arrival at Mulberry Street. The cause of the eclipse, ironically, was his determination to enforce a law about which he was not enthusiastic and which he felt must be enforced only because laxity was breeding corruption.

The law in question required that all saloons remain closed on Sunday—and in practice it was honored only in the breach, for any saloon that wished to pay the police for the privilege was allowed to receive Sabbath-day customers at the back door without interference. Roosevelt was no prohibitionist, but he was determined to stamp out this source of police corruption. "I shall procure the enforcement of the Sunday closing law not by spurts but by steadily increasing rigor," he announced. "If it proves impossible to enforce it, it will be only after the experiment of breaking many a captain of the police in the endeavor to secure the enforcement has first been tried."

Nothing could have pleased his enemies more. The Sunday drought reduced drunkenness, but it also deprived thousands of New Yorkers of their favorite Sunday relaxation. Worse, it hit hardest at the poor man, because persons of means were still free to drink on a Sunday at their clubs or have wine with their dinners at plush hotels. In vain Roosevelt protested that he was "enforcing honestly a law that hitherto has been enforced dishonestly." The politicians and the press contended that the Sunday saloon restriction was a "blue law" that was never intended to be enforced. Otherwise virtuous citizens made it plain that they preferred their Sunday drink to an honest police force. "Every discredited politician, every sensational newspaper, every timid fool who could be scared by clamor was against us," Roosevelt recalled.

The protests took different forms. Many New Yorkers crossed the Hudson to do their Sunday drinking unmolested in New Jersey. There were indignant protest meetings at which the appointment of a new commissioner was demanded. In the German section the citizenry staged a protest parade but made the mistake of inviting Roosevelt, who attended and all but stole the show with his good-humored performance. When a Tammany man protested that "the law should be enforced, but with intelligence and discrimination," Roosevelt replied: "That is a good deal like believing in truthful mendacity." By the end of 1895, Roosevelt was admitting to Henry Cabot Lodge that "I have not one New York City newspaper or one New York City politician on my side" and that "Whitelaw Reid was given orders that in the *Tribune* I am not to be mentioned save to attack me, unless it is unavoidable." But he added: "I shall continue absolutely unmoved on my present course and shall accept philosophically whatever violent end may be put to my political career."

In the end the Sunday drinking issue was settled by a compliant city magistrate who ruled that drinking was permissible with meals and that any food whatever comprised a meal, which, as Roosevelt complained, meant that eating one pretzel could entitle a man to seventeen beers.

By this time, however, the commissioner's enemies were attacking on other fronts. At the behest of Tammany, members of the force had started trying to make Roosevelt look ridiculous by invoking long-forgotten blue laws at the expense of Sunday purveyors of flowers, shoe shines, and ice cream sodas. Rumors were started that ice could no longer be sold on the Sabbath, and the New York *World* fabricated a harrowing story about a woman whose child had died because ice was unobtainable. When, early in 1896, Roosevelt sent a letter to President Cleveland commending his strong stand on Venezuela, the hard-pressed Chief Executive thanked him by return mail and closed with a masterpiece of understatement. "It seems to me," said Cleveland, "that you and I have both been a little misunderstood lately."

The misunderstandings on Mulberry Street were scarcely less frequent as the year progressed. Enforcement of the Sunday laws brought the already tense relationships within the four-member police board close to the breaking point. The constant bickering was "doing more to depress than elevate the tone of the force," said Dr. Parkhurst. Nor was the situation helped when the board had to face a host of new problems caused by the so-called Raines Law, a state act which sought to tighten regulations governing Sunday drinking in hotels by defining a hotel as a building with a dining room and at least ten bedrooms. Within the year some 2000 new "hotels" sprang up in the city—many of them saloons which merely partitioned off ten bedrooms upstairs to meet the requirement for Sunday drinking and then, adding insult to injury, used the bedrooms for prostitution.

By the time this crisis arose, however, Roosevelt's attention was being increasingly focused on the national political scene. In July of 1896 he offered his services to the political wirepuller Mark Hanna, whom he found "well-meaning" but "shrewd and hard-headed," and in the fall he was sent out as a principal stump speaker to some of the wavering sections of the Middle West. Although Roosevelt in later years was to embrace many of the "radical" ideas championed by the Democrats in 1896, he felt a deep and instinctive contempt for William Jennings Bryan and his Populist followers at the time. He campaigned with enthusiasm for William McKinley, the Republican candidate, and likened Bryan to Jefferson Davis and to the leaders of the reign of terror in the French Revolution.

The Republican campaign against Bryan and free silver brought fruit. William McKinley was elected by an overwhelming majority. The victory rewarded Roosevelt with the post of Assistant Secretary of the Navy.

HOW THE RICH LIVED. A party at the home of Mrs. Frank Leslie, the four-times-married "Empress of Journalism." Her Thursday-evening receptions were a New York social institution. Mrs. Leslie loved men because "they are the spice of the earth," and she loved diamonds because "there is imprisoned in the heart of the diamond—a soul." Her extra-marital affairs and her extravagant jewelry—one necklace contained three thousand diamonds—were the talk of the town. When she died, she left $1,000,000 to further women's suffrage.

THE JAPANESE ROOM in William Henry Van-derbilt's mansion on Fifth Avenue. The building of the palace cost an estimated $1,750,000, the interior decorations—executed by 600 artisans—another $800,000. A contemporary journalist, in awe of all this splendor, wrote in *Collier's:* "The Vanderbilts have come nobly forward and shown the world how millionaires ought to live." They certainly did. And the world—admitted to the art gallery of the mansion on Thursdays—gasped at the collected treasures, admired the seven paintings by the French artist Meissonier for which Vanderbilt had paid $188,000.

HOW THE POOR LIVED. A dark alley between tenement houses in New York, the playground of the children of the poor, a breeding ground for typhoid fever and crime. The congestion in the teeming tenements of the lower East Side was estimated at 330,000 persons per square mile. Here Russian and Polish Jews, who came to America to escape the pogroms of their native lands, crammed the buildings from garret to cellar. An investigating commission found that in some rooms there lived as many as fourteen human beings.

SWEATSHOP IN THE TENEMENTS. Here people ate, slept and worked; here sick adults, healthy adults, sick children, healthy children lived together in close quarters. A French visitor wrote about it saying that one could "hardly endure the air of these shops, where the odor of ill-cared bodies mingled with the odor of spoiled food." For making a dozen pairs of children's trousers, a man was paid $.75; if he worked from dawn to nightfall he could make eighteen trousers (and this only if he was not losing more than one half hour for his meals and rest). Thus, on a good day, he earned all of $1.12.

NEW YORK IN THE NINETIES

A metropolis, one of the largest cities in the world, and yet somewhat provincial. A city of wealth and a city of the poor. Part of it as Irish as Dublin, part of it as Jewish as Lemberg, part of it as Hungarian as Budapest, and some of it as Italian as Naples.

Women wore their skirts to the ground, sweeping the pavement as they walked. Young men with incomes of $5,000 or more lived in luxurious bachelor apartments—sitting room, bedroom, bathroom—paying $1,000 to $1,200 rent for a year, which included heat, light, and maid service.

Elegant homes were furnished in oriental fashion. Society followed the fad of Turkish divans, brass coffee trays, Moorish bric-a-brac, heavy hangings, and soft rugs. Some of the apartments had an atmosphere much more like the harems of Eastern potentates than homes of New Yorkers.

A GREAT DEPARTMENT STORE IN ITS YOUTH

NSOM CABS AT MADISON SQUARE

VERS' LANE
CENTRAL PARK

ROOSEVELT UPHOLDS THE LAW, a cartoon by Thomas Nast in *Harper's Weekly*. "Last Sunday I spent in town with Jacob Riis," reported he to Cabot Lodge, "driving and walking about for nine hours to see for ourselves exactly how the Excise Law was enforced. I had no idea how complete our success was; not four percent of the saloons were open and these were doing business with the greatest secrecy and to a most limited extent. We have really won a great triumph so far . . . The *World* and *Journal* nearly have epilepsy over me; and they are united in portraying me as spending my Sundays heavily in the Union League Club."

Roosevelt was not a prohibitionist, but he saw that the violation of the Excise Law led to extortion by the police. And as he proceeded with the enforcement, his zeal and enthusiasm grew.

★

FIFTH AVENUE and corner Fifty-ninth Street in 1895, at the time Roosevelt was police commissioner of the city. The streets were still quiet and New Yorkers were not yet in a hurry. They strolled leisurely along the Avenue, dressed in their best clothes. One could still cross the Square without fear of coming to harm from the traffic.

THE VIRTUOUS POLICE COMMISSIONER,
as caricatured in the New York *Herald* by C. G. Bush.
Father Knickerbocker—peeved because the law
which forbade saloonkeepers to sell liquor on Sunday
was for the first time being strictly enforced—reminds
Roosevelt of Shakespeare's lines: "Art any more than
a steward? Dost thou think, because thou art virtuous, there shall be no more cakes and ale?"

THE DEFENDER OF THE LAW

After Roosevelt began his drive against the saloons
which disregarded the law forbidding the sales of
liquor on Sunday, he encountered the animosity of
all those who could not obtain their Sunday drink.
The Germans and the Irish were particularly vociferous in their opposition. They resented the curtail-
ments of their small pleasures. They failed to see
how the strict enforcement of the Excise Law would
help police reforms; they regarded it as an intrusion
in their personal liberties, and turned against Police
Commissioner Roosevelt, whom they held responsible
for the outrage.

He became a target for cartoonists, a butt for
criticizing newspaper writers.

MULBERRY STREET, where police headquarters—a gloomy building with underground dungeons—was located. From here Police Commissioner Theodore Roosevelt set out to watch for policemen who were taking it easy on duty, who were drinking in saloons, or who received bribes from street-walkers. Because of his nightly prowlings, reporters called him "Roosevelt-al-Raschid." He had great fun roaming around the city and had fascinating adventures, even though each trip meant "going forty hours at a stretch without any sleep."

"THE CHAMBER OF HORRORS." A cartoon by Bush in the New York *Herald*, September 1895, showing the prominent figures of the Police Department. The first figure on the left is Police Commissioner Roosevelt, holding his three colleagues—Andrews, Grant, Parker—under his arm while his foot is pressing down on the bottle. The third figure from the left is "Easy Boss" Platt with Edward Lauterbach, his willing mouthpiece in city affairs.

THE PRESIDENTIAL CAMPAIGN OF 1896

William McKinley, the Republican candidate, stayed at home in Canton, Ohio, where he addressed his supporters from the front porch of his house with pleasant, pious platitudes. Supported by the business and financial interests, who were steadfastly for a solid gold-backed currency, he won the election with 271 electoral votes against his opponent's 176.

THE DEMOCRATIC CANDIDATE, William Jennings Bryan, pleaded for silver coinage at a ratio of sixteen ounces of silver to one ounce of gold. Supported by western farmers and mining interests, he argued for a reduction in value of the dollar so mortgages could be repaid in cheaper money.

CHAPTER XXI

ASSISTANT SECRETARY OF THE NAVY

"There is one thing I *would* like to have, but there is no chance of my getting it. McKinley will never give it to me. I should like to be Assistant Secretary of the Navy." Thus spoke Roosevelt to his friend Maria Longworth Storer. Yet, President McKinley had hardly begun his term when he appointed Roosevelt to the post.

Before he received the appointment Roosevelt promised to be a faithful subordinate to the Secretary of the Navy, the courteous and gentlemanly John D. Long; but with the nation's steadily worsening relations with Spain, he found that to keep his pledge was more than difficult.

His sympathy, like the sympathy of most Americans at the time, was with the downtrodden Cubans, who were in rebellion against their corrupt and despotic Spanish overlords. Though the American attitude toward the Cuban people was based mainly on humanitarian motives, other, and less idealistic, considerations helped push the United States down the road to war. One was economic; our trade with Cuba, amounting to more than $100,000,000 in 1893, was badly disrupted by the insurrection. Another was geo-political; we felt an increasing need to control the Caribbean area, both to provide bases for a growing Navy and to protect the approaches to what already appeared to be the ordained site of an Isthmian canal linking the Atlantic and Pacific oceans. And still another one was the relentless propaganda campaign of the popular press. Led by Pulitzer's New York *World* and Hearst's New York *Journal,* a steady diet of Cuban atrocity stories was served to the unsuspecting public, recounting the inhumanities of General Weyler, the Spanish commander who herded thousands of non-combatant Cubans into concentration camps. The campaign for "Cuba Libre!" and the reports on the cruelty of "Butcher Weyler" increased circulation, thus more and more lurid tales were printed, selling more newspapers and fomenting the war spirit against Spain.

Like President Cleveland before him, McKinley held that the United States should remain neutral. This was not the opinion of the Assistant Secretary of the Navy. Theodore Roosevelt, convinced that the United States must fight Spain, divided his energies between trying to swing others in the administration to his belief and doing his utmost to bring the Navy up to maximum strength. Secretary Long said: "His ardor sometimes went faster than the President or the department approved."

It was less than three months after he took up his duties in the Navy Department that Roosevelt delivered at the Naval War College an address that summed up his views on military preparedness—views similar to those he had first suggested in his *History of the Naval War of 1812*. "Cowardice in a race, as in an individual," he said, "is the unpardonable sin, and a wilful failure to prepare for danger may in its effects be as bad as cowardice. The timid man who cannot fight and the selfish, shortsighted or foolish man who will not take the steps that will enable him to fight, stand on almost the same plane." He went on to state that diplomacy is "utterly useless" without force behind it, and that "the diplomat is the servant, not the master, of the soldier." And he concluded that "no national life is worth having if the nation is not willing, when the need shall arise, to stake everything on the supreme arbitrament of war, and to pour out its blood, its treasures, its tears like water rather than to submit to the loss of honor and renown." Roosevelt's speech was widely praised. The highly critical Washington *Post* commented: "Well done, nobly spoken! Theodore Roosevelt, you have found your proper place at last—all hail!"

Throughout the summer of 1897 he fought tirelessly for bigger naval appropriations, convinced that war would soon come. By September he was eagerly planning the strategy, suggesting to Secretary Long that in the event of hostilities the main fleet should converge on Cuba while a flying squadron should attack the coast of Spain itself. Two months later, in a letter to Navy Commander Kimball, he declared that he would welcome hostilities with Spain not only for humanitarian reasons but also because of "the benefit done to our people by giving them something to think about which isn't material gain, and especially the benefit done our military forces by trying both the Army and Navy in actual practice."

By this time the Spanish government in Madrid was thoroughly alarmed by the bellicose attitude of America. General Weyler was recalled, and proposals for Cuban home rule were offered; President McKinley, his hopes for peace revived, asked that Spain "be given a reasonable chance" to reform her policies. Early in February of 1898, however, events took another turn for the worse when an indiscreet letter written by Enrique de Lôme, the Spanish Minister in Washington, was intercepted by a Cuban revolutionary agent and turned over to the New York *Journal*. The letter described President McKinley as being "weak and a bidder for the admiration of the crowd, besides being a would-be politician who tries to leave a door open behind himself while keeping on good terms with the jingoes in his party." The yellow press raged.

Then, at 1:30 on the morning of February 16, 1898, Secretary Long was awakened to read a dispatch that smashed to bits any possibility of reconciliation with Spain. The battleship *Maine*, riding at anchor in Havana Harbor, had been blown up and sunk with the loss of 260 lives. Whether the tragedy was plotted by the Spaniards, whether it was the work of Cuban provocateurs, or whether it resulted from an internal explosion has never been determined, but the well-nigh universal assumption in America at the time was that the Spanish government was guilty. The war fever was rising, and the yellow press redoubled its efforts to fan the flames of jingoism.

The President and his Cabinet were still for peace. Roosevelt urged war.

"Being a jingo," he wrote to a friend the day after the *Maine* disaster, "I will say, to relieve my feelings, that I would give anything if President McKinley would order the fleet to Havana tomorrow." And he said that the *Maine* "was sunk by an act of dirty treachery on the part of the Spaniards," although he had no evidence that this was the fact. A few days later, hearing that a group in Congress was suggesting curtailment of the battleship construction program, he told Long that such a decision "would mean that we have reached the last pitch of national cowardice and baseness."

Such pronouncements did not soothe Long's worries about his assistant. On February 25, when he took a day's rest away from the office, he sent Roosevelt a personal note of instruction not to take "any step affecting the policy of the administration without consulting the President or me." He could have written his instruction in the sand. On that very day Roosevelt sent a cable to Commodore Dewey, the commander of the Asiatic Squadron, ordering him to "Keep full of coal" and in the event of war "to see that the Spanish Squadron does not leave the Asiatic coast," and take up "offensive operations in the Philippine Islands." Thus, when the Secretary of the Navy returned to his office the next day, he was faced with an accomplished fact. Long noted in his diary that Roosevelt "in his precipitate way has come very near causing more of an explosion than happened to the *Maine*," adding: "It shows how the best fellow in the world—and with splendid capacities—is worse than no use if he lacks a cool head and discrimination."

Through the month of March, McKinley continued to resist the demand for war. Such shilly-shallying made Roosevelt desperate about the President, who, in his opinion, had "no more backbone than a chocolate eclair." To his brother-in-law, Captain Cowles, Roosevelt wrote that "I have advised the President in the presence of his Cabinet, as well as Judge Day and Senator Hanna, as strongly as I knew how, to settle this matter instantly by armed intervention." And when Mark Hanna, at a Gridiron Club dinner, pointed out the heavy human and material costs of war, the Assistant Secretary of the Navy retorted: "We will have this war for the freedom of Cuba, Senator Hanna, in spite of the timidity of the commercial interests."

Roosevelt's fears that war would be averted proved groundless. On March 28 a board of inquiry report attributing the *Maine* disaster to a submarine mine was submitted to Congress, and the national war cry of "Remember the *Maine!*" reverberated all over the land. Meanwhile the Spanish government made frantic efforts to avoid the clash of arms. On April 9 it suspended hostilities against the Cuban rebels, and the American Minister in Spain reported to President McKinley that the issue could be settled through peaceful means.

But it was too late. McKinley did not possess the moral strength to resist the demand for armed intervention. On April 11 he sent his war message to a wildly cheering Congress. Roosevelt was elated; the war he sought had finally come. Within days he resigned his post, ordered a uniform, half a dozen pairs of spectacles, and some horses, and was off to join the Rough Riders.

ASSISTANT SECRETARY OF THE NAVY. It was not easy for Roosevelt to obtain the coveted appointment. President McKinley, who declared that "there will be no jingo nonsense under my administration," was hesitant to name him to the post. When Bellamy Storer, a mutual friend, went to see McKinley on Roosevelt's behalf, McKinley said: "I want peace, and I am told that your friend Theodore . . . is always getting into rows with everybody. I am afraid he is too pugnacious."

Senator Cabot Lodge, the faithful friend, worked tirelessly on Roosevelt's behalf in Washington, using all his influence. He wrote Roosevelt that "the only thing I can hear adverse is that there is a fear that you will want to fight somebody at once." When Lodge told his friend that John Long, the Secretary of the Navy, was not against his becoming the Assistant Secretary of the Navy, Roosevelt promised that he would work hard and "stay at Washington hot weather or any weather, whenever he wants me to stay there, and go wherever he sends me, and my aim should be solely to make his administration a success." There was one last obstacle—Thomas Collier Platt, the boss of the New York political machine. Lodge advised Roosevelt to see the old man. "He wants really more than anything else to feel that you are not shoved in over his head and that your idea in going there is not to make war on him." Platt was ready to support Roosevelt's appointment if it "was not charged to him or New York." He was happy to help him go to Washington and thus rid New York of the obnoxious and troublesome police commissioner. In the first week of April, Cabot Lodge wired his friend that the appointment would be forthcoming and Roosevelt replied with pleasure: "Sinbad has evidently landed the old man of the sea."

As you will see by the heading of this letter, I am now Assistant Secretary of the Navy. Cabot Lodge *plus Procter & a few others* got me in, though the New York machine vigorously opposed me. My chief, Secretary Long, is a perfect dear, and I think his views of foreign policy would entirely meet your approval. I see a good deal of Proctor, who is a trump, as ever. I am staying with the Lodges. Mrs. Lodge looks so well. All this winter I have seen a great deal of Bob. I am now mourning the fact that during this summer I shall hardly be at all with Mrs. Roosevelt and the children, but I greatly enjoy the work here. During my two years as police commissioner I think I may say I accomplished a great deal, but gradually

things have so shaped themselves that I couldn't do anything more.

Goodbye; and do come here and see us some time.

Always yours,

Theodore Roosevelt

Mr. Cecil Spring Rice,
British Embassy,
Berlin, Germany.

A NOTE TO AN OLD FRIEND, written April 27, 1897, about his appointment. Cecil Spring-Rice, the British diplomat who had been Roosevelt's best man at his London wedding to Edith Carow in 1886, was now attached to Great Britain's Embassy in Berlin, Germany.

THE FAMILY

More than in being a public servant, he took pride in being a devoted husband and a good father. He loved his children, and the children adored him. In letters to family and friends, Roosevelt constantly referred to them and their doings.

Besides Alice, the daughter from his first marriage, there were now four more: Theodore, Jr. (with glasses), born on September 13, 1887; Kermit, born October 10, 1889; Ethel, born August 13, 1891 (both on Mrs. Roosevelt's lap), and Archibald (held by his father), born April 9, 1894. Quentin was not born until November 19, 1897.

May 3, 1897.

Captain A. T. Mahan, U. S. N.,

160 West Eighty-sixth Street,

New York City, N. Y.

My dear Captain Mahan:

This letter must, of course, be considered as entirely confidential, because in my position I am merely carrying out the policy of the Secretary and the President. I suppose I need not tell you that as regards Hawaii I take your views absolutely, as indeed I do on foreign policy generally. If I had my way we would annex those islands tomorrow. If that is impossible I would establish a protectorate

over them. I believe we should build the Nicaraguan canal at once, and in the meantime that we should build a dozen new battle ships, half of them on the Pacific Coast, and these battle ships should have large coal capacity and a consequent increased radius of action. I am fully alive to the danger from Japan, and I know that it is idle to rely on any sentimental good will towards us. I think President Cleveland's action was a colossal crime, and we should be guilty of aiding him after the fact if we do not reverse what he did. I earnestly hope we can make the President look at things our way. Last Saturday night Lodge pressed his views upon him with all his

A REMARKABLE LETTER, published here in facsimile for the first time, reveals Roosevelt's thoughts on America's role in world affairs.

The letter went to Captain Alfred Thayer Mahan, (1840–1914) America's most influential advocate of sea power. Roosevelt, sharing Mahan's views on naval expansion, first wrote to him in 1890 when Mahan published *The Influence of Sea Power Upon History, 1660–1783*, "the clearest and most instructive general work of its kind."

When the Senate hesitated to approve the Hawaiian annexation treaty, Roosevelt communicated with Mahan (December 9, 1897): "It seems incredible that such shortsighted folly should obtain among our public men, but it does. If we refuse these islands, then I honestly hope England will take them, if only to bring back to our people the knowledge of their folly." And in another letter (December 14, 1897) Roosevelt told Mahan that he was sharing his bitter feelings, "but I take a grim consolation in thinking that we have acted quite as foolishly during the past hundred years as we possibly can act now, and yet we have lived through trial after trial and so we shall continue to do. At any rate your creed and mine is and must be, resolute to do our best to stand by our country to the utmost of our power, and to accept whatever comes."

Admiral Beardslee quite the man for the situation there, but Captain Barker, of the OREGON, is, I believe, excellent in point of decisions, willingness to accept responsibility, and thorough knowledge of the situation. But there are big problems in the Indies also. Until we definitely turn Spain out of those islands (and if I had my way that would be tomorrow), we will always be menaced by trouble there. We should acquire the Danish Islands, and by turning Spain out should serve notice that no strong European power, and especially not Germany, should be allowed to gain a foothold by supplanting some weak European power. I do not fear England; Canada, is a hostage for her good behavior; but I do fear some of the

ers. I am extremely sorry to say that
re is some slight appearance here of the
ire to stop building up the Navy until
finances are better.   Tom Reed, to my
onishment and indignation, takes this
w, and even my chief, who is one of the
t high-minded, honorable and upright
tlemen I have ever had the good fortune
serve under, is a little inclined toward

I need not say that this letter must
strictly private. I speak to you with
greatest freedom, for I sympathize with
r views, and I have precisely the same
a of patriotism, and of belief in and
e for our country. But to no one else
epting Lodge do I talk like this.

ngth. I have been getting matters in shape on
Pacific coast just as fast I have been allowed.
wn belief is that we should act instantly before
two new Japanese warships leave England. I would
the OREGON, and, if necessary, also the MONTEREY
her with a deck load of coal or accompanied by a
ing ship) to Hawaii, and would hoist our flag over
island, leaving all details for after action. I
press these views upon my chief just so far as
ill let me; more I cannot do.
As regards what you say in your letter, there is
one point to which I would take exception. I
realize the immense importance of the Pacific
. Strictly between ourselves, I do not think

As regards Hawaii I am delighted to be
able to tell you that Secretary Long shares
our views.   He believes we should take the
islands, and I have just been preparing
some memoranda for him to use at the Cabinet
meeting tomorrow. If only we had some good
man in the place of John Sherman as Secretary of State there would not be a hitch,
and even as it is I hope for favorable action.   I have been pressing upon the Secretary, and through him on the President, that
we ought to act now without delay, before
Japan gets her two new battle ships which
are now ready for delivery to her in England.
Even a fortnight may make a difference.
With Hawaii once in our hands most of the
danger of friction with Japan would disappear.

The Secretary also believes in building the Nicaraguan canal as a military measure, although I don't
know that he is as decided on this point as you and I
are; and he believes in building better ships on the Pacific
slope.

Faithfully yours,

Theodore Roosevelt

THE EXPLOSION OF THE *MAINE*. On February 15, 1898, the United States battleship *Maine,* while on a "friendly visit" in Havana harbor, blew up. Though the cause of the tragedy (taking the lives of 258 crewmen and two officers) could never be determined, American public opinion put the blame squarely on the Spanish government.

All over the country the cry went up *"Remember the* Maine," and the cry grew in intensity as Congress hesitated to declare war. But the pressure was so great that within two months the United States and Spain were engaged in conflict. Discussing the explosion, Woodrow Wilson asserted that war came "not because a vessel of the American Navy had been destroyed in a port of Spain, but because opinion leaped upon the provocation of that tragic incident from quiet inquiry to hot impatience with regard to all the ugly Cuban business. . . . It was a war of impulse, as any one might see who had noted how unprepared the country was for what it had suddenly undertaken."

ON FEBRUARY 17, 1898, the *Journal* printed over a million copies.

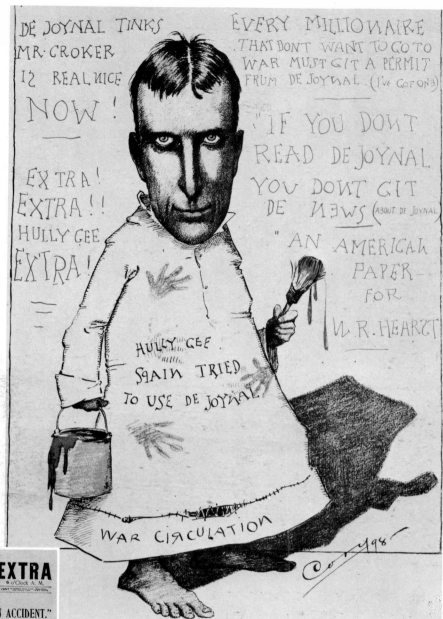

LE COUNTRY THRILLS WITH THE WAR FEVER,
YET THE PRESIDENT SAYS "IT WAS AN ACCIDENT."

Many States Report the Militia Ready and Anxious for Service---A Careful Poll of Congress
Overwhelming Majority for Immediate Intervention---An Emphatic Protest Against the
of Timidity and Delay---Spain's Particularly Humble Apology for the De Lome
Letter, with the Evident Desire of Averting Trouble---Solemn Funeral of
the Maine's Victims in Havana, Refuses to Appear Before the
Spanish Admiralty Board That Is to
Inquire Into the Loss of
Our Big Battleship.

KINLEY at midnight allowed this statement to be made of his views on the cause of the explosion on the Maine:
information now in his possession, the President believes that the Maine was blown up as the result of an accident, and he hopes the
y will develop that fact. If it is found that the disaster was not an accident, prompt and decisive steps will be taken in the premises
of the Naval Court will develop the cause, and until that is submitted nothing will be done."

E OF THE MAINE. REFUSES TO APPEAR BEFORE THE SPANISH COURT OF INQUIRY.
---Captain Sigsbee, of the Maine, has flatly refused to obey the summons of the Spanish Admiralty Board, to appear at the inquiry over

the Captain received the summons yesterday and that he immediately called upon Consul-General Lee.
is reported, advised Captain Sigsbee not to honor the summons.
sent to the Admiralty Board, couched in courteous but firm language, that the United States captain will not certify before the
-miner sends him explicit orders to do so.
is responsible for the issuance of the summons, so he was first consulted by the Board as to the advisability of such a course.
.. is was cabled the Journal yesterday, was to forestall the coming investigation by the United States Government. The Court of
retary Long is now on its way here. This action of Captain Sigsbee will probably be the means of delaying investigation by the Govern
ough to allow the United States officials to begin their own work in the matter.
nish officials to-night there is considerable talk about Captain Sigsbee's action, much unfavorable comment being heard. If the Captain
e Maine's survivors to appear and testify the Spanish inquiry will be nothing more or less than a farce.

RIT IS GROWING STRONGER AND STRONGER ALL OVER THE ENTIRE COUNTRY.
IN CAN FURNISH 13,902 IN 24 HOURS. | GOV. LEEDY WOULD LEAD KANSAS TROOPS.

W. RANDOLPH HEARST—"THE YELLOW KID"

The owner of the New York *Journal* wanted to outsell *The World*, owned by Joseph Pulitzer. Whatever Pulitzer tried—if it proved successful—Hearst tried also. After *The World* started a comic strip with a bald-headed, flap-eared kid in a yellow nightgown, Hearst lured away Outcault, the originator of the cartoons, so the *Journal*, too, had its yellow kid. To increase circulation, the rival owners used every means in the trade: sensationalism, murder, love stories and jingoism.

Hearst sent a bevy of correspondents to Cuba to report on the atrocities of the Spaniards in words and in pictures. When the artist Frederic Remington asked his boss to allow him to return home, since war did not seem to be materializing, Hearst wired him: "You furnish the pictures and I'll furnish the war."

ON FEBRUARY 18, 1898, this was the front page of Hearst's paper.

NAVY DEPARTMENT,

WASHINGTON,

February 25, 1898.

These are trying times. In the evening Roosevelt,
whom I had left as Acting Secretary during the afternoon,
came around. He is so enthusiastic and loyal that he is,
in certain respects, invaluable, yet I lack confidence
in his good judgment and discretion. He goes off very
impulsively and, if I have a good night tonight, I shall
feel that I ought to be back in the Department rather than
take a day's vacation.

A MOMENTOUS DECISION. On the afternoon of February 25, 1898, while Secretary Long was away from the office, Roosevelt as Acting Secretary of the Navy, sent this cable to Admiral Dewey, the head of the Asiatic Squadron: "Order the Squadron except Monocacy to Hong Kong. Keep full of coal. In the event of declaration war Spain, your duty will be to see that the Spanish squadron does not leave the Asiatic coast and then offensive operations in Philippine Islands. Keep Olympia until further orders." The same evening—as is evident from Long's private diary—Roosevelt must have told his superior what he had done; and while Secretary Long lacked confidence in his assistant's "good judgment and discretion," he did not revoke the order.

Washington, D. C., Saturday, February 26th, 1898.

- : -

I had a splendid night last night, and return to the
office, both because I feel so much better, and because
during my short absence I find that Roosevelt, in his
precipitate way, has come very near causing more of an explosion than happened to the Maine. His wife is very ill
his little boy is just recovering from a long and dangerous illness, so that his natural nervousness is so much
accentuated that I really think he is hardly fit to be
entrusted with the responsibility of the Department at
this critical time. He is full of suggestions; many of
which are of great value to me, and his spirited and
forceful habit is a good tonic for one who is disposed to
be as conservative and careful as I am. He means to be
thoroughly loyal, but the very devil seemed to possess
him yesterday afternoon. Having the authority for that
time of Acting Secretary, he immediately began to launch
peremptory orders, distributing ships, ordering ammunition, which there is no means to have, to places where
there is no means to store it; sending for Captain

Barker to come on about the guns of the Vesuvius, which
is a matter that might have been perfectly arranged by
correspondence; sending messages to Congress for immediate legislation, authorizing the enlistment of an unlimited number of seamen, and ordering guns from the
Navy Yard at Washington to New York, with a view to arm-
ing auxiliary cruisers which are now in peaceful commercial pursuit. The only effect of this last order would
be to take guns which are now carefully stored, ready for
shipment any moment, and which could be shipped before in any
they could possibly be put on any vessel, and to dump them
in the open weather in the New York Navy Yard, where they
would be only in the way and under no proper care. He has
gone at things like a bull in a china shop, and with the
best purposes in the world, has really taken what, if he
could have thought, he would not have for a moment have
taken, and that is the one course which is most dis-
courteous to me, because it suggests that there had been
a lack of attention which he was supplying. which shows
how the best fellow in the world and with splendid capacities is worse than of no use if he lack a cool head
and careful discretion.

TWO PAGES from Secretary Long's private diary written on February 26, 1898, a day after Theodore Roosevelt ordered Admiral Dewey to be ready for war. (Publication by courtesy of Dr. Margaret Long.)

*SECRETARY LONG IGNO
REPORTERS AS HE ENT
THE NAVY BUILDING*

W. A. Rogers.

APRIL, 1898.

THURS. 14.

FRI. 15.

SAT. 16.

APPOINTMENTS.

APRIL, 1898.

SUN. 17.

MON. 18.

TUES. 19.

WED. 20.

ROOSEVELT'S DIARY. The entry on April 16, nine days before Congress voted its war resolution against Spain reads: "The President still feebly is painfully trying for peace. His weakness and vacillation are even more ludicrous than painful. Long is at last awake; and anyway I have the Navy in good shape. But the army is awful. The War Dept. is in utter confusion. Alger has no force whatever, & no knowledge of his department. But he wishes war, at least. Miles is merely a brave peacock. They both told me they could put 100,000 men in Tampa in 24 hours! The folly, & lack of preparation, are almost inconceivable. Reed, backed by Cannon and Boutelle, is malignantly bent on preventing all preparation for war, so far as he can. I really believe that if it does come, he wishes it to be a failure." Roosevelt was strongly critical of President McKinley, who in his opinion had "no more backbone than a chocolate eclair." He was impatient, thinking the Cuban problem could not be solved through peaceful means. Roosevelt urged quick and decisive action—no more political dillydallying, but a firm and unequivocal stand—in other words, war.

Washington, D. C., Monday April 25th, 1898.

- : -

My Assistant Secretary, Roosevelt, has determined upon resigning, in order to go into the army and take part in the war. He has been of great use; a man of unbounded energy and force, and thoroughly honest, which is the main thing. He has lost his head to this unutterable folly of deserting the post where he is of most service and running off to ride a horse and, probably, brush mosquitoes from his neck on the Florida sands. **His heart is right, and he** means well, but it is one of **those cases of aberration-** desertion - vain-glory; **of which he is utterly unaware.** He thinks he is **following his highest ideal, whereas,** in fact, as without exception **every one of his friends ad-** vises him, he is acting like a fool. **And, yet, how absurd** all this will sound if, by some turn of fortune, he should accomplish some great thing and strike a very high mark.

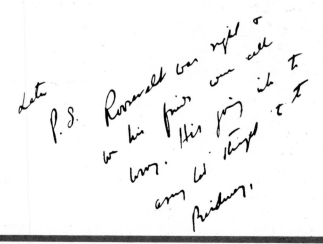

"ROOSEVELT WAS RIGHT" reads the handwritten postscript in Secretary Long's diary; "we his friends were all wrong. His going into the army led straight to the Presidency." (This first reproduction of the revealing diary is by courtesy of Secretary Long's daughter.)

Navy Department,

Washington, D. C.   April 30, 1898 189

Brooks Brothers,

Twenty-second St.& Broadway, New York.

Can you make me so I shall have it here by next Saturday a blue cravennet regular lieutenant-colonel's uniform
without yellow on collar, and with leggings? If so make it.

Theodore Roosve

Charge Mr Roosevelt

CHAPTER XXII

ROUGH RIDER

"While I think I could face death with dignity," wrote Roosevelt to his friend Dr. W. Sturgis Bigelow on March 29, 1898, "I have no desire before my time has come to go out into the everlasting darkness . . . So I shall not go into a war with any undue exhilaration of spirits or in a frame of mind in any way approaching recklessness or levity. . . . One of the commonest taunts directed at men like myself is that we are armchair and parlor jingoes who wish to see others do what we only advocate doing. I care very little for such a taunt, except as it affects my usefulness, but I cannot afford to disregard the fact that my power for good, whatever it may be, would be gone if I didn't try to live up to the doctrines I have tried to preach."

And though his friends warned that to relinquish his post in the Navy Department might mean the end of his political career, Roosevelt's ears were deaf to such warnings. Determined to prove himself as a soldier on the battlefield, he left his wife—who has just recovered from an operation—he left his children, he left his political career.

Congress had authorized the recruitment of three volunteer cavalry regiments in the states and territories of the West and Southwest. General Russell A. Alger, the Secretary of War, was ready to put the Assistant Secretary of the Navy at the head of one of the regiments, but Roosevelt declined the honor, proposing that his friend Leonard Wood, a young Army surgeon, should be given the command, while he was content with the rank of a lieutenant colonel.

Within a few days the outfit that came to be known as the Rough Riders was formed—the most extraordinary fighting force ever assembled in America. From the ranches and outposts of the West came hard-riding cowboys, iron-tough gamblers, and recruits whose relations with the law were strained at best. From the fashionable centers of the East came adventurous college boys, polo players, Long Island fox hunters. By the spit-and-polish standards of the regular Army it was a motley and ill-disciplined regiment. But the men were physically tough; they were good shots and good horsemen; they were eager to fight. And while they were training in San Antonio, Texas, the first spectacular victory of the war was won in the Philippines by Commodore Dewey—thanks in no small measure to the state of readiness he had assumed on Roosevelt's orders. Dewey left Hong Kong with his squadron and on the night of April 30 slipped into Manila Bay, where the Spanish fleet lay at anchor. At dawn he closed in to a range of two and one half miles before issuing his famous order: "You may fire when ready, Gridley." Five times his ships passed the Spanish fleet, raking it with gunfire; and when the order was given to "draw off for breakfast," the backbone of Spanish resistance had been broken.

By the end of May, Roosevelt and his regiment moved on to the embarkation point of Tampa, Florida, where Roosevelt enjoyed a four-day visit from his wife and caused consternation among the regular Army officers by dining at the hotel with non-commissioned officers.

On June 22 the Rough Riders—sans their horses—landed in Cuba at the village of Daiquiri, near Santiago on the island's southerly tip. Two days later, advancing through a thick jungle in mountainous terrain at Las Guásimas, they had their baptism of fire. Though the skirmish was brief, Richard Harding Davis, the correspondent who accompanied the regiment, termed it "the hottest, hastiest fight I ever imagined." Sixteen Rough Riders lost their lives, another fifty were wounded.

But it was on July 1 and 2, at San Juan Hill just outside Santiago, that the Rough Riders endured their greatest test with the capture of the Spanish entrenchments at the summit of the hill. Roosevelt referred to that day at San Juan as "the greatest day of my life," and surely it was. Mounted on horseback so his men could see him, he led the infantry charge under heavy fire and held the newly captured entrenchments against all Spanish counterattacks. When the smoke of the battle cleared, fifteen out of the five hundred Rough Riders were dead and seventy-three were wounded—a higher casualty rate than was suffered by any other regiment during the entire Spanish-American War.

Still, though the infantry fought hard, the war was not decided by their bravery. It was the Navy who delivered the final blow, it was the Navy who won the decisive battle. In mid-May the main Spanish fleet, under Admiral Cervera, had taken refuge in Santiago Harbor, where it was bottled up by an American fleet under Admiral Sampson. With the American land forces approaching Santiago, Cervera made a dash for the open sea. It was a disastrous decision. The ramshackle Spanish boats were sitting ducks for the American Navy. Though American marksmanship was pitifully poor, within hours the Spanish fleet was annihilated.

That the United States won the war was a miracle. The inefficiency of the War Department's planning was incredible: for want of khaki clothing, the troops fought in heavy winter uniforms during a tropical summer; supply services were so mismanaged that the soldiers in the combat area were not only ill-equipped but ill-fed; sanitation in the camps was so primitive that disease killed thirteen times as many men as enemy bullets. What saved the day was not American efficiency but the incompetence of the Spaniards, whose Navy was untrained and who used only a minute fraction of the 200,000 troops they assembled in Cuba.

Roosevelt, who after San Juan Hill was promoted to a colonelcy, raged against the War Department's bungling. In his diary, before leaving Tampa for Cuba, he complained that "there is no head, no energy, no intelligence in the War Department," and he warned Senator Lodge that "military disaster" might result if adequate food and supplies were not made quickly available to the troops.

By mid-July, when Santiago surrendered, an alarming wave of yellow fever began taking a heavy toll among the American troops. The medical officers wanted to move the soldiers from the unsanitary camp to a northern climate, but the War Department insisted that they should be left in Cuba for the summer. Roosevelt, by tacit agreement with General Shafter, composed a letter of complaint, which Shafter turned over to an Associated Press correspondent. Other division and brigade commanders signed a "Round Robin" to the War Department, demanding the removal of the Army from Cuba. Thus, when at last the troops were allowed to return to the States, Roosevelt was given the main credit for it and hailed as a national hero.

Before Roosevelt and the Rough Riders were shipped north, Spain signed a preliminary peace treaty on terms dictated by President McKinley, though protesting that "this demand strips us of the very last memory of a glorious past." In October formal negotiations began in Paris, with America represented by a five-man commission that included Undersecretary of State Day and editor Whitelaw Reid of the New York *Tribune*. The treaty granted Cuba independence, and Spain assumed Cuba's debt of 400 million dollars; Puerto Rico and Guam were ceded to the United States; the Philippine Islands were annexed ("to educate the Filipinos and uplift and Christianize them"). The taking of the Philippines, which consequently forced us to wage a war in the islands against the natives was bitterly opposed by such anti-imperialists as Bryan, Godkin, Carl Schurz, and Mark Twain, but the party in power felt that it was America's destiny to rule over the Philippines.

The signing of the Treaty of Paris marked our emergence as a world power. The old sense of isolation was gone; we were now committed to rely on our own Navy rather than England's to enforce the Monroe Doctrine, and we were educated by our military mistakes into creating an adequate standing Army with a permanent general staff.

The Spanish-American War was the most popular in our history. "It has been a splendid little war," wrote John Hay to Roosevelt, "begun with the highest motives, carried on with magnificent intelligence and spirit, favored by that Fortune which loves the brave." Hay's words expressed the feeling of all America. It was a victorious war of only a few weeks, covering the fighters with glory, and with less than three hundred combat casualties to pay for it.

To Roosevelt the war had been a glorious adventure, a vindication of his physical courage and his abilities as a leader, and he made no great effort to conceal his pride. "I do not want to be vain," he had written Senator Lodge from Cuba, "but I do not think anyone else could have handled this regiment quite as I have." Later, when he wrote a book about himself and the Rough Riders, Finley Peter Dunne's Mr. Dooley read it thoughtfully and concluded: "If I was him I'd call th' book 'Alone in Cubia.'" As alternative titles Mr. Dooley suggested "Th' Biography iv a Hero be Wan who Knows" or "Th' Darin' Exploits iv a Brave Man be an Actual Eye-Witness." But however much the humorists joked about him, the battle of San Juan Hill made Roosevelt one of the most popular men in America.

THE DAY WAR BEGAN: IN CUBA. The sun shines and it is pleasant to stroll after the day's work with the girl one loves. The thought of war seems far away; in peacetime it is so hard to imagine what war is like. But within the island the guerrillas were fighting savage battles; within the island Spanish soldiers at the behest of their superiors were killing Cubans; within the island thousands and thousands were herded into dreaded concentration camps. Spain ruled with heavy hand over her dependency; Cuba was desolate, with a quarter of the population exterminated, while those who were living suffered from disease and starvation. How to improve such conditions? The answer was: by war. So war it was.

298

THE DAY WAR BEGAN: IN NEW YORK. Fifth Avenue is peaceful on this April morning. The sun shines and it is pleasant to stroll down the street with the girl one loves. The thought of war seems far away; in peacetime it is so hard to imagine what war is like. But already the Navy had sailed to Cuba to blockade its port, and Congress had voted for President McKinley's war resolution. The American people became war-minded—the sensation-loving newspapers, the business community, the conservatives, and the reformers demanded the punishment of Spain. "Save the downtrodden Cubans from their Spanish oppressors," cried the headlines. How to do it? The answer was: by war. So war it was.

"YOU MAY FIRE WHEN READY, GRIDLEY," ordered Admiral Dewey at nineteen minutes to six on the morning of May 1, 1898, after his fleet had passed the silent guns of Corregidor and sneaked inside the harbor of Manila. Soon the guns of the warships were blazing; soon the Spanish fleet lay prostrate in the bay. Roosevelt, who as Assistant Secretary of the Navy had ordered Dewey to be ready for war, was elated by the victory. The battle of Manila Bay elevated the United States to one of the great naval powers of the world.

THE ASIATIC SQUADRON commanded by Admiral George Dewey, in battle formation. The American fleet entered Manila Bay under cover of darkness and smashed the Spanish ships in a short encounter. The people back home recited:

Oh, dewy was the morning
Upon the first of May
And Dewey was the admiral
Down in Manila Bay.

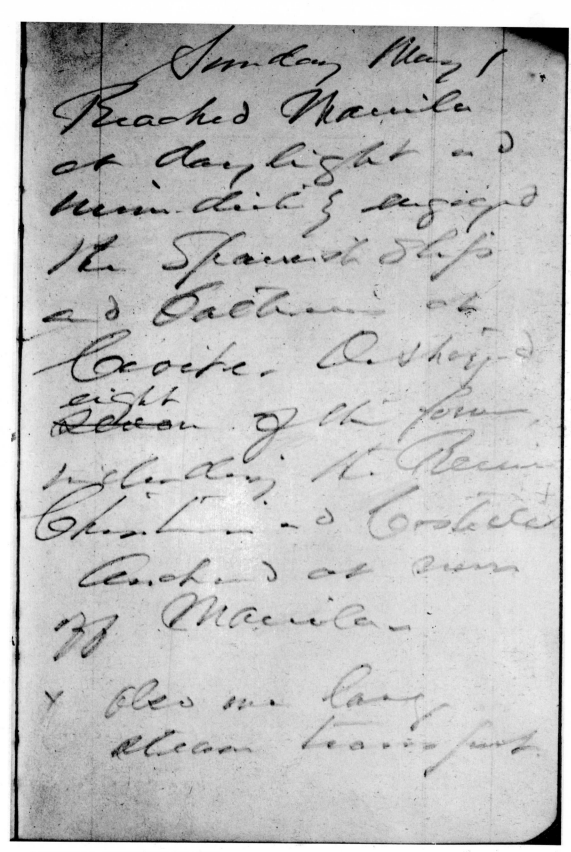

ADMIRAL DEWEY'S DIARY
on May 1, 1898, the day he defeated the Spanish fleet at Manila.

OFF TO THE WAR. After Congress declared war, the President called for 125,000 men. The youth of the country flocked to the colors; war was still a romantic escapade, a heroic dream. Theodore Roosevelt, too, pined for adventure; he was impatient to sail to Cuba and free the suppressed Cubans from their Spanish overlords. "It will be awful," he wrote in a letter (excerpt reproduced on the right page), "if the game is over before we get into it."

how Will feels; it will
be awful if the game is
over before we get into it.

THE ROUGH RIDERS, under Colonel Leonard Wood and Lieutenant Colonel Theodore Roosevelt (at the head of the troops), were the first volunteer regiment organized, armed, and equipped for the Spanish-American War. From the ranches and outposts of the West came hard-riding cowboys and iron-tough gamblers; from the East came college boys and polo players thirsting for adventure. It was a motley crew at first, but with a remarkable *esprit de corps* and with a deep affection for their leaders. "I suppose every man tends to brag about his regiment,"

LUNCHEON AT SAN ANTONIO.

wrote Roosevelt later, "but it does seem to me that there never was a regiment better worth bragging about than ours."

After leaving the Navy Department in the first week of May, Roosevelt joined the regiment in San Antonio, Texas, where the Rough Riders received their training. The men drilled, but what a bore it was! They had joined the army to fight, not to exercise on the parade ground. They wanted to go to war; they wanted to be heroes but there was nothing heroic, nothing romantic in San Antonio.

The regiment was better outfitted for the hot climate in the brown canvas fatigue uniform of the cavalry than were the regulars, who had to wear woolens more suited for the arctic regions. However, they were still uncomfortable, and they complained and grumbled. One hot afternoon after Roosevelt had drilled a squadron, the men got so thirsty that their commander bought beer for them. In the evening Colonel Wood reprimanded Roosevelt, who agreed with him. "You are right, sir! I consider myself the damnedest ass within ten miles of this camp."

THE BIRTH OF A HERO

If a ship could be sunk in the narrow part of the channel leading to Santiago, the Spanish fleet would be bottled up inside the harbor, unable to escape; at the same time, the obstacle would keep other Spanish warships—particularly the *Pelayo*—from entering the harbor and bringing help to the ships in distress.

Admiral Sampson, who conceived this idea, dispatched Lieutenant Richmond Pearson Hobson, an assistant naval constructor, and seven other volunteers on the old collier *Merrimac* to accomplish the feat. Hobson planned to steam past Morro Castle, then turn his vessel crosswise, drop anchor, and explode it with ten torpedoes.

At three-thirty in the morning of June 3 the small group set out on their dangerous mission and reached the harbor's entrance not long thereafter. By then the steering gear of their ship had been shot away by the Spanish shore batteries. Desperately, Hobson tried to sink his helpless vessel, but as only two of the torpedoes could be exploded, the *Merrimac* drifted straight down the channel. When at last it sank—aided by hits from the guns on land—it went down in the wrong spot, leaving the entrance to Santiago Harbor still free.

Hobson and the volunteers left their ship, jumping into the water, where they floated holding onto their life raft. At dawn a Spanish steam launch came out to rescue them, with Admiral Cervera, the commander of the Spanish fleet, himself giving a hand in pulling them into the boat. They were made prisoners of war, and Hobson—like Lieutenant Rowan who carried the celebrated message to Garcia, the Cuban insurgent leader—became a national hero.

BLOCKING THE HARBOR

After the battle of Santiago, in which the American fleet caused havoc to its adversaries, the Spaniards in Santiago Harbor hit on the same idea as Admiral Sampson's a few days before. They, too, wanted to block the harbor entrance, their aim now to keep the American fleet outside. The attempt was made with the three-thousand-ton cruiser *Reina Mercedes*—but, like the *Merrimac*, it sank outside the channel, leaving the entrance free.

FAREWELL SERMON AT TAMPA. Before their embarkation to Cuba, Chaplain Brown addresses the troops. Standing by the trees in the background are Major Dunn, General Wheeler, Lieutenant Colonel Roosevelt, and Colonel Wood.

The troops were happy to leave Tampa. They had no proper accommodations, as no effort had been made to set up a camp there. They simply formed in lines—a row of tents and a row of horses at their picket lines. Some who had money took rooms in the Tampa Bay Hotel, the rest slept on the ground—what wet ground it was—plagued by flies, tarantulas, and centipedes. Many of them contracted typhoid and typhus-malaria, many of them so sick that—instead of going to Cuba—they were sent to hospitals or back home.

GETTING TO THE WAR WAS NO EASY MATTER. "We were up the entire night standing by the railway track at Tampa, hoping for trains that did not come. At dawn we were shifted to another railway track, and then owing to some energetic work of Wood and myself succeeded in getting the troops on empty coal cars, on which we came down the wharf," wrote Roosevelt. On arrival, the Rough Riders found the wharf jammed and all in a "higgledly-piggledly" state. The quartermaster general allotted them a transport but "advised us to seize her instantly if we hoped to keep her." While Wood requisitioned a ship, Roosevelt with four hundred men took possession of it "in the very nick of time to head off the 71st regiment, which was also advancing for the purpose."

THE ROUGH RIDERS ON THE *YUCATAN*. Utter confusion marked the embarkation of the troops at Tampa. Ships which should have carried 750 men were filled with twice that number. A soldier chalked on the side of the boat: "Standing room only," to which another added, "And damned little of that." Roosevelt wrote: "We are in a sewer."

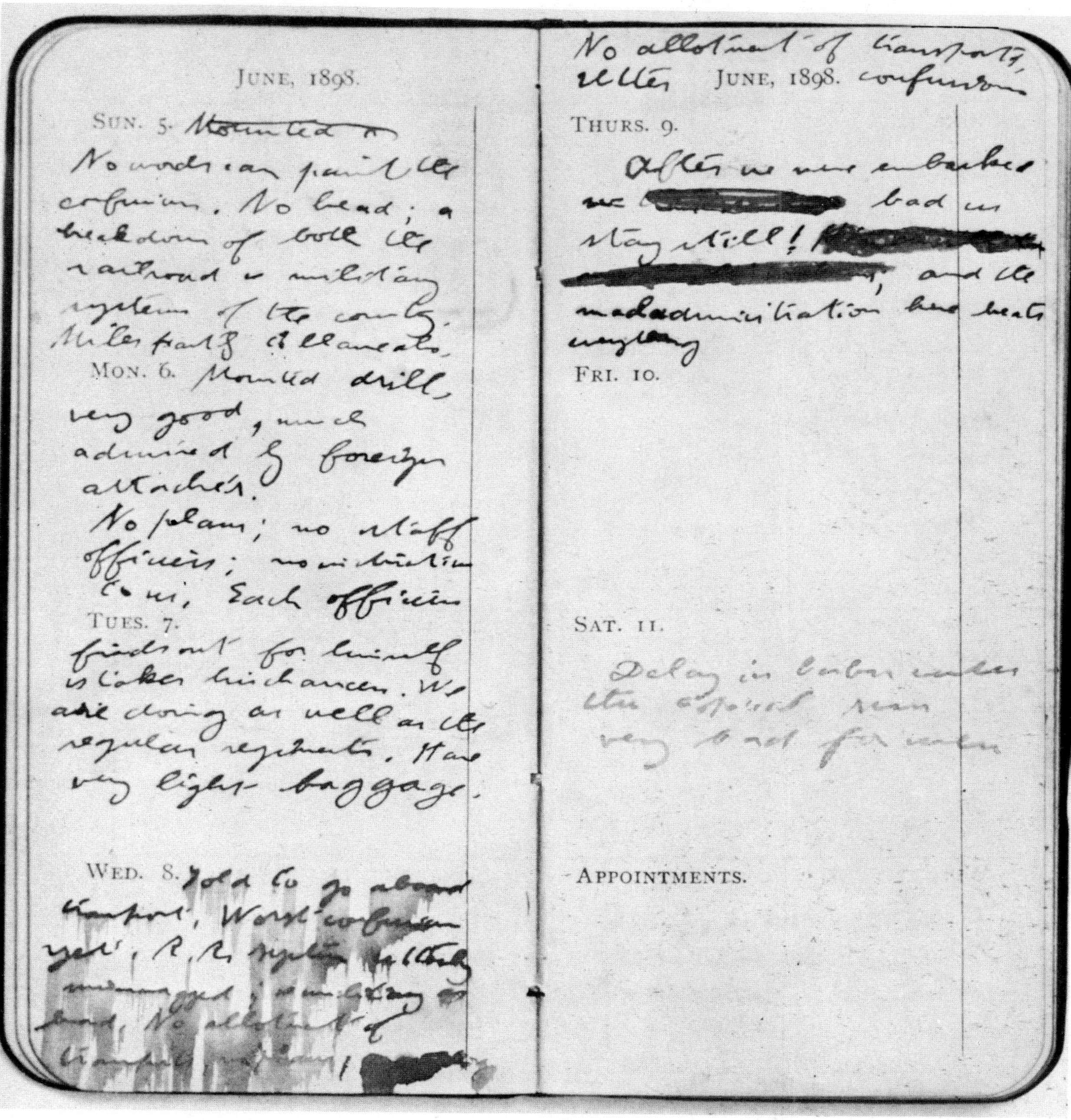

JUNE, 1898.

SUN. 5. ~~Mounted~~ No words can paint the confusion. No head; a breakdown of both the railroad & military systems of the country. Miles partly to blame also.

MON. 6. Mounted drill, very good, much admired by foreign attachés. No plans; no staff officers; no [illegible]. Each officer finds out for himself & takes his chances. We are doing as well as the regular regiments. Have very light baggage.

TUES. 7.

WED. 8. Told to go aboard transport. Worst confusion yet. R.R. system totally unmanaged; [illegible] No allotment of transports; no plans!

No allotment of transports, utter confusion.
JUNE, 1898.

THURS. 9. After we were embarked we [redacted] bad as stay still! [redacted], and the maladministration here beats anything

FRI. 10.

SAT. 11. Delay in harbor under the [illegible] very bad for men

APPOINTMENTS.

THE DIARY OF ROOSEVELT while he and his men waited in Tampa to be shipped to Cuba reveals the abysmally poor planning of the expedition. Its most recurrent word is "confusion."

The entry on June 5 says: "No words can paint the confusion. No head; a breakdown of both the railroad and military systems of the country. Miles partly to blame also."

On June 8: "Worst confusion yet. . . . No allotment of transports; no plans."

On June 9 the troops embarked. Packed on board were 15,058 enlisted men, 819 officers, and some additional clerks, teamsters, packers, and stevedores, along with 2,295 horses and mules, 114 six-mule army wagons, but only seven ambulances. For days the transports—on order of the War Department—remained in the harbor, a delay Roosevelt considered "very bad for men." Not until June 14 did they set sail. The situation was aptly summed up by a general who commented: "This is God Almighty's war, and we are only His agents."

THE BATTLEFIELD OF THE WAR.

On May 25 the American fleet reached the shores of Cuba. The Spanish fleet, under the command of Admiral Cervera, was inside Santiago Harbor.

On June 1 Admiral Sampson arrived with the *New York* and the *Oregon* and took a position opposite the harbor's entrance, placing his ships in a semi-circle, watching the channel day and night.

On June 3 Lieutenant Hobson was given orders to sink the *Merrimac* in view of the Spanish batteries at Morro Castle and Socapa.

On June 22 the first six thousand American troops landed at Daiquiri (on the far left), fifteen miles from Santiago. Next day they marched into Siboney and established the main American base. On June 24 the first land battle of the war was fought at Las Guásimas. After a fearful engagement the Spaniards retreated toward Santiago. General Wheeler, the

CASTLE

SOCAPA

MAZAMORRA

LA BATTERY

SMITH KEY

HERMITANO

EL COBRE

IAGO HARBOR

CAIMANES

former Confederate leader, who was in command, shouted excitedly: "We've got the Yankees on the run," forgetting that he was not fighting the Civil War but the Spaniards.

The engagement at Las Guásimas was followed between July 1 and 3 by the twin battles of El Caney and San Juan Hill. The way to Santiago was clear.

On July 3 the American Navy decisively defeated the Spanish fleet as it attempted to escape from Santiago Harbor. "The fleet under my command offers the nation, as a Fourth of July present, the whole of Cervera's fleet," read Admiral Sampson's announcement.

On July 3 General Shafter—the head of the American armed forces in Cuba—asked General Toral for the surrender of the Spanish land forces. On July 17, after a truce, the Spanish army officially surrendered, and the war was over.

THE BATTLE OF SAN JUAN HILL. Richard Harding Davis, the celebrated war correspondent, vividly recounted the charge. He wrote that the Rough Riders "had no glittering bayonets, they were not massed in regular array. There were a few men in advance, bunched together, and creeping up a steep, sunny hill, the top of which roared and flashed with flame.... It was more wonderful than any swinging charge could have been."

REACHING THE TOP OF SAN JUAN HILL, as pictured by Frederic Remington. After the capture of the blockhouse, Roosevelt called on his men to charge the next line of Spaniards, who ran before them. "When we reached the trenches we found them filled with dead bodies in the light blue and white uniforms of the Spanish regular army."

REINFORCEMENTS. A day after the battle of San Juan Hill, the much-needed reinforcements arrived to hold the thin line. The 9th Massachusetts and 34th Michigan regiments were rushed to the front and dug in. "We have won so far at a heavy cost," wrote Roosevelt, "but the Spaniards fight very hard and charging their intrenchments against modern rifles is terrible." The success of the battle brought advancement to the leaders. Wood became brigadier general, Roosevelt was made a colonel.

ROOSEVELT'S ENTRY in his war diary on July 1, the day of the battle of San Juan Hill. "Rose at 4. Big battle. Commanded regiment. Held extreme front of firing line." Two days later he wrote to Cabot Lodge: "I commanded my regiment, I think I may say, with honor. We lost a quarter of our men . . . how I have escaped I know not; I have not blanket or coat; I have not taken off my shoes even; I sleep in the drenching rain, and drink putrid water."

He was contented; he had proved himself on the battlefield. His hat, full of holes, was draped with a blue bandanna, shading his neck from the sun. Boots mud-soaked, shirt bathed in sweat, he was a soldier.

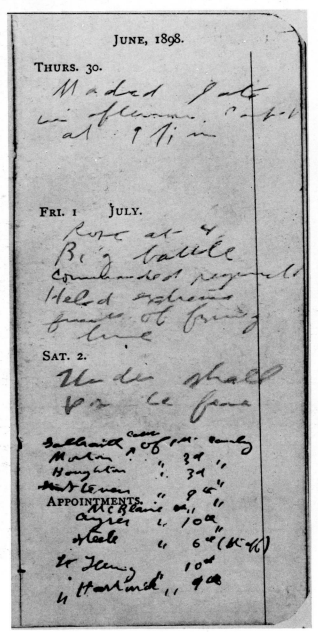

AFTER THE BATTLE OF SAN JUAN HILL
Roosevelt poses with the Rough Riders on the very spot where they fought. The picture was taken by William Dinwiddie, one of the outstanding photographers of the Spanish-American War.

316

In the attack on the San Juan hills, the American forces numbered 6,600 men, facing 4,500 Spaniards. Roosevelt's Rough Riders had 490 men in the battle, bound together by their common experience.

They were like children, proud of their accomplishment, and sang lustily:

"Rough, rough, we're the stuff,
We want to fight, and we can't get enough,
Whoo-pee."

THE LEADER OF THE AMERICAN FORCES IN CUBA, General William R. Shafter, was a fat, jovial man, his corpulence serving the correspondents with an easy butt for ridicule. While en route to the war he read the account of the British expedition of 1741, which landed at Guantanamo with 5,000 men and attempted to take Santiago. At that time Lord Vernon, the British general (after whom Washington's Mount Vernon was named), made the fatal mistake of ordering his men to repair the roads as they were advancing toward the city. And though the Spanish troops offered scant opposition, two thousand of the English "died on their feet" during the march. The expedition had to be abandoned when the remnants of the disease-stricken and exhausted Britishers were still sixteen miles from Santiago.

General Shafter, keeping in mind the failure of the English campaign, was determined to avoid the mistake of Lord Vernon. He was not impetuous; he was careful, and his mind worked slowly. He would not be rash, he would not make a risky landing at the entrance of Santiago Harbor as Admiral Sampson suggested, and he would not attack Santiago until he had ample ammunition and provisions on hand. He knew that "the campaign was a race between the physical vigor of the men and the Cuban malarial fever that lay in wait for them." To a man of Roosevelt's temperament, such a cautious attitude was distasteful. "Not since the campaign of Crassus against the Parthians has there been so criminally incompetent a general as Shafter," wrote Roosevelt to Cabot Lodge after the battle of San Juan Hill. And two days later: "It is criminal to keep Shafter in command. He is utterly inefficient, and now he is panic struck." Roosevelt heaped his abuse on Shafter because the general kept on negotiating with the Spaniards, because he tried to bring an end to the war without any further fighting. In reality, Shafter—not a heroic man —did a commendable job; without risking a single American life, he captured Santiago.

THEIR FIGHT IS DONE. After the Spanish army surrendered to the American forces, the Cuban guerrillas crowded in long lines before the arsenal at Santiago, where they had been ordered to turn in their arms. For years they had fought their oppressors, for years they had kept the Spanish troops at bay, for years they had sacrificed themselves for the freedom of their land. Now, with the war over, they were to return to their homes and take up life as they had left it. They were free men now—free forever of the harsh Spanish rule.

IN THE NEWSROOM of the White House, President McKinley waits for the news from Cuba. The Spanish-American War was one of the shortest in history, lasting only twenty-three days. The first land battle at Las Guásimas was fought on June 24; on July 15 the Spanish army was ready to surrender.

The losses of the American expeditionary force were no more than 243 killed and 1,445 wounded, but more than twice that number died after the end of the war, of diseases which the men had contracted in Cuba.

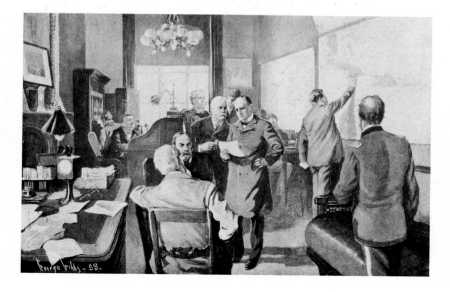

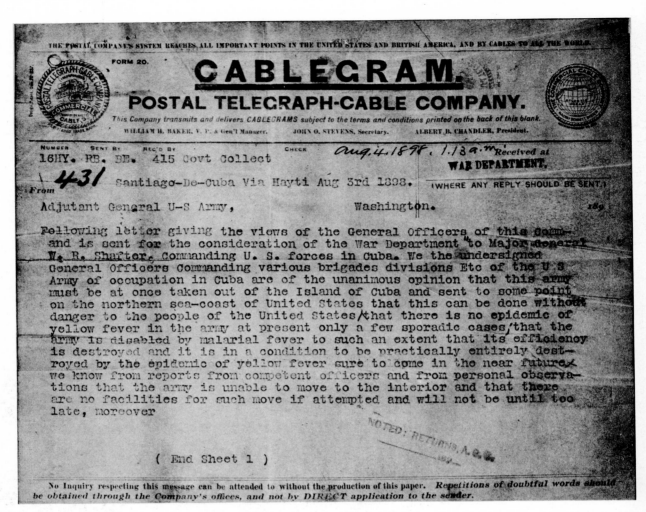

THE POSTAL COMPANY'S SYSTEM REACHES ALL IMPORTANT POINTS IN THE UNITED STATES AND BRITISH AMERICA, AND BY CABLES TO ALL THE WORLD.

FORM 20.

CABLEGRAM.

POSTAL TELEGRAPH-CABLE COMPANY.

This Company transmits and delivers CABLEGRAMS subject to the terms and conditions printed on the back of this blank.

WILLIAM H. BAKER, V. P. & Gen'l Manager.   JOHN O. STEVENS, Secretary.   ALBERT B. CHANDLER, President.

NUMBER   SENT BY   REC'D BY   CHECK

16HY. RB. BE. 415 Govt Collect   Aug. 4. 1898. 1.13 a.m. Received at

WAR DEPARTMENT.

431   Santiago-De-Cuba Via Hayti Aug 3rd 1898.   (WHERE ANY REPLY SHOULD BE SENT.)

From

Adjutant General U-S Army,   Washington.

Following letter giving the views of the General Officers of this Comm-
and is sent for the consideration of the War Department to Major General
W. R. Shafter, Commanding U. S. forces in Cuba. We the undersigned
General Officers Commanding various brigades divisions Etc of the U S
Army of occupation in Cuba are of the unanimous opinion that this army
must be at once taken out of the Island of Cuba and sent to some point
on the northern sea-coast of United States that this can be done without
danger to the people of the United States that there is no epidemic of
yellow fever in the army at present only a few sporadic cases, that the
army is disabled by malarial fever to such an extent that its efficiency
is destroyed and it is in a condition to be practically entirely destroyed by the epidemic of yellow fever sure to come in the near future
we know from reports from competent officers and from personal observations that the army is unable to move to the interior and that there
are no facilities for such move if attempted and will not be until too
late, moreover

NOTED: RETURNS, A.G.

(End Sheet 1)

No Inquiry respecting this message can be attended to without the production of this paper. Repetitions of doubtful words should
be obtained through the Company's offices, and not by DIRECT application to the sender.

THE ROUND ROBIN OF THE OFFICERS URGED THE TROOPS' IMMEDIATE RETURN

THE ROUND ROBIN. The letter of the general officers in Cuba, urging the return of the ailing troops.

After the surrender of Santiago a severe form of malarial fever spread among the American expeditionary force; more than four thousand men were on the sick list. General Shafter implored the War Department to order the army home, but the Secretary of War, fearing that they would bring with them the germ of yellow fever, replied: "The troops must all be put in camps as comfortable as they can be made and remain, I suppose, until the fever has had its run." In a meeting of division and brigade commanders and the chief medical officers, who were unanimously for the return of the troops, General Shafter proposed "some authoritative publication which would make the War Department take action before it was too late to avert the ruin of the army."

Roosevelt—the only one among the high officers who was to return to civilian life and therefore could freely criticize the War Department—was the obvious man to issue such publication. He agreed to give an interview to the press, but General Wood advised him to make his statement in a letter to General Shafter. Roosevelt followed the advice and penned a letter, which was handed then to the Associated Press correspondent, who cabled it to America.

"To keep us here," wrote Roosevelt, "in the opinion of every officer commanding a division or a brigade, will simply involve the destruction of thousands." He urged that with fifteen hundred cases of malarial fever, the men should be recalled to a cooler climate in the northern part of America. "Six weeks on the North Maine coast," Roosevelt wrote, "where the yellow-fever germ can not possibly propagate, would make us all as fit as fighting-cocks, as able as we are eager to take a leading part in the great campaign against Havana in the fall, even if we are not allowed to try Porto Rico."

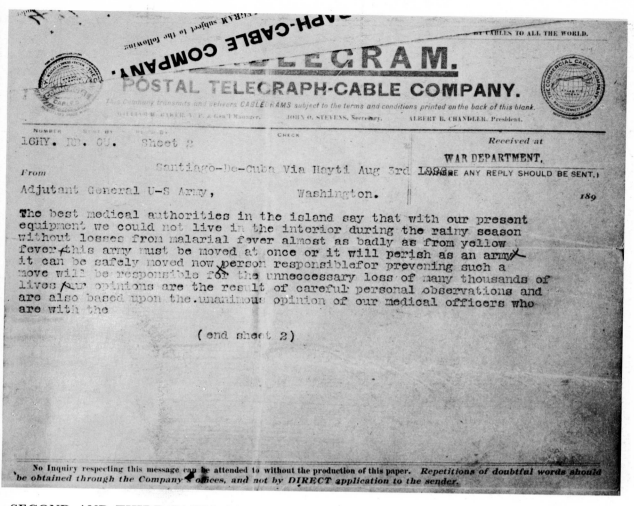

SECOND AND THIRD PAGES OF THE CABLE WHICH WAS SENT TO WASHINGTON

After Roosevelt's letter was already in the hand of the Associated Press man, General Wood dictated a statement in identical terms—the celebrated Round Robin—which was signed by Roosevelt and seven generals.

As it happened, days before the Secretary of War received the officers' communication, he had already issued orders for the return of the troops. Thus, neither Roosevelt's letter nor the Round Robin could have had any bearing on his decision. Still, in the mind of the public it was Colonel Roosevelt who was instrumental in getting the boys home—a feat which increased his popularity.

THE END OF WAR IN PUERTO RICO
The campaign lasted only two weeks; it consisted of six skirmishes, in which only four Americans were killed and forty wounded. On August 13 the hostilities came to an end.

THE TAKING OF WAKE ISLAND
The American flag was raised on Wake Island on July 4, 1898, by General F. V. Greene and a small landing party. A special correspondent for *Harper's Weekly*, who accompanied the expedition on the *China*, described the coral atoll as a barren waste stretching along for twenty miles, "with an oblong lagoon, cut from the sea by shallow reefs, over which the waves constantly break, eating their way into the heart of the island. A dreary, sun-beaten spot. . . ." And he mused: "Perhaps this heretofore unclaimed island may some day be used as a telegraph post, or even a coaling station. It lies well on the way to Manila and therefore has been visited only by a few exploring expeditors."

THE ANNEXATION OF HAWAII. U. S. Minister Sewall presenting to President Dole, at the Palace, Honolulu, an official copy of the act of annexation, August 12, 1898. Immediately thereafter the Hawaiian flag was hauled down and replaced by the Stars and Stripes.

THE TAKING OF THE PHILIPPINES.
The detachment of First Colorado Volunteers advancing to attack Fort San Antonio Abad in the Philippines on August 13, 1898.

A week before, Admiral Dewey asked the Spanish governor general in Manila to surrender the city. Though the reply was negative, the governor general—in fear of the insurgents—sent word that the Spanish troops would not offer serious resistance.

Aguinaldo, the head of the Philippine insurgents and the self-proclaimed President of the independent Philippine republic, demanded that his troops and the American forces should jointly occupy the islands.

But President McKinley directed the leaders of the American forces that there should be no joint occupation. "The insurgents and all others must recognize the military occupation and authority of the United States." Thus the Spanish flag came down and the Stars and Stripes went up over Manila.

"WE HAVE HAD A BULLY FIGHT"

Colonel Theodore Roosevelt as he landed at Montauk Point from the military transport *Miami*. On the pier he perceived Mrs. John A. Logan, the mother of a fellow officer, and he greeted her warmly.

To an officer who welcomed him, Roosevelt said: "I am feeling disgracefully well. I feel positively ashamed of my appearance when I see how badly off some of my brave fellows are."

He moved with the troops to the detention camp at Montauk Point—Camp Wikoff. Constantly in the public eye, a national hero, he was soon visited at the camp by New York politicians, who within days made him the official Republican candidate for the gubernatorial office of New York State.

HOME AT LAST. The 24th Infantry—a gallant regiment of colored troops—marches into the Montauk camp after their triumphant return from Cuba.

8-YEAR-OLD
Dwight D. Eisenhower at the time Theodore Roosevelt fought in the Spanish-American War.

13-YEAR-OLD
Harry S. Truman, as he looked a year before the Spanish-American War.

24-YEAR-OLD
Winston Churchill in 1898. The next year he was a news correspondent in the Boer War.

★

40-YEAR-OLD
Theodore Roosevelt, as he looked in 1898 when

PHOTOGRAPHING THE COLONEL was the favorite pastime of the visitors who came to the Montauk camp of the Rough Riders. And Roosevelt posed obligingly with men and animals alike. He was the most popular man in the camp and welcome copy for newspapermen.

PRESIDENT MCKINLEY VISITED the camp at Montauk on September 4. When he perceived Roosevelt, he left his carriage and shook T. R.'s hand.

ADMIRING THE SNAPSHOTS. Roosevelt and the Rough Riders were on the most cordial terms. He called most of them by their first names.

"MY REGIMENT WILL BE MUSTERED OUT IN A FEW DAYS," wrote he to his sister, "and then I shall be footloose. Just at the moment there is a vociferous popular demand to have me nominated for Governor, but I very gravely question whether it materializes."

FAREWELL TO THE ROUGH RIDERS. On September 15, 1898, the troops were mustered out at Camp Wikoff. In the morning a delegation of soldiers fetched Roosevelt to a table outside his tent, on which was a mysterious object wrapped in an army blanket.

From the ranks stepped Will S. Murphy of M Troop and, on behalf of the troops, presented the colonel "as a very slight token of admiration, love and esteem in which you are held by the officers and men of your regiment, a bronco buster in bronze."

When the cheering subsided, Roosevelt made a little speech. "I am proud of this regiment beyond measure," he began. "I am proud of it because it is a typical American regiment. The foundation of the regiment was the cow puncher, and we have got him here in bronze," he continued. Then he went on:

"No gift could have been so appropriate as this bronze of Frederic Remington. The men of the West and Southwest—horsemen, ridemen and herders of cattle—have been the backbone of this regiment, which demonstrates that Uncle Sam has another reserve of fighting men to call upon if the necessity arises.

"Outside of my own immediate family . . . I shall never show as strong ties as I do toward you. I am more than pleased that you feel the same toward me."

The Rough Riders cheered, and the men who stood behind them watching the ceremony cheered too; they belonged to the 9th and 10th colored cavalry regiments. Recognizing them, Roosevelt complimented the colored men on their heroism. He recalled: "The Spaniards called them 'smoked Yankees' but we found them to be an excellent breed of Yankee."

"Boys," Roosevelt said to his men as he concluded, "I am going to stand here, and I shall esteem it a privilege if each of you will come up here. I want to shake your hands—I want to say good-by to each one of you in person." With wet eyes, the men filed before him.

THEY SERVED HIM WITH THEIR PENS
Roosevelt with two of the best-known war correspondents: Stephen Bonsall and Richard Harding Davis, in whose dispatches the Colonel was always pictured as a hero. On the right is Major Dunn.

TEDDY THE HERO—an imaginary painting of the Battle of San Juan Hill in which the dashing, galloping Roosevelt is leading his column into battle. The painter cared little for accuracy; he disregarded the fact that the Rough Riders had no horses in Cuba. But pictures like this were extremely popular; they created the hero image of Roosevelt, the fearless Rough Rider, making him a legendary figure.

TEDDY THE TERROR—as pictured in *Life* on August 4, 1898, the very day the Round Robin telegram was dispatched to the War Department.

THE RESULT
OF THE WAR

THE SPANISH-AMERICAN WAR molded the United States into a colonial nation. The country's "Manifest Destiny," enforced by its victories on the battlefields and on the high seas, brought forth four dependencies: Cuba, Puerto Rico, the Philippines, and Hawaii. An embarrassed Uncle Sam is pictured in this *Puck* cartoon looking at the basketful of infants. "Gosh!" he cries out. "I wish they wouldn't come quite so many in a bunch; but if I've got to take them, I guess I can do as well by them as I've done by the others!" The "others," dancing on the left, are labeled Texas, California, and New Mexico.

THE OFFICIAL END OF THE WAR. On April 11, 1899, in President McKinley's office, Secretary of State John Hay signed the memorandum of ratification on behalf of the United States. A few months earlier Hay wrote to his friend Theodore Roosevelt the oft-quoted sentence: "It has been a splendid little war, begun with the highest motives, carried on with magnificent intelligence and spirit, favored by that fortune which loves the brave."

The peace negotiations began on July 26, 1898. On August 10 President McKinley submitted a protocol which asked for "the evacuation of Cuba by Spain with the relinquishment of sovereignty, the cession of Porto Rico and one of the Ladrone Islands to the United States as indemnity, and the occupation by the United States of Manila and Manila Bay." Spain signed it on August 12.

On October 1, when the peace commission met in Paris, McKinley had no fixed plan for the Philippines. With little help from the politicians, he turned to God. "I went down on my knees and prayed Almighty God for light and guidance more than one night," he said. "And one night late it came to me this way—I don't know how it was, but it came: (1) that we could not give them back to Spain—that would be cowardly and dishonorable; (2) that we could not turn them over to France or Germany—our commercial rivals in the Orient—that would be bad business and discreditable; (3) that we could not leave them to themselves—they were unfit for self-government—and they would soon have anarchy and misrule over there worse than Spain's was; and (4) that there was nothing left for us to do but to take them all and to educate the Filipinos, and uplift and civilize and Christianize them, and by God's grace do the very best we could by them as our fellowmen for whom Christ also died." In this way the Philippines became an American dependency.

On December 10 Spain signed the treaty; on February 6, 1899, the U. S. Senate ratified it.

CHAPTER XXIII

GOVERNOR OF NEW YORK

In the summer of 1898, Senator Thomas Collier Platt, the all-powerful Republican boss of New York State, was faced with a grave dilemma. He had to decide on a candidate for the New York governorship, and he had none. He would have liked to see the renomination of Governor Frank S. Black, but he knew that Black could not be re-elected; his extravagant administration of the state's canal system had caused such an outcry that his chances for winning the election were poor. Platt had to find a new candidate.

The name which reached him most frequently and for which there was a real popular clamor was that of Theodore Roosevelt, the Colonel of the Rough Riders, the hero of San Juan Hill.

Chauncey M. Depew, President of the New York Central Railroad and influential figure in New York politics, told Platt: "If you nominated Governor Black, and I am addressing a large audience—and I certainly will—the heckler in the audience will arise and interrupt me saying: 'Chauncey, we all agree with you about the Grand Old Party and all that, but how about the canal steal?' I have to explain that the amount stolen was only a million, and that would be fatal. But if Colonel Roosevelt is the candidate I can say to the heckler with indignation and enthusiasm: 'I am mighty glad you asked that question. We have nominated for governor a man who has demonstrated in public office and on the battlefield that he is a fighter for the right and is always victorious. If he is elected you know and we all know from his demonstrated characteristics—courage and ability—that every thief will be caught and punished, and every dollar that can be found will be restored to the public treasury.' Then I will follow the colonel leading his Rough Riders up San Juan Hill and ask the band to play 'The Star-Spangled Banner.'"

So Platt sent his emissary, Lemuel Ely Quigg, to see Roosevelt at his tent at Montauk and sound him out. Quigg asked the Colonel whether he would accept the Republican nomination for governor. Roosevelt beamed. "Would I?" he roared. "I would be delighted." And Quigg replied: "Then count on Senator Platt's support. Come to the Fifth Avenue Hotel and see him."

That Roosevelt should become "Platt's candidate" upset the reform element in New York, who had expected his leadership in their fight for good government. But Roosevelt was forever a faithful Republican; he did not leave the party in 1884 when the Republicans chose Blaine as their presidential candidate, and he would not disassociate himself from Senator Platt and his party now. Forced to decline the nomination of the independents, he turned his back on his former political allies, soon speaking of the Reverend Dr. Parkhurst as "that silly goose" and lumping Carl Schurz and Editor Godkin together with "the idiot variety of 'Goo-Goos'" (the advocates of Good Government).

After a strenuous campaign, in which he toured the state in his flag-bedecked special train, Roosevelt defeated his Democratic opponent, Augustus Van Wyck, the candidate of Tammany Hall, by the slim margin of 18,000. Thus, at the age of forty he returned to Albany, installing himself and his family in the governor's mansion.

Before his nomination he gave a promise to consult Platt on all appointments and policy matters. "He religiously fulfilled this pledge," Platt said later in his autobiography, "although he frequently did just what he pleased." Usually the two men met over breakfast at the Fifth Avenue Hotel in New York City. Roosevelt came down from Albany to meet the Senator at "Amen's Corner," the nickname for the niche reserved for Platt at the hotel. These breakfasts were vigorously criticized as evidence of the Governor's subservience to the Senator, but Roosevelt said: "My object was to make it as easy as possible for him to come with me. As long as there was no clash between us there was no object in seeing him; it was only when a clash came or was imminent that I had to see him. A series of breakfasts was always a prelude to some active warfare."

And warfare it was from the beginning. The first run-in with Boss Platt came when the new governor appointed his own public works commissioner and not the man Platt had chosen for him. This—as Roosevelt recalled —"produced an explosion." But there was a far bigger explosion several months later when, casting about for a strong reform issue, Roosevelt championed a twice-defeated bill to impose a special tax on public service corporations in proportion to the value of their franchises. Since most of the big corporations were paying the party organization for protection against just such legislation, Platt pleaded and threatened in the strongest terms for the governor to desist. Roosevelt would not listen. When the enraged speaker of the Assembly tore up his message rather than read it, he followed up his first message with a second one, forcing the Legislature to pass it.

The outraged Platt sent Roosevelt a severely critical letter. "You were a little loose on the relations between capital and labor, on trusts and combinations, and, indeed, on those numerous questions which have recently arisen in politics affecting the security of earnings and the right of a man to run his own business in his own way, with due respect of course to the Ten Commandments and the Penal Code," wrote Platt. And he accused Roosevelt that his stand on the franchise tax had caused businessmen to "wonder how far the notions of Populism, as laid down in Kansas and Nebraska, have taken hold upon the Republican party of the State of New York."

Roosevelt answered the charges squarely, his reply reflecting his emerging philosophy on the whole issue of government and business. "I do not believe that it is wise or safe for us as a party to take refuge in mere negation and to say that there are no evils to be corrected," he wrote. Republicans should oppose "improper corporate influence" on the one hand while opposing the "demagogy and mob rule" of Populism on the other. Firmly in the saddle, he would not be subservient to Platt and the Republican machine.

The other major battle of the two men came early in the following year when the Governor made it known that he would not reappoint Insurance Commissioner Lou Payn, whose term was about to expire. Payn, a former lobbyist for Jay Gould, was financially involved with some of the very companies his office was supposed to regulate. To Platt, Payn's reappointment seemed essential; the insurance companies under Payn's jurisdiction were the biggest customers for the securities issued by corporations on the Republican preferred list.

Senator Platt realized that for him and his forces another gubernatorial term of Roosevelt would be disastrous. In two more years the headstrong Rough Rider could virtually destroy the state's Republican machine. The idea presented itself: why not "kick him upstairs" to the Vice Presidency where he could do no harm to the party and where his name and fame would be an asset?

To achieve this two obstacles had to be overcome. One was the reluctance of Roosevelt himself, who had no desire to be put on the shelf. He told Platt: "The more I have thought it over the more I have felt that I would a great deal rather be anything, say a professor of history, than vice president." The other difficulty was the unwillingness of Mark Hanna, the top leader of the party, to put the name of "that crazy cowboy" on the Republican ticket.

But by the time the Republican convention opened in Philadelphia, there was such an overwhelming demand for Roosevelt's nomination that both Hanna and Roosevelt had to acquiesce to the wishes of the delegates. Thus Roosevelt was nominated by acclamation despite Hanna's angry warning that there would now be "only one life between this madman and the White House."

Henry Cabot Lodge, who had been confident from the first that the Vice Presidency would lead to "more important things," had assured his friend that "the way to make a precedent is to break one." Still Roosevelt felt that the Vice Presidency marked the end of his political career.

Nonetheless, he pitched into the campaign with his usual extraordinary vigor, his appetite for the fight greatly whetted by the fact that the Democrats had renominated William Jennings Bryan on a platform denouncing the "imperialism growing out of the Spanish War." Before he completed his tour, he had traveled more than 21,000 miles on his special train, had made a thousand speeches, and had been seen or heard by more than three million people. "'Tis Tiddy alone that's runnin'," observed Mr. Dooley, "an' he ain't a-runnin', he's gallopin'."

The contest was won by the McKinley-Roosevelt ticket, with an 849,000 plurality, the largest Republican victory in more than a quarter century. Boss Platt could breathe easily—his unmanageable governor was removed to Washington, and for a long time—if not forever—was relegated to the political graveyard. Or so he thought.

CAMPAIGNING FOR THE GOVERNORSHIP

"I am not having an entirely pleasant campaign," wrote Roosevelt to Cabot Lodge. "I may win yet, and I am going in to do everything that can be done." He toured the state in a flag-bedecked train, escorted by Rough Riders and heralded by buglers. Stumping the state relentlessly, he spoke on national issues and told his audiences that a vote against Republicans would be a vote against "the flag we fought for this summer." Still, things went badly until a remark of Tammany boss Richard Croker served him with a good campaign issue. Croker refused to support the

TROUBLES ABOUT TAXES. As Roosevelt had signed two affidavits to avoid payment of taxes, one in Oyster Bay, the other in New York City, lawfully he was ineligible for the New York governorship.

EDITING THE COLONEL.

THE POWER BEHIND THE THRONE— Senator Thomas C. Platt—who, from his home at 49 Broadway, "ruled" the state of New York.

renomination of a Supreme Court Justice because that man showed "undue independence" and no consideration for Tammany Hall. It was a clear attack on the nonpartisan judiciary, and the angered electorate voted against the Tammany candidate, Augustus Van Wyck. Thus, Roosevelt was elected.

THE GOVERNOR OF NEW YORK riding in the Dewey celebration. Admiral Dewey, the hero of Manila Bay, was given a tumultuous welcome by the New Yorkers, but the Rough Rider hero of San Juan Hill was not neglected by the cheering audience—even if in this photograph nobody seems to be looking at Roosevelt, who led the colorful procession attired in a formal suit and a silk top hat, dignified, solemn, looking every inch a governor.

Jany. 26th, 1900.

Mr. Henry L. Sprague,
    Union League Club,
               N.Y. City.
Dear Harry:--
        Your letter of the 25th really pleased me. Of course, I shall not feel real easy until the vote has actually been taken, but apparently everything is now all right. I have always been fond of the West African proverb: "Speak softly and carry a big stick; you will go far." If I had not carried the big stick the Organization would not have gotten behind me, and if I had yelled and blustered as Parkhurst and the similar dishonest lunatics desired, I would not have had ten votes. But I was entirely good humored, kept perfectly cool and steadfastly refused to listen to anything save that Payn had to go, and that I would take none but a thoroughly upright and capable man in his place. Unless there is some cataclysm, these tactics will be crowned with success. As for the Evening Post, Parkhurst

best to try to get me to take action which would have ensured Payn's retention and would have resulted therefore in a very imposing triumph for rascality. They have often shown themselves the enemies of good government, but in this case I do not think they are even to be credited with good intentions. They were no more anxious to see dishonesty rebuked than a professional prohibitionist is to see the liquor law decently administered.

    With warm regards,

        Faithfully yours,

        Theodore Roosevelt

THE FIRST MENTION OF THE BIG STICK. In a letter to Henry L. Sprague, who served with him in the New York Assembly, Roosevelt wrote on January 26, 1900: "I have always been fond of the West African proverb: 'Speak softly and carry a big stick; you will go far.'" The phrase later became a Roosevelt trade-mark; he was drawn with the big stick in hundreds of cartoons, and people referred to his "big stick" policies.

Roosevelt used the proverb in connection with the celebrated Payn affair. Louis F. Payn had been Superintendent of Insurance. When his term came to a close, Roosevelt would not reappoint him. But to Boss Platt, Payn's reappointment seemed essential; the insurance companies under Payn's jurisdiction were the biggest customers for the securities issued by corporations on the Republican preferred list, and Payn was thus a needed link between business and politics. Platt threatened Roosevelt with political destruction if he denied Payn's reappointment; still Roosevelt would not yield. In his eyes Payn was involved in dishonest practices when, out of a seven-thousand-dollar-a-year salary, he "saved enough to enable him to borrow nearly half a million dollars from a trust company, the directors of which are also the directors of an insurance company" under his supervision.

On the night before the governor was to send in the name of his own candidate, Francis Hendricks, to the Senate for confirmation, a Platt lieutenant met with him at the Union League Club for a final appeal. Roosevelt declined. "You know it means your ruin," said the man. "Well, we'll see about that," replied Roosevelt. "You understand the fight will begin tomorrow and will be carried on to the bitter end," continued the agent. By then Roosevelt had started for the door. "Hold on!" said the agent. "We accept. The senator is very sorry, but he will make no further opposition." And Roosevelt later recalled in his *Autobiography:* "I never saw a bluff carried more resolutely through to the final limit."

STRUGGLE BETWEEN PLATT AND ROOSEVELT

"HANDS OFF, TOMMY! I'll do the driving," exclaims Governor Roosevelt in this New York *Herald* cartoon, when Senator Thomas Platt—the New York political boss—attempts to take over the reins from his hands. Roosevelt would not be thwarted.

THE BULL TEDDY gores toreador Platt in this C. G. Bush cartoon of the *World*. Boss Platt, with whom Roosevelt constantly clashed on legislative and patronage matters of the state, cries out: "Peace is beautiful but visionary! It is not for this age."

SVENGALI PLATT hypnotizes Roosevelt in this Davenport cartoon of the *Journal*. "He wept with delight when Platt gave him a smile, and trembled with fear at his frown," reads the caption, alluding to the demoniac Svengali in Du Maurier's *Trilby*.

"THE EASY BOSS." In this C. G. Bush cartoon of the New York *World*, Platt leads the reluctant governor into the corporation paddock after Roosevelt called an extra session of the legislature to deal with the controversial franchise tax on corporations.

WILL HE
OR
WON'T HE?

ROOSEVELT SAYS "NO"

Platt and other New York party leaders, in their desire to ease Roosevelt out of the gubernatorial chair, proposed that he be "kicked upstairs" and made a vice-presidential candidate. Roosevelt, fighting against their move, issued the statement printed on the right on February 13, 1900.

ROOSEVELT'S EMPHATIC "NO!"

Governor Makes the Definite Announcement That Under No Circumstances Will He Accept the Nomination for the Vice Presidency.

ALBANY, Monday.—Governor Roosevelt gave out to-day this statement relative to the Vice Presidency:—

"In view of the continued statements in the press that I may be urged as a candidate for Vice President, and in view of the many letters that reach me advising for and against such a course, it is proper for me to state definitely that under no circumstances could I or would I accept the nomination for the Vice Presidency.

"It is needless to say how deeply I appreciate the honor conferred upon me by the mere desire to place me in so high and dignified a position, but it seems to me clear that at the present time my duty is here in the State whose people chose me to be Governor. Great problems have been faced and are being partly solved in this State at this time, and if the people so desire I hope that the work thus begun I may help carry to a successful conclusion."

Governor Roosevelt, in giving out his statement, said:—"I am happy to state that Senator Platt cordially acquiesces in my views in the matter."

April 23rd, 1900.

Dear Cabot:—

I send you the inclosed as a sample of the literally hundreds of letters that I am receiving. All my friends in the West seem to be hostile to my taking the vice presidential nomination.

By the way, I did *not* say that I would not under any circumstances accept the vice presidency. I have been careful to put it exactly as you ~~know~~.

Always yours,

Theodore Roosevelt

Hon. H. C. Lodge,
            Senate Chamber,
                    Washington, D.C.

P. S.   Since writing the above the letter from Proctor came which I also send to you. I find also that Silas Wright refused the nomination of Vice President on the ticket with Polk after he had been nominated, came back and ran for Governor and was elected by a larger majority than that by which Polk carried the State.

I think that one feature of the present situation is overlooked viz: that if I am now nominated for vice president, it will be impossible to get it out of the heads of a number of people that

2.

the Machine had forced me into it for their own sinister purpose and that I had yielded from weakness, as they know I do not want the position of Vice President.

HE DOES NOT SAY "NO"

Two months after Roosevelt issued the statement that "under no circumstances could I or would I accept the nomination for the Vice Presidency," he sent a note to Henry Cabot Lodge saying, "I did *not* say that I would not under any circumstances accept the vice-presidency." Roosevelt remonstrated with his friend, who advised him to take the vice-presidency as "it is the true stepping stone for you either toward the Presidency or the Governor Generalship of the Philippines." Roosevelt argued that "if I am now nominated for vice-president, it will be impossible to get it out of the heads of a number of people that the machine had forced me into it for their own sinister purpose and that I had yielded from weakness, as they know I do not want the position of Vice President." Yet, he accepted it.

A DEPRESSED ROOSEVELT sits with a gloomy expression between Senator Thomas C. Platt and Republican State Chairman Benjamin B. Odell at the Republican national nominating convention in Philadelphia. He was certain that the vice presidential nomination would end his political career.

He was in a quandary whether he should accept it or not. His friends Nicholas Murray Butler and Albert Shaw implored him to issue an unequivocal statement declining it, but Roosevelt told reporters that "if the nomination came to me by acclamation I cannot possibly decline it." After Senator Mark

THOMAS C. PLATT, the head of New York's political machine, tried to keep an iron grip on Roosevelt, but when he failed he eased him into the vice-presidency.

H. CABOT LODGE, Roosevelt's most faithful and intimate friend, regarded him as presidential timber therefore urged him to accept the vice-presidential post.

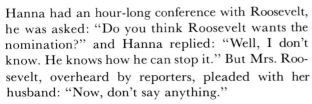

Hanna had an hour-long conference with Roosevelt, he was asked: "Do you think Roosevelt wants the nomination?" and Hanna replied: "Well, I don't know. He knows how he can stop it." But Mrs. Roosevelt, overheard by reporters, pleaded with her husband: "Now, don't say anything."

THE RELUCTANT ROOSEVELT fights in desperation against the vice-presidential nomination.

THE REPUBLICANS ASSEMBLED IN PHILADELPHIA to choose their candidate for President and Vice-President. That President McKinley would be renominated was never in doubt. The question was who would be his running mate. Vice-President Garret A. Hobart had died in office, and the Republicans were not of one mind about his successor. Senator Allison and Secretary of the Interior Bliss, who were offered the nomination, had declined to accept it.

Governor Theodore Roosevelt, one of the delegates-at-large (indicated by the arrow), was proposed by the New York boss, Thomas C. Platt, who wanted to get rid of the unmanageable governor and make him Vice-President. Platt, cynically supported by Matt Quay of Pennsylvania, fought for Roosevelt's nomination, even though the New York governor—so he protested—was reluctant. But when Roosevelt walked into the hall holding onto his wide-brimmed campaign hat, which so resembled the headgear of the Rough Riders, a politician whispered to his neighbor, "That's an acceptance hat."

Mark Hanna, the dominant force in the convention, violently opposed Roosevelt. "Don't any of you realize," he asked those who tried to persuade him, "that there's only one life between this madman and the White House?" But as Platt was adamant in his determination to get Roosevelt out of New York, Mark Hanna had to acquiesce.

As Roosevelt rose to second McKinley's nomination, the convention gave him a tremendous ovation; it was now obvious that the tide for his vice-presidency could not be stemmed. After the event, Hanna supposedly told McKinley: "Now it is up to you to live."

MARK HANNA ADDRESSES THE DELEGATES and puts President McKinley's name before them for renomination. The convention gave a rousing approval to his proposal. For the Republicans, McKinley was the ideal candidate. Solid, self-assured, smug—he was the symbol of prosperity. Thus, the Republican ticket became "William McKinley, a western man with eastern ideas, and Theodore Roosevelt, an eastern man with western characteristics."

TWENTY THOUSAND MEN cheered in the convention hall when the western delegations marched up and down the aisles, chanting in unison: "We want Teddy! We want Teddy." The feeling of the delegates was so strong, that if the bosses blocked Roosevelt's nomination, McKinley's re-election would have been in jeopardy. Mark Hanna said to newspapermen the night before Roosevelt's nomination: "Boys, you can't stop it any more than you could stop Niagara."

AS THEY SAW HIM

This was how people remembered him. This was Roosevelt, the campaigner: his rimless eyeglasses with the dangling cord, his tie awry, his hand clutching the wide-brimmed hat, his high-pitched voice with the Harvard accent coining phrases against William Jennings Bryan and the policies of the Democrats. He said: "The success of the party representing the principles embodied in the Kansas City platform would bring about the destruction of all the conditions necessary to the continuance of our prosperity."

The photograph was taken on July 5, 1900, at the place where Abraham Lincoln debated with Stephen A. Douglas—before the "Old Main" building of Knox College at Galesburg, Illinois. The campaign was still in an early stage. After the Republican ticket was chosen, Roosevelt wrote to Mark Hanna, who masterminded the campaign: "I am as strong as a bull moose and you can use me up to the limit, taking heed of but one thing and that is my throat. Two years ago in the New York campaign I only managed to hold out just barely to the end and could not have spoken for three days longer. Of course then I had to make some three hundred speeches in four weeks and carry the whole campaign on my own shoulders, so the case is not quite the same now. Still I do not want my throat to give out."

346

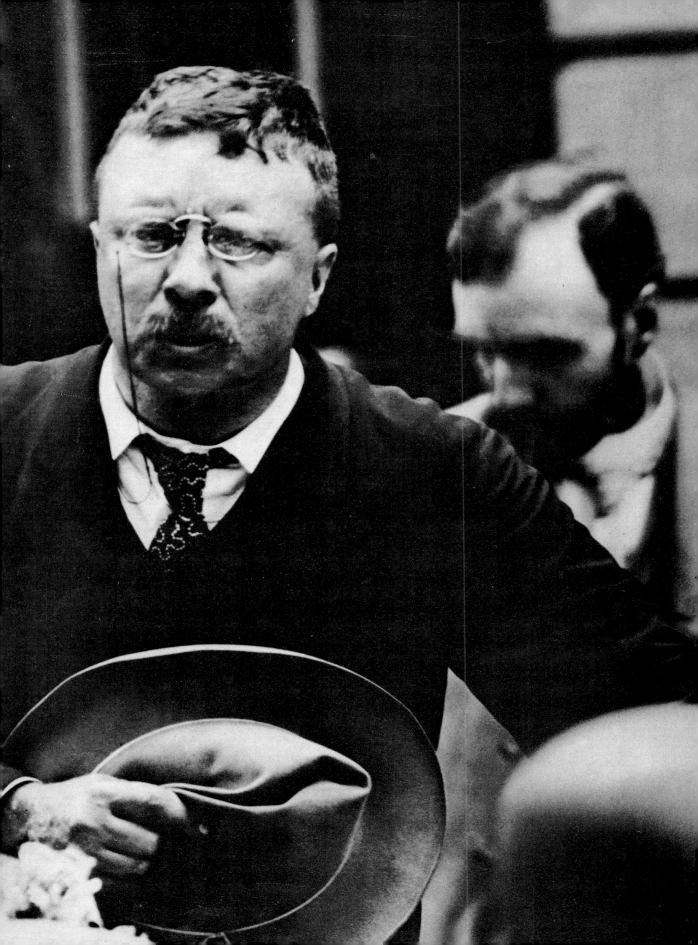

Michigan girls at Saginaw watch Roosevelt. From Mrs. Roosevelt's campaign scrapbook.

CAMPAIGNING. Tradition frowned upon a President making stump speeches in behalf of his re-election, thus the brunt of the campaign had to be borne by the vice-presidential candidate. Theodore Roosevelt dove into the contest like a duck into water. The Democrats accused President McKinley that he had abandoned America's traditional anti-empire policy and subjugated millions of defenseless people. Roosevelt reminded his listeners that McKinley clearly stated in his acceptance letter that "no blow has been struck except for liberty and humanity and none will be," and that the ten million people who had come under the American flag were not subdued but liberated "from the yoke of imperialism." Roosevelt told his audiences: "We are not taking a single step which in any way affects our institutions or our traditional policies." The question was not "whether we shall expand— for we have already expanded—but whether we shall contract."

For him, more important than the imperialist issue was "that of securing good government and moral and material well-being within our own borders. Great though the need is that the nation should do its work well abroad, even this comes second to the thorough performance of duty at home." He emphasized the need for an honest and responsible government, a government which would keep the need of the citizens at heart.

It was an arduous campaign, and Roosevelt enjoyed the speechmaking to the hilt. He had an intense dislike of Bryan and he blasted him with his usual vehemence. "What a thorough-faced hypocrite and demagogue he is, and what a small man!" wrote he to Cabot Lodge.

THE REPUBLICAN CAMPAIGN POSTER boasted that McKinley was right in 1896 when he would not open up "the mints of the United States to the silver of the world." But it neglected to say that, owing to new gold discoveries, the silver issue was no longer relevant.

THE ISSUES OF THE CAMPAIGN. For the Democrats the paramount issues were imperialism and legislation against the trusts. For the Republicans they were prosperity and the full dinner pail. For Roosevelt—as he repeated in his speeches—they were the honor and decency of the political leaders, a flag to be revered and respected, and, naturally, the depravity of the Democratic opponents, who must be defeated come what may.

THE CAMPAIGN SLOGAN of the Republicans was once again "The Full Dinner Pail." "Four years more of the full dinner pail," screamed the posters, even though the abundance the campaign orators were talking about was mostly in their imagination. Workers earned little; the farmers struggled against hard times. Prosperity affected only the small upper class. Hardly a few weeks before the election, Mark Hanna, with banker J. Pierpont Morgan's help, averted a strike of the anthracite miners, persuading mine owners to grant their employees a ten-per-cent wage increase.

THE ROUGH RIDERS ESCORTED Theodore Roosevelt wherever he journeyed. They lined up at his platform, cheered him and pumped his hand, asked him for jobs and favors, rode next to his train. Roosevelt enjoyed such campaigning immensely. This scene, found in Mrs. Roosevelt's campaign scrapbook of 1900, was taken at Watertown, South Dakota.

"HIS RUNNING MATE" reads the caption under this C. G. Bush cartoon in the New York *World*. To the American public it seemed that Theodore Roosevelt, who addressed meetings all over the country, was running for the presidency rather than McKinley, who during the entire campaign remained silent.

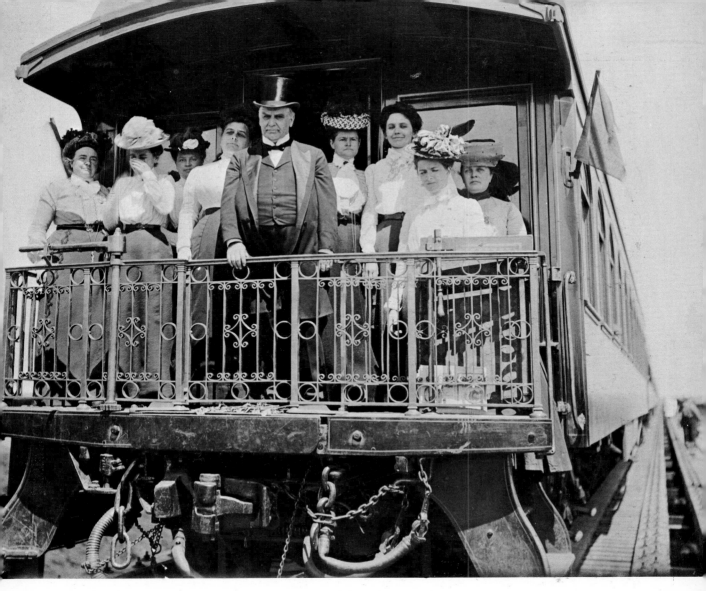

CERTAIN OF HIS ELECTION, President McKinley kept away from the campaign. But he showed himself to the people and allowed his photograph to be taken with all the visiting delegations.

THE RESULT of the election was a thumping victory for the Republican ticket. William McKinley and Theodore Roosevelt defeated William Jennings Bryan and Adlai G. Stevenson. (Stevenson, the grandfather of another candidate of later times, had previously served as Vice-President under Grover Cleveland.) The Republicans had 7,219,525 popular votes against the Democrats' 6,358,737, their largest plurality in twenty-eight years. In the electoral college the McKinley-Roosevelt ticket received 292 votes against Bryan-Stevenson's 155.

MARCH 4, 1901: The inauguration of President McKinley as he is sworn in by Chief Justice Melville Weston Fuller. Between the two stands a somber Theodore Roosevelt. It was not a happy day for him. For a man of Roosevelt's temperament, the vice-presidency had little to offer. It was an office—as John Adams, the country's first Vice-President put it—"the most insignificant . . . that ever the invention of man contrived."

If Roosevelt was in a gloomy mood, Thomas Platt, who had eased him out of the gubernatorial chair at Albany, was in a happy one. As he walked to the inauguration, with a broad smile he remarked to a friend that he was attending "to see Roosevelt take the veil."

CHAPTER XXIV

VICE PRESIDENT

Of all the jobs he held, Roosevelt liked the Vice Presidency the least. It was a post of limited scope, of small possibilities. There was little that he could do, and he felt that his political life was over. Not since Martin Van Buren in 1836 had a Vice President succeeded a President, and this time the situation was different—McKinley was no Andrew Jackson.

But while Roosevelt saw his future in dark colors, his friends thought differently. They believed that he would be the exception to the rule; they were confident that he could break precedent and would be the first Vice President to be nominated for the Presidency. "I have no doubt that you will be the nominee in 1904," wrote his friend William Howard Taft, and Senator Lodge advised him to handle himself with caution so that there would be nothing against him when the time came.

The year 1901, when Roosevelt took office under McKinley, was to be a fateful one for him, and it was already proving an interesting one for the nation. In January a great oil boom had begun in the previously untapped state of Texas when a well spouting 200 feet into the air was brought in near Beaumont. A government report showed that there was now an astonishing total of nearly 10,000 motor cars in the nation, and that one family in 66 was now equipped with a telephone. A month before McKinley's inauguration Governor-General Leonard Wood of Cuba, Roosevelt's former comrade-in-arms, had launched the Army's historic attack against yellow fever on the infested island. And on the very eve of the inaugural, J. P. Morgan & Company announced the formation of a monster combine to be known as U. S. Steel Corporation, with an unprecedented capitalization of $1,400,000,000. "God made the world in 4004 B. C.," went a current witticism, "but it was reorganized in 1901 by James J. Hill, J. Pierpont Morgan, and John D. Rockefeller."

The most controversial public issue at the opening of the McKinley administration was raised but not settled in the campaign of the previous fall: the issue about the fate of the new territories which the United States had acquired overseas as a result of the Spanish-American War. The treaty signed at Paris had given us unlimited control over Puerto Rico and the Philippine Islands—and in the case of the Philippines our decision not to grant independence had pushed us into a bloody and demoralizing guerrilla war with the native liberation forces headed by Emilio Aguinaldo. The position of the McKinley administration, and presumably of a majority of Americans, was reflected by Kipling's injunction of two years earlier to "take up the White Man's burden"—a viewpoint amplified in a much-quoted speech by young Senator Albert J. Beveridge of Indiana, who pictured America as "the trustee, under God, of the civilization of the world." Yet this expansionist philosophy was bitterly contested by many others who felt that our Philippine policy of "pacification by force" was a total denial of what we had claimed to be fighting for in the war with Spain. Because of the intensity of feelings on this issue and the moral questions it raised, there was wild celebrating across the nation when, barely three weeks after McKinley's inaugural, the Philippine Insurrection was finally brought to an end by Major-General Frederick Funston's dramatic capture of Aguinaldo, who subsequently took an oath of allegiance to the United States. It was mainly due to the bitterness of the Philippine controversy that Americans thereafter turned increasingly away from the expansionist notions for which Beveridge had been cheered but a year earlier.

Immediately after the inauguration, Roosevelt had taken up the Vice President's duties as president of the Senate. The Senate session, as it happened, was only a five-day affair, devoted primarily to confirming various presidential appointments. The brevity of the session suited Roosevelt admirably, for he had little interest in the role of a parliamentary umpire and had frequently remarked when his vice-presidential candidacy was under discussion that he would find it both boring and exasperating to preside over debates in which he could not actively participate. As Chauncey Depew rather mildly put it, Roosevelt conspicuously lacked the "equable temper" desirable in such a situation. Nonetheless, his first appearance as Senate president was made into something of a family affair, with Edith, the children and a dozen other members of the Roosevelt clan watching in awe from the gallery. "He was very quiet and dignified," Mrs. Roosevelt reported to her sister.

A fortnight later the Vice President was back with the family at Oyster Bay, his official duties presumably over with until December, when Congress would reconvene. The prospect of four more years of such inactivity still chilled him, and he began exploring the idea of resuming the law school studies he had begun at Columbia two decades earlier, partly to fill his time profitably and partly as an economic anchor to windward in the event that no worthwhile opportunity for continued public service were to present itself after completion of his term as Vice President. By May he had made arrangements to undertake legal studies upon his return to Washington in the fall under the guidance of Chief Justice White of the Supreme Court. Meanwhile, he lived what he rather apologetically termed a life of "unwarranted idleness" at Sagamore Hill, interspersed with several speaking tours and a hunting trip to Colorado in August. Late that month Edith took the children, who had been suffering from various minor ailments, to the Tahawus Club in the Adirondack Mountains for some invigorating mountain air, while Roosevelt went off on a speaking tour with plans for joining them in the mountains early in September.

All of a sudden this peaceful life was cut short by a tragic event. At 4 o'clock in the afternoon of September 6, as President McKinley was greeting visitors at a reception in his honor at Buffalo's Pan-American Exposition, the half-crazed anarchist Leon Czolgosz approached him with a revolver concealed under a handkerchief. As McKinley reached out to shake hands with him, Czolgosz fired, pumping two bullets into the President's body. One of the bullets was harmless, merely grazing McKinley's chest, but the other penetrated the wall of his stomach. An emergency operation was performed at the hospital of the Exposition, after which the President was removed to the home of a political friend.

The news reached Roosevelt that afternoon at Isle La Motte, on Lake Champlain, where he was attending the annual outing of the Vermont Fish and Game League. He immediately took a special train to Buffalo, arriving there the following day. To his relief, the news was good; the President's doctors were confident that McKinley would recover. To his sister Bamie, Roosevelt reported that "the President is coming along splendidly," adding: "Awful though this crime was against the President it was a thousand-fold worse crime against this Republic and against free government all over the world." Two days later he informed Lodge in Paris: "Long before you receive this letter I believe the last particle of danger will have vanished; nor do I anticipate even a long convalescence." As there was no emergency, Roosevelt left Buffalo the following day to join his family in the Adirondacks and continue his vacation.

But less than a week later, early on the morning of Friday, September 13, the President's condition took a severe turn for the worse and an urgent message was sent to Albany, where a courier was dispatched to notify the Vice President. The day before, Roosevelt, with Edith, Kermit, Ethel, and three friends, had started an overnight trip into the Mount Marcy area. Roosevelt, with the menfolk of the party, had gone to the summit and was on his way down early in the afternoon when a guide reached him with the fateful message. Signed by Secretary of War Elihu Root, it said: "The President appears to be dying, and members of the Cabinet in Buffalo think you should lose no time in coming." It was night time before Roosevelt made the 35-mile trip from the clubhouse to the nearest railroad, traveling in a buckboard at breakneck speed through the darkness on rough mountain roads. On boarding his special train in North Creek just before dawn, he learned that President McKinley had died at 2:15 that morning.

Arriving in Buffalo early that afternoon, Roosevelt repaired to the place where the dead President lay, and paid his respects to Mrs. McKinley. Then, at about 3 o'clock, he joined the Cabinet members in the study of the Ansley Wilcox residence. "I will show the people at once that the administration of the government will not falter in spite of the terrible blow," he declared, his face grim and impassive. "I wish to say that it shall be my aim to continue, absolutely unbroken, the policy of President McKinley for the peace, the prosperity, and the honor of our beloved country." He then took the oath of office administered by Judge John R. Hazel of the United States District Court.

Theodore Roosevelt was now President of the United States.

WORRIED ABOUT THE FUTURE

On May 16, 1901, not long after the beginning of his vice-presidential term, Roosevelt wrote this letter to Governor Hugh S. Thompson, pondering about his future career:

"If I get through the Vice Presidency I should like to get some position in a college where I could give lectures on United States history to graduates, and at the same time start to write a history of the United States. Although a republican politician, I really believe I could do absolute justice, or very nearly absolute justice, as between section and section. South Carolina has never received the proper recognition for the great part she played long before the lead she took in the nullification and secession movements." In his dark moments he felt that his political career would be finished with the end of the vice-presidential term. What was he to do after that? To become a writer? To become a professor? To become a lawyer?

PRESIDING OVER THE SENATE

This Berryman cartoon in the Washington *Post* caricatures Roosevelt as the president of the Senate. The public could not think of him as an impartial arbitrator; for the American people, Roosevelt was the dashing, fighting hero of San Juan Hill.

THE IMAGE OF THE VICE-PRESIDENT. To cartoonists, Roosevelt was a much
stronger personality than McKinley. But Roosevelt had a low opinion of the vice-presidential
office. His main duty was to preside over the Senate, and as he was a thoroughgoing partisan
with scant knowledge of parliamentary law and a temper at a low boiling point, he made a
poor showing in the post. Fortunately for him, his rule was of short duration—lasting from
March 5–9, after which a recess was called. When the Senate reconvened, Roosevelt was
already President and relieved of Senate duties. A newspaper account of the period tells an
amusing incident of his senatorial rule. Convinced that all Democratic senators were ob-
structionists, he once, when a vote was taken, bowed to the Republican side and said: "All in
favor will say Aye," then turning to the Democratic side he called: "All those opposed say No."

359

THE LAST S
The President
way to a recep
the Pan Am
Exhibition in
falo. A few m
after this phot
was taken, M
ley was felle
an assassin's

J. DART WALKER
BUFFALO

THE ASSASSIN AND THE PRESIDENT
On September 6, as McKinley was attending a public reception in Buffalo's Temple of Music, Leon Czolgosz, an anarchist, moved toward him and discharged a revolver hidden in a handkerchief.

BEFORE THE TEMPLE OF MUSIC a large crowd was waiting to greet President McKinley.

THE MILBURN RESIDENCE in Buffalo. It was here that the President, after struggling for his life for a full week, died on September 14, 1901.

OUTSIDE THE HOUSE. Theodore Roosevelt and Mr. Milburn confer. They were waiting on the lawn for the doctor's report on McKinley's condition.

THE VICE-PRESIDENT gives an interview to the press. Roosevelt had to answer a variety of questions thrown at him by the ever-present newspapermen.

VICE-PRESIDENT ROOSEVELT
On September 6, 1901, the day the assassin shot the President, Roosevelt was a

AS HE ARRIVES IN BUFFALO FOR A VISIT TO THE WOUNDED PRESIDENT MCKINLEY
dinner guest of the Vermont Fish and Game League on Isle la Motte in Lake Champlain. It was there that a telephone message reached him with the news. He left immediately, hurrying to Buffalo.

363

WHERE ROOSEVELT TOOK THE OATH OF THE PRESIDENCY on September 14, 1901: The parlor of the Wilcox residence in Buffalo. The night before, when McKinley's condition worsened, Roosevelt was summoned from the Adirondacks, where he went after the doctors assured him that the President would pull through. By relays he was brought down in bouncing buckboards over tortuous roads. One driver said of the wild ride: "I made the last sixteen miles in one hour and forty-three minutes. It was the darkest night I ever saw. I could not even see my horses except the spots where the flickering lantern light fell on them." But Roosevelt urged him on: "Push along! Hurry up! Go faster."

THE NEW PRESIDENT
ON HIS MOUNT "BLEISTEIN
AT THE CHEVY CHASE C

Part 3:

PRESIDENT

CHAPTER XXV

THE FIRST BATTLES

While the ordinary man's attitude toward the new President was one of curiosity and expectation, that of the financier and big businessman was of trembling fear and jittery concern. The business moguls who, in the words of Henry Adams, had regarded McKinley as "nothing more than a very supple and highly paid agent," were ill at ease about the "damned cowboy" who now was the head of the state. Could they rely on him? The watchword of the 1900 campaign had been "stand pat," and Mark Hanna considered the outcome "a clear mandate to govern the country in the interests of business expansion." But Roosevelt had too many of the earmarks of a reformer, a boat-rocker, a meddlesome political adventurer.

President McKinley was still alive when Douglas Robinson, Roosevelt's brother-in-law, sent Roosevelt a long letter by messenger, telling him that in New York's financial circles there was a fear that if he became President he might change matters so "as to upset the confidence." And after McKinley's death, Hanna himself urged the new President to "go slow."

Roosevelt was thoroughly amenable to these pleas. He told the grief-stricken Hanna that he would not attempt anything out of the ordinary, and he pledged his word to continue his predecessor's policies. Wall Street took heart, and the "stand-pat" newspapers waxed lyrical. "Theodore Roosevelt is a man on whom the American people can rely as a safe and sagacious successor to William McKinley," wrote the conservative New York *Sun*. And Mr. Hanna praised the new President: "Mr. Roosevelt is an entirely different man today from what he was a few weeks since. He has now acquired all that is needed to round out his character—equipoise and conservatism."

However, to more perceptive observers the omens of trouble were not difficult to perceive, for Roosevelt exhibited from the first a brash self-confidence that had not been seen at the White House in many a year. His manner was informal and—to the delight of the newspapermen—outspoken. He saw scores of visitors a day, listening to them attentively and dispatching them with machine-gun rapidity. "Every day or two," remarked one reporter, "he rattles the dry bones of precedent and causes sedate senators and heads of departments to look over their spectacles in consternation." A few days after moving into the White House he shocked a delegation of Congressmen by telling them that "if I cannot find Republicans I am going to appoint Democrats"—and two weeks later he proved it by making Thomas Goode Jones, a Democrat from Alabama, a federal judge. Soon conservative Southerners were stirred to fury when they learned that the President had invited Booker T. Washington, the distinguished Negro educator, to the White House—an act which the Memphis *Scimitar* termed "the most damnable outrage ever."

Senators and Congressmen who asked him illegitimate favors were firmly shown the door. A Texas Senator came in seeking promotion for an Army colonel who, he said, was favored by the entire Legislature of Texas despite the disapproval of his superior officers. "I don't give a damn for his superior officers!" said the Senator, to which Roosevelt replied: "Well, Senator, I don't give a damn for the Legislature of Texas." Before long, Finley Peter Dunne's "Mr. Dooley" was proposing an "emergency hospital f'r office-holders an' politicians acrost th' sthreet fr'm th' White House."

Roosevelt's eagerly awaited first message to Congress covered a score of subjects but was strangely mild in content. It dealt at some length with the growing power of the great industrial trusts—the biggest domestic issue of the time —but the tone was that of caution. To the puzzled Mr. Dooley the message's equivocal words seemed to say that "th' trusts are heejous monsthers built up be th' inlightened intherprise iv th' men that have done so much to advance progress in our beloved country. On wan hand I wud stamp thim undher fut; on th' other hand not so fast."

Three months later, however, all those who had found the message so reassuring suffered a severe shock. Without warning to Wall Street—indeed, without discussing it with his Cabinet—Roosevelt authorized Attorney General Philander Knox to invoke the Sherman Anti-Trust Act against the Northern Securities Company, the new giant holding company which represented a merger of the vast Harriman and Hill railroad empires.

The corporation lawyers who had formed Northern Securities were certain that it was invulnerable to legal attack; they based their opinion on the American Sugar Refining case six years earlier, when the Supreme Court had said in effect that the trusts were immune from prosecution because the federal power to regulate interstate commerce did not include the power to regulate acquisitions of stock. But when the Northern Securities suit was finally decided in 1904, the Supreme Court reversed its former verdict by a 5–4 margin. The new decision meant that the government had the right to control powerful business combinations.

From the outset, one of Roosevelt's strongest assets was his skill in molding public opinion and his readiness to appeal to the people over the heads of Congress. Soon after launching the Northern Securities case, he undertook a succession of speaking tours in which he repeatedly stated his deepening conviction that the nation must seek a middle course between "the demagogue who raves against wealth" and the plutocrat who denies that social evils exist. "When you can make it evident," he said in Boston, "that all men, big and small alike, have to obey the law, you are putting the safeguard of law around all men." The electorate approved such language. As the mid-term elections of 1902 approached, it seemed evident that Roosevelt would win a Republican endorsement from the voters but for one obstacle.

That obstacle was a coal strike which had begun in the anthracite fields of eastern Pennsylvania on May 12, 1902, and dragged on through the summer and early fall with no end in sight. Some 140,000 miners, newly organized in the United Mine Workers, were involved in it, but the political danger came not from the workers but from the coal-consuming public. Lodge, writing Roosevelt in alarm, predicted "political disaster in New England" and quoted a typical constituent as saying: "We don't care whether you are to blame or not. Coal is going up and the party in power must be punished."

In essence, the issue at the mines was union recognition. Repeatedly in the months before the strike was called, John Mitchell, the level-headed young president of the union, had asked the operators to meet with him to discuss wages and various grievances; just as often, the operators had told him they would deal with their workers only as individuals, not as a union.

George F. Baer, president of the mine-owning Philadelphia & Reading Railroad, was the spokesman for the operators. He was haughty, arrogant, and full of his own importance. When Mitchell proposed arbitration by several prominent clergymen, Baer replied: "Anthracite mining is a business and not a religious, sentimental, or academic proposition."

At the height of the strike, on September 3, Roosevelt suffered an accident at Pittsfield, Massachusetts, which almost proved fatal. He was forced to return to Washington and be confined to a wheel chair. In this condition he invited the spokesmen of the operators and the miners to discuss a settlement with him. The meeting proved to be a bitter and fruitless one. Mitchell suggested that the President name an arbitration commission and offered to abide by whatever decision such a group might make. But the coal operators would not hear of such a proposal. They denounced Mitchell as an "outlaw" and an "instigator of violence and crime." Baer even went so far as to rebuke the President for asking them to "waste time negotiating with the fomenters of this anarchy." Roosevelt held his temper with difficulty. "If it wasn't for the high office I hold," he noted, "I would have taken him by the seat of the breeches and the nape of the neck and chucked him out the window."

In the face of this seemingly hopeless situation, the President planned to send an army of 10,000 regulars into the coal fields, dispossess the operators, and dig the coal without regard to interference from the owners, strikers, or even the courts. When Secretary of War Elihu Root, a former Wall Street attorney, heard of the plan, he asked for permission to try once more to arrange a settlement through J. P. Morgan. Root and the banker met on Morgan's yacht, *The Corsair*, in New York harbor, and when they disembarked, Morgan had agreed to bring pressure on the mine operators to accept arbitration by a commission to be appointed by the President.

The country approved the way Roosevelt handled the issue. The *Review of Reviews* described his performance as "the greatest event affecting the relations of capital and labor in the history of America."

SOCIAL LIFE IN WASHINGTON

A WHITE HOUSE RECEPTION as seen by Charles Weber, an artist for *Leslie's Weekly,* where the drawing appeared on January 16, 1902. Roosevelt enjoyed the company of people, so did his daughter Alice (next to him) and Mrs. Roosevelt (next to Alice). There were dinners and parties, receptions and levees. When the President was criticized about the cost of such entertainments, he replied that all these sundry expenses were paid for out of his private pocket. "Apparently people do not understand . . . that I pay the butcher, the baker, and the grocer at Washington just as I do at Oyster Bay; and the protest is apparently against my having people whom I like lunch or dine with me at the White House."

INVITED TO DINNER. The very day he took office, Roosevelt wrote to Booker T. Washington, the Negro educator, suggesting a conference. The President wanted to talk about appointments in the South, to be based on merit. A month later he invited Dr. Washington to have dinner at the White House, an invitation which created an uproar in the South. "The most damnable outrage ever committed," cried a Memphis newspaper. "A studied insult," headlined the New Orleans *Picayune.* Roosevelt retorted testily that he would ask Dr. Washington to his dinner table as often as he pleased, but it did not take him long to realize that the invitation was a political mistake which he did not repeat again.

STATE BANQUET FOR PRINCE HENRY

The German Prince Henry came to the United States in February 1902 on a good-will tour to offset the anti-German feelings in the country.

The official reason for the Prince's visit was to take over the yacht built in an American shipyard for his brother, the German Emperor. President Roosevelt entertained him lavishly, and "took him out for a first-class two hours' ride in the rain." When it was suggested that Alice Roosevelt, who was to christen the vessel, should also make a short speech, Roosevelt told the amused John Hay: "I hesitated, as the only motto sufficiently epigrammatic that came to my mind was 'Damn the Dutch!!!'"

REINCARNATION

The ghost of President McKinley stands behind his successor, guiding his decisions. On taking office Roosevelt declared that he would continue "absolutely unbroken" the policy of McKinley. And when Mark Hanna wrote him to "go slow," Roosevelt promised to do so.

Roosevelt asked all members of the McKinley Cabinet to keep their posts; he did not replace any of them. John Hay remained Secretary of State; Lyman J. Gage, Secretary of Treasury; Elihu Root, Secretary of War; John D. Long, Secretary of Navy; Ethan A. Hitchcock, Secretary of Interior; James Wilson, Secretary of Agriculture; Philander C. Knox, Attorney General.

FIGHTING PLUTOCRATS

Roosevelt held that "Of all forms of tyranny the least attractive and the most vulgar is the tyranny of mere wealth, the tyranny of plutocracy." Determined to check the rise of the financial giants whose power overshadowed that of the federal government, he initiated a suit for the dissolution of the newly formed Northern Securities Company, which aimed at a railroad monopoly in the Northwest. Under the label of the $400,000,000 holding company, the bankers J. P. Morgan and Kuhn and Loeb Company had merged Edward H. Harriman's Union Pacific with James J. Hill's Northern Pacific and Great Western.

The suit, filed in St. Paul and won by the government, was appealed, and the U. S. Supreme Court decided that the merger of the railroads was in violation of the Sherman Anti-Trust Act, ordering the dissolution of the Northern Securities.

"It seems hard," said railroad baron Hill, ". . . that we should be compelled to fight for our lives against the political adventurers who have never done anything but pose and draw a salary."

NEW YORK HERALD, THURSDAY, FEBRUARY 20, 1902.—

PRESIDENT ASTONISHES FINANCIERS

Mr. Roosevelt Directs Attorney General Knox to Bring Suit to Dissolve the Northern Securities Merger.

BILL IN EQUITY SOON TO BE FILED

J. Pierpont Morgan, James J. Hill and Their Associates Will Be Made the Defendants.

STRONG INFLUENCES THRUST TO ONE SIDE

Powerful Interests Work in Vain to Prevent Action Taken by President.

NOW PREPARING FOR CASE

Government Will Ask for Dissolution of the Merger and Restoration of Stocks.

HERALD BUREAU,
No. 734 FIFTEENTH STREET, N. W.,
WASHINGTON, D. C., Wednesday.

President Roosevelt's much talked of activity in inquiring whether any laws of the United States were violated and any interests of the public endangered by the railroad merger represented in the Northern Securities Company has developed into action.

The whole question will be tested by the Department of Justice, acting under direct orders from the President. This was made clear in a statement issued by Attorney General Knox to-night, in which he said he was preparing a bill in equity to test the validity of the merger, of which he was in much doubt. The Attorney General says:—

Some time ago the President requested an opinion as to the legality of this merger, and I have recently given him one to the effect that in my judgment it violates the provisions of the Sherman act of 1890, whereupon he directed that suitable action should be taken to have the question judicially determined.

A bill in equity is now in course of preparation, which will be filed within a very short time, which will ask that the merger effected through the exchange of shares of the Northern Securities Company for shares of the two railroad companies be dissolved and such shares ordered re-exchanged, to restore the stocks of the two railroad companies to their original holders.

The two railroad companies, the Northern Securities Company, J. Pierpont Morgan and James J. Hill and their associates, stockholders in the two companies, will be the defendants in the bill.

The district in which the proceedings will be instituted has not yet been determined. Most likely it will be in Minnesota.

This means that the President has decided that the matter must go to the highest courts. It is regarded as a rather momentous decision.

Great Interests Disregarded.

President Roosevelt has put aside some of the most important financial interests and influences in the country, who have been using extraordinary measures to induce him to keep hands off. The great financiers of the country have been representing to the President and his friends that the merger, while it may not be entirely legal, is not against public policy, and that more could be gained by letting it proceed than to stir up trouble in Wall street.

President Roosevelt has not been entirely blind to appeals against stirring up business distrust, but he has taken the broad stand that if business distrust must follow the preventing of such acts as are shown in the Northern Securities merger then those who are engaged in promoting them should have taken into consideration that view before they consummated them.

When the deal was on the leaders in it came to Washington at various times, and are understood to have talked with the President about their project. They sought, it is said, to get some light as to what he would do. He is said to have taken the position that no man need fear him unless that man contemplated violating the law. The deal went on and the President, who is something of a progressive reformer, and has made many utterances on the subject of safeguarding the interests of the public against great combinations of capital, was taunted with the fact that the greatest railroad combination in the United States had come into being since he entered the White House.

Asked for Investigation.

When Attorney General Douglass, of Minnesota, and those associated with him in Governor Vansant's effort to dissolve the Northern Pacific merger, came to Washington, they asked the President to give his assistance. He is said to have replied that he could not commit himself, but that if the merger was against public policy and against the interests of the public, and at the same

P. C. KNOX.
Attorney General of the United States, Who Will Bring Suit Against the Great Northern Railroad Combination.

FINANCIER J. P. MORGAN, one of the powers behind the Northern Securities Company, was stunned when he heard that the President asked for the company's dissolution. "If we have done anything wrong send your man [Attorney General Knox] to my man [his lawyer] and they can fix it up," he told Roosevelt, treating the President as if he were a rival operator. He wanted to know whether his other interests would be attacked. "Not," replied Roosevelt, "unless we find out . . . they have done something that we regard as wrong."

Philadelphia & Reading Railway Company.
President's Office.

Reading Terminal, Philadelphia. 17th July 1902.

My dear Mr. Clark:-

I have your letter of the 16th instant.

I do not know who you are. I see that you are a religious man; but you are evidently biased in favor of the right of the working man to control a business in which he has no other interest than to secure fair wages for the work he does.

I beg of you not to be discouraged. The rights and interests of the laboring man will be protected and cared for - not by the labor agitators, but by the Christian men to whom God in His infinite wisdom has given the control of the property interests of the country, and upon the successful Management of which so much depends.

Do not be discouraged Pray earnestly that right may triumph, always remembering that the Lord God Omnipotent still reigns, and that His reign is one of law and order, and not of violence and crime.

Yours truly,

Geo. F. Baer

President.

Mr. W. F. Clark,

Wilkes-Barre,

Pennsylvania.

AN AMAZING LETTER, by the spokesman of the coal barons: "The rights and interests of the laboring man will be protected and cared for . . . by the Christian men to whom God in his infinite wisdom has given the control of the property interests of the country. . . ."

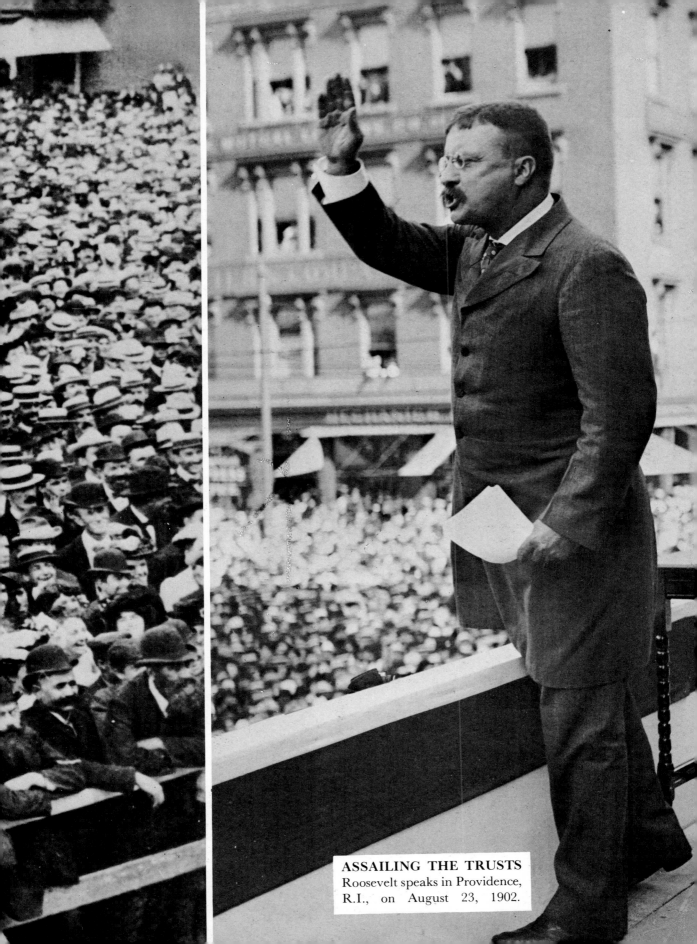

ASSAILING THE TRUSTS
Roosevelt speaks in Providence, R.I., on August 23, 1902.

TOURING THE COUNTRY

Roosevelt was a new kind of President. He was a doer. First he acted, then went before the public and explained his actions. In the summer of 1902 he departed on a tour that took him through the New England states and the Middle West. In his addresses he spoke against the swollen wealth and against the trusts, he spoke against the rich that got richer. The political oracles considered his trip as a campaign tour for the 1904 presidential nomination.

IN CHARACTERISTIC SPEAKING POSES

AT BANGOR, MAINE on August 1902. Three days later he journey with Winston Churchill to Verm

NARROW ESCAPE FROM DEATH

THE PRESIDENT'S BROKEN LANDAU

ONE OF THE HORSES WAS KILLED

WITH SWOLLEN FACE, HE GOES ON

AN HOUR LATER HE SPOKE IN LENOX

THE PITTSFIELD ACCIDENT

On September 3 Roosevelt, while driving in an open landau with Massachusetts Governor Murray Crane and presidential secretary George B. Cortelyou, barely escaped death. An electric railway car outside Pittsfield, Mass., collided with his carriage, and the impact threw all the men in the vehicle onto the road. Secret Service man William Craig, sitting on the driver's box beside the coachman, fell from his seat in front of the trolley and was run over. Cortelyou was severely wounded in the back of his head; Roosevelt's lip was cut, his face and leg bruised; only Governor Crane was unharmed.

The accident occurred because people on the electric car urged the motorman to drive as near to the President as possible. Thus, when the track, which was running down the center of the road, turned toward the right in a narrow bend, the racing trolley could not stop in time to avoid colliding with the presidential carriage. (The place of the collision was not far from the house where Herman Melville wrote *Moby Dick*.) According to the newspaper report, "the car struck the rear wheel of the carriage on the left side and ploughed through the front wheel of the vehicle, which received the full force of the blow. The carriage was upset in the twinkling of an eye and one horse fell dead on the tracks."

Half an hour later the presidential party resumed the journey to Lenox, where the President made a short speech, reassuring his listeners that he was not hurt. Then he proceeded through Great Barrington and New Milford to Bridgeport, Conn., where 30,000 people had assembled at Seaside Park to greet him. The meeting over, Roosevelt joined Mrs. Roosevelt, Kermit, Ethel, and his mother-in-law, waiting for him on the gunboat *Sylph,* which took the family across the Sound to Oyster Bay.

Sympathy messages came from all parts of the world. Emperor Wilhelm II of Germany sent his felicitations, as did King Edward VII of England. Thanking Edward for his wire, Roosevelt cabled him: "My hurts were trivial." This seemed so at first, but soon afterwards the bruised leg began to swell, an abscess developed and had to be drained. For weeks Roosevelt was confined to a wheel chair.

380

THE DAY HE ENTERED THE HOSPITA
at Indianapolis (September 23) Roosev
spoke at Tipton, Indiana, on his polici

SURGERY AT INDIANAPOLIS

Two days after the Pittsfield accident Roosevelt was on the road again. His journey took him south; he spoke at Wheeling, W. Va., and addressed the convention of the Brotherhood of Locomotive Firemen in Chattanooga. Before returning to his home, he made speeches at Asheville and Greensboro, N.C. He remained at Oyster Bay only a week, then was off again—this time he was traveling west. He spoke on the trusts and on tariff in Cincinnati, on Cuban reciprocity and the Philippine problems in Detroit, and on the creation of a tariff commission in Indiana.

On September 23 he addressed the Spanish-American War veterans at Indianapolis' Tomlinson Hall. For the past few days his left leg, which he injured in Pittsfield, had caused him some pain. The doctors who were summoned at Indianapolis found that the bruise had developed into a small abscess and urged an operation to drain the leg and reduce the swelling. Roosevelt followed their advice and entered St. Vincent's Infirmary. The medical bulletin issued after the operation said that "there was found to be a circumscribed collection of perfectly pure serum in the middle third of the left anterior tibial region, the sac containing about two ounces, which was removed."

While the doctors worked on the leg, Roosevelt was in high spirits. He always loved the unusual, and for him an operation was unusual. He joked with the surgeons and the Sisters. He was given a local anesthetic, then an aspirator (a syringe that works backwards) was inserted into the swollen leg. Though he gritted his teeth, he would not keep silent. He told the surgeons that if they desired any expert information on the subject, "he could inform them that something was happening in the vicinity of his shinbone."

Soon Governor Durbin and other politicians were admitted to the room. Roosevelt apologized to them that he had to cut short his tour, but the danger of blood poisoning had forced him to listen to his doctors' advice.

In the evening the President was taken to his special train and put into bed with his leg propped up on pillows. A reporter noted: "He at once began to read a book." When he reached Washington—though confined to a wheel chair—he pursued life as actively as ever. A great problem waited for solution: the settling of the anthracite coal strike.

INDIANAPOLIS' COLUMBIA CLUB, where the doctors examined Roosevelt and advised surgery.

ST. VINCENT'S HOSPITAL, where on September 23 an operation was performed on his infected leg.

AN EFFORT TO END THE COAL STRIKE

On October 3 the wheel-chair-ridden President summoned the coal operators and the representatives of the miners to his temporary residence in Washington. It was the first time in American history that a Chief Executive personally interfered in a labor dispute. On Roosevelt's left is John Mitchell of the United Mine Workers. Standing on the right is George F. Baer, president of the Philadelphia & Reading Railroad and spokesman for the mine operators.

A HISTORIC OCCASION

Ten days after the abortive conference with the operators, J. Pierpont Morgan, the banker, came to Washington to discuss with the President the settling of the coal strike. Roosevelt repeated to the financier that if the operators would not accept the proposal of an arbitration commission, he would send General Schofield with 10,000 soldiers to the mine fields, dispossess the mine owners, and run the mines under military rule. Returning to New York, J. P. Morgan persuaded the coal barons to accept arbitration.

Personal.

October 17, 1902.

Dear Cabot:

On the suggestion of Foulke I shall write you one incident while it is fresh on my mind, in connection with this coal strike. The wild advice I have received in reference to it is really extraordinary. I must show you a letter from Stuyvesant Fish which is as startling of its kind as anything I have ever read. Also another of good Dr. Van Dyke which is to the effect that if federal troops are sent into the district they should enforce altruism at the bayonet's point on the operators.

The crisis came at the last moment. Between the hours of 10 P.M. and 1 A.M. I had Perkins and Bacon on here, on behalf of Morgan, but really representing the operators. Neither Morgan nor anyone else had been able to do much with those wooden-headed gentry, and Bacon and Perkins were literally almost crazy. Bacon in particular had become so excited that I was quite concerned over his condition. The operators had limited me down, by a fool proviso, to five different types of men, including "an eminent sociologist". This was a ridiculous proviso because I could have appointed bad men in every case and yet kept to its letter; and

-2-

they ought to have given me a free hand. The miners, on the other hand, wanted me to appoint at least two extra members myself, or in some fashion to get Bishop Spalding (whom I myself wanted), a labor union man on the commission. I regarded their contention as perfectly reasonable, and so informed Bacon and Perkins and the operators. The operators refused point blank to have another man added, and Bacon and Perkins came on nearly wild to say that they had full power to treat on behalf of the operators, but that no extra man should be added. Finally it developed that what they meant was that no extra man should be added if he was a representative of organized labor; and argue as I could, nothing would make them change; although they grew more and more hysterical, not merely admitted, but insisted that the failure to agree mean probable violence and possible social war. It took me about two hours before I at last grasped the fact that the mighty brains of these captains of industry had formulated the theory that they would rather have anarchy than tweedledum, but that if I would use the word tweedledee they would hail it as meaning peace. In other words, that they had not the slightest objection to my appointing a labor man as "an eminent sociologist", and adding Bishop Spalding on my own account, but they preferred to see the Red Commune come than to have me make Bishop Spalding or anyone else an "eminent sociologist" and add the labor man. I instantly told them that I had not the slightest objection whatever to do

HOW THE COAL STRIKE CAME TO AN END

While the operators were ready to accept a five-man arbitration commission, they were not willing to see a representative of labor on the board. Roosevelt, in a last-effort letter to J. P. Morgan, said that with "a little ingenuity" he could appoint a board acceptable to both sides, and proposed increasing the number of commissioners to seven. That brought about a crisis.

"Between the hours of 10 P.M. and 1 A.M.," wrote the President to Cabot Lodge two days later, "I had Perkins and Bacon on here, on behalf of Morgan, but really representing the operators. Neither Morgan nor anyone else had been able to do much with these wooden-headed gentry, and Bacon and Perkins were literally almost crazy. . . . The operators had limited me down, by a fool proviso, to five different types of men, including "an eminent sociologist." This was a ridiculous proviso. . . . The miners, on the other hand, wanted me to appoint at least two extra members myself. . . . I regarded their contention as perfectly reason-able, and so informed Bacon and Perkins and the operators. The operators refused point blank to have another man added. . . . Finally it developed that what they meant was that no extra man should be added if he was a representative of organized labor; and argue as I could, nothing would make them change. . . . It took me about two hours before I at last grasped the fact that the mighty brains of these captains of industry had formulated the theory that they would rather have anarchy than tweedledum, but that if I would use the word tweedledee they would hail it as meaning peace. In other words, that they had not the slightest objection to my appointing a labor man as "an eminent sociologist," and adding Bishop Spalding on my own account, but they preferred to see the Red Commune come rather than to have me make Bishop Spalding or anyone else the "eminent sociologist" and add the labor man. I instantly told them that I had not the slightest objection whatever to doing an absurd thing when it was necessary to meet the objection of an absurd mind on some vital point, and that I would

384

3

absurd thing when it was necessary to meet the objection of an
[ab]surd mind on some vital point, and that I would cheerfully ap-
[poi]nt my labor man as the "eminent sociologist". It was almost
[imp]ossible for me to appreciate the instant and tremendous relief
[thi]s gave them. They saw nothing offensive in my language and
[not]hing rediculous in the proposition, and Pierpont Morgan and
[Bae]r, when called up by telephone, eagerly ratified the absurdity;
[and] accordingly, at this utterly unimportant price we bid fair to
[com]e out of as dangerous a situation as I ever dealt with.
    Love to Nannie,

                    Ever yours,

                    Theodore Roosevelt

. H. C. Lodge, U.S.S.,
   Nahant, Mass.

[P.]S.

    In secrecy, Stuyvesant Fish's proposition was that the bi-
[tum]inous miners were entitled to get all the benefit they could
[out] of the stoppage of the anthracite coal supply, and that with
[all] due respect to my humanitarian motives, he must protest on be-
[hal]f of the operators, miners and carriers engaged in the bitumi-
[nou]s coal trade against any effort of mine to secure a settlement

4

which would interfere with the legitimate extension of their business! The only analogy I could think of would be a protest by
the undertakers against the improper activity of the Government
quarantine officers in preventing the admittance of Asiatic cholera
to our shores.

    As for the multitude of creatures who want me to "sieze the
coal barons by the throat," on the one hand, or on the other hand,
to "stamp out the lawlessness of the trades unions" by the instant
display of force under the penalty of being considered a demagogue - why, I couldn't begin to enumerate them.

                    T. R.

cheerfully appoint my labor man as the "eminent
sociologist". . . . Pierpont Morgan and Baer, when
called up by telephone, eagerly ratified the absurdity; and accordingly, at this utterly unimportant
price we bid fair to come out of as dangerous a
situation as I ever dealt with."

Thus, on October 16, with Roosevelt appointing
the commission, the strike finally came to an end.

THE ARBITRATION COMMITTEE AT WORK

In a railroad car moving from place to place in the
coal district the seven members of the commission
interviewed miners and listened to their grievances.
From left to right: General John M. Wilson, Labor
Commissioner Carroll D. Wright, E. E. Clark
(showing his back), Judge George Gray, Edward
W. Parker, Bishop John L. Spalding, and Thomas
H. Watkins. On March 22, 1903, the commission
awarded a 10 per cent wage increase to the miners
but denied recognition of the United Mine Workers.

LINES FOR COAL. It was now October. Ever since May 12, 147,000 miners had been idle in one of the longest strikes the country had ever known. Schools closed, factories and engine rooms were in dire need of fuel, hospitals cold. The discontent of the people grew, there was an ugly spirit in the air, the anger against the coal operators mounted. "Unless the strike is ended and fuel is reduced in price," wrote one New York newspaper, "there is a general impression that weather sufficiently cold to cause real suffering among the poor will drive thousands to the coal yards, where rioting will occur if they are denied the right to help themselves." But the price of coal rose to $25 a ton, and those who could acquire a quarter of a ton considered themselves lucky. The reserve policemen at every station were increased.

On the whole, the country sympathized with the strikers; it understood the legitimacy of their grievances. A miner in the coal fields earned not more than $10 a week. There were numerous fatal accidents in the mines—441 in 1901 alone—and no workman's compensation. The housing accommodations in the company towns were at times preposterous, the prices in the company stores unfair, the weighing of the coal not equitable.

When Roosevelt showed that he would not bow to the will of the arrogant operators and insisted on arbitration, his firmness was acclaimed by all those who were critical of the operators' behavior. His settling of the strike enhanced his stature; he had accomplished a deed that no other President had dared before—he interfered in a dispute between capital and labor and forced the captains of industry to respect the rights and needs of the general public.

CHAPTER XXVI

THE AMERICAN EMPIRE

The problems Roosevelt had inherited from the McKinley administration did not stop at the water's edge. The Spanish-American War had made the United States an imperial power with large overseas possessions. It was a novel experience and, after the first flush of heady adventure wore off, a somewhat disconcerting one. New questions had to be solved, new policies had to be formulated. What should we do in the Philippines, what should we do in Cuba, what should we do in Puerto Rico?

In the Phillipine Islands, which we bought from Spain for $20,000,000, we were compelled to fight a bloody insurrection. The natives were led by Emilio Aguinaldo, who, with the encouragement of Admiral Dewey, had overrun the islands shortly after the Battle of Manila Bay and had declared the independence of the Philippines. When our policy became annexation rather than liberation, armed conflict with Aguinaldo's troops was inevitable. The fighting, much of it guerrilla warfare, dragged on for three years, with unspeakable cruelty on both sides. The American casualties exceeded the total of the entire Spanish-American War, and the Filipino losses were far greater, including hundreds of thousands of noncombatants who died from famine and disease as a result of the devastation of their farmlands.

At home, thoughtful citizens were shocked by the picture of America in the role of the hated oppressor, and by the excesses of such generals as "Hell Roaring Jake" Smith, who was eventually court-martialed for telling his men to make the island of Samar "a howling wilderness" and to "kill everything over ten." Mark Twain said bitterly that the stars on the American flag should be replaced by the skull and crossbones, and Andrew Carnegie wrote to a friend in the administration: "You seem to have about finished your work of civilizing the Filipinos; it is thought that about 8,000 of them have been civilized and sent to Heaven; I hope you like it." The Boston *Transcript* expressed the sentiments of countless conscientious citizens with this verse:

> O Dewey at Manila
> That fateful first of May
> When you sank the Spanish squadron
> In almost bloodless fray,
> And gave your name to deathless fame;
> O glorious Dewey, say,
> Why didn't you weigh anchor
> And softly sail away?

The fighting came to a virtual standstill when on March 27, 1901, the American General Frederick Funston captured Aguinaldo "by decoys, the forging of letters and other ruses, fit for kidnappers and bank crooks rather than soldiers of the United States." Roosevelt, at this time still governor of New York, firmly believing that the Filipinos would be better off under American rule, congratulated Funston warmly: "I take pride in this crowning exploit of a career filled with feats of cool courage, iron endurance and gallant daring."

As though to atone for the suppression of the independence movement, America undertook the job of Filipino reconstruction with zeal and generally beneficial results. On July 4, 1901, civil administration was instituted with the kindly Judge William Howard Taft as governor. Native leaders were appointed to important administrative posts. Modern sanitation brought about astonishing reductions in the mortality rate of Manila and other cities. Baseball became a national pastime, extending even to remote tribal areas where the Moro chieftains insisted upon doing the batting and leaving the menial task of base-running to their servants. An enormous education program was launched. Nonetheless, our Philippine adventure had proved excessively costly in an economic as well as a moral sense. Between 1898 and 1902 our expenditures in the islands totaled more than $190,000,000.

In Cuba our experience was considerably happier. When Congress, on the eve of the Spanish war, passed the resolution authorizing the use of American troops to liberate Cuba, it declared its intent to "leave the government and control of the island to its people." To the astonishment of cynical Europeans, we began taking steps toward that end as soon as hostilities ended. In the autumn of 1900, General Leonard Wood, the military commander of the island, arranged for a convention of nationalist leaders, and they proceeded to adopt a constitution modeled on our own.

One thing marred this idealism, however. At the insistence of the McKinley administration—and over vigorous objections from many Cuban nationalists and American anti-imperialists—the new constitution was modified by the so-called Platt Amendment. The effect of the amendment was to give the United States a virtual veto power over Cuban relations with foreign powers and to authorize us to intervene in her national affairs when and if we felt it necessary for the preservation of stable government.

The third major American acquisition resulting from the war with Spain was Puerto Rico. Military occupation of the island ended in 1900 with the passage of the Foraker Act, which provided for a House of Delegates elected by the people and a governor and executive council appointed by the American President.

One of the thorniest of the many problems raised by the American acquisitions was the constitutional question. This the Supreme Court answered in the spring of 1901 when it handed down its decision in the so-called Insular Cases. The issue in point was whether the U. S. Constitution should "follow the flag," conferring on new subjects overseas the same rights and privileges accorded to American citizens. The Court, amid a confusing welter of concurring and dissenting opinion, declared that as most Americans did not want to consider Puerto Ricans and Filipinos as constitutional equals, it was for the

President and Congress to run American colonies whichever way they desired. As Mr. Dooley summed it up: "No matter whether the constitution follows th' flag or not, th' Supreme Court follows th' illiction returns."

The lands taken from Spain were not the only overseas acquisitions to receive extensive attention. The Hawaiian Islands, their importance as a naval base greatly increased by our purchase of the Philippines, were annexed in 1898 and received full territorial status two years later. And Alaska, which had been popularly regarded as little more than a vast wasteland since its purchase from the Russians in 1867 for half a cent an acre, suddenly leaped into the headlines with the discovery of gold in the Klondike River area in 1897. The following year, a gold fever swept across the nation, and thousands of Americans joined the stampede to the frozen North, most of them poorly equipped for the rigors of an Alaskan winter. The 20,000 prospectors brought back picturesque tales for the newspapers but not a great deal of wealth—though there were colorful exceptions like the much-publicized "Sweetwater Bill" Gates, who presented his sweetheart with her weight in gold upon his return to San Francisco.

America was expanding, America was flexing its muscles.

With the acquisition of the Philippine Islands the United States had become a Far Eastern power with, inevitably, a new and vital interest in the fate of China, which appeared on the point of being gobbled up by Japan and the major European powers. The American Secretary of State at the time was John Hay, a remarkably able and scholarly statesman who had gone from an Illinois law practice to become a secretary to Abraham Lincoln and had subsequently made a high reputation as a writer, historian, and diplomat. In the face of the competing claims of the great powers in China, Hay and the British Foreign Office joined forces in enunciating what came to be known as the Open Door policy, under which the powers grudingly agreed to respect each other's rights in China. Soon afterward, a Chinese secret society called the Boxers massacred some 300 Occidentals near Peking in an effort to drive the "foreign devils" out of their country. The United States joined in a successful punitive expedition against the Boxers, but when in July of 1900 the episode threatened to provide Germany, Russia, and Japan with an excuse for the total dismemberment of the weak Chinese nation, Hay sent a circular note to the major powers amplifying the Open Door policy and guaranteeing in the name of the United States and Great Britain the political integrity of China.

In a sense, the Open Door was symbolic of the American attitude toward overseas expansion. It expressed our new status as a world power, but at the same time it showed our distaste for joining the rest of the powers in the scramble for additional colonies. Our expansionist fever, which began in 1898, was waning fast by 1900. Americans had no desire to take on further responsibilities beyond their borders; they had no desire to grow into a colonial and imperialist nation.

THE CAPTURE OF MALOLOS by the American forces on March 31, 1899. The revolutionary Philippine government fled northward; their House of Congress was set on fire by American soldiers.

THE WAR IN THE PHILIPPINES

After the overthrow of Spanish rule, the Philippines hoped the United States would grant them independence. But when American policy became annexation rather than liberation, armed conflict with the native troops became inevitable. From February 1899 until March 1901, when the rebel leader, Emilio Aguinaldo, was captured, the war in the Philippines went on, with casualties far larger than in the entire Spanish-American War. Back at home

PHILIPPINE CASUALTIES
after the battle of Malolos.

A FILIPINO PRISONER is interrogated by our soldiers. It was a cruel war, with unspeakable atrocities on both sides. Many Filipinos helped the insurgents against the American "conquerors."

bipartisan anti-imperialist leagues protested against "prosecuting a ruthless war in a savage manner on a helpless race."

Roosevelt, concerned about such attacks, wrote to Senator Hoar: "I am encouraging in every way the growth of the conditions which now make for self-government in the Philippines and which, if the Filipino people can take advantage of them, will assuredly put them where some day we shall say that if they desire independence they shall have it."

AMERICAN TROOPS
in battle position in Pasig.

THE PACIFICATION OF THE PHILIPPINES

When President McKinley had chosen William Howard Taft to govern the Philippines, Taft was hesitant to accept the honor. He had a distinguished legal career, which took him from Superior Court Justice of Ohio to Judge on the Circuit Court. He liked being a Circuit Court Judge and had no desire to change. But once he became the governor of the Philippines, he won the respect and admiration of the people he governed, and he encompassed real compassion and sympathy for them.

Taft's administration improved the Philippine economy, instituted a limited self-government for the islands, established an educational program. His sanitary measures cut down the mortality rate; the building of roads and harbors made life easier for the "little brown brothers."

But his greatest success was the settling with the Vatican the land ownership of the Dominican and Franciscan friars, a major grievance of the Filipinos. These clerics, who under Spain's dominion largely ruled the country, were hated by the natives. When Aguinaldo's revolutionary government came into being, their lands were confiscated. Many of the friars, fearing retribution, fled, and Taft agreed with the wish of the population that they should not return. The question was how to compensate the Vatican for their holdings. To bring an end to the issue, Taft traveled to Rome in 1902; and after protracted negotiations he signed an agreement whereby the United States was to pay $7,239,000 for 410,000 acres of land formerly owned by the friars. This land was then sold to the Filipinos at a fair price and "with easy payments for a number of years."

Thus when President Roosevelt recalled Taft in late 1904 to make him his Secretary of War, his departure was accepted with genuine sorrow by the Filipinos. For the full month before his leaving, there were celebrations in his honor, the most spectacular among them a semi-Spanish-Venetian fiesta on the Pasig River, on which occasion Taft welcomed his guests in the costume of a Venetian doge.

THE LEADERS OF THE PHILIPPINE INSURRECTION. IN THE CENTER: EMILIO AGUINALD

GOVERNOR TAFT AS VENETIAN DO
at one of the elaborate farewell pa
in the Philippines in December 1

THE ALASKA CONTROVERSY

Roosevelt inherited this dispute with Great Britain from the McKinley administration. Canada—after gold was discovered in the Klondike region in 1896—claimed a valuable strip of land in southern Alaska. Roosevelt felt that it was a wholly "false claim" and that Canada had no more "right to the land in question than they have to Aroostook County, Maine, or than we have to New Brunswick."

The English suggested arbitration, but Roosevelt would not hear of it, and the argument between the two countries dragged on for years. Roosevelt finally agreed that six "impartial jurists of repute"—three from the United States and three from Great Britain and Canada—should meet in London and determine the boundary lines; but he told the three "impartial" American jurists—Henry Cabot Lodge, Elihu Root, and George Turner, "not to yield any territory whatever."

And he threatened that if the commission could not agree on the boundary, the American Congress would be forced to "give me the authority to run the line as we claim it, by our own people, without any further regard to the attitude of England and Canada."

On October 20, 1903, the tribunal handed down its decision—the English Lord Chief Justice voting with the Americans—upholding the American position. It was a signal victory for Roosevelt.

★

Below:

THE ALASKA TRIBUNAL at its final session in the London Foreign Office. At the head table are the six commissioners: 1. Lord Alverstone, the English Lord Chief Justice; 2. Elihu Root, the American Secretary of War; 3. Senator Henry Cabot Lodge of Massachusetts; 4. Sir Louis Jette; 5. Allen B. Aylesworth, of England; 6. George Turner, ex-Senator from the state of Washington.

Right:

THE KLONDIKE GOLD RUSH OF 1898
which precipitated the Alaskan boundary controversy between the United States and Great Britain.

AS ROOSEVELT SEEMED TO HIS OPPONENTS

A cartoon by Charles R. Macauley in the Democratic New York *World*. With his right hand Roosevelt balances the globe, while his left is holding the big stick. To his friend George Otto Trevelyan the President unburdened himself: "I am trying to make tropical American peoples understand that on the one hand they must behave themselves reasonably well, and on the other I have not the slightest intention of doing anything that is not for their own good."

CHAPTER XXVII

THE BIG STICK DIPLOMACY

Roosevelt, an apt phrase maker, was ever willing to use his phrases as weapons in his political battles. Through forceful diplomacy, and through his readiness to brandish the big stick when necessary, he soon redefined the Monroe Doctrine and showed the colonial powers of Europe that the Western Hemisphere was not a safe place to exercise any extraterritorial ambitions.

Even as he assumed the Presidency, one major test of the Monroe Doctrine was shaping up in South America. Through a revolution in 1899 Venezuela had fallen into the hands of Cipriano Castro, who in Roosevelt's terminology became "an unspeakably villainous little monkey." Under Castro's dictatorship the state fell far behind in meeting her financial obligations to the citizens of other nations, and in July of 1901 Germany asked Venezuela to submit the matter to arbitration at the Hague Tribunal for International Disputes. After this was declined, and after the protracted negotiations yielded nothing, Germany and England decided on stronger measures. On December 13, 1902, they blockaded five Venezuelan ports, captured several gunboats, and submitted the town of Puerto Cabello to a British bombardment. In the face of these actions, Castro agreed to arbitration—a step strongly endorsed by the United States—and the claims were adjudicated without further military measure.

This, at least, is one version of the affair. Thirteen years later, in 1915, Roosevelt put it in a very different light by contending that Germany, not Venezuela, had refused to submit to arbitration, and that Germany backed down and agreed to go to the Hague only when he, Roosevelt, informed the German Ambassador that the American fleet would be sent to prevent any occupation of Venezuelan territory. This version, which assumes Germany's motive to have been seizure of new territory in South America, was publicized by Roosevelt during World War I, when his feelings against Germany were exceedingly intense.

The Venezuelan affair illustrated a problem that imposed continual strains on the Monroe Doctrine. Unstable Latin-American regimes, often in the hands of revolutionary parties, were prone to disregard debts or damages owed to foreigners, and this in turn provided European powers with an easy excuse for interfering in their internal affairs. In December of 1901, at the outset of the Venezuelan controversy, Roosevelt sought to keep this problem within bounds by declaring in a message to Congress that the coercion of a Latin-American state did not violate the Monroe Doctrine provided the coercion did not "take the form of the acquisition of territory by any non-

American power." Or, as he had put it some six months earlier in a private letter: "If any South American country misbehaves toward any European country, let the European country spank it." The one reservation was that the "spanking" could not include occupation.

In the wake of the Venezuelan controversy, however, Roosevelt decided that this was not enough. By 1904 he had come to feel that if and when the Latin-American countries needed spanking, the United States rather than European powers should do it. This concept came to be known as the "Roosevelt Corollary" to the Monroe Doctrine, and the President described it in these words: "Brutal wrong-doing, or an impotence which results in a general loosening of the ties of civilized society, may in America, as elsewhere, ultimately require intervention by some civilized nation, and in the Western Hemisphere the adherence of the United States to the Monroe Doctrine may force the United States, however reluctantly, in flagrant cases of such wrong-doing or impotence, to the exercise of an international police power."

Though such pronouncement drew sharp criticism from the anti-imperialists at home and was denounced throughout Latin America as an attempt of American imperialistic expansion, to the President it seemed elementary common sense. "If we are willing to let Germany or England act as the policeman of the Caribbean," he wrote to Elihu Root, "then we can afford not to interfere when gross wrong-doing occurs. But if we intend to say 'Hands off' to the powers of Europe, sooner or later we must keep order ourselves." Someone, he reasoned, had to play the role of stern father toward the weak and unstable nations of the hemisphere. Far better that the role should be played by the United States, which had no territorial ambitions in South America, than by the land-hungry European nations.

Shortly after enunciating this expansion of the Monroe Doctrine, Roosevelt proceeded to apply it to the "black Republic" of Santo Domingo, where political disorder and mismanagement were chronic. "There was always fighting, always plundering," Roosevelt wrote, "and the successful graspers for governmental powers were always pawning ports and custom-houses, or trying to put them up as guarantees for loans. . . . So utter was the disorder that on one occasion when Admiral Dewey landed to pay a call of ceremony on the president, he and his party were shot at by revolutionists in crossing the square, and had to return to the ships, leaving the call unpaid." By the close of 1904 Santo Domingo's habit of defaulting on debts to foreign creditors had raised the threat of punitive action by various European powers, and the republic appealed to the United States for help.

Roosevelt's reply was to arrange in February of 1905 a protocol under which the United States took charge of the Dominican customhouses, turning over 45 per cent of the customs receipts to Santo Domingo and putting the remainder in a sinking fund in New York for the benefit of foreign creditors. Although the President insisted that he was merely trying to forestall European intervention and that he had no desire to annex Santo Domingo, the Senate declined to ratify the protocol. Roosevelt disregarded the Senate's wishes, and for the next twenty-eight months he carried out his plan by an executive agreement. As a financial arrangement the protocol worked admirably; customs receipts more than doubled under American management, and European claims were settled within a few years. As a diplomatic arrangement it headed off a threat of European intervention, but committed us to a policy of continual involvement in the internal affairs of Central American and Caribbean states.

"I felt," so Roosevelt wrote to John Hay on April 2, 1905, "that much less trouble would come from action; but beyond doubt we shall have flurries in connection with revolutionary uprisings and filibustering enterprises, as we assume the protection of the custom-houses."

Although Roosevelt was generally an eager champion of arbitration in disputes between other nations, he tended to be considerably less eager when the United States was a party to the dispute. This was demonstrated by the controversy involving the boundary between Alaska and British Columbia, which achieved importance after the discovery of gold in the Klondike. Throughout the year of 1902 Roosevelt maintained his contention that the claims were "an outrage, pure and simple," and that there was no justification for the Anglo-Canadian request for arbitration. To the Englishman Arthur H. Lee's question why America should not arbitrate, Roosevelt replied that "there are cases where a nation has no business to arbitrate. If we suddenly claimed a part of Nova Scotia you would not arbitrate."

In January 1903, however, he reluctantly consented to a treaty calling for appointment of six "impartial jurists of repute" to fix the boundary line, with three of the jurists to represent England and Canada and three to represent the United States. To the consternation of the British and Canadians, Roosevelt appointed as the American "impartial jurists of repute" Secretary of War Root, ex-Senator George Turner of Washington, and the anti-Anglophile Senator Lodge. In the end (and over the objections of the two Canadian commissioners, who declined to sign the document), and with the English Lord Chief Justice voting with the Americans, the boundary line was drawn substantially on Roosevelt's terms. Years later the President wrote to Admiral Mahan that "the settlement of the Alaskan boundary settled the last serious trouble between the British Empire and ourselves. . . ."

The "big stick" approach to diplomacy was the object of much criticism, and some aspects of it—most notably the "Roosevelt Corollary" to the Monroe Doctrine—were eventually repudiated by subsequent administrations. But it is important to remember that his assumption of the role of hemispheric police chief was not a manifestation of commercial imperialism in the European sense. If the business interests of America abroad benefited from his diplomacy, that was incidental. In foreign policy, as in domestic, he tended to view problems in highly moral terms, and in most cases he managed to find a clear-cut "right" and "wrong" to justify his position. Roosevelt regarded the big stick as the righteous billy-club of a policeman whose duty was to enforce law and order in an essentially wicked world.

FOREIGN POLICY UNDER ROOSEVELT

"THAT'S A LIVE WIRE, GENTLEMEN!" SAYS UNCLE SAM TO BRITAIN AND GERMANY

THE VENEZUELAN AFFAIR

At the opening of the century Venezuela's financial affairs were in a dismal state. Large debts for public work were accumulated; and when the foreign cred-

"IT'S UP TO YOU TO CAGE HIM!"

itors were unable to collect their bills, their governments assumed them. Great Britain, Germany, and Italy pressed Venezuela for payment, but received only promises. In July 1901 Germany proposed arbitration of the issue before the Hague Tribunal. Venezuela refused. For more than a year the negotiations continued. On December 7, 1902, Venezuela was handed a last ultimatum; on December 13, German and English warships were in Venezuelan waters, bombarding the fort of Puerto Cabello. This made Venezuela ask for arbitration; on December 16 both Great Britain and Germany accepted the offer and the controversy was resolved.

Roosevelt's part in the affair was that of an intermediary. He said: "If any South American State misbehaves toward any European country, let the European country spank it; but I do not wish the United States or any other country to get additional territory in South America." But when at one point he felt that Germany hesitated to accept arbitration, he threatened the German Ambassador in Washington with sending the American fleet to Venezuela, making it certain that Germany would not attempt the seizure of any territory in the Western Hemisphere.

THE BIG STICK IN THE CARIBBEAN SEA—ANOTHER WILLIAM A. ROGERS CARTOON

THE SANTO DOMINGO INCIDENT

In 1903 the Republic of Santo Domingo was not able to meet her financial obligations. Payments to foreign creditors were stopped. As President Roosevelt had no desire to see a repetition of the Venezuelan affair, he suggested to the Dominican government that the United States be entrusted with the charge of custom receipts, from which Santo Domingo's creditors would then be paid.

Though the American Senate refused to sanction such an arrangement, Roosevelt carried it out under an executive agreement. For twenty-eight months the United States supervised Santo Domingo's custom receipts, paid the creditors, and stabilized that country's finances. When Roosevelt was accused of setting a precedent for imperialistic ventures, he said: "I want to do nothing but what a policeman has to do in Santo Domingo. As for annexing the island, I have about the same desire to annex it as a gorged boa constrictor might have to swallow a porcupine wrong-end-to."

It was the Santo Domingo affair which brought forth in 1904 Roosevelt's corollary to the Monroe Doctrine: "Brutal wrong doing, or an impotence

which results in a general loosening of the ties of civilized society, may finally require intervention by some civilized nation, and in the Western Hemisphere the United States cannot ignore this duty."

"IS THIS WHAT WE WANT?"

401

"GO AWAY, LITTLE MAN, AND DON'T BOTHER ME," says the caption of this Charles Green Bush cartoon in the New York *World*. The gun is being pointed at the tiny figure of Colombia, for whom Roosevelt had little use. "To talk of Colombia as a responsible Power to be dealt with as we would deal with Holland or Belgium or Switzerland or Denmark is a mere absurdity," wrote Roosevelt some years after the event to William R. Thayer, the biographer of John Hay. "The analogy is with a group of Sicilian or Calabrian bandits; with Villa and Carranza at this moment. You could no more make an agreement with the Colombian rulers than you could nail currant jelly to a wall—and the failure to nail currant jelly to a wall is not due to the nail; it is due to the currant jelly. I did my best to get them to act straight. Then I determined that I would do what ought to be done without regard to them. The people of Panama were a unit in desiring the Canal and in wishing to overthrow the rule of Colombia. If they had not revolted, I should have recommended Congress to take possession of the Isthmus. . . ." Roosevelt was outraged that Colombia opposed him.

CHAPTER XXVIII

"I TOOK PANAMA"

The dream of an Isthmian canal to link the Atlantic and Pacific oceans at Central America had fired people's imaginations for centuries. In 1850 the United States and Great Britain had agreed in the Clayton-Bulwer Treaty that any such undertaking would be a joint operation. Twenty-six years later, in 1876, a French stock company bought from Colombia a concession to build a canal across the province of Panama, and the operation was put under the direction of Ferdinand DeLesseps, the hero of Suez. But by 1888, after spending more than a quarter of a billion dollars, the company declared bankruptcy.

The United States had become increasingly apprehensive that an Isthmian canal so near to its borders should be built under foreign auspices. Thus, after protracted negotiations with Great Britain, a treaty was concluded (the Hay-Pauncefote Treaty of 1901) by which Great Britain relinquished her rights leaving the construction, operation, and fortification of any Isthmian canal to the United States.

From the outset most experts in America favored the building of a canal across Nicaragua rather than along the ill-fated route in Colombia. But when, in 1894, the bankrupt Universal Inter-Oceanic Canal Company was reorganized as the New Panama Canal Company (with the sole purpose of selling its concession from the Colombian government to the United States), the propaganda for a Colombian canal caused a reversal in the thinking of the people. The canal company hired William N. Cromwell, a New York attorney, as its lobbyist (an assignment for which he later collected a fee of $800,000), and his behind-the-scenes work was so successful that in the Republican platform of 1900 the words "an Isthmian canal" were substituted for the "Nicaragua canal." The $60,000 campaign contribution given by Cromwell to the Republicans from the canal company's fund probably helped to effect the change.

Still, the battle for the Colombian route was not yet won. The obstacle to it was that ancient obstacle of mankind—money. For a while it looked as though the New Panama Canal Company would be worsted by its own greed. In response to inquiries from President McKinley's Isthmian Canal Commission in 1901, it set the price of its rights at $109,141,000, whereupon the commission, contending that $40,000,000 was as much as the rights were worth, recommended the use of the Nicaraguan route. At this point the flamboyant French engineer Philippe Bunau-Varilla, working with Cromwell for the Colombian route, persuaded the directors of the canal company to cut their price to the suggested $40,000,000. With the lower price, many who had originally favored Nicaragua were now for a canal through Colombia. President Roosevelt was one of them.

Those who pressed for the Nicaraguan route suffered a severe disappointment when in May 1902 the volcano Mount Montombo in Nicaragua erupted, a sign from Heaven against that state. Bunau-Varilla hurriedly called on all the stamp dealers in Washington and, within a matter of hours, had presented each member of the Senate with a Nicaraguan stamp showing a volcano "belching forth in magnificent eruption," a bad place to build a canal. Presently Congress passed the Spooner Act, authorizing the purchase of the Panama Company's concession for $40,000,000—provided Colombia would cede to the United States a strip of land across the Isthmus of Panama.

By January 22, 1903, Colombia's chargé d'affaires in Washington was ready to sign what came to be known as the Hay-Herran Treaty, granting the United States a 100-year lease on a six-mile-wide strip of land across the Isthmus of Panama. For this favor Colombia was to receive $10,000,000 besides annual payments of $250,000. But when the treaty reached the Colombian Congress, that body rejected it by a unanimous vote.

This refusal threw Roosevelt into a more than usual rage. Even before the rejection of the American offer he had remarked that "those contemptible little creatures in Bogotá ought to understand how much they are jeopardizing things and imperiling their own future." And when Colombia refused to ratify the treaty the President told his Secretary of State that "we may have to give a lesson to those jack rabbits." Roosevelt believed that the United States was not only morally but legally justified in "interfering summarily and saying that the canal is to be built and that they must not stop it," even if such a feat could be brought about only through a revolution.

As it turned out there was no need for Roosevelt to indulge in any open "instigation of a revolt." An uprising was already under way, stirred up by Bunau-Varilla and Cromwell, secure in the knowledge that Washington would welcome it. By mid-October Roosevelt was given the word that a revolt in Colombia was forthcoming. However, even if it failed, "we should at once occupy the Isthmus anyhow, and proceed to dig the canal."

Room 1162 of the Waldorf-Astoria Hotel in New York City became "the cradle of the Panama Republic." There Bunau-Varilla set up his headquarters, there he drew up a declaration of independence and a Panamanian constitution, there the "agile and discreet fingers" of his wife stitched the future flag of liberation. There, also, on October 14, came Dr. Manuel Amador, company physician of the Panama Railroad and Steamship Company, soon to be President of the new republic. Bunau-Varilla told Amador that $100,000 would be provided to underwrite the revolt, which was to take place on November 3. The exact date was set after the volatile Frenchman had learned from Secretary of State Hay that the Navy had ordered several ships of the Pacific fleet to proceed to Colombian waters. Later the date of the rebellion had to be postponed by twenty-four hours to allow time for the U.S.S. *Nashville* to reach the Atlantic side of the Isthmus.

All the preparations were carefully mapped out. General Huertas, head of the Colombian Army detachment in Panama City, was to be the rebel commander in chief, and his soldiers would receive $50 apiece for joining him. To supplement the bribed Huertas soldiers a revolutionary "army" made up of 300 railway section workers and the 287-man fire brigade of Panama City was pressed into action. The American naval commanders were instructed to prevent the landing of troops within 50 miles of Panama. And when—regardless of all precautions—500 Colombian troops landed at Bogotá, they were quickly bribed and prevailed upon to sail away instead of marching into Panama City.

Everything went according to plan; within hours the rebels were successful. On November 4 the troops of General Huertas were paid their $50 apiece in gold by Dr. Amador, who told them: "The world is astonished by your heroism! . . . Long live the Republic of Panama! Long live President Roosevelt!" There was no bloodshed. The only casualties were a Chinaman and his dog, killed by a shell fired from a Colombian gunboat.

With Panama's independence proclaimed by the revolutionists, Roosevelt and his Secretary of State worked with remarkable speed. One hour and fifteen minutes after the White House had received word that independence had been achieved, the American Consul in Panama City was instructed to extend *de facto* recognition to the new regime. Bunau-Varilla, who had remained in the United States, installed himself as Panamanian Minister to Washington. By November 17 he had concluded a treaty with the American Secretary of State, setting up the canal zone and conferring on the Republic of Panama the $10,000,000 down payment that had originally been offered to Colombia. And, of course, the stockholders of the New Panama Canal Company were to receive the $40,000,000 guaranteed by the Spooner Act.

Americans in general, intrigued by the prospect of an Isthmian canal, had no inclination to examine with critical eye the means that were used to achieve it, though there was a large and vocal minority which bitterly censured the President for what seemed an immoral land grab at the expense of a weaker nation. To these critics Roosevelt replied sharply that the Colombian political leaders were "inefficient bandits," and he claimed that, far from inciting the revolutionists, he had "simply ceased to stamp out the different revolutionary fuses that were already burning."

Eight years later, in a candid speech at the University of California, Roosevelt confessed: "If I had followed conventional, conservative methods, I should have submitted a dignified state paper of approximately two hundred pages to the Congress and the debate would have been going on yet, but I took the canal zone and let Congress debate, and while the debate goes on the canal does also." It was this statement that helped Colombia to wage a campaign for the payment of an indemnity from the United States. For years Roosevelt's friends in the Senate blocked the Wilson administration's effort to apologize to Colombia and to pay the indemnity. After Roosevelt was dead, the Harding government paid $25,000,000 to Colombia. As "conscience money" it was slight. The worth of the Panama Canal to the United States was many times that sum.

THE FIRST EFFORT TO BUILD A CANAL

It was in Colombia across the province of Panama, and it ended in disaster. The prime mover behind it was DeLesseps, the successful builder of the Suez Canal. From 1879 till 1888 the work went on. That year, after more than a quarter of a billion dollars had been spent, the company went bankrupt, a victim of poor management, unlucky engineering, and the ravages of yellow fever. Machinery was abandoned to fill the ditches, and everything came to a halt. In 1894 the bankrupt company had been reorganized as the New Panama Canal Company, started to dig again, and hoped to sell its concession from the Colombian government to the United States for the asking price of $109,141,000. In June 1901 the Spooner Act authorized the purchase of the Panama Company's concession for $40,000,000, provided Colombia would cede to the United States a strip of land across the Isthmus of Panama. And if Colombia refused, the canal would be built through Nicaragua.

THE CULEBRA CUT—A SECTION OF THE PANAMA CANAL

"The people of the United States and the people of the Isthmus and the rest of mankind will all be the better because we dig the Panama Canal and keep order in the neighborhood," wrote Roosevelt to Cecil Spring-Rice in January 1904. Around the same time he told Samuel W. Small: "To my mind this building of the canal through Panama will rank in kind, though not of course in degree, with the Louisiana Purchase and the acquisition of Texas. I can say with entire conscientiousness that if in order to get the treaty through and start building the canal it were necessary for me forthwith to retire definitely from politics, I should be only too glad to make the arrangement accordingly, for it is the amount done in office, and not length of time in office, that makes office worth having." Some years later, in 1911, in viewing the events in retrospect, Roosevelt declared: "I took the Isthmus, started the Canal, and then left Congress, not to debate the Canal, but to debate me."

SHADE OF THE IMMORTAL GEORGE—"WHERE'S MY HATCHET?"

AN ANTI-IMPERIALIST CARTOON. The Colonel of the Rough Riders plants a seedling tree with fruits labeled Philippines, Panama, Porto Rico, Santo Domingo, Hawaii, Guam. About his imperialist beliefs Roosevelt wrote: "Nations that expand and nations that do not expand may both ultimately go down, but the one leaves heirs and a glorious memory, and the other leaves neither." And he argued that "every expansion of a great civilized power means a victory for law, order and righteousness. This has been the case in every instance of expansion during the present century, whether the expanding power were France or England, Russia or America. In every instance the expansion has been of benefit, not so much to the power nominally benefited, as to the whole world. In every instance the result proved that the expanding power was doing a duty to civilization far greater and more important than could have been done by any stationary power."

CHAPTER XXIX

TOWARD THE PRESIDENCY
OF HIS OWN

The Presidency is an elective office, and Roosevelt was President only by accident. This troubled him. He desired to become President in his own right, he wanted to be sent to the White House by the mandate of the people. To attain his goal he laid careful plans, and he worked toward it with great diligence. Historically, the precedents were against him; no previous Vice President who had come into the high office through the death of his predecessor had ever been nominated for the Presidency. Neither John Tyler nor Millard Fillmore, Andrew Johnson nor Chester A. Arthur were able to succeed themselves. Roosevelt felt that these precedents were of a past era and that there were new rules which applied to him.

He campaigned for his election in many different ways. He courted the newspaper correspondents, holding press conferences and establishing a special room in the White House for their use. He went before the people on extensive speaking tours, outlining his policies and political philosophy, and by his energy, his versatility, his informality, and his outspokenness won their admiration.

He expected the support of the rank and file, but he was apprehensive about the business and financial leaders. During a speaking tour in 1903 he told a friend: "They've finished me. I have no machine, no faction, no money." He was prone to indulge in picturing his future in gloomy colors, even though at every stop of his tour tremendous crowds gathered around his platforms. In such a mood, the cheers meant nothing. "They came to see the President much as they would have come to see a circus," he remarked sadly.

Roosevelt realized that he had to gain the support of big business and of Wall Street, that he must lure "the captains of industry" and the "malefactors of great wealth" into his fold. Thus, he began to make conciliatory gestures toward them, and he compromised whenever his conscience permitted it. On the tariff question, which he determined to be "a mere matter of expediency" rather than a moral issue, he kept silent so that neither the low-tariff supporters from the West nor the high-tariff priests of the East should be offended. He backed the Elkins Act, which forbade the granting of rebates to shippers, an essentially weak bill, drawn up with the aid and consent of the railroads themselves, who had no desire to reduce the excessive freight rates. One of his biggest political compromises came early in 1904, when by executive order he provided pensions for all veterans between the ages of 62 and 70, whether disabled or not, at an annual cost of some $5,000,000. Meanwhile, he included among his political appointments a number of men quite frankly chosen for their ability to enlist Roosevelt-pledged delegates to the nominating convention.

As he worried about his prospects of becoming President in his own right, his concern turned upon the figure of Mark Hanna, the chairman of the Republican National Committee, the man who might block his way. It was true that various big business interests hoped to boom Hanna for the Presidency as a means of getting rid of Roosevelt, but Hanna realized Roosevelt's hold on the voters, and he knew that he could not challenge him without splitting the party in two.

Nevertheless, Roosevelt watched Hanna's moves with suspicion, and when the opportunity presented itself he went after the Senator and in a masterful political stroke eliminated him as a rival for the nomination. A few months later Hanna died, giving Roosevelt the opportunity to select a new chairman of the Republican National Committee—a post of great importance in view of the forthcoming presidential campaign. He chose his former private secretary, George B. Cortelyou, who a year earlier had left his staff to head the newly created Department of Commerce and Labor. Cortelyou's appointment —actively opposed by Senator Platt and the Old Guard—proved Roosevelt's domination over the Republican organization. It reflected his determination to have the chairmanship in the hands of a man who "will manage the canvass on a capable and absolutely clean basis," as "my canvass cannot be managed on any other lines either with propriety or with advantage. If I win this year it will be because the bulk of the people believe I am a straightforward, decent and efficient man. . . ."

Thus, when the Republicans assembled in Chicago for their convention, there was no other candidate before them but Roosevelt, and they nominated him by acclamation. The pervading dullness of the proceedings was relieved by an episode that dramatized the Roosevelt administration's forthright approach to diplomatic questions. In far-off Morocco the wealthy American citizen Ion Perdicaris had been kidnaped by the bandit chieftain Raisuli. The chief treated Perdicaris well, and when the dispute between him and the Sultan of Morocco (the reason for the kidnaping) had been resolved he was ready to release his captive. It was then that Secretary of State Hay, after consultation with Roosevelt, sent to the American Consul in Tangiers the peremptory message: "We want Perdicaris alive or Raisuli dead." The message, when it reached the Republican convention, created a jubilant uproar. "It was magnificent—magnificent!" Senator Depew exclaimed in behalf of his fellow delegates. And Secretary Hay recorded in his diary: "My telegram to Gunmere had an uncalled-for success. It is curious how a concise impropriety hits the public."

The platform of the Republicans, built to the President's specifications by Senator Lodge, pictured the party as the guardian of the Monroe Doctrine and the champion of economic prosperity. Its policies were not radical nor reactionary—they were middle-of-the-road.

The Democrats, meeting in St. Louis, were firmly under the control of the "Safe-and-Saners"—the Eastern conservatives who had joined forces to prevent Bryan from seizing the nomination for a third time. Their platform accused Roosevelt of various unlawful and unconstitutional actions and spoke of his administration as "sporadic, erratic, sensational, spectacular and arbitrary." For their presidential candidate they chose conservative Judge Alton B. Parker of New York, whom the Bryan faction termed as being "under the control of the Wall Street element." For the second place they nominated ex-Senator Henry G. Davis of West Virginia, a man of eighty-two and of considerable wealth. Republicans soon chided their opponents for nominating "an enigma from New York and a reminiscence from West Virginia."

One of the reasons for Parker's nomination was the Democrats' hope that he would appeal to the normally Republican big businessmen who distrusted the erratic Roosevelt. Logically, such strategy should have worked; actually it did not. The conservative New York *Sun,* summing up Wall Street's attitude, printed a one-line editorial—only five words. It said: "Theodore! with all thy faults—." Later the newspaper explained that it preferred "the impulsive candidate of the party of conservatism to the conservative candidate of the party which the business interests regard as permanently and dangerously impulsive."

As election day drew near Roosevelt grew alarmed. Every contest filled his heart with dark foreboding. This time he became apprehensive that the State of New York with its heavy electoral vote might turn Democratic. Obsessed with what Secretary Hay diagnosed as the traditional "October scare" common to political candidates, the President made personal appeals to such capitalists as Edward H. Harriman, the railroad king, and steel man Henry C. Frick. Harriman hurriedly raised $250,000 for the Republican campaign chest. Eight years later, when a Senate committee analyzed the Republican receipts, it was found that nearly three fourths of the money (over two million dollars) was collected from big corporations and trusts.

Cortelyou's collections from big business provoked the Democratic candidate to charge that the donors were being "blackmailed" by promises of political immunity. Roosevelt struck back with an indignant denial in which he described the charges as "monstrous" and concluded: "The assertion that there has been made any pledge or promise or that there has been any understanding as to future immunities or benefits in recognition of any contribution from any source is a wicked falsehood."

The result of the election showed that Roosevelt need not have been scared. The Democrats carried no states outside the Solid South, and even Missouri broke precedent by going Republican. The electoral margin was 336 to 140, while Roosevelt's popular majority of 2,540,067 was the largest in the history of presidential elections. The President, who voted at Oyster Bay and then returned to Washington to receive the election returns at the White House, was elated. In the flush of victory he told reporters: "Under no circumstances will I be a candidate for or accept another nomination," a statement which he was to regret later.

To his son Kermit he wrote: "I am stunned by the overwhelming victory we have won. I had no conception such a thing was possible." And to his wife he summed up the cause of his deep satisfaction with the words: "I am no longer a political accident."

THE TRUSTBUSTER

"The Northern Securities suit is one of the great achievements of my administration," wrote Roosevelt to George Cortelyou, and he added, "for through it we emphasized in signal fashion, as in no other way could be emphasized, the fact that the most powerful men in this country were held to accountability before the law." Roosevelt felt that "a moral standard" must be set up for the very rich, who in "their greed and arrogance . . . and the corruption in business and politics have tended to produce a very unhealthy condition of excitement and irritation in the popular mind. . . ." So he wrote in his letter to William Howard Taft on March 15, 1906. Roosevelt focused public attention on the wrongdoing of the trusts, instigating twenty-five suits against them, demanding their dissolution, which led to indictments under the Sherman Act. And the American electorate approved the "trust-busting" President's vigorous fight against the large industrial combinations.

OUCH!—A BERNARD GILLAM CARTOON IN *JUDGE*, APRIL 16, 1904

April 29, 1903:
TAKING HIS CASE BEFORE THE PEOPL
Explaining his legislative program in Hannibal, M

APRIL 2: AT EVANSTON, ILLINOIS

MAY 8: AT LOS ANGELES, CALIFORNIA

THE GREAT WESTERN TOUR
APRIL 1—JUNE 5, 1903

APRIL 8: AT YELLOWSTONE PARK

MAY 17: AT YOSEMITE

JUNE 1: AT OSCEOLA, IOWA

MAY 5: AT SANTA FE, NEW MEXICO

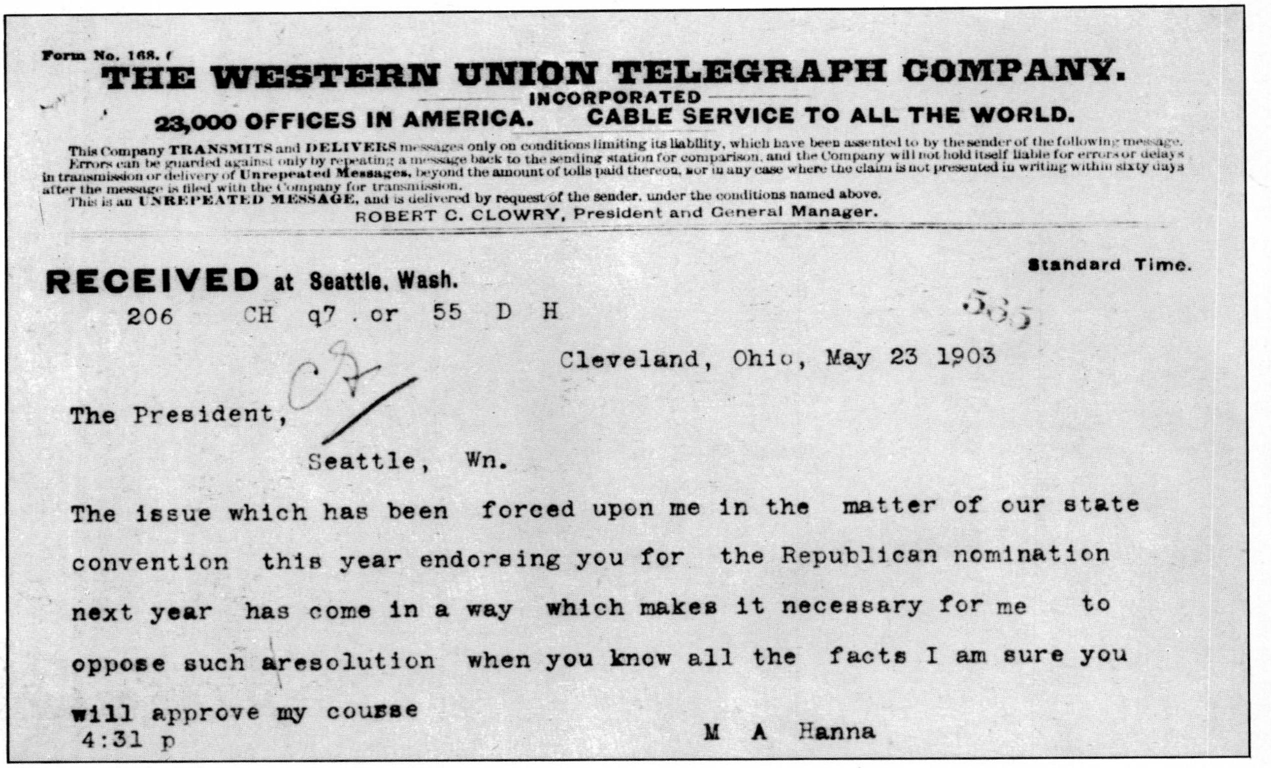

RECEIVED at Seattle, Wash.   Standard Time.
206   CH q7 . or 55 D H   535

Cleveland, Ohio, May 23 1903

The President,

Seattle, Wn.

The issue which has been forced upon me in the matter of our state

convention this year endorsing you for the Republican nomination

next year has come in a way which makes it necessary for me   to

oppose such aresolution when you know all the facts I am sure you

will approve my course
4:31 p   M A Hanna

JOCKEYING FOR THE NOMINATION. While Roosevelt toured the West, attempting to secure his nomination in 1904, politicians intrigued behind the scenes. The man whom Roosevelt most feared was the Republican National Chairman, Senator Mark Hanna of Ohio. He had forebodings that Hanna, supported by conservative Republicans and Wall Street interests, might either become a candidate himself (which Hanna denied) or might block his nomination. When Joseph B. Foraker, the junior senator of Ohio, precipitated a showdown by suggesting that the Ohio State Convention endorse Roosevelt a year ahead of time, Hanna sent the above telegram to the President, who was then in Seattle.

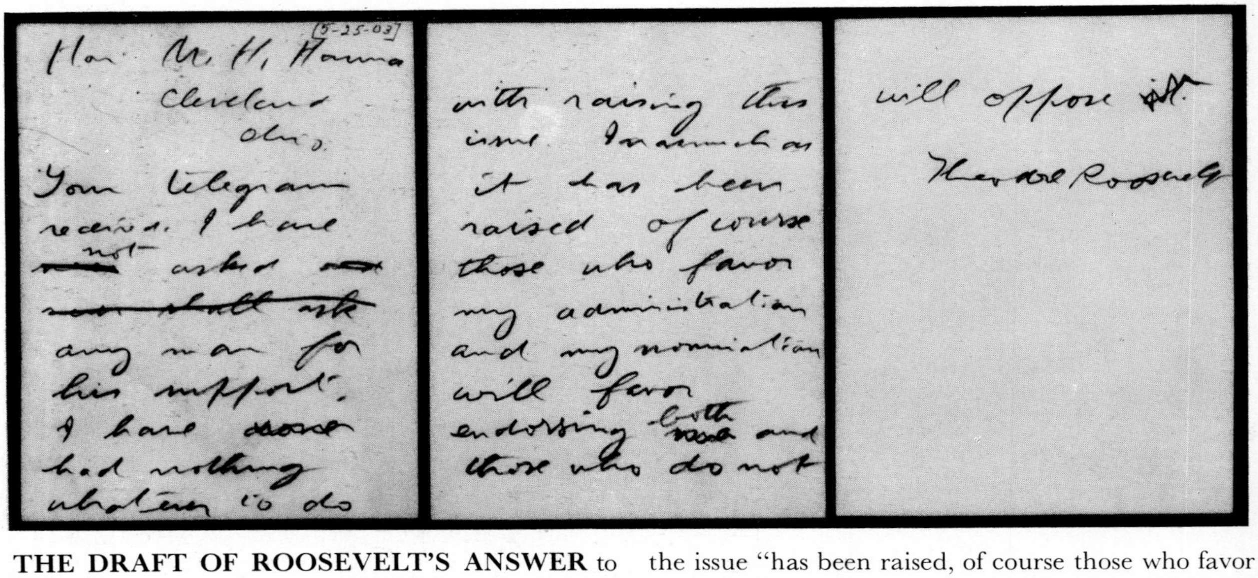

THE DRAFT OF ROOSEVELT'S ANSWER to Senator Hanna. "I have not asked any man for his support," the President told Hanna. But inasmuch as the issue "has been raised, of course those who favor my administration and my nomination will favor endorsing both and those who do not will oppose."

416

THE OUTMANEUVERED HANNA surrendered. Forced by his colleague, Senator Foraker, on one side and by President Roosevelt on the other, he acknowledged defeat. To the President's telegram he answered: "In view of the sentiment expressed I shall not oppose the endorsement of your administration and candidacy by our State Convention."

Roosevelt was elated. He had showed "that the time had come to stop shilly shallying" and he had let the Republican Chairman know "that I did not intend to assume the position, at least passively, of a supplicant to whom he might give the nomination as a boon." And he confessed to intimates that the affair gave him "a new and vivid interest in life."

THE REPUBLICAN TICKET In their Chicago convention the Republicans nominated Theodore Roosevelt for the Presidency and Charles W. Fairbanks of Indiana for the second place.

They were opposed by Alton B. Parker and Henry G. Davis, the choice of the Democrats. Parker, presiding judge of the New York Court of Appeals, was a conservative, "safe and sane" candidate, while the 81-year-old Davis of West Virginia was nothing more than an extremely wealthy man. Still, the opposition could not beat the "unsafe" Roosevelt with the "safe" Parker. Outside the Solid South the Democrats did not carry a single state.

PUTTING THE SCREWS ON! A cartoon by Joseph Keppler in *Puck* shows George B. Cortelyou, the Republican National Chairman, squeezing money out of the trusts. When later an investigation was held, it came to light that 72 per cent of the $2,195,000 which Cortelyou collected for the Republican campaign fund came from large corporations. The directors of Standard Oil contributed $100,000; E. H. Harriman donated $50,000 and collected $200,000 more. J. P. Morgan gave $150,000; George J. Gould, $100,000; Henry C. Frick, $50,000. Joseph Pulitzer's New York *World* wondered publicly whether the reason for the big businessmen's contributions was the hope of buying protection. The newspaper wanted to know how much money the beef, the paper, the coal, the sugar, and other trusts contributed. But Roosevelt and Cortelyou remained silent; they would not answer the *World*.

HE'S GOOD ENOUGH FOR ME! HOMER DAVENPORT'S FAMOUS CARTOON IN 1904.

PRESIDENT ON HIS OWN

NO THIRD TERM! Dalrymple's cartoon in *Judge* refers to Roosevelt's statement which he issued on election night: "On the 4th of March next I shall have served three and a half years and this three and a half years constitutes my first term. The wise custom which limits the President to two terms regards the substance and not the form. Under no circumstances will I be a candidate for or accept another nomination." Years later he told a friend: "I would cut my hand off right there," indicating his wrist, "if I could recall that written statement."

ALL HIS OWN! A CARTOON IN *PUCK*

AVE THEODORE! WAS THE TITLE OF JOS

Inauguration day was a jubilant one for Roosevelt. The night before, he said to a friend: "Tomorrow I shall come into my office in my own right. Then watch out for me!" John Hay, once Lincoln's secretary, presented him with a ring which supposedly contained some of Lincoln's hair, cut from his head after the assassination, and the deeply touched Roosevelt wore it when he took the oath.

Riding down Pennsylvania Avenue, the bands played "There'll Be A Hot Time in the Old Town

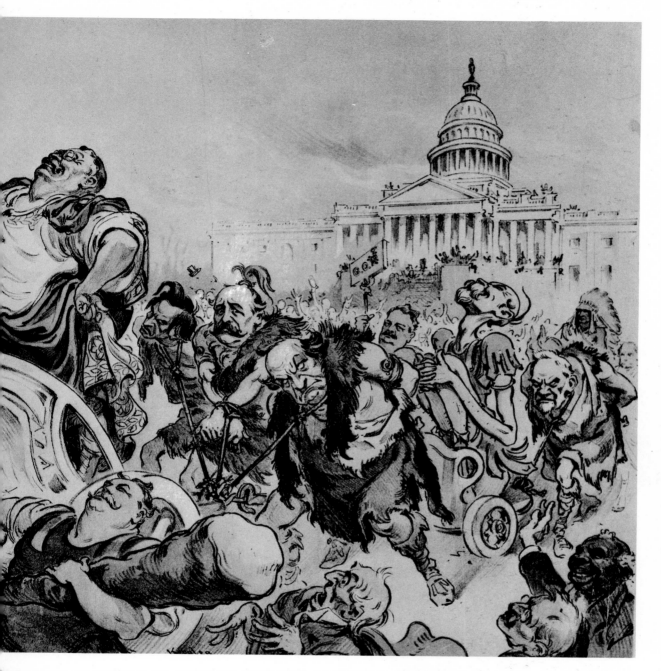

EPPLER'S CARTOON IN *PUCK* IN WHICH ROOSEVELT APPEARED AS ROMAN EMPEROR

Tonight"; thirty members of his old regiment as his special guard of honor were galloping next to his carriage. "And there was every variety of civic organization," he described the event to George Otto Trevelyan in England, "including a delegation of coal miners with a banner recalling that I had settled the anthracite coal strike; Porto Ricans and Philippine Scouts; old-style Indians, in their war paint and with horses painted green and blue and red and yellow, with their war bonnets of eagles' feathers and their spears and tomahawks, followed by the new Indians, the students of Hampton and Carlisle; sixty or seventy cowboys; farmers clubs; mechanics clubs—everybody and everything. Many of my old friends with whom I had lived on the ranches and worked in the roundups in the early days came on to see me inaugurated."

And to his father's brother he wrote: "How I wish Father could have lived to see it too! You stood to me for him and for all that generation . . ."

CHAPTER XXX

AMERICA IN 1905

At the time Theodore Roosevelt was elected to the Vice Presidency—the year was 1900—the *Literary Digest* editorialized: "The ordinary 'horseless carriage' is at present a luxury for the wealthy; and altho its price will probably fall in the future, it will never, of course, come into as common use as the bicycle." Five years later—the year was 1905—when Roosevelt took the oath as President in his own right, this prophecy seemed already absurd. Some 78,000 automobiles were in use across the nation; quantity production methods were already bringing the "rich man's toy" within reach of families of modest income.

These, too, were the years in which man's timeless dream of learning to fly leapt toward incredible fruition. In 1903 the whole world had skeptically watched as a distinguished American scientist, Professor Samuel P. Langley, attempted to launch from atop a houseboat near Widewater, Virginia, a flying machine built with a War Department subsidy. The plane plunged into the sea "like a handful of mortar," fulfilling, as one newspaper put it, the "fondest expectations of its critics." Humorists had a field day; they suggested that the vehicle should have been hitched to the price of beef, that it might have flown had it been launched upside down. "Here is $100,000 of the people's money wasted on this scientific navigation experiment," snorted Congressman Robinson of Indiana, "because some man, perchance a professor wandering in his dreams, was able to impress the officers that his scheme had some utility."

Yet just nine days after Langley's final fiasco, while the world was still laughing, two persistent and mechanically inclined brothers did what the public knew couldn't be done. On December 17, 1903, on the windswept sand dunes of Kitty Hawk, North Carolina, Wilbur and Orville Wright put a flying machine aloft for 12 seconds. The initial flight covered only 120 feet; for the first time a machine carrying a man had flown by its own power.

Almost simultaneously with the birth of the air age came a development that was to rival the automobile in its revolutionary effect on American manners and mores. Before the turn of the century Thomas A. Edison's moving-picture device, the kinetoscope, had been installed in box-like slot machines for the amusement of customers in penny arcades. By 1900 the pictures were being projected on open screens in theaters where they served as "chasers" between vaudeville acts. Three years later the real possibilities of motion pictures were recognized when Edwin S. Porter, Edison's cameraman, produced the melodrama *The Great Train Robbery*. Improvised five-cent theaters known as "nickelodeons" sprang up all over the country, and by the end of the decade movies were well on their way to becoming an established form of entertainment.

The legitimate stage prospered as never before. Maude Adams, Ethel Barrymore, Julia Marlowe, Ada Rehan, Richard Mansfield, William Gillette, John Drew, E. H. Sothern played before full houses. On the musical stage the biggest name was Victor Herbert, whose initial success had come with *Babes in Toyland* in 1903, while Florenz Ziegfeld was preparing to put musical comedy on a new basis with the first of his *Ziegfeld Follies,* produced in 1907. In opera the year 1905 marked the debut of a native American soprano, Geraldine Farrar, and a wave of excitement over the talents of a young Italian tenor, Enrico Caruso, who had completed his first American tour and whose voice would soon be projected through Edison's new-fangled "gramophone" to countless Americans who never saw him in the flesh.

One reason for the growth of the entertainment industry was the fact that the average American of 1905 had more leisure time than his forebears of a generation, or even a decade, earlier. The six-day week was being modified by a half-holiday on Saturday; and while the ten-hour day was still common, the federal government had presaged its passing, specifying an eight-hour day for government contractors. Meanwhile, the new inventions in transportation greatly increased the public's opportunities for the enjoyment of leisure. For a few pennies, city dwellers could take the electric trolley cars to beaches and amusement parks on the outskirts of town. With the increased leisure, also, came an increased interest in sports, and particularly in "spectator sports." Organized baseball, a thriving industry before the turn of the century, was enhanced with the introduction of the World Series in 1903, and college football was already being deplored on the grounds of professionalism and overemphasis. "Baseball and football matches," reported James Bryce in 1905, "excite an interest greater than any other public events except the Presidential election, and that comes only once in four years."

Except for a few genteel diversions like lawn tennis and sidesaddle horseback riding, women were still excluded from most sports. In politics their influence was negligible. Though ex-President Cleveland said that "sensible and responsible women do not want to vote," the "weaker sex" had already obtained that right in Wyoming, Utah, Colorado, and Idaho. More significantly, women were becoming a vital factor in the work force. By the end of the decade more than eight million of them were employed.

In their clothing there was little emancipation. In dry weather skirts were still expected to come within an inch or two of the ground. The bustle was rapidly going out of style (though a newspaper item of 1905 reported that a Minneapolis woman waiting for a train had "lost her bustle in which was five hundred dollars"). Boned collars were much in style, as were "peek-a-boo" waists. Hats were customarily enormous variations on the sailor hat, and hair was curled and puffed up with the aid of "rats" or rolls. In men's clothing dark blue serge was still the standard, and derby hats were reaching a peak of popularity. A few daring men were beginning to wear wrist watches, though this was generally frowned on as a sign of effeminacy.

Despite the phenomenal growth of Chicago and other cities, New York remained the undisputed center of fashion and fashionable society. Along Fifth

Avenue and on Riverside Drive the great barons of the new industrialism displayed their wealth with proud vulgarity in palaces that dwarfed many of the city's public buildings. The Vanderbilt family's mansions occupied six blocks of frontage; Carnegie's establishment at the corner of 91st Street boasted fifty rooms and a miniature golf course; Charles Schwab's residence on Riverside Drive—completed in 1905—contained seventy-five rooms, forty baths, and a refrigerator capable of holding twenty tons of beef; Henry C. Frick's mansion, that was to make Carnegie's "look like a miner's shack," was in construction—when completed nearly a decade later, it had cost close to $17,000,000.

Throughout the first decade of the century Mrs. William Astor remained the unquestioned empress of New York society. Her social prime minister, Ward McAllister (who once said that "a fortune of only a million is respectable poverty"), originated the term "Four Hundred" to describe the number of persons who could be comfortably accommodated in her ballroom; and for the better part of two decades the guest list for her lavishly dull annual ball was accepted as the Who's Who of New York society. Mrs. Astor's principal rival was Mrs. Stuyvesant Fish; her extravagant entertainments presided over by her social factotum, Harry Lehr, included a lavish "dog dinner" at which the dogs of Mrs. Fish's friends were invited to feast on *pâté de foie gras* and similar delicacies. But even Lehr's talent for conspicuous waste was outdone when James Hazen Hyde, the insurance tycoon, staged at Sherry's a $100,000 costume ball modeled in every detail on the court entertainments of Louis XIV.

Such extravagance contrasted bitterly with the poverty of New York's hundreds of thousands of slum dwellers. The effort to provide decent housing for the city's working people had scarcely begun; the population density of more than one thousand persons per acre in lower Manhattan exceeded even the congestion of overpopulated cities of India. In many of the tenements most of the bedrooms were windowless, and bathtubs were a rarity.

To these dark, foul-smelling, demoralizing slums flocked an ever-increasing flood of immigrants from abroad. In 1905, for the first time, the total number of immigrants exceeded one million, with Italy and eastern Europe as the principal sources. Many of the newcomers went to work in the sweatshops of New York; others were absorbed by the textile mills of New England, the steel mills of Pittsburgh, the stockyards of Chicago, and the bituminous coal fields of Pennsylvania. Illiterate and unfamiliar with the law, the immigrant was a natural target for unscrupulous employers and tradesmen. "Right off the boat" became a standard term for a gullible person; it was even reported that one designing New York taxi driver put an immigrant on the Third Avenue elevated, collected several hundred dollars from him, and told him the train would take him to Kansas City.

It was the wide disparity between irresponsible wealth and grinding poverty that bred the progressive movement which began in the early 1890s and gathered its greatest force in the first decades of the twentieth century.

IN NEW YORK CITY

A FASHIONABLE ARTIST'S STUDIO. Charles Dana Gibson, the creator of the popular Gibson girls.

THE CHILDREN'S PLAYGROUND. The youngsters have no eyes for the dead horse on the pavement.

A MOVIE SET in New York's Vitagraph studio, where many of the early film-dramas were made.

THE CHANGING SCENE ON FIFTH AVENUE
Compare this picture taken in 1905 with other Fifth Avenue pictures on pages 190, 276 and 299.

CORRECT FIRST POSITION FOR ENTERING CAR—GRASP GUARD-RAIL WITH LEFT HAND, LIFT SKIRT WITH RIGHT, AND PLACE LEFT FOOT ON STEP.

SECOND POSITION—BRING RIGHT FOOT SMARTLY FROM GROUND INTO CAR, STILL RETAINING HOLD OF RAIL AND SKIRT.

THIRD POSITION—STAND ERECT IN VEHICLE, HOLDING SKIRT WITH BOTH HANDS AND FACING THE FRONT.

FOURTH POSITION—COMFORTABLY SEATED IN THE AUTOMOBILE AND READY FOR THE START.

PROPER WAY TO ALIGHT—GRASP RAIL WITH RIGHT HAND AND SKIRT WITH LEFT—PLACE LEFT FOOT ON STEP AND LOWER RIGHT FOOT TO GROUND.

INCORRECT AND DANGEROUS METHOD—GRASPING DASHBOARD WITH LEFT AND SKIRT WITH RIGHT HAND.

TAKE A LETTER, MISS KINNEY. Women secretaries became the mode. They handled the newfangled devices—the telephone, the typewriter and other office equipment—better than their male counterpart. They were neat, too, in white aprons and starched blouses.

LADIES PREFERRED dark veils to protect their delicate nostrils when playing a game of tennis.

OPERATING TELEPHONES was another of the professions in which the fair sex was predominant.

W TO ENTER THE AUTO

age of photographic instruction

eslie's Weekly, March 31, 1904.

MOVING ON LAND...

MILLIONAIRES TOOK A FANCY TO THE HORSELESS CARRIAGE. At the opening of the century only wealthy people bought automobiles, although the prices of the early vehicles were not prohibitive. Here John Jacob Astor drives one of his first cars.

AN EARLY ADVERTISEMENT. Miss Frances Belmont, one of the girls of the celebrated Floradora Sextet, in an air-cooled Franklin car of 1904. A Floradora girl in an automobile was an advertising man's dream.

FORD IN HIS FIRST CAR
It was in 1896 that the machinist Henry Ford, in a shed behind his Detroit house, came up with a gasoline-engine vehicle. Ford's dream was a universal car, to be sold cheaply and in quantities. In 1903 he organized his own company.

EXPERIMENTS IN FLYING. The brothers Wilbur and Orville Wright took up aeronautics as a pastime. Influenced by the German Otto Lilienthal's experiments, they built gliders; in 1902 they were able to fly their machine for 26 seconds, covering a run of 622½ feet.

THE WRIGHT BROTHERS—Orville and Wilbur —in Europe, where in 1908 and 1909 they demonstrated their machine. In France and in Italy hundreds of thousands turned out to see their plane take to the air. European countries started to manufacture the Wrights' invention, but not until late 1910 did an American company begin to make aeroplanes, producing about two of the craft each month.

THE BICYCLE SHOP in Dayton, Ohio, where the first motor-driven aeroplane was designed. The machine was tested at Kitty Hawk, N.C., on December 17, 1903. It flew! Orville wired his father: "Success four flights Thursday morning all against twenty-one mile wind. Started from level with engine power alone. Average speed through air thirty-one miles longest fifty-nine seconds. Inform press. Home Christmas."

A MEDICAL SCHOOL FOR WOMEN. On January 14, 1904, *Leslie's Weekly* published the above picture of the Woman's Medical College of Pennsylvania, calling it a "remarkable clinic, at which the patient, the operators, and the witnesses were all women."

THE CITY ROOM of the Brooklyn *Daily Eagle* at the time Roosevelt became President "in his own right." The press at this time was overwhelmingly and enthusiastically behind Roosevelt; only a few conservative newspapers, foremost among them the New York *Sun,* were against him. He was riding the crest of the wave; he was at the height of his popularity. Newspapermen were his friends; they admired and they loved him because he gave them colorful copy, he created news, he served them with spicy controversies, zestful excitement, and sheer fun.

"GET A HORSE! AND IF A HORSE IS NOT AVAILABLE, A DONKEY WILL DO!"
As motor cars multiplied, so did the jokes about them. It was easy to make fun of the helpless vehicles bogged down on impossible roads and no experienced mechanic in a hundred miles.

AWE-INSPIRING was the sight of Roy Knabenshue's balloon. On June 30, 1906, the aviator made a successful ascent in his airship at Toledo. He started from the fairgrounds and flew three miles against a heavy wind, and after twenty-five minutes in the air he landed on the roof of a ten-story office building.

Two weeks before, Knabenshue sailed around the dome of the Capitol at Washington. At that time so many senators and representatives left their desks to watch the spectacle that for an hour it was not possible to get a quorum in either assembly.

ENRICO CARUSO (1873–1921)

the Italian grand opera tenor from Naples, the eighteenth son of his parents and the first who survived infancy, opened his first season at the Metropolitan Opera on November 21, 1903, singing in *Rigoletto*. The world of music immediately acclaimed him.

MAUDE ADAMS (1872–1953)

became the darling of theater audiences when she played Peter Pan in the fairy tale by James Barrie, which ran on Broadway from the fall of 1903 until the summer of 1906. After that she appeared in *Quality Street, What Every Woman Knows,* and other Barrie plays.

FLORADORA was one of the most successful musicals at the turn of the century. It starred six attractive, vivacious, and charming young ladies—the Floradora Sextet—who soon became the talk of the nation. It was opened in 1901, continued the following year, and before it closed had chalked up a record of 547 performances. After New York, the company played most of the big cities of America. At the tour's end in 1905 the popular demand in New York was still so great that the musical was obliged to return to Broadway.

ETHEL BARRYMORE (1879–1959)
the daughter of Maurice and Georgiana Drew Barrymore and the sister of John and Lionel, belonged to
the celebrated "royal family" of actors. In 1905,
around Roosevelt's inauguration, she appeared in
Ibsen's *A Doll's House*. "Ibscene," wrote one critic.

THE SEASON OF 1905 was studded with remark-
able dramatic plays. Mrs. Fiske played with George
Arliss of London (on the right) in *Leah Kleschna*.
David Warfield drew packed houses with *The Music
Master*, held over from the previous year. Forbes
Robertson played Hamlet, "the only Hamlet of the
modern world." Sarah Bernhardt played *Magda*,
Sappho, *Phèdre*, and *La Dame aux Camelias*. Bernard
Shaw's *Mrs. Warren's Profession* was suppressed by the
police after its first showing in New York on October 31.

LILLIAN RUSSELL (1861–1922)
was the toast of Broadway when she played Lady
Teazle in the musical version of Sheridan's *The School
for Scandal*. On the stage since 1879, she thrilled
audiences not only with her beauty and acting, but
with the amorous adventures of her private life.

SOCIETY. Members of the elegant Four Hundred have a friendly chat before the Casino of Newport, R.I., which was then one of the most fashionable summer resorts of the nation.

THE VANDERBILTS

Millionaire Alfred Gwynne Vanderbilt I was a coaching enthusiast. Once, in 1901, he and James Hazen Hyde raced their tallyhos from New York to Philadelphia. The race required 78 horses; it took 9 hours 25 minutes one way and 10 hours 10 minutes for the other, with a six-minute "rest" between. Next to Vanderbilt is his first wife, Elsie French, who divorced him in 1908, receiving a settlement of ten million dollars. Behind him, in the center, is his sister Gladys, who later became the wife of the celebrated Hungarian diplomat Count László Széchenyi.

TENNIS ENTHUSIASTS. Alice Roosevelt, the leading light of American society, arrives with two of her friends at the Newport Casino to be a spectator at the seasonal matches.

THE HARRIMANS

Railroad executive Edward Henry Harriman, like other prominent New Yorkers of wealth, enjoyed the sport of driving a four-in-hand. Coaching clubs, imitating their English counterparts, became the order of the day. Madison Square and the nearby hostelries were the center of the coaching fraternity. From clubs and other approved stations the drags paraded up Fifth Avenue, entering Central Park at 59th Street. On the sidewalks crowds watched the picturesque prancing of the four horses, the immaculate drivers, and their beautifully dressed lady companions.

CONEY ISLAND WAS THE MOST POPULAR HOT-WEATHER PLACE

BY THE SEA, by the sea, by the beautiful sea,
You and I, you and I, oh! how happy we'll be!
When each wave comes a-rolling in,
We will duck or swim, and we'll float and fool around the water . . ."

THE SUMMERS WERE HOT, vacations were short. One worked six days a week on an average of ten hours a day. Families traveled little—the cheap Ford was not yet available. An outing to Coney Island on the streetcars was an event long to be remembered. Mother cooked and packed a huge picnic lunch. And what a picnic it was! Even Father had to admit that Mother's cooking was best.

439

THE
FAIR
SEX
IN THE
EARLY
PART
OF THE
CENTURY

RICH GIRLS. A society darling (on the left), the only one of the fabulous Cryder triplets still unmarried, poses for the photographer in a hansom at New York's Central Park.

★

SPORT GIRLS. Georgiana Bishop (on the right) won the Women's Amateur Golf Championship in 1904 against Mrs. L. Callan, whose powerful swings were a wee bit short.

WORKING GIRLS. A charming photograph of four stenographers enjoying their luncheon break in downtown New York. It was taken by the photographer Edwin Levick in 1903.

MARK TWAIN'S BIRTHDAY

NEW YORK'S LITERATI celebrated Mark Twain's seventieth birthday at Delmonico's restaurant on December 5, 1905. The lady on the right is Emily Post. Around the table clockwise are James MacArthur, John A. Mitchell, May Sinclair, S. M. Gardenshire, Hamilton W. Mabie.

★

ANOTHER TABLE OF WELL-WISHERS. Clockwise from the center: Florence Morse Kingsley, Philip Verrill Mighels, Frederick Trevor Hill, Frances Powell Case, Edwin Markham, and Churchill Williams. On the right, before the window, Dorothy Canfield and William D. Orcutt.

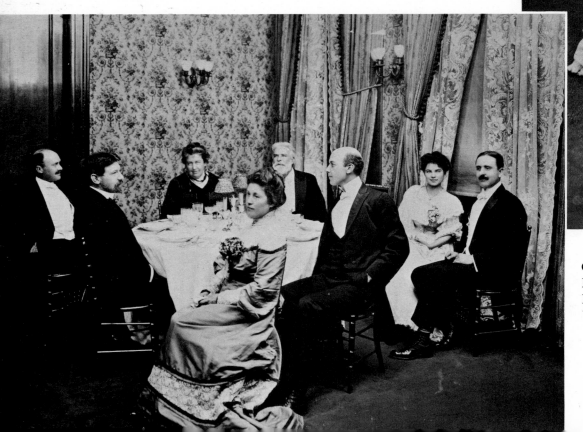

ON NOVEMBER
MARK TWAIN
BECAME SEVEN
YEARS OLD

THE CELEBRANT AND HIS FRIENDS

Clockwise from Mark Twain are Kate Douglas Riggs, Rev. Joseph H. Twichell, Bliss Carman, Ruth Mc-Enery Stuart, Henry Mills Alden, Henry H. Rogers, and Mary E. Wilkins Freeman.

Theodore Roosevelt was invited to attend the dinner, but he sent his regrets. Once he called Mark Twain a "prize idiot" (because of his stand on the China issue), another time "a man wholly without cultivation and without any real historical knowledge" (because of his book on King Arthur's Court). But now that the writer had reached the age of seventy, the President thought him "one of the citizens whom all Americans should delight to honor. . . . May he live long, and year by year may he add to the sum of admirable work that he has done."

AND THE IMMIGRANTS POURED IN. The country offered opportunities and the promise of a good life. In the year 1905 the number of immigrants who came from Europe was 1,026,499, the majority Italians but a large number from Hungary, Slovakia, Poland, and Western Russia. The largest number of immigrants arriving at the shores of the New World was recorded in May, when in a single day 12,039 disembarked in New York Harbor. America was growing with great speed; it needed men to work, it needed men to build.

CHAPTER XXXI

PEACEMAKER

"In foreign affairs we must make up our minds that, whether we wish it or not, we are a great people and must play a great part in the world. It is not open to us to choose whether we will play that part or not. We have to play it. All we can decide is whether we shall play it well or ill."

This expressed one of Roosevelt's deepest convictions. That he spoke thus in 1905 was appropriate, for it was in that year that he stepped into the role of global statesman. On two sides of the world he played the peacemaker between great powers: in the Far East, where he stage-managed the treaty that ended the Russo-Japanese War, and in North Africa, where he played a leading part in de-fusing the Moroccan crisis and averting, at least temporarily, a military showdown between the colonial powers of Europe.

In handling the foreign policy reins, Roosevelt was considerably aided by his close personal friendship with two foreign diplomats whose honesty and discretion he relied upon heavily. One was Count Speck von Sternburg, known affectionately as "Specky" to the Roosevelts since 1890, a bright young aristocrat who had been made secretary of the German legation in Washington at the President's suggestion. The second was Cecil Spring-Rice, the "Springy" who was best man at Roosevelt's second marriage in England and who, as a British diplomat stationed at St. Petersburg, was now a trusted if roundabout middleman between the White House and No. 10 Downing Street. He also developed a close friendship with Jules Jusserand, the French Ambassador in Washington. These close relationships established the direct lines of communication which the President needed for his personal style of diplomacy.

The first challenge to his diplomatic skill came from the Far East, where the Russo-Japanese War had begun in February 1904. The roots of the war were many and tangled, but the major cause was a bitter commercial rivalry in North China and Manchuria. Czar Nicholas of Russia had been tacitly encouraged in his truculent Far Eastern policies by Kaiser Wilhelm II of Germany, who tried to divert Russia from Germany's eastern frontier.

At first, President Roosevelt was pleased with the succession of Japanese victories. He believed that Japan's growing strength in the Far East constituted a healthy counterweight to Russian power. And he had a low regard for Czar Nicholas, whom he thought "a preposterous little creature."

But as the Japanese success took on the complexion of an unqualified Russian rout, Roosevelt's satisfaction with the war began to wane. Though his sympathies were with Japan, he realized that an overwhelming victory by either side would make an added threat to the territorial integrity of China and to American interests in the Philippines. Thus, when the Japanese captured Port Arthur in the first month of 1905 and proceeded to their victory at Mukden, Roosevelt felt that the war must be brought to an end. He was not alone in this view. The French were getting alarmed; the Kaiser, too, felt things had gone far enough; and even the Japanese were finding the war a heavy strain on their manpower and economy. Moreover, France and England were by this time beginning to fear that they might need Russia's help against Germany in the event that the crisis which was beginning to shape up in Morocco took a desperate turn.

At first, to peace overtures both Russia and Japan turned a deaf ear. Neither country was ready to enter negotiations. Roosevelt kept sounding out the belligerents without success. However, after the Japanese won a smashing naval victory in the Sea of Japan in May—a victory Roosevelt termed more overwhelming than Trafalgar or even the defeat of the Spanish Armada—Japan notified the American President that it would accept his good offices as a mediator for peace. Two weeks later, in a letter to Senator Lodge, Roosevelt was still picturing Russia as "so corrupt, so treacherous and shifty, and so incompetent, that I am utterly unable to say whether or not it will make peace." Nevertheless, both Russia and Japan agreed to send plenipotentiaries to a conference in the United States. "I have led the horses to water, but heaven only knows whether they will drink or start kicking one another beside the trough," wrote Roosevelt to a friend.

Meanwhile, an interesting—though unpublicized—footnote had been added to the complex negotiations. Secretary of War Taft, who had stopped off in Japan on his way to the Philippine Islands, received assurances that Japan had no interest in the Philippines. Taft, on the other hand, told the Japanese Prime Minister that the United States concurred with Anglo-Japanese policy in the Far East and had no objection if Japan would exercise suzerainty over the unstable Korean empire. This secret understanding was significant both as an example of Roosevelt's free-wheeling diplomatic methods and as a further demonstration of his partiality in the Russo-Japanese controversy.

On August 5, 1905, the Russian and Japanese envoys were formally received by the President in the wardroom of the U.S.S. *Mayflower,* anchored in the harbor at Oyster Bay. The ceremony was so carefully planned that even the wardroom chairs were removed from around the table lest there be any controversy about precedence in seating arrangements. At the close of the buffet luncheon the President proposed a solemn toast to "a just and lasting peace," after which the envoys departed for Portsmouth, New Hampshire, to begin their peace conference.

Three weeks of negotiation brought forth the agreement that Japan was to be given Port Arthur and a protectorate in Korea. However, Russia firmly refused to pay an indemnity as desired by Japan. When the conference seemed about to founder on this issue, Roosevelt persuaded both sides to accept a compromise under which Japan waived indemnities in exchange for the southern half of the island of Sakhalin, off the Siberian coast. The proposal was accepted, and on September 5 the delegates signed the peace treaty. The world looked upon Roosevelt as a great man; congratulations came to him from kings and commoners alike. In England, Edward VII told the American Ambassador that he was "simply lost in admiration for the President."

Even before the Russo-Japanese peace was signed, Roosevelt had stepped into the middle of another great-power dispute by settling an ugly controversy that had arisen over control of the nominally "independent" state of Morocco. The President's role in this drama was played so secretly that its full import did not become known until many years later; but in the opinion of Secretary Root it was of far greater importance to the world than his role in ending the Russo-Japanese War. To the extent that the Moroccan settlement staved off World War I and helped bind us irrevocably to the Anglo-French alliance, this judgment seemed to be based on solid foundation.

In essence, the Moroccan crisis was an offspring of French acquisitiveness and German frustration. At the turn of the century all the major European powers had extensive commercial interests in Morocco, when in 1904 England and France signed a treaty designed to freeze out their rivals. Under the publicly announced provisions of the treaty, England agreed to give France a free hand in Morocco in exchange for a free British hand in Egypt; under secret provisions, which came to light later, the two powers agreed to Morocco's eventual partitioning. To the ambitious Kaiser Wilhelm of Germany, this Anglo-French entente looked like another crucial step in the dreaded encirclement of his imperial dreams. He visited Morocco and expressed hopes for the independence of that state. Now, France refused the Kaiser's demand for a conference to discuss neutral rights in Morocco, and her decision was backed by England.

The shaken Kaiser turned to Roosevelt, asking for his intervention in behalf of his proposal for a conference, arguing that all he sought in Morocco was an "open door" policy of the sort America supported in China. The Kaiser's message reached Roosevelt while he was on a hunting trip in Colorado. His first inclination was to do nothing. But when he returned to Washington, all signs pointed toward a European war. Such a conflagration, Roosevelt knew, would wreck his pacification efforts in the Far East. Thus, he accepted the Kaiser's request and interfered in the conflict. He asked the French Ambassador to persuade his government to agree to a Moroccan conference that would allow the Kaiser "to save his face." The result of Roosevelt's proposal was the Algeciras Conference, where Henry White represented the American interests. To him Roosevelt wrote: "I want to keep on good terms with Germany and if possible to prevent a rupture between Germany and France. But my sympathies have at bottom been with France and I suppose will continue so." At the conference table America's weight generally leaned toward the Anglo-French side, and Germany had to settle for small crumbs of prestige. The Kaiser got his conference, and France got Morocco.

The value of President Roosevelt's two great foreign policy adventures of 1905 is open to dispute. Yet the fact remains that in both the Far East and North Africa the immediate effect of his interventions was peace.

THE RUSSO-JAPANESE WAR

JAPANESE OBSERVERS watch the effect of the Japanese guns on Port Arthur from a balloon.

THE HUMAN PYRAMID of Japanese so storms over a high stone wall outside Port Ar

THE RUSSIAN ARMY marches through Manchuria. A photograph by war correspondent Bulla.

1200 JAPANESE DEAD littered the battl after the savage battle of Tashihkiao on Jun

The war began on February 9, 1904, with Japan's night attack on the Russian fleet in Port Arthur. The Japanese fleet, commanded by Vice-Admiral Togo, inflicted heavy losses on the Russians and bottled up their fleet inside the harbor. Hearing the news, Roosevelt wrote to his eldest son: "I was thoroughly well pleased with the Japanese victory, for Japan is playing our game." In his opinion, Russia had "behaved very badly in the Far East, her attitude toward all nations including us, but

AMPAGNE AND SHELLS. A Russian officers'
y in Port Arthur is disrupted by enemy fire.

MANTLET AND SHEARS. Japanese soldiers hiding behind mantlets destroy Russian barbed wire.

HE PALACE OF THE CZAR. Ladies of the
ocracy sew garments for the Russian wounded.

MOBILIZATION IN SIBERIA. An artist of the
French *L'Illustration* depicts soldiers leaving Omsk.

especially toward Japan, being grossly overbearing."
A week later he told Elihu Root that "the Japs
showed themselves past masters in the practical
application of David Harum's famous gloss on the
'Do unto others' injunction. They did it fust! Oh, if
only our people would learn the need of preparedness, and of shaping things so that decision and
action can alike be instantaneous. Mere bigness, if it
is also mere flabbiness, means nothing but disgrace."
But as the war went on, Roosevelt's attitude changed.

THE PRESIDENT IN COLORADO

After Roosevelt instructed the American Ambassador in Russia to offer his services to bring about peace between Russia and Japan, he left Washington on April 4 for a hunting trip in the Southwest. Before his departure he assured the country that there was no need to worry as he had "left Taft sitting on the lid," a phrase which was gleefully acknowledged by political commentators and cartoonists.

Four days later he sent Taft a confidential note from "En Route," saying that he expected the Japanese would materially increase their demands after their victory over the Russians under General Kuropatkin at Mukden. "My own view is that the Russians would do well to close with them even now; but the Czar knows neither how to make war nor to make peace. If he had an ounce of sense he would have acted upon my suggestion last January and have made peace then. There is nothing for us to do now but to sit still and wait events."

And while he waited for events to develop, he had "unalloyed pleasure" in "coursing wolves in Oklahoma," being in the saddle for eight or nine hours every day. Then he journeyed to Colorado for a long-anticipated bear hunt with his friends Dr. Alexander Lambert and Phil Stuart (riding behind him).

THE KAISER IN TANGIER

Wilhelm II's visit in Morocco at the end of March 1905 and his remark in Tangier that the Sultan of Morocco was an independent monarch created great apprehension in European diplomatic circles. It was only a year previously that France and England had made a secret agreement to eliminate German interest in Morocco, and now the German Kaiser came

out as protector of the Sultan—an ill omen for the future and for peace. It was rumored that Germany and Russia were secretly allied, and though these rumors proved to be untrue, the mere possibility of a German-Russian alliance made France tremble with fright. She needed Russia's friendship; she needed that country as an ally against Germany. And Great Britain, in her desire to keep the balance of power in Europe, was also fervently courting Russia. Thus, diplomats, ambassadors, foreign ministers in the European capitals maneuvered for position. As all three great European powers sought Russia's friendship, they had a vital interest in the cessation of the Russo-Japanese War. It remained for Roosevelt to be the peacemaker and bring representatives of the two warring nations to a conference in America.

451

芝離宮に於ける米國佳賓及接待員

後列　中佐リイ氏　大佐エドワーダ氏　少將リブツス氏　寺島伯　陸軍大將タフト氏　大尉トムソン氏　松手式部官　大將クレール氏

前列　ポ一トルマシ嬢　寺島伯爵夫人　ルーズヴエルト嬢　宮崎中宮内官間夫人　ツミラソン嬢

ROOSEVELT'S ENVOY IN JAPAN. William Howard Taft and his party, among them Roosevelt's daughter Alice (in the center), visited Japan in the summer of 1905 on the way to the Philippines. Taft urged the Japanese to make peace with the Russians.

MUTSUHITO, EMPEROR OF JAPAN, WITH HIS WIFE, AND HIS SON

THE PEACEMAKER. On August 5, 1905, President Roosevelt arrived at the *Mayflower,* lying in the harbor of Oyster Bay, to meet the Japanese and Russian envoys. "Whether they will be able to come to an agreement or not I can't say. . . . Of course Japan will want to ask more than she ought to ask, and Russia to give less than she ought to give. . . . But there is a chance that they will prove sensible, and make a peace, which will really be for the interest of each as things are now." Thus wrote Roosevelt to his son Kermit. The delegates left in separate ships for Portsmouth, N.H., the place of the peace conference.

RUSSIA AND JAPAN MAKE PEACE

MEETING THE ENVOYS of Japan and Russia on board the *Mayflower* at Oyster Bay before they began their conferences. On the left, the leaders of Russia's delegation: Count Witte and Baron Rosen; on the right, the Japanese Baron Komura and Minister Takahira.

Once Roosevelt wrote to his friend Lodge: "The more I see of the Czar, the Kaiser and the Mikado, the better I am content with democracy, even if we have to include the American newspaper as one of its assets—liability would be a better term."

ENOUGH OF THE BLOODSHED!—a Spanish cartoon in Barcelona's *Hojas Selectas*. "Now, be good, boys, and throw yourselves at the feet of this divinity." Roosevelt, though attacked by Japan for not letting her secure an indemnity, was hailed by the civilized world. For his contribution in bringing Japan and Russia together, he was the first American statesman to receive the Nobel Peace Prize.

THE PEACE NEGOTIATIONS BETWEEN

On Roosevelt's insistence the representatives of the two warring nations sat down at a conference table to negotiate the terms of peace. In front are the Japanese envoys: Messrs. Adatchi and Otchai, Baron Jutaro Komura, Minister for Foreign Affairs, Minister Kogoro Takahira, Aimaro Sato. On the opposite side of the table, the Russians: Mr. Plancon, C. Nabokoff, Count Serge Witte, Baron Roman Rosen, Russian Ambassador to the United States, J. J. Korostovetz.

After the peace treaty was concluded, Roosevelt

RUSSIA AND JAPAN BEGAN IN PORTSMOUTH, NEW HAMPSHIRE, ON AUGUST 9, 1905

was blamed by both Russia and Japan of bringing the war to an end prematurely. "The Russians claimed that they were just getting into their stride, while the Japanese asserted that had the war continued a few months more they would have been able to obtain a huge indemnity." But Roosevelt knew that "The truth was that the Japanese had to have peace. Their money was exhausted. So was their credit. . . . When I intervened Japan was on the verge of collapse. She was bled white." And Russia was in no better state. "If the war went on," so

Roosevelt thought, it was "likely that Russia would be driven west of Lake Baikal."

In the treaty of peace, signed on August 23, the Russians agreed to cede half of Sakhalin to Japan, surrender their lease of the Kwantung Peninsula and Port Arthur, evacuate Manchuria, and recognize Japan's suzerainty in Korea.

Roosevelt felt the securing of the peace greatly increased America's prestige, "and as far as I am personally affected I have received infinitely more praise for it than in my opinion I deserve. . . ."

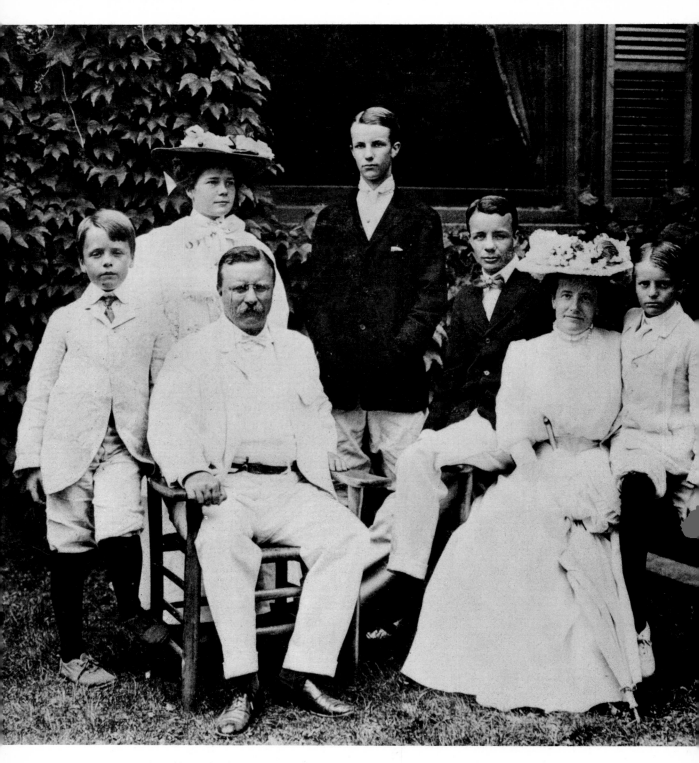

THE FAMILY AT SAGAMORE HILL IN 1907. The children from left to right: Quentin, Ethel, Kermit, Theodore, Jr., and Archibald. "Home, wife, children," wrote Roosevelt some years later to his eldest son, "they are what really count in life. I have heartily enjoyed many things; the Presidency, my success as a soldier, a writer, a big game hunter and explorer; but all of them put together are not for one moment to be weighed in the balance when compared with the joy I have known with your mother and all of you. . . ."

456

CHAPTER XXXII

FAMILY MAN

If the years of Theodore Roosevelt's Presidency were told only in terms of political controversies and diplomatic adventures, the story would not be complete. His public policies shaped our national development and projected us into a new role in world affairs, yet they were only one measure of a personality that was unique in its time and, indeed, in American history.

No other President has rivaled his diversity of interests or his physical energy; and none made a deeper imprint on the outlook and opinions of his contemporaries. "Roosevelt, more than any other living man within the range of notoriety," said Henry Adams, "showed the singular primitive quality that belongs to ultimate matter—the quality that mediaeval theology assigned to God—he was pure act." And he was not only in the political field "pure act." He had opinions on almost every subject and an extraordinary flair for expressing them forcefully. As one national magazine summed it up in 1906: "The scrapes he gets into, the scrapes he gets out of; the things he attempts, the things he accomplishes, the things he demolishes; his appointments and his disappointments; the rebukes that he administers and those he receives; his assumptions, presumptions, omnisciences and deficiencies, make up a daily tale which those of us who survive his tenure of the presidential office will doubtless miss, as we might miss some property of the atmosphere we breathe." Julian Street spoke for millions in labeling him "the most interesting American," and John Morley, the British historian, after a visit to the White House said: "The two things in America which seem to me the most extraordinary are Niagara Falls and President Roosevelt."

Roosevelt was an omniverous reader of books and periodicals, and he talked about them constantly. Writers who spoke critically of him were likely to receive long letters of rebuttal; authors whose work interested him were asked to the White House to discuss their ideas. "I am delighted to show any courtesy to Pierpont Morgan or Andrew Carnegie or James J. Hill," the President once remarked in explaining his guest lists, "but as for regarding any one of them as, for instance, I regard Professor Bury, or Peary, the arctic explorer, or Rhodes, the historian—why, I could not force myself to do it, even if I wanted to, which I don't." He liked to surround himself with people of thought rather than people of wealth. As Owen Wister put it, "For once in our history, we had an American salon."

The President regarded the White House as "a bully pulpit," and the preaching from his pulpit was not limited to political matters alone. He preached the virtue of simplified spelling, though Congress indignantly rebelled when he ordered the Government Printer to adopt such phonetic changes as "tho" for "though" and "thru" for "through." He preached with equal vigor against what he termed the "nature fakers" who wrote what purported to be factual children's books attributing human emotions and reasoning powers to animals. He preached the doctrine of the strenuous life, with daily demonstrations to the delight of the public and cartoonists. He preached, also, the virtues of large families and the sacredness of the American home.

He was a moralist, firmly believing in moral principles. He wrote: "If courage and strength and intellect are unaccompanied by the moral purpose, the moral sense, they become merely forms of expression for unscrupulous force and unscrupulous cunning. If the strong man has not in him the lift toward lofty things his strength makes him only a curse to himself and to his neighbor." And he said to his son Kermit: "If a man does not have an ideal and try to live up to it, then he becomes a mean, base and sordid creature, no matter how successful." For Theodore Roosevelt "morality, decency, clean living, courage, manliness, self-respect—these qualities are more important in the make-up of a people than any mental subtlety." He pleaded: "We ought not to tolerate wrong. It is a sign of weakness to do so, and in its ultimate effects weakness is often quite as bad as wickedness. But in putting a stop to wrong we should, so far as possible, avoid getting into an attitude of vindictive hatred toward the wrongdoer." Such were his fundamental tenets, forming a base to his philosophy on life.

He believed in the sanctity of marriage. He said: "When the ordinary decent man does not understand that to marry the woman he loves, as early as he can, is the most desirable of all goals, the most successful of all forms of life entitled to be called really successful; when the ordinary woman does not understand that all other forms of life are but makeshift and starveling substitutes for the life of the happy wife, the mother of a fair-sized family of healthy children; then the state is rotten at heart." He was against divorce and argued his point. "I do unqualifiedly condemn easy divorce. I know that the effect on the 'Four Hundred' of easy divorce has been very bad. It has been shocking to me to hear young girls about to get married calmly speculating on how long it will be before they get divorces." He was for families, the larger the merrier. "The woman who shrinks from motherhood is as low a creature as a man of the professional pacifist, or poltroon type, who shirks his duty as a soldier." But he had decided opinions about the offspring of "the wrong people." He wished that "the wrong people could be prevented entirely from breeding; and when the evil nature of these people is sufficiently flagrant, this should be done. Criminals should be sterilized, and feeble-minded persons forbidden to leave offspring behind them."

For the role of the wife in the family he had great respect. "I have mighty little use for the man who is always declaiming in favor of an eight-hour day for himself who does not think anything at all of having a sixteen-hour day for his wife." And he held that males must share responsibility in bringing up children. Once he asked a naturalist whether the male wolf took any interest in the female during pregnancy and whether he ever took care of the cubs.

When the naturalist said that he had observed the wolf doing both Roosevelt shouted in delight: "I'm glad to hear it! I think better of him."

In matters of morality Roosevelt assiduously practiced what he preached, and nowhere was this more evident than in his family life, which was a separate and hallowed compartment of his existence. "I have had the happiest home life of any man I have ever known," he once wrote, and he regarded it as perhaps the greatest achievement of his career. Writing to his son Kermit, after the 1904 election, he said: "It was a great comfort to feel, all during the last days when affairs looked doubtful, that no matter how things came out the really important thing was the lovely life I have with Mother and you children, and that compared to this home life everything else was of very small importance from the standpoint of happiness." He never—so his daughter says—showed the slightest interest in any woman other than his wife. He was the cleanest-living man. In his entire life there were but two women —Alice, his first wife, and, after her death, Edith, his second. And even before he married Edith, he went through soul-searching agonies, walking the floor for three days, "pounding one fist into the other palm, expostulating the while to himself: 'I have no constancy. I have no constancy.'"

He adored his family. His children shared his exuberance, and this produced a continuous flow of colorful newspaper stories. The nation read with delight about Quentin smuggling Algonquin, a calico pony, up the White House elevator and into his brother's bedroom, or his scaring the wits out of some Congressmen by bringing a four-foot king snake into the anteroom of his father's office. When Archie, whose engaging personality made him the public's particular favorite, nearly died of diphtheria shortly after his thirteenth birthday, the New York *Times* said that "all Washington, on getting up these mornings, eagerly scans the newspaper with the query, 'How's Archie?'"

Early in Roosevelt's Presidency the New York *Herald* reported: "It has been an extraordinary change for the strenuous young Roosevelts, this transformation from the quiet country life of Oyster Bay to the dazzling, bewildering atmosphere of the national capital." Actually, the "quiet life of Oyster Bay" was not entirely lost to the Roosevelt children when their father became President. The rambling house at Sagamore Hill became the summer White House; and despite the ever-present Secret Service men and the streams of official visitors who made their way up the hill from the village railroad station, life there remained in most respects as idyllic as ever. "There could be no healthier and pleasanter place in which to bring up children," Roosevelt wrote in his *Autobiography*. "It was real country and—speaking from the somewhat detached point of view of the masculine parent—I should say there was just the proper mixture of freedom and control in the management of the children. They were never allowed to be disobedient or to shirk lessons or work; and they were encouraged to have all the fun possible. They often went barefoot, especially during the many hours passed in various enthralling pursuits along and in the waters of the bay. They swam, they tramped, they boated, they coasted and skated in winter, they were intimate friends with the cows, chickens, pigs and other live stock."

He entered into their pastimes with the enthusiasm of a man who was always half child himself. It was truly a remarkable sight, reported a visiting newspaper man from Chicago, to see "the President of the United States at the head of this young band of savages on their way to the woods or to the target grounds." For the Roosevelt children and their numerous small cousins (the J. West Roosevelts and the Emlen Roosevelts were Sagamore Hill neighbors), the big event of the summer was the annual overnight camping trip down the bay—a trip that was always under the personal command of "Father," who prepared the supper and told stories of his Western adventures around the campfire before his charges fell asleep under the stars. And no matter how heavy the press of official business, nothing was permitted to interfere with the leisurely family breakfast each morning or with the walk or drive which he took every afternoon with his wife, whose serene and well-ordered management of the Sagamore Hill household was a constant and valued counterweight to his exuberance.

In her role as first lady Mrs. Roosevelt shied away from the limelight, devoting much of her attention to the task of trying to keep its glare from interfering with a normal upbringing for the children. Inevitably, her very lack of ostentation exposed her to some feline jibes. Mrs. Stuyvesant Fish, the New York society leader, remarked: "The wife of the President, it is said, dresses on $300 a year, and she looks it." But for the most part the nation respected her self-effacing traits, and her friends spoke with admiration of her graciousness and her effectiveness as a sage if unobtrusive partner to her husband in affairs of state as well as affairs of the family. "Never, when he had his wife's judgment, did he go wrong or suffer disappointment," said Mark Sullivan.

Next to the President himself, easily the most colorful member of the family was the headstrong and imperious Alice, a young lady of 17 at the time the Roosevelts moved into the White House. Intelligent, beautiful, vigorously independent, she soon found the heady life of the rich far more to her liking than the wholesome atmosphere of Sagamore Hill. Writing to his sister Corinne at the end of the summer of 1903, the President mentioned that Alice had been "spending most of her time in Newport and elsewhere, associating with the Four Hundred—individuals with whom the other members of her family have exceedingly few affiliations." The newspapers, in which she was referred to as "Princess Alice," kept an amused and generally admiring audience of millions informed of her adventures—her romances, her irrepressible comments on the passing scene, her trips about the countryside at the dizzying speed of thirty miles an hour in a Panhard racer automobile. When she openly smoked a cigarette, it was the sensation of the year. Her name was appropriated by the clothing trade, which produced the new shade of "Alice blue," just as her father's nickname had been used by the makers of "Teddy bears."

"I can do one of two things," Roosevelt once remarked to a friend with mock concern. "I can be President of the United States or I can control Alice. I cannot possibly do both." In the summer of 1905 Alice joined Mr. and Mrs. William Howard Taft and a delegation of Congressmen and wives in a much-publicized tour of the Far East; and the following February she married one of the gentlemen who was with the party on the voyage—Congressman Nicholas Longworth, talented scion of one of Ohio's first families.

The "strenuous life" which Roosevelt both preached and practiced was not only strenuous physically but intellectually as well. It was significant that the devoted group of younger officials who surrounded and advised him during his White House years were popularly named the "Tennis Cabinet"—an apt term to distinguish them from the older and less vigorous men who comprised the regular Cabinet. Nothing short of the gravest affairs of state was allowed to interfere with his daily exercise, though he would not permit photographers to take his picture on the tennis court. At Sagamore Hill the tennis was supplemented by riding, rowing, lumbering, and hiking. In Washington he rode or hiked when time and weather permitted; or if confined to the White House, he practiced boxing, wrestling, and jujitsu. It was as a result of a boxing bout at the White House that he all but lost the sight of his left eye.

Of all the President's outdoor pastimes, perhaps the most characteristic of all were his "obstacle walks," a form of exercise which he first devised at Sagamore Hill to entertain and toughen his children and their cousins. The rules were simple; the hikers proceeded from the starting point to the objective in a beeline without stopping and without permitting any natural obstacle to divert their course. In Washington the "obstacle walks" were generally taken at Rock Creek, and it was counted a considerable honor—though an exhausting one—to be invited to accompany him. It was partly as an outgrowth of this pastime that he tried on one occasion to combat the indolent habits of the swivel-chair Army officers in Washington by issuing an order that they must establish their physical fitness by marching fifty miles in a three-day period or, in the case of cavalry officers, riding one hundred miles in the same period. When the order was widely attacked as tyrannical and capricious, the President, in company with three Army officers, rode more than one hundred miles in a single day over the back roads of Virginia through freezing rain and sleet to prove that the test was not unduly demanding.

It was such episodes that made him the most controversial and provocative public figure of his time. People could revere him or deplore him, condemn his actions or praise them, but no one could ignore him. The enormous range of his interests, and his endless reservoirs of combative energy, projected him into every phase of national life; and whether the issue was big or little, he was generally to be found in its storm center. "Roosevelt," as one of his far-from-worshipful contemporaries acknowledged, "has the knack of doing things, and doing them noisily, clamorously; while he is in the neighborhood the public can no more look the other way than the small boy can turn his head away from a circus parade followed by a steam calliope."

THE NEWLYWEDS. On February 17, 1906, twenty-two-year-old Alice Roosevelt married thirty-six-year-old Nicholas Longworth, scion of a Cincinnati family and Republican congressman from the First Ohio District. The wedding—one of the most brilliant of the early part of the century—was held at the White House, as Roosevelt said, "against a background which bristled with 'officialdom.'"

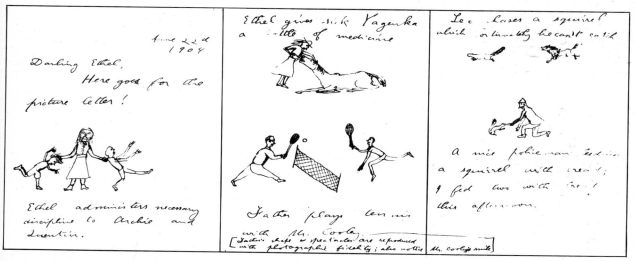

ONE OF HIS PICTURE LETTERS

Ever since he was a child Roosevelt had liked to draw funny little sketches in his letters, illustrating the events he described. And when he became a father, he delighted his five children with such letters, some of the most charming he ever penned.

HE WEDDING PICTURE

ice remembers that the draping of her
in was arranged by her cousin Franklin.

ROOSEVELT'S MOST CHERISHED ACHIEVEMENT was the building of the Panama Canal. Though the Canal was not opened to commercial traffic until August 1914, it was during his administration that the plans were adopted and the bulk of the work done.

In November of 1906 the President and his wife paid a visit to the Canal Zone to see with his own eyes how the project was progressing. It was the first time in the country's history that an American President had traveled outside American territory while in office. Roosevelt went everywhere; he inspected the huge machinery, he took a seat inside the giant steam shovels.

When Roosevelt visited Panama the project was still in its early stage, the Commission being preoccupied mainly with assembling the enormous amounts of equipment, expanding and organizing the complex railroad network required to move materials and men, and with the building of accommodations for the 45,000 construction workers.

CHAPTER XXXIII

BUILDING THE CANAL

The construction of the Panama Canal was the biggest, costliest, and most difficult public works project ever undertaken by the American people. Of all Roosevelt's achievements, it was the one closest to his heart. He approached it with an almost missionary belief in its importance to humanity. Years after the Panamanian revolt, when he acknowledged that "I took the Isthmus," he emphasized that he was of "a wholly unrepentant frame of mind" on the subject. "The ethical conception upon which I acted," he said, "was that I did not intend that Uncle Sam should be held up while he was doing a great work for himself and all mankind."

Customarily the canal is pictured as one of history's greatest engineering feats. But while the engineering problems were numerous and of great scope, they were not unprecedented or even very intricate. Far more frustrating and time-consuming were the mechanics of the undertaking—the endless problems of labor, of supply, and particularly of public health in a tropical and disease-ridden climate. Plagued by malaria and yellow fever, Panama was one of the foulest pestholes in the world. This more than anything else was the reason why the French attempt to build the canal under the direction of Ferdinand DeLesseps in the eighties turned into a tragic fiasco.

The first question which President Roosevelt and Congress had to answer was whether the great new waterway should be a sea-level canal or a lock canal. Lawmakers, engineers, and the public-at-large debated the issue for many months. The international board of inquiry recruited by the President was unable to come to agreement. Roosevelt pondered over the issue and, after examining all the evidence, decided on a lock canal. He reasoned that though a sea-level canal would cost slightly less to operate and would be less vulnerable in time of war, a lock canal would cost half as much to build and could be built in half the time. Thus, influenced and pressured by the impetuous President, the Senate by a vote of 36 to 31 approved the lock plan; and the House fell into line.

The health problem in the Canal area was one of the greatest obstacles to the progress of the undertaking. At the suggestion of a group of prominent doctors Roosevelt instructed the seven-man Canal Commission to place all sanitation work under the jurisdiction of General William C. Gorgas, who had been victorious over yellow fever in Cuba some three years before. But when Gorgas set about the work of eradicating from the forty-mile-long Canal Zone the Stegomyia mosquito—the small insect which transmitted the disease—he was opposed by the Canal Commission, who regarded the mosquito theory as nonsense. The commissioners believed that the only way to drive disease from the Canal Zone was by eliminating filth, burying garbage, and painting all buildings. Gorgas's pleas for chemicals, crude oil, and metal screening went unheeded.

Early in 1905 a yellow-fever epidemic struck the Zone. Chief Engineer John F. Wallace threatened to resign; workmen put down their tools and demanded passage back to the States; incoming laborers refused to disembark from the ships. Gorgas, even though he had warned his superiors of the danger of epidemics, was saddled with most of the blame. It was a curious state of affairs to have the prophet accused while the guilty men played the role of prosecutor.

The President, increasingly dissatisfied with the sluggishness of the Canal Commission, enmeshed in constant controversy and administrative red tape, decided that it was time to take matters into his own hands. As Congress was unwilling to provide for a smaller governing body with a less divided authority, he dismissed the first commission and replaced it with a new one headed by Theodore P. Shonts, a hard-driving railroad builder from the Middle West. Shonts' ideas about yellow fever were no different from those of the preceding commissioners. He, too, believed that if Gorgas—instead of fighting mosquitoes —would concentrate on cleaning up Panama City and the other settlements in the Canal area, yellow fever would no longer be a hazard. Fortified by this belief, he sent a memorandum to Secretary of War Taft, asking for the dismissal of Gorgas; Taft, endorsing the memorandum, passed it on to the President at Sagamore Hill.

This put Roosevelt on the horns of a dilemma. He had promised Shonts absolute authority in running the Canal Commission, therefore he was reluctant to override the first major exercise of that authority; at the same time he was strongly inclined to agree with the beliefs of Gorgas about yellow fever. Discussing the problem with his personal physician, Dr. Alexander Lambert, who had accompanied him on a bear hunt in Colorado only a few months before, he was advised to let Gorgas prove the theory in practice.

Roosevelt needed no further urging. He made up his mind to back Gorgas, and gave his word to stick with him. Thus, with the President behind him, Gorgas went on with his campaign against the Stegomyia mosquito throughout the summer. By early fall he knew that his efforts were successful.

The next plague to be overcome was malaria. Gorgas intensified his attacks against the disease, which was propagated by the Anopheles, another variety of mosquito. Again he ran into resistance from the Canal Commission. The commissioners complained that the campaign against malaria was costing the American taxpayers ten dollars for every mosquito killed. Yet Gorgas persisted, and he proved his point. By 1914, when the first ships passed through "the big ditch," the death rate from all causes in the Canal Zone was the astonishingly low figure of 6 per thousand—against 14.1 per thousand in the United States —a signal success due mainly to the foresight of Gorgas.

Late in 1906, President Roosevelt himself paid a visit to the Canal Zone with Mrs. Roosevelt in order to obtain firsthand knowledge of the project and its progress. At the time of his visit the grand plan of the canal was clear; its key feature was to be a huge lake created at eighty feet above sea level by damming the Chargres and Rio Grande rivers. From this body of water—Gatun Lake—the canal's descent to the Atlantic and Pacific was to be achieved by a system of locks at both ends.

Administrative problems continued to impede progress. Early in 1907 John F. Stevens, chairman and chief engineer of the Canal Commission, resigned. Roosevelt saw that he must solve the administrative problems, once and for all. The enormous job in Panama required a firm, co-ordinated administration by a permanent staff that would stay with it until it was done; but because of the complex problems and the distastefulness of life in the hot and undeveloped area, the personnel turnover averaged about ninety per cent a year, an ominously high figure.

The President appointed a third commission, composed primarily of Army and Navy engineers, "who will stay on the job till I get tired of having them there, or till I say they may abandon it." To the post of chairman and chief engineer he named Lieutenant Colonel George W. Goethals, a senior officer in the Army Engineers and a recognized expert on canal construction. By executive order Goethals was given supreme authority over all matters connected with the canal. To the other members of the commission the President put the matter frankly. "If at any time you do not agree with Colonel Goethals' policies," he told them, "do not bother to tell me about it—your disagreement with him will constitute your resignation." Goethals was given a free hand, and the policy worked.

In such a way, Congress—which had steadfastly rejected Roosevelt's proposals to change the multi-headed commission system in favor of a one-man control—was effectively circumvented. Time has proved the soundness of Roosevelt's decision. Armed with authority, technical competence, and an iron sense of responsibility, Goethals played the part of a benevolent tyrant with striking success from the first. He overcame staggering technical difficulties —particularly in the mountainous section known as the "Culebra Cut," where there was a succession of nearly disastrous landslides. The difficulties at Culebra proved conclusively the wisdom of the bitterly debated decision to build a lock canal instead of trying to cross the mountains at sea level. "There is not enough money in the world to construct a canal at sea level," Goethals had said at the height of the controversy, "and if constructed, it could not be kept open."

By the time the Panama Canal was completed, the cost to the American taxpayers totaled $223,000,000, not including the $40,000,000 paid to the French canal company and the $10,000,000 given to the Republic of Panama for the Canal Zone. Yet its significance could not be measured in dollars. The canal, a monument to American technical proficiency, became the most enormous economic and military asset to the United States. That it was transformed from a seemingly Utopian plan into bold reality was greatly due to the courageous and determined leadership of Theodore Roosevelt.

HE SAW EVERYTHING FOR HIMSELF—MOVING AROUND IN AN OPEN CAR

INSPECTING THE CONSTRUCTION OF THE PANAMA CANAL

"I went over everything," wrote Roosevelt to his son Kermit from his tour of the Panama Canal in November 1906, "that I could possibly go over in the time at my disposal. I examined the quarters of married and single men, white men and negroes. I went over the ground of the Gatun and La Boca dams; went through Panama and Colon, and spent a day in the Culebra Cut, where the great work is being done. There the huge steamshovels are hard at it; scooping huge masses of rock and gravel and dirt previously loosened by the drillers and dynamite blasters, loading it on trains which take it away to some dump, either in the jungle or where the dams are to be built. They are eating steadily into the mountain, cutting it down and down. Little tracks are laid on the side-hills, rocks blasted out, and the great ninety-five ton steamshovels work up like mountain howitzers until they come to where they can with advantage begin their work of eating into and destroying the mountainside. With intense energy men and machines do their task, the white men supervising matters and handling the machines, while the tens of thousands of black men do the rough manual labor where it is not worth while to have machines to do it. It is an epic feat, and one of immense significance."

It was only a year previously that a yellow-fever epidemic had struck the Canal Zone, causing panic among the construction workers. Chief Engineer John F. Wallace, who had

468

ON A TUGBOAT WITH T. P. SHONTS (RIGHT), HEAD OF THE PANAMA COMMISSION

taken the precaution of having his coffin sent to Panama, threatened to resign, and General William C. Gorgas—the man who had cleared Cuba of the disease and who was now fighting the mosquitoes in the Panama Canal area—was blamed for the epidemic. Members of the Panama Canal Commission ridiculed Gorgas's efforts and demanded his resignation. Roosevelt had to decide whether to let Gorgas go or to uphold him. He consulted his friend Dr. Alexander Lambert, who told him: "If you fall back on the old methods of sanitation, you will fail, just as the French failed. But if you back up Gorgas and his ideas and let him pursue his campaign against the mosquitoes you will get your Canal." The President followed the advice; he told Gorgas to keep on with his fight against the Stegomyia mosquito. It was a tremendously important decision—and it meant success. Gorgas kept on, and by the early fall of 1905 he felt confident enough to tell a group of surgeons who were examining the corpse of a yellow-fever victim in a government hospital: "Take a good look at this man, boys, for it's the last case of yellow fever you will ever see. There will never be any more deaths from this cause in Panama," a prediction which proved to be accurate.

After Gorgas eradicated yellow fever, he went on to fight against malaria, propagated by another variety of mosquito. Again the Canal Commission resisted him, and again the General proved his point. Thus, when Roosevelt came to inspect the progress of the construction he saw that things were proceeding well and that his dream was taking shape.

CHAPTER XXXIV

CRUSADING AGAINST "THE PREDATORY RICH"

"I have a definite philosophy about the Presidency," Roosevelt told the British historian Trevelyan. "I think it should be a very powerful office, and I think the President should be a very strong man who uses without hesitation every power that the position yields." Roosevelt was not afraid to use such powers and to use them forcefully. Seeking to temper the worst social and economic effects of American industrialism, he wielded the "big stick" against big business as no President had done before him.

Wall Street looked upon him as a dangerous socialist. This was an exaggeration. Roosevelt's "Square Deal" was essentially a middle-class program, aimed as much at "unruly labor leaders" as at "the predatory rich." He was profoundly disturbed by the growth of the radical movement in America, and he attributed it largely to the "dull, purblind folly" of men who accepted the privileges of great wealth without accepting its responsibilities. He himself would have liked to be a middle-of-the-road umpire who would keep the rich from exploiting the poor so that the poor would not be induced to seize power and exploit the rich.

Roosevelt tended to view this more as a moral than as an economic or a social problem. In his opinion monopoly was not evil in itself; there were "good" trusts and "bad" ones, and the duty of government was to force the bad ones to become good by making them follow what he deemed to be the path of "righteousness." This copybook approach amused many of his more skeptical friends. Speaker of the House Thomas B. Reed once told him: "If there is one thing more than another for which I admire you, Theodore, it is your original discovery of the Ten Commandments." And John Hay noted in his diary: "Knox says the question of what is to become of Roosevelt after 1908 is easily answered. He should be made a bishop."

That the trend toward monopoly was getting out of hand was evident from the latest government studies, which showed that while in 1900 there were 185 manufacturing combinations, or trusts, with a total capitalization of about three billion dollars, by 1904 their number had grown to 318 with a total capitalization of more than seven billion dollars, or approximately two fifths of the manufacturing capital in the nation. In theory these consolidations produced economic benefits, in practice such benefits tended to go neither to the consumer in terms of lower prices nor to the worker in terms of better pay, but to a handful of industrialists and financiers, who reaped tremendous profits

PANAMA
lying to President Amador's
come on November 14, 1906.

471

and established increasing control over the economic life of the nation. By 1905 the United States Steel Corporation, the biggest octopus of all, controlled no less than 170 subsidiary companies.

In no field was the tendency toward consolidation greater than in transportation, where at the time of Roosevelt's election six railway systems had obtained control of three quarters of the nation's railroad mileage without achieving any improvements in service, rates, or wages. In his message to Congress the President asked that teeth be put into the long-dormant Interstate Commerce Act by giving the Interstate Commerce Commission power to "summarily and effectively prevent the imposition of unjust or unreasonable rates." Meanwhile, under the terms of the Elkins Act of 1903 he instituted suits against the nation's four biggest meat-packing companies for receiving secret freight rebates at the expense of their competitors. A suit was also brought against the Standard Oil Company, which was accused of rebates totaling nearly one million dollars a year.

The 1906 session of Congress saw the introduction of a bill by Representative William Hepburn of Iowa containing the provisions Roosevelt had demanded. The Hepburn Bill passed the House easily, but when it came before the Senate it was opposed by a powerful block of "Railway Senators." The strategy of Senator Aldrich, the son-in-law of John D. Rockefeller, who led the fight against the bill, was to amend the rate-making process, make it cumbersome and costly, and subject it to review by the courts. To embarrass the President, "Pitchfork Ben" Tillman, a radical Southern Democrat whom Roosevelt disliked, was put in charge of the measure.

For two months the Hepburn Bill was bitterly debated in the Senate. Senator Foraker alone made eighty-six speeches against it. In the end it looked as though Roosevelt might win a complete victory over the "standpat" Republican leadership; still, when the showdown came, he compromised rather than risk alienating the most powerful men in his own party.

His compromise was branded a "betrayal," a "surrender," and a "sellout." Yet the Hepburn Bill as passed represented an important advance in railroad regulation. It provided for broader judicial review than Roosevelt wanted; but it gave the Interstate Commerce Commission power to set maximum rates for the first time; it provided stiff penalties for violation of Commission orders; it extended the Commission's authority over most aspects of railroading.

And while Roosevelt battled for railroad regulation he also assailed the trusts, demanding that "all corporations engaged in interstate commerce should be under the supervision of the national government" and even suggesting that the Constitution should be amended to such purpose. For such a radical position he could find no support in Congress. Thus all he could do was to institute prosecutions under the Sherman Anti-Trust Act.

The most dramatic of the President's victories over predatory business interests was the federal meat-inspection bill. When it seemed that the meat packers might cripple it with amendments, Roosevelt released a portion of his examiners' report about the unsanitary conditions in the Chicago packing houses and threatened to publish the remainder if the packers refused to call off their lobbyists. His threat and the fact that meat sales in the country and abroad were already suffering from the bad publicity led to the passage of the bill. By its momentum it also forced favorable action on the Pure Food Bill, which had been gathering dust for some years in a House pigeonhole. Denounced by Senator Aldrich as an infringement on "the liberty of all the people of the United States," this bill provided the first effective controls over the widespread use of adulterants in foods, drugs, and liquors.

The 1906 session of Congress, "the most ferocious, the most loquacious, and one of the most industrious" sessions on record, represented the high tide of Roosevelt's pressure on big business. As the booming prosperity of the century's early years had given way to a financial depression in 1907, financiers blamed the slump on the President's "undermining of public confidence." Roosevelt replied indignantly: "If trouble comes from having the light turned on, remember that it is not really due to the light but to the misconduct which is exposed." Nothing, he declared, could "alter in the slightest degree my determination that for the remaining sixteen months these policies shall be persevered in unswervingly." To William Allen White he wrote: "If we meet hard times . . . I shall probably end my term of service as President under a more or less dark cloud of obloquy. If so, I shall be sorry, of course, but I shall neither regret what I have done nor alter my line of conduct in the least degree." Nevertheless, the panic of 1907 made him slacken his attacks.

Of economic and financial matters, Roosevelt had little knowledge. However, on the issue of conservation, where he assumed a comparable role as a protector of the public interest against the private, he was an expert. Both his lifelong interest in nature and his firsthand acquaintance with the wilderness areas of the West contributed to an intense and unrelenting concern for the preservation of the nation's forest and water resources. He had the good fortune to have at his command the devoted services of many dedicated conservationists, of whom the most able was Gifford Pinchot, the man who devised and executed much of the President's program.

At the outset of Roosevelt's Presidency there was, for all practical purposes, no conservation policy. "The habit of deciding, whenever possible, in favor of private interests against the public welfare was firmly fixed," he wrote in his *Autobiography*. "The relation of the conservation of natural resources to the problems of national welfare and national efficiency had not yet dawned on the public mind." But by the time he left the White House, he had added 150,000,000 acres to the national forests, had launched large-scale reforestation and irrigation programs serving more than 3,000,000 acres of the West, had pushed through legislation to check the wholesale depletion of mineral resources, and had brought to a halt the systematic looting of the public preserves by an unholy alliance of railroad operators, timber barons, and ranchers.

The battle for conservation was less dramatic than the battles with Wall Street and the trusts, nevertheless it was part of the same crusade against exploitation by a predatory minority. Roosevelt's victories on this front were of lasting value.

CARTOONIST'S PET

"SOMEBODY'S GOT TO TURN BACK"
Cartoon by Zim in *Judge* at the time when Roosevelt's fight for railroad regulation got under way.

NO MOLLYCODDLING HERE
The big stick in action against the Beef Trust, the Oil Trust, the Railroads, and "Everything In General."

CHRISTMAS AT THE WHITE HOUSE—
Roosevelt on his hobbyhorse marked Anti-Railroad Rebate Laws. Around the room the toys are labeled: Panama Canal, Cuban Treaty, Tariff Revision, New Immigration Laws, Reciprocity, Porto Rico, Chinese Immigration, Square Deal for the South, Trust Question, Venezuelan Troubles, Insurance Scare, Cut Government Expenditures—pointing to the issues of the first four years of his administration.

If the cartoon had been drawn four years later— at the end of Roosevelt's term "in his own right"—

AN AMUSING CARTOON BY FLORHI WHICH *JUDGE* PRINTED ON DECEMBER 23, 1905

the artist could have added many more toys, so many more were Roosevelt's achievements and the important events in which he played a prominent part. There would have been labels on his negotiations for the Russo-Japanese peace treaty, on conservation and irrigation, on the administration of the Philippines, on his stand in the controversy with Japan, on simplified spelling, on nature fakers, on his quarrels with Mrs. Bellamy Storer and General Miles, on muckrakers and the Pure Food Bill, and

a number of other related and unrelated subjects.

Roosevelt was always doing things, always in the midst of things. "Whatever I think it is right for me to do, I do. I do the things that I believe ought to be done. And when I make up my mind to do a thing, I act." There was no doubt about it.

One marvels at his versatility. There was hardly any subject under the sun about which he did not hand down an opinion. He was equally at home in discussing science, literature, history, philosophy.

MUCKRAKERS

UPTON SINCLAIR, whose realistic novel *The Jungle* in 1906 led to investigation of the Chicago meat-packing industry.

IDA M. TARBELL, whose history in *McClure's* of the Standard Oil Company in 1902 pioneered a new kind of journalism.

THOMAS LAWSON, whose *Frenzied Finance* revealed the manipulations of financiers in Amalgamated Copper stock.

LINCOLN STEFFENS, whose disclosures on corruption in local politics were contained in his volume *The Shame of the Cities.*

RAY S. BAKER exposed dishonesty in rate-setting practices of the lines in his 1906 book, *The Railroads on Trial.*

CHARLES RUSSELL uncovered the shady activities of the beef trust in *The Greatest Trust in the World,* published in 1905.

DEMANDING REFORMS

The ruthlessness of modern finance, the corruption in business, and the graft in politics demanded corrective measures. Writers and journalists woke the country to the machinations of great corporations and the rottenness in political life; with Samuel S. McClure's founding of a 15-cent magazine, the literature of such exposures found a home and a platform. The first successful attempt was Ida M. Tarbell's "History of the Standard Oil Company," which *McClure's Magazine* printed in 1902, shedding light on the abuses of that huge trust. Then came Lincoln Steffen's "Enemies of the Republic," a disclosure of graft in the government of the cities. As the circulation of *McClure's* rose, other magazines followed its lead. Their policy of exposure flourished, paving the way for many of Roosevelt's reforms.

But when sensational magazines like *Everybody's* printed Thomas W. Lawson's vituperative "Frenzied Finance," or *Cosmopolitan* published David Graham Phillips's "The Treason of the Senate," Roosevelt felt that the writer went too far. He wanted to make it clear that he would not be a part of "the lunatic fringe" that rushes into the comet's tail of every reform movement. In a speech on March 17, 1906, before the Gridiron Club, he quoted from Bunyan's *Pilgrim's Progress* about "the man with the muckrake ... who could look no way but downward." The phrase stuck—all exposé writers became "muckrakers."

THE PACKING-HOUSE SCANDAL

When a commission, appointed by Roosevelt, reported "revolting" conditions in the Chicago packing houses, with "meat shovelled from filthy wooden floors, piled on tables rarely washed . . . gathering dirt, splinters, floor filth," public indignation forced the passing of a Meat Inspection bill. At about the same time, Upton Sinclair's novel *The Jungle* dramatized the abuses in stockyards and packing houses, preparing a climate for the meat inspection bill.

ONE OF HIS GREAT ACHIEVEMENTS

The Reclamation Act of 1902 provided that proceeds from the sales of public lands in sixteen Western states should go into a special irrigation fund. With the money, huge tracts of land were reclaimed, irrigated, and sold to settlers. In such a way, thousands of acres of sagebrush-covered wasteland were turned into fertile agricultural areas—a proud achievement of Roosevelt's irrigation policy.

CONSERVATION

"When, at the beginning of my term of service as President," wrote Roosevelt, "... I took up the cause of conservation, I was already fairly well awake to the need of social and industrial justice; and from the outset we had in view, not only the preservation of natural resources, but the prevention of monopoly in natural resources, so that they should inhere in the people as a whole." In June 1902 the Reclamation Act was signed, which provided for irrigation in the West by the government, the cost to be repaid by the settlers and kept as a revolving fund for further work. During Roosevelt's administration almost 150 million acres—mostly timberland—were added to the 45 million acres previously held as permanent government reserves, an efficient forest service was organized, and sanctuaries were set up for the preservation of wildlife—all in the face of constant opposition from Congress and people in the West who had been counting on using the land and its resources for their own personal profit.

THE AMERICAN SAMSON. Delilah Roosevelt: "I must get these shears to work together before I can do any hair-cutting." By J. S. Pughe in *Puck,* December 13, 1905.

One of Roosevelt's greatest political battles was fought over the regulation of the railroads. He wanted fair rates for all railroad shippers without discrimination, and desired "to set up a moral standard." There was a mounting feeling in the country against the "rebates" of the railroads, given to powerful companies but denied to smaller ones, with hardly any two shippers paying the same rates. The system worked against the farmers and small businessmen and was grossly unjust. President Roosevelt asked Congress for a law which "shall summarily and effectively prevent the imposition of unjust and unreasonable rates."

THE INFANT HERCULES AND THE STANDARD OIL SERPENTS. F. A. Nanki-vell's cartoon in *Puck,* May 23, 1906, shows Roosevelt with Rockefeller and Rogers.

On March 4, 1906, while the railroad regulation was being debated in the Senate, the President made public the report of the Bureau of Corporations on the Standard Oil Company. This report revealed "that the Standard Oil Company has benefited enormously up almost to the present moment by secret rates" amounting to at least three quarters of a million a year. On March 18 the Senate finally passed the Hepburn Act, which strengthened the Interstate Commerce Commission's rate-making powers and gave it jurisdiction over pipelines, Pullman operation, and other important transportation matters.

THE RECENT FLURRY IN THE SENATE—J. S. PUGHE IN *PUCK*, MARCH 21, 1906

FIGHTING FOR THE RAILROAD BILL

The battle between Roosevelt and the Senate raged over the control of the railroad companies' rate-fixing power. Roosevelt demanded that his Interstate Commerce Commission be given "the power to revise rates and regulations." Senator Aldrich, the son-in-law of Rockefeller, leading the Senate opposition, fought the President's contention. Aldrich pleaded for court decision about unfair rates—which in the final outcome would have proven ineffective. But Roosevelt stood by his demand—he battled manfully against the many-headed senatorial monster (see cartoon by J. S. Pughe on the left) and won a victory. Though the radical provisos of the Hepburn bill were modified by the Senate, the passing of it represented a great step forward in the regulation of the railroads. Still, the fundamental issue was not solved—to determine rates through the evaluation of railroad properties and the cost of service. That was left until a much later day.

480

A SHORT INTERVIEW IN THE WHITE HOUSE

Now, Mr. Railroadman, stock watering must stop —

Rates are too high —

They must come down

Safety must be guaranteed —

I hope I impress my meaning on you —

Good day!

THE PANIC OF 1907

In 1907 the booming prosperity of the Roosevelt years gave way to severe financial unrest. Those who opposed Roosevelt pointed a finger at the President who "undermined public confidence." Edward Harriman told reporters: "I would hate to tell you to whom I think you ought to go for an explanation of all this." And Roosevelt retorted that certain malefactors of great wealth continued "to bring about as much financial stress as possible" to embarrass the government. Both Roosevelt and Harriman indulged in partisan recriminations. The causes of the economic unrest lay deeper—it was neither caused by the government nor by the malefactors of great wealth; it had been a world-wide phenomenon.

The crisis reached its climax in the third week of October when the Knickerbocker Trust Company of New York failed and numerous other banks trembled on the brink of disaster. On October 22, Secretary of Treasury Cortelyou hurried to New York, where he met with J. P. Morgan and other bankers. He assured the financiers that the Treasury would deposit $25,000,000 of its surplus funds in the New York national banks; after this Morgan, Harriman, Rockefeller, and others invested even larger funds in institutions which they deemed worthy of saving.

Early in November it became evident that the brokerage house of Moore & Schley was in grave difficulties because it held as collateral $5,000,000 worth of stock of the Tennessee Coal and Iron Company which it was unable to turn into cash. Morgan and his colleagues, who at this time seemed to rule over the nation's financial policies, came up with the idea that the United States Steel Corporation should purchase the Tennessee Coal and Iron Company and thus validate its securities.

Elbert H. Gary and Henry C. Frick, the president and a director of U. S. Steel, rushed to Washington to see Roosevelt. Early Monday morning—November 4—they saw the President and told him that in an effort to save "a certain business concern" and stem the tide, they would have to purchase the stock of Tennessee Coal and Iron for $40,000,000, but would do it only if the government would give assurance that the merger would not lead to prosecution under the Sherman Act.

Although the merger increased U. S. Steel's share of the market from 50 per cent to 60 per cent, Roosevelt acquiesced. His assurance was telephoned to New York, where Morgan and his partners awaited the news. Within minutes the sale was made, and the stock market catastrophe avoided.

THE RUN OF THE WORRIED DEPOSITORS

A subsequent congressional investigation revealed that Judge Gary misrepresented the situation to the President and that the Morgan interests bought the

ON THE TRUST COMPANY OF NORTH AMERICA IN WALL STREET ON OCTOBER 25, 1907

Tennessee Coal and Iron because it was a bargain at $40,000,000 and not because they desired to save Moore & Schley. But by then the financial panic of 1907 was long over, and nobody could do anything about the hundreds of millions that Morgan and his colleagues had made on the transaction.

"WALL STREET PAINTS A PICTURE OF THE PRESIDENT" — A CARTOON IN *COLLIER'S*

CHAPTER XXXV

WAR CLOUDS
IN THE PACIFIC

Roosevelt's good offices on behalf of Japan were little appreciated in that country. The Japanese were at first grateful for his bringing the representatives of the two warring nations to a conference, but at the conclusion of the peace treaty they became resentful because they were not able to secure indemnity payments from Russia. For this they blamed Roosevelt and the American people. In September 1905 there were severe anti-American riots in Japan.

Friction between the two countries was further inflamed when, ten months later, Japanese seal-hunting poachers raided the Pribilof Islands off Alaska and were driven back by an American patrol. Five Japanese lost their lives in the encounter.

Nor was the feeling of Americans toward Japan friendlier. There was a steady anti-Japanese agitation on the West Coast, where infiltration of Japanese immigrants caused fears that the cheap Oriental labor would undermine the standard of American living. Newspapers—printing lurid tales of the "Yellow Peril" and stirring the readers to near-hysteria—fomented these flames of hate.

When on October 11, 1906, the San Francisco Board of Education issued an order excluding Japanese pupils from the city's school system, matters came to a head; war between the two nations became a possibility. To the emphatic protest of the Japanese government, Roosevelt replied on October 26: "Thru the Department of Justice we are already taking steps in San Francisco to see if we cannot remedy the matter thru the courts. . . ." And he promised: "I shall exert all the power I have under the Constitution to protect the rights of the Japanese who are here, and shall deal with the subject at length in my message to Congress."

To his son Kermit he wrote: "I am being horribly bothered about the Japanese business. The infernal fools in California, and especially in San Francisco, insult the Japanese recklessly, and in the event of war it will be the Nation as a whole which will pay the consequences. However I hope to keep things straight. I am perfectly willing that this Nation should fight any nation if it has got to, but I would loathe to see it forced into a war in which it was wrong."

His eyes on the future, he told Senator Eugene Hale that if Japan is "sufficiently irritated and humiliated by us she will get to accept us instead of Russia as the national enemy whom she will ultimately have to fight; and under such circumstances her concentration and continuity of purpose, and the exceedingly formidable character of her army and navy, make it necessary to reckon very seriously with her. It seems to me that all of this necessitates our having a definite policy with regard to her; a policy of behaving with absolute good faith, courtesy and justice to her on the one hand, and on the other, of keeping our navy in such shape as to make it a risky thing for Japan to go into war with us. . . ."

After lengthy negotiations with public leaders in San Francisco and the government in Tokyo, a compromise was effected by which San Francisco agreed to rescind its segregation policy and Tokyo agreed to prohibit the influx of Japanese laborers to the United States, limiting emigration mainly to merchants and students. Furthermore, Roosevelt promised to push through Congress legislation barring immigration of Japanese laborers from Hawaii, Mexico, and Canada. Unhappily, the compromise did not mark the end of the troubles. Agitation against the Japanese continued, and in the early summer of 1907 these feelings erupted into riots in which Japanese restaurants and restaurant keepers were attacked in San Francisco.

Roosevelt held that the San Franciscans' insult of the Japanese was wanton and foolish, therefore "everything we can do must be done to remedy the wrongs complained of." To Cabot Lodge he wrote: "I shall continue to do everything I can by politeness and consideration to the Japs to offset the worse than criminal stupidity of the San Francisco mob, the San Francisco press, and such papers as the New York *Herald.* I do not believe we shall have war; but it is no fault of the yellow press if we do not have it. The Japanese seem to have about the same proportion of prize jingo fools that we have."

The President received alarming reports through his diplomatic pipelines. According to one account, a Japanese diplomat in Russia declared that his country was ready to move against the Philippine Islands, Alaska, and even the Pacific Coast. According to other reports from the British Intelligence service, Japan was preparing war against the United States. From Kaiser Wilhelm II came word that 10,000 Japanese soldiers, disguised as laborers, were already in Mexico, ready to move into United States territory.

Throughout the crisis Roosevelt remained calm, maintaining a consistently conciliatory attitude toward Japan. At the same time, he was ready to show that his conciliatory attitude should not be interpreted as a sign of American weakness, for he was quite convinced (as he explained to Secretary of State Root) that "the only thing which will prevent war is the Japanese feeling that we shall not be beaten." He decided to send the American battle fleet on a trip around the world to demonstrate the nation's naval prowess to the world in general and to Japan in particular.

Although the Japanese crisis was the principal motive for the battle fleet's voyage, it was by no means the only one. "In the first place," Roosevelt wrote to Root, "I think it will have a pacific effect to show that it can be done; and in the next place, after talking thoroughly over the situation with the naval board I became convinced that it was absolutely necessary for us in time of peace to see just what we could do in the way of putting a big battle fleet in the Pacific, and not make the experiment in time of war." Later he wrote in his *Autobiography:* "It seemed to me evident that such a voyage would greatly benefit the Navy itself; would arouse popular interest in and enthusiasm for the Navy; and would make foreign nations accept as a matter of course that our fleet should from time to time be gathered in the Pacific, just as from time to time it was gathered in the Atlantic, and that its presence in one ocean was no more to be accepted as a mark of hostility to any Asiatic power than its presence in the Atlantic was to be accepted as a mark of hostility to any European power."

The fleet's voyage was an immense undertaking; the complexity of its organization and supply enormous. Foreign naval experts were firm in their belief that it could not be done. At home vigorous objections were raised, especially from the Eastern Seaboard, where people became alarmed at the removal of the fleet from the waters of the Atlantic. In the Senate the chairman of the Committee on Naval Affairs announced that money for the voyage would not be appropriated, to which the President replied that he already had enough funds to send the fleet to the Pacific, and that if Congress declined to appropriate additional funds, the fleet would be left there. "I will tolerate no assault upon the Navy or upon the honor of the country," Roosevelt said, "nor will I permit anything so fraught with menace as the usurpation by any clique of Wall Street Senators of my function as Commander-in-Chief." For the success or failure of the undertaking he accepted full responsibility. "I determined on the move without consulting the Cabinet, precisely as I took Panama without consulting the Cabinet. A council of war never fights, and in a crisis the duty of the leader is to lead and not to take refuge behind the generally timid wisdom of a multitude of councillors."

The fleet, composed of sixteen battleships and lesser vessels, with crews totaling some twelve thousand officers and men, steamed out of Hampton Roads on December 16, 1907. The fears that the voyage would bring Japanese retaliation were dispelled when Japan extended an invitation for the naval officers and men to visit her shores. By the time the ships had sailed from Japan to the Philippines and back home through the Mediterranean, the war clouds that had looked so ominous a few months before had disappeared.

On Washington's birthday of 1909, sixteen months after they had set out on their historic trip, the battleships returned to Hampton Roads—an occasion of national pride and rejoicing. Once again the President, now but ten days from the end of his reign, watched the proceedings from the deck of the *Mayflower*. "Over a year has passed since you steamed out of this harbor, and over the world's rim," he told the officers and men of Admiral Sperry's flagship, "and this morning the hearts of all who saw you thrilled with pride as the hulls of the mighty warships lifted above the horizon. . . . We welcome you home to the country whose good repute among nations has been raised by what you have done." Later, to the admirals and skippers assembled in the *Mayflower* cabin, he put his deep pride into more concrete terms. "Isn't it magnificent?" he said. "Nobody after this will forget that the American coast is on the Pacific as well as on the Atlantic."

TROUBLE WITH JAPAN

THE TEST CASE. When the nine-year-old Japanese Keikichi Aoki was refused admission by Miss M. E. Dean, Principal of the Reading Primary School in San Francisco, the federal government brought suit against the San Francisco Board of Education. Roosevelt wrote Elihu Root that the suit "should be prest as rapidly as possible." The prosecution was later abandoned when the United States reached a "Gentlemen's Agreement" with Japan.

JAPANESE WAR SCARE
This cartoon by Louis M. Glackens in *Puck* on October 23, 1907, alludes to President Roosevelt's contention that "the war talk is due entirely to newspapers, which seek to increase their sales, and which for political reasons attack the government."

THE SCARECROW OF THE PACIFIC. J. S. After the conclusion of the Russo-Japanese peace treaty in Portsmouth, relationships between Japan and the United States deteriorated, as Japan mistakenly believed that America had blocked their demand for indemnity payments from Russia. In anti-American rioting at Tokyo, four American churches were burned by the enraged mob.

The feeling against Japan in the United States—especially on the West Coast—was not friendlier. The agitation in California against the Japanese

PUGHE'S CARTOON OF 1907, IN *PUCK*, DEPICTS OUR NAVY'S RACE TO JAPAN

mounted, and Hearst's San Francisco *Examiner* fanned the discontent with its "Yellow Peril" articles.

Things came to a head in October 1906 when the San Francisco Board of Education excluded Japanese pupils from the city's school system. The Japanese government protested against this as a violation of the Japanese-American Treaty of 1894. Roosevelt felt that Japan was not treated fairly. "I am being horribly bothered about the Japanese business," wrote he to his son Kermit. "The infernal fools in

California, and especially in San Francisco, insult the Japanese recklessly, and in the event of war it will be the Nation as a whole which will pay the consequences."

The dispute ended in a compromise; San Francisco agreed to rescind its segregation policy, and Japan prohibited the influx of Japanese laborers to the United States. Still the agitation against the "Yellow Peril" had not come to an end; it erupted again a year later, with severe rioting in San Francisco.

"THE MOST IMPORTANT SERVICE that I rendered to peace" was Roosevelt's comment about his ordering the fleet around the world. Sixteen vessels under Rear Admiral Robley D. Evans left on December 16, 1907, with Roosevelt watching their departure from the *Mayflower*. The fleet's voyage had a twofold purpose: (1) to impress Japan that America would not be intimidated; (2) to create sentiment in Congress for increased naval expenditures. Both aims were realized. Japan did not shoot at the American vessels, but feted the officers and men, and Congress appropriated funds for two new battleships.

CHAPTER XXXVI

THE END OF THE REIGN

"There are plenty of people who really want me to run for a third term who, if I did run, would feel very much disappointed in me and would feel that I had come short of the ideal they had formed of me," wrote Roosevelt to his son Kermit. Regardless of pressures, he would not renege on the promise given after his election. He would not be a candidate or accept another nomination.

Curiously enough, the economic setbacks and the increasing hostility of Congress had increased the people's admiration for him. The New York *Times,* polling newspaper editors across the nation, reported that he was "stronger with the people than ever before." The third-term tradition, said the *Times,* "will not in the slightest degree avail against the wave of popular favor that now promises to make Mr. Roosevelt the candidate of next year. With the spirit he has invoked and stirred, tradition counts for nothing."

Determined to be "a full president right up to the end," Roosevelt's power over Congress nonetheless became weak as his reign was nearing its close. During the congressional session which began at the end of 1907, he sent a total of twenty messages to Capitol Hill, and most of them were disregarded by the lawmakers. A year later, at the "lame duck session," the struggle between the executive and legislative branches of the government descended to the level of childish bickering when Roosevelt asked the repeal of an act which, among other things, forbade the Secret Service to investigate the affairs of Congressmen. The House, by the overwhelming vote of 212 to 35, rejected the presidential message—a stinging rebuke to the President.

As Congress became less receptive to Presidential proposals, the suggestions themselves became more radical. Because of his own growing disenchantment with the leaders of the business community, and in response to public unrest resulting from the financial panic, Roosevelt came forward with a series of boldly progressive pronouncements. He argued that both an income and an inheritance tax "should be part of our system of federal taxation." He vigorously criticized the Supreme Court for invalidating the Employers' Liability Act of 1906 and reversing the $29,000,000 fine that had been levied against Standard Oil for accepting railroad rebates. And he sent Congress an outspoken message urging sharp restrictions on "gambling in the stock market," legislation allowing the Interstate Commerce Commission to determine the physical valuation of railroads as a means toward more comprehensive rate-making, and limitations on the use of injunctions against labor unions.

It was in this message that the President described as his aim "the moral regeneration of the business world." The economic distress, he argued, was due not to any anti-business policy in the White House, as had been alleged, but rather to "the speculative folly and flagrant dishonesty of a few men of great wealth."

When speculation about a third term had become persistent, presidential secretary William Loeb told his chief that the only way to squelch such rumors was to choose a successor. In other words, the President would have to run a candidate against himself in order to be sure that the Republican convention would not find itself so divided between competing candidacies that it would stampede him for a third term.

Roosevelt's preference as political heir would have been Elihu Root, his Secretary of State. "I would walk on my hands and knees from the White House to the Capitol to see Root made President," he had once told a friend; but he knew that Root, who was a former corporation lawyer, could never be chosen. Thus he turned to the faithful William Howard Taft, the man who had served him as governor-general of the Philippines, as Secretary of War, and as an invaluable trouble-shooter and envoy-at-large. The affable Taft had great administrative abilities, but no political acumen and none of Roosevelt's crusading zeal. He would have preferred to be on the Supreme Court rather than to become President. Yet persuaded by his ambitious wife, his half-brother, and other friends he kept himself available for the Presidency by declining all offers of a judicial appointment.

Early in 1908, Roosevelt started to organize the campaign for Taft's nomination, channeling abundant publicity toward the heir-apparent and even employing his patronage power to ensure the selection of Taft-pledged delegates. By the spring of that year, control over the Republican convention was assured, and Roosevelt felt that "all opposition to Taft had died down." Still he remained cautious; he would take no chances. He saw to it that his friend Senator Cabot Lodge was installed as chairman of the convention and would keep the reins in his hand. He knew that if Taft failed to win on the first ballot, "there is a chance of a stampede to me, and if it really gets underway nothing that I could do would stop it." Such a scare came when, the day before the balloting, Senator Lodge's reference to Roosevelt as "the best abused and the most popular man in the United States today" provoked forty-nine minutes of frenzied cheering. Lodge could restore order over the convention only by warning the delegates that "anyone who attempts to use his name as a candidate for the Presidency impugns both his sincerity and his good faith."

The convention, bowing to Roosevelt's will, nominated Taft. They would have nominated anyone whom their idol suggested.

The campaign was dull. Taft was not a dynamic candidate, and William Jennings Bryan, chosen by the Democrats to oppose him as a third-time nominee could no longer arouse the interest of the electorate. Roosevelt, who had promised not to be a "busybody," was puzzled and disappointed because Taft "does not arouse the enthusiasm which his record and personality warranted us in believing he would arouse." He urged him: "Hit them hard, old man!"—an admonition of little avail. Some excitement was injected in the contest when William Randolph Hearst, running as a splinter candidate on the Independence Party platform, made public a series of letters apparently proving that Senator Foraker had been on the payroll of Standard Oil Company. Roosevelt, wanting "to put a little vim into the campaign by making a publication of my own," attacked Foraker sharply, even though Taft wondered whether it was fair to "hit a man when he is down."

The result of the election was a Republican victory, and a great victory for Roosevelt. His influence was so strong that the people, trusting him, voted for his hand-picked successor. Taft won with 321 electoral votes against Bryan's 162. "The first letter I wish to write is to you," came a message from the President-elect to Roosevelt, "because you have always been the chief agent in working out the present state of affairs, and my selection and election are chiefly your work."

The election brought the exciting years in the White House to a close. An English journalist asked Roosevelt about his future plans and he answered: "When people have spoken to me as to what America should do with its ex-Presidents, I have always answered that there was one ex-President as to whom they need not concern themselves in the least, because I would do for myself. It would be to me a personally unpleasant thing to be pensioned and given some honorary position. I emphatically do not desire to clutch at the fringe of departing greatness." His plans were made. He had agreed to write twelve articles a year at $1000 apiece for *The Outlook,* a weekly journal of opinion. He would go big-game hunting in Africa—"my last chance for something in the nature of a 'great adventure.'" And upon his return he would fight for political, social, and industrial reform "just as I have been fighting for it for the twenty-eight years that I have been in politics."

Parting from the Presidency was not an easy task for a man who, by his own testimony, had "enjoyed it to the full." On the last day of December in 1908 he said in a note to Taft: "Ha! Ha! *You* are making up your Cabinet. *I* in a lighthearted way have spent the morning testing the rifles for my African trip. Life has its compensations!" But the regrets were at least as great as the anticipations. On March 1, 1909, he gave a luncheon to his "Tennis Cabinet," and when he offered a fond farewell toast to the thirty-one guests who had been his closest and most devoted comrades through the previous seven and one half years, many of them wept unashamedly. Three days later, on the eve of the inaugural, President-elect and Mrs. Taft were guests at a dinner which Taft remembered as "that funeral."

Yet in a letter to his son Kermit, Roosevelt spoke cheerfully about leaving the Presidency. "I have had a great run for my money," he said, "and I should have liked to stay in as President if I had felt it was right for me to do so; but there are many compensations about going, and Mother and I are in the curious and very pleasant position of having enjoyed the White House more than any other President and his wife whom I recall, and yet being entirely willing to leave it, and looking forward to a life of interest and happiness after we leave."

HE QUARRELED WITH...

HE QUARRELED WITH...

LIEUTENANT GENERAL NELSON A. MILES,

"a brave peacock" in the Roosevelt language, who clashed with the President when he voiced an opinion on the findings of a Naval Court of Inquiry. The Court, investigating the conduct of Rear Admirals William T. Sampson and Winfield S. Schley at the battle of Santiago, found Schley guilty of errors in judgment. Admiral Dewey, one of the judges, dissented. At this point General Miles, who had no connection with the inquiry and whose opinion was not asked, entered the fray, declaring that he would rather take the judgment of Admiral Dewey than that of the final finding of the Naval Court of Inquiry. Elihu Root, the Secretary of War, got furious. It was not Miles's business to criticize the Court's finding. Such behavior was "subversive of discipline." Root consulted Roosevelt, who approved his suggestion to censure Miles. The General hurried to the White House to defend his action, but the President told him bluntly that his conduct had "been not merely silly but insubordinate and unmilitary." Miles, soon to be forced into retirement, left the meeting a broken man. Roosevelt had never liked the General, holding him responsible for some of the mismanagement in the Spanish-American War.

MARIA LONGWORTH STORER,

a close friend of the Roosevelts and a meddlesome woman. As wife of the American Ambassador in Vienna, she worked relentlessly to have Archbishop Ireland of St. Paul, Minnesota, elevated to Cardinal, inferring to the Vatican that this was the wish of President Roosevelt as well. When in March 1906 she desired to see the Pope as the accredited agent of the American government "to secure a Cardinal's hat for Archbishop Ireland," Roosevelt's temper flared. Members of the Cabinet urged him to recall Ambassador Storer at once, but, reluctant to dismiss the man who had once helped him to secure the post of Assistant Secretary of the Navy, the President sent a letter to the Ambassador and included a note for his wife. In this he asked a written promise that she would no longer interfere in diplomatic matters. The Storers, hurt and angry, left the letter unanswered. Roosevelt wrote once more; and when the second communication was disregarded, he demanded the Ambassador's resignation. Some months later the Storers issued a pamphlet in which they printed some of Roosevelt's letters to them, whereupon Roosevelt released many more letters which showed that his behavior in the matter was correct.

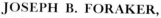

JOSEPH B. FORAKER,

with whom Roosevelt disagreed over the Negro troops' dismissal because of the Brownsville affair.

On the night of August 14, 1906, shooting broke out at Brownsville, Texas, in which one man was killed, two men were wounded, allegedly shot by men belonging to three all-Negro companies stationed at Fort Brown. When none of the soldiers would confess, the President gave his authorization for the dishonorable discharge of all three companies.

In the Senate, Foraker attacked Roosevelt and his unjust order, claiming it was based on insufficient and false information. Though Roosevelt explained that "the opposition to me on Brownsville was simply a cloak to cover antagonism . . . about trusts, swollen fortunes and the like," this was not the case.

At a Gridiron Club dinner in Washington on January 26, 1907, Roosevelt and Foraker faced each other and made bitter speeches. To his son-in-law Roosevelt wrote: "That scoundrel, Foraker, is doing all the damage he can with the negroes. . . . A blacker wrong . . . than Foraker and his friends have committed it would not be possible to imagine."

But later, during the Barnes trial, Roosevelt lauded Foraker as an honest man who had his respect.

EDWARD H. HARRIMAN,

the railroad man, for years had friendly relations with Roosevelt. The two clashed when a personal letter of Harriman was printed in the New York *World* on April 2, 1907, regarding the 1904 election.

In his letter to a friend, which was sold to the newspaper for $150, Harriman said that in the fall of 1904 Roosevelt "told me that he understood the campaign could not be carried on without sufficient money, and asked me if I would help them in raising the necessary funds." Harriman was ready to collect the funds if Chauncey Depew, whose re-election to another Senate term split the Republican ranks, could "be taken care of in some other way." Roosevelt supposedly promised to name Depew as Ambassador to France, whereupon Harriman contributed $50,000 for the campaign and brought in another $200,000. But after the Republicans won the election, Roosevelt would not keep his side of the bargain.

Roosevelt retorted that this was not so, charged Harriman with lying, and heaped his choicest epithets on the unfortunate railroad man. He emphatically stated that he "never requested Mr. Harriman to raise a dollar for the Presidential campaign of 1904," and disavowed any promise to appoint Depew.

WHAT HE THOUGHT OF TOLSTOY

"First as to Tolstoy's immorality. Have you ever read his Kreutzer Sonata . . . ?" he asked Lawrence Abbott. "The man who wrote that was a sexual and a moral pervert. It is as unhealthy a book, as vicious in its teaching to the young, as Elinor Glyn's *Three Weeks* or any other piece of pornographic literature. . . . I think that the love of the really happy husband and wife . . . is the loftiest and most ennobling influence that comes into the life of any man or woman. . . . The cheapest . . . and most repulsive cynicism is that which laughs at, or describes as degraded, this relation."

★

WHAT HE THOUGHT OF EMILE ZOLA

"Of course the net result of Zola's writings has been evil. Where one man has gained from them a shuddering horror at existing wrong which has impelled him to try to right that wrong, a hundred have simply had the lascivious, the beast side of their natures strengthened and intensified by them."

WHAT HE THOUGHT OF DANTE

"When Dante deals with the crimes which he most abhorred, simony and barratry, he flails offenders of his age who were of the same type as those who in our days flourish by political or commercial corruption; and he names his offenders, both those just dead and those still living, and puts them, popes and politicians alike, in hell. There have been trust magnates and politicians and editors and magazine writers in our own country whose lives and deeds were no more edifying than those of the men who lie in the third and the fifth chasm of the eighth circle of the Inferno; yet for a poet to name those men would be condemned as an instance of shocking taste. . . . I must say I should thoroughly enjoy having a Dante write of a number of our present-day politicians, labor leaders, and Wall Street people! When he came to deal with the worst offenders among our newspaper editors and magazine writers, I hope he would not dignify them by putting them in a circle of flame, but leave them in the circles of pitch and of filth."

WHAT HE THOUGHT OF SHAKESPEARE

"You will . . . be amused to hear that at last, when fifty years old, I have come into my inheritance in Shakespeare. I never before really cared for more than one or two of his plays; but for some inexplicable reason the sealed book was suddenly opened to me on this trip. . . . I still balk at three or four of Shakespeare's plays; but most of them I have read or am reading over and over again. . . ."

WHAT HE THOUGHT OF WALT WHITMAN

". . . a warped, although a rugged, genius of American poetry. . . .

"Of all the poets of the nineteenth century, Walt Whitman was the only one who dared use the Bowery—that is, use anything that was striking and vividly typical of the humanity around him—as Dante used the ordinary humanity of his day; and even Whitman was not quite natural in doing so, for he always felt that he was defying the conventions and prejudices of his neighbors, and his self-consciousness made him a little defiant. . . . Whitman wrote of homely things and every-day men, and of their greatness, but his art was not equal to his power and his purpose. . . ."

WHAT HE THOUGHT OF LONGFELLOW

"He is more than simply sweet and wholesome. His ballad-like poetry, such as 'The Saga of King Olaf,'

LITERARY FIGURES

'The Discovery of the North Cape,' 'Belisarius,' and others, especially of the sea, have it seems to me the strength as well as the simplicity that marks Walter Scott and the old English ballad writers. . . .

"Longfellow's love of peace was profound; but he was a man, and a wise man, and he knew that cowardice does not promote peace, and that even the great evil of war may be a less evil than cringing to iniquity."

WHAT HE THOUGHT OF HOLMES
"Oliver Wendell Holmes, of course, is the laughing philosopher, the humorist at his very highest, even if we use the word 'humor' only in its most modern and narrow sense."

WHAT HE THOUGHT OF LOWELL
"I like his literary essays; but what a real mugwump he gradually became, as he let his fastidiousness, his love of ease and luxury, and his shrinking from the necessary roughness of contact with the world, grow upon him! I think his sudden painting of Dante as a mugwump is deliciously funny. I suppose that his character was not really strong, and that he was permanently injured by association with the Charles Eliot Norton type, and above all by following that impossible creature, Godkin."

WHAT HE THOUGHT OF WHITTIER
"It seems to me that all good Americans should feel a peculiar pride in Whittier, exactly because he combined the power of expression and the great gift of poetry, with a flaming zeal for righteousness which made him a leader in matters of the spirit no less than of the intellect."

WHAT HE THOUGHT OF W. J. LONG
"It may be that I have helped Long from the financial standpoint, for that lying scoundrel is too shamelessly dishonest to mind the scorn of honest men if his infamy adds to his receipts; and of course it advertises him to be in a controversy with me. But I think I have pretty well destroyed his credit with all decent men of even moderate intelligence."

WHAT HE THOUGHT OF E. A. ROBINSON
"I hunted him up, found he was having a very hard time, and put him in the Treasury Department. I think he will do his work all right, but I am free to say that he was put in less with a view to the good of the government service than with a view to helping American letters." And he wrote to him: "I expect you to think poetry first and Treasury second."

WHAT HE THOUGHT OF GORKY
The Russian writer came to the United States in April 1906 to raise funds in the cause of Russian emancipation. In New York he was expelled from his hotel for sharing his rooms with Madame Andreiava, a Russian actress who was not his legal wife. When Gorky asked for an interview, Roosevelt refused to see him. He wrote sharply: "Gorky in his domestic relations seems to represent with nice exactness the general continental European revolutionary attitude, which in governmental matters is a revolt against order as well as against tyranny, and in domestic matters is a revolt against the ordinary decencies and moralities even more than against conventional hypocrisies and cruelties."

★

WHAT HE THOUGHT OF DICKENS
"It always interests me about Dickens to think how much first-class work he did and how almost all of it was mixed up with every kind of cheap, second-rate matter. I am very fond of him. There are innumerable characters that he has created which symbolize vices, virtues, follies, and the like . . . therefore I think the wise thing to do is simply to skip the bosh and twaddle and vulgarity and untruth, and get the benefit out of the rest. Of course one fundamental difference between Thackeray and Dickens is that Thackeray was a gentleman and Dickens was not. But a man might do some mighty good work and not be a gentleman in any sense."

A FEW SHOTS AT THE KING'S ENGLISH. A cartoon by E. W. Kemble in *Collier's Weekly* in September 1906, shortly after Roosevelt tried to introduce spelling reforms in printing government documents.

SIMPLIFIED SPELLING

This was one of Roosevelt's most amusing controversies. Brander Matthews of Columbia University persuaded him to join the ranks of the spelling reformers, and Roosevelt took up the fight at once. At first the suggested changes were moderate and embraced only 300 words. For example: honour, parlour, labour were to be written without the "u." Programme and catalogue were to be program and catalog. The "re" in theatre, centre, sabre was to be reversed; instead of cheque and comptroller, it would be check and controller. In some words like surprise and compromise, "s" was to become "z." Double letters in instill, fulfill, distill were eliminated, whiskey shortened to whisky, mamma to mama. The changes most resisted were "tho," "thoro," and "thru."

"Nothing escapes Mr. Rucevelt," wrote "Marse Henry" Waterson in the Louisville *Courier*. "No subject is tu hi for him to takl, nor tu lo for him to notis."

A MEMO BY ROOT

Elihu Root could take the liberty of teasing the President by sending him a note in simplified spelling, not long after Roosevelt ordered the Public Printer to use new spellings for 300 words.

When Congress reassembled and the President sent his annual message in the new spelling, the storm broke. The lawmakers adopted a resolution forbidding the printing of public documents in orthography not accepted by standard dictionaries. After the rebuke, Roosevelt withdrew his order but promised to continue using the new spelling in his own private correspondence.

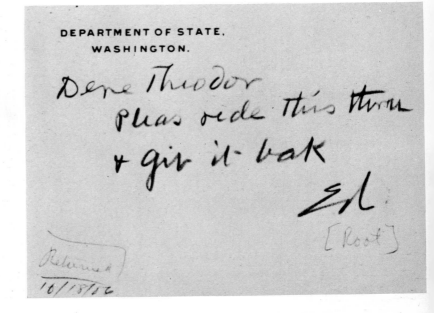

498

A "POINT TO POINT" WALK in Washington's Rock Creek Park was a part of Roosevelt's regular exercise. "Over and through, never around" was his motto, and those who accompanied him could barely keep up with the pace he set over jutting rocks and through swollen streams. Once his heart gave out while climbing, and his companions had to pull him up a cliff and wait forty minutes for him to recover.

THE "BEARDED LADY" was Roosevelt's description of Charles Evans Hughes, who would have liked to receive the Republican nomination in 1908.

"IF ONLY THERE WERE THREE OF YOU," Roosevelt once wrote to Taft. But he warned his friend of too much publicity on the golf course.

"THE COURTSHIP OF BILL TAFT." A cartoon by Joseph Keppler in *Puck* on April 24, 1907, which made America chuckle. In it "John Alden" Roosevelt speaks for "Miles Standish" Taft, and Priscilla asks, "Why don't you speak for yourself, Theodore?" Still, no decision was reached.

Early one morning a year later, Roosevelt's secretary, William Loeb, Jr., told the President that "we must have a candidate. If things continue to drift along as now, our friends may lose control." Roosevelt replied that the man whom he would like to see

as his successor was Elihu Root, the Secretary of War. "I would walk on my hands and knees from the White House to the Capitol to see Root made President," he once remarked. But when Loeb came to Root with the message, Root said: "Please tell the President that I appreciate deeply every word, but I cannot be a candidate. It would mean a fight in the convention and I could not be elected. I've thought it all out. Thank the President, but tell him I am not in the running."

After Root's refusal Roosevelt told Loeb: "We had better turn to Taft. See Taft and tell him of our talk today—tell him all of it so he will know my mind."

Taft accepted Roosevelt's endorsement with joy. And when the Republican Nominating Convention met in Chicago, the delegates ratified the President's choice on the first ballot. In the election Taft defeated William Jennings Bryan, whom the Democrats nominated for the third time, and Eugene V. Debs, also a third-time contender for the Socialist party. Taft's popular vote was 7,677,788; Bryan's, 6,407,982; Debs's, 420,890; and Chapin's, 252,511.

AN ENGLISH CARTOONIST'S COMMENT ON ROOSEVELT'S SUCCESSOR

Bernard Partridge, who four and a half decades before had assailed Abraham Lincoln in *Punch*, now used his sharp pen against Theodore Roosevelt. In the biting cartoon "The Heir Presumptive," which the English weekly printed on June 17, 1908, President Roosevelt tells Taft: "There, sonny, I've fixed you up so they won't know the difference between us."

ALONE I DIDN'T DO IT! is the title of this superb Partridge cartoon in *Punch* on November 11, 1908, after the news reached England that William Howard Taft had been elected to the American Presidency. Taft defeated William Jennings Bryan, the three-time Democratic candidate, with 321 electoral votes against his opponent's 162. In the caption under the drawing, the breathless but triumphant President-elect says: "Thank you, Teddy!"

TWO OF ROOSEVELT'S FAVORITE CARTOONS

"IT WILL END THIS SIDE UP," a cartoon by Westerman in the *Ohio State Journal*, indicating how the American people felt about Roosevelt and Congress.

"HIS FAVORITE AUTHOR," a cartoon by Lowry in the Chicago *Chronicle*. Roosevelt put this one in a frame and hung it on his study wall at Oyster Bay.

MARCH 2, 1909: THE LAST MEETING WITH THE CABINET

CELEBRATING THE 100TH ANNIVERSARY OF ABRAHAM LINCOLN'S BIRTH
President Roosevelt on February 12, 1909, journeyed to Hodgenville, Ky., where he
spoke in honor of "the mightiest of the mighty men who mastered the mighty days."

THE END OF THE REIGN

FAREWELL, TEDDY! Weeping newspaper correspondents say good-by to the President. They know that never again will they have such good copy.

★

ONE OF HIS LAST OFFICIAL ACTS. On February 22, 1909, at Hampton Roads, Va., Roosevelt welcomed the fleet from its voyage around the world. "Not until some American fleet returns victorious from a great sea battle," prophesied he, "will there be another such homecoming and such a sight."

A SNOWY INAGURATION. A bitter storm blew on March 4, 1909; snow and ice cut Washington off from

the rest of the world. The weather was so severe that the ceremonies had to be held inside the Senate chamber. Taft said sadly: "I always knew it would be a cold day when I became President of the U.S." But Roosevelt was in high spirits in anticipation of his African trip, "the realization of a golden dream."

Part 4:

PRIVATE CITIZEN

HE OLD AND THE NEW
heodore Roosevelt poses with President-
lect William H. Taft on March 4, 1909.

CHAPTER XXXVII

THE GREAT ADVENTURE
AND ITS AFTERMATH

William Howard Taft was installed in Washington, and Theodore Roosevelt was on his way to Africa. After seven and one half years in the White House he was once more a private citizen.

Despite the popular toast in the clubs of the rich "Health to the lions!" and the forebodings of his anxious friends, the safari in Africa was a success. For eleven months he and his party traveled "rifle in hand over the empty, sunlit African wastes" experiencing, as he phrased it, "the joy of wandering through lonely lands; the joy of hunting the mighty and terrible lords of the wilderness, the cunning, the wary and the grim." Though he was not conditioned to the tropical climate, he was ill for only five days during the entire trip. He was watched wherever he went; his every move was recorded in the press. "The people," Senator Lodge wrote to him, "follow the account of your African wanderings as if it were a new Robinson Crusoe."

As soon as the expedition disbanded in Khartoum—it was in the middle of March 1910—Roosevelt became embroiled in the controversy over the British rule in Egypt. Invited to address a native officers' club, he spoke with "unmistakable plainness as to their duty of absolute loyalty, and as to the ruin which would come to both Egypt and the Sudan unless the power and prestige of the English rule were kept undiminished." The speech embittered the Egyptian Nationalists, struggling to lift the yoke of British imperialism.

Originally, he had planned to return home, but the demands for lectures were so pressing that he could not avoid accepting some of the invitations. Oxford University asked him to deliver the Romanes lecture; the Sorbonne in Paris wanted him to give an address; Kaiser Wilhelm insisted that he should speak in Germany. And Roosevelt himself felt that he should deliver an address in Norway, giving his belated thanks for the Nobel Peace Prize. Invitations poured in from the royal rulers of Europe. "I soon found," said he in amusement, "that while the different rulers did not really care a rap about seeing me, they did not like me to see *other* rulers and pass them by." And so he set out for a grand tour of the continent.

It was a happy trip, the trip through Europe; the ex-President's unaffected candor fascinated kings and commoners alike. "I thoroughly liked and respected almost all the kings and queens I met," Roosevelt said. "They struck me as serious people with charming manners, devoted to their people and anxious to justify their own positions by the way they did their duty." But his respect was mixed with a degree of pity for "the tedium, the dull, narrow routine of their lives," which he felt forced them into the role of a "kind of sublimated American vice-president." In dealing with the immensely complex questions of protocol at court functions, he insisted that his status as ex-President entitled him to no special precedence whatever. "To me," he declared, "there is something fine in the American theory that a private citizen can be chosen by the people to occupy a position as great as that of the mightiest monarch and to exercise a power which may surpass that of Czar, Kaiser, or Pope, and that then, after having filled this position, the man shall leave it an unpensioned private citizen, who goes back into the ranks of his fellow-citizens with entire self-respect, claiming nothing save what on his own individual merits he is entitled to receive."

Not everything went smoothly. Roosevelt was Roosevelt, and he loved a good fight. Thus, in Rome he was embroiled in "an elegant row" with the Vatican. The reason: Pope Pius X would not receive him without a promise that he would not visit the American Methodist missionaries who talked of the Pope as "the whore of Babylon." Though Roosevelt had no intention of visiting the Methodists, he told the Vatican that he could not submit to "any conditions which limit my freedom of conduct." He deplored the excessive zeal of the Methodist missionaries, but he also rebuked Papal Secretary Merry del Val, whom he described as a "furiously bigoted reactionary." By his actions he showed the world "that I feared the most powerful Protestant Church just as little as I feared the Roman Catholics."

From Italy the tour took him to Austria-Hungary, France, Belgium, Holland, the Scandinavian countries, and finally to Germany. Everywhere he went he attracted large crowds and intense curiosity; everywhere his attempts to explain that an ex-President has no more authority than any other American citizen were "greeted with polite but exasperating incredulity."

Particular interest focused on his visit to Germany, where Kaiser Wilhelm's growing belligerence in the face of military encirclement was causing increasing concern to the British and French. "The Germans," in Roosevelt's opinion, "did not like me and did not like my country; and under the circumstances they behaved entirely correctly, showing me every civility and making no pretense of an enthusiasm that was not present." No cheering crowds followed him about, as in other nations, but he was warmly received by the Kaiser, "an able and powerful man," who asked how he was regarded in the United States. Roosevelt told him: "In America we think that if you lived on our side of the water you would carry your ward and turn up at the convention with your delegation behind you—and I cannot say as much for most of your fellow sovereigns!"

The English greeted him with good-humored affection. His Romanes lecture in Oxford, a treatise on the parallels between the evolution of animal life and the evolution of civilization, was introduced by Lord Curzon, the chancellor of the University. Curzon said that Roosevelt's "onslaughts on the wild beasts of the desert have been not less fierce nor less successful than over the many-headed hydra of corruption in his own land"—an encomium which the chancellor topped off with this couplet:

> Before whose coming comets took to flight
> And all the Nile's seven mouths turned pale in fright.

As if to justify this tribute to his vigor, Roosevelt essayed to counsel the British on empire management in a speech he delivered at the Guild Hall on being made a Freeman of the city of London. England, he declared, should decide whether it had a right to control Egypt or not. This speech created an uproar, with Englishmen both attacking and defending him.

During his trip in Europe, King Edward VII of England died, and President Taft asked Roosevelt to represent the United States at the funeral. Like most royal funerals, it was a giant pageant more than an occasion of genuine grief, and the ex-President made little effort to restrain his enormous amusement at the studied posturings of the royal guests as they jostled for precedence and vented their petty jealousies against one another. Years later at Sagamore Hill he delighted friends and visitors with his anecdotes about how the domineering Kaiser put the lesser monarchs through their paces and about the contempt with which the better established kings and queens regarded the pathetic little "bush league czars from the Balkans." By the time the funeral was over, Roosevelt had had enough of royal pageants. "I felt," he said, "that if I met another king I should bite him."

In early June it was time to go home. Letters had come by the thousands from all parts of the country, asking him to address meetings or give lectures. Taft had written as well—a letter of political sorrow. Roosevelt knew of Taft's growing troubles with Congress and his growing troubles with the progressive wing of the party. Now he learned about them from the President himself. And while Roosevelt was sailing toward America, a versifier in *Life* expressed the feelings of many a citizen:

> Teddy come home and blow your horn,
> The sheep's in the meadow, the cow's in the corn.
> The boy you left to tend the sheep
> Is under the haystack fast asleep.

As his ship, the *Kaiserin Augusta Victoria*, sailed into New York Harbor, some 2500 dignitaries, Congressmen, Senators, and governors, were at hand to greet him. The nation showed its affection by a spectacular demonstration. A huge parade, with ex-Rough Riders as an honor guard, escorted him up Broadway and Fifth Avenue between lines of cheering citizens. It was the most fervent reception of his career.

With his return, press and public speculated about his future. What would he do? They were curious to know: Would he back Taft or would he join the insurgents?

OFF TO THE GREAT ADVENTURE. March 23, 1909, the day Theodore Roosevelt left for Africa, was a great day in Hoboken, New Jersey. He was fifty years old, but as eager as a young boy for adventure. The pier was dark with people—Rough Riders, political friends, delegations of all kinds had come to shake his hand and bid him farewell. President Taft sent Archie Butt, his military aide, with a bon voyage letter and gold ruler inscribed: "Theodore Roosevelt from William Howard Taft. Good Bye—Good Luck—and a Safe Return."

THE LUGGAGE of the expedition contained a wide variety of objects from rifles, maps, and taxidermist equipment to boxes of champagne and whisky.

The expedition's expenses, at first estimated at $75,000, were covered by the Smithsonian Institution in Washington with money donated by sponsors, Andrew Carnegie heading the list.

Roosevelt signed up with *Scribner's Magazine* to write articles on his African experiences for $50,000. When he heard about this, King Edward of England remarked: "President Roosevelt is coming out as a penny-a-liner."

*A DAVENPORT CARTOON
IN THE NEW YORK EVENING MAIL,
THE DAY ROOSEVELT SET OUT FOR AFR*

"HIST! SEE WHO'S COMING!"

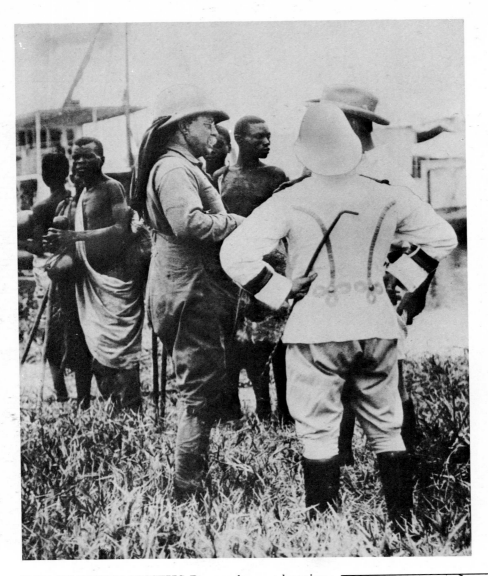

FOR ELEVEN MONTHS Roosevelt went hunting and searched for rare specimens of animals in the jungles of Africa. In his articles for *Scribner's* and in his subsequent book, *African Game Trails,* he left a vivid description of those eleven months. His "list of game shot with the rifle during the trip" added up to 296 animals. Among these were 9 lions, 8 elephants, 13 rhinoceroses, 7 hippopotami, 6 buffaloes, 15 zebras, and 28 gazelles. (Kermit's bag was 216.)

On the last day of February 1910 the expedition began the return trip down the Nile. "We reached Khartoum on the afternoon of March 14, 1910," wrote Roosevelt, "and Kermit and I parted from our comrades of the trip with real regret; during the year we spent together there had not been a jar, and my respect and liking for them had grown steadily. Moreover, it was a sad parting from our faithful black followers, whom we knew we should never see again."

WHAT ARE THEY DOING AT HOME?
A Cunningham cartoon in the Washington *Herald.*

516

THE FAMILY IS TOGETHER AGAIN. The Roosevelts, with their daughter Ethel, inspect the well from which Slatin Pasha had to drink during his long imprisonment. Rudolf Carl von Slatin, one of the most fabulous personalities in the Middle East, was Roosevelt's host during his three days of sightseeing in Khartoum. An Austrian, he came to the Sudan in 1879 at the instigation of the English Governor General Gordon. Soon he became governor of Dara, then governor general of Darfur. In December 1883 hostile Arab tribes captured him, and for eleven years they kept him as their prisoner. When he escaped in 1900, he was named inspector general of the Sudan, remaining in this post until the outbreak of the First World War in 1914.

The Roosevelts were welcomed by Slatin Pasha "with more than mere friendly enthusiasm." They were entertained lavishly and they were shown around the country. Mrs. Roosevelt, with Ethel, came to Khartoum to join her husband and her son Kermit. They arrived on March 14, and it was a joyous reunion after such a long separation. During his whole stay in Africa, Roosevelt was "dreadfully homesick" for his wife. To his friend Spring-Rice he wrote: "Catch me ever leaving her again, if I can help it."

Now that Mrs. Roosevelt was at his side, his happiness was complete. He showed her the desert, he made her ride on a camel, he took her on a sightseeing tour.

After he delivered two addresses praising the British rule in the Sudan, the party journeyed to Wady Halfa and from there to Cairo where the "great adventure" came to an end.

THE PIGSKIN LIBRARY which Roosevelt carried with him in an aluminum and oilcloth case weighed less than sixty pounds. The books revealed his literary interest, ranging from Homer to Macaulay and Carlyle, from Shakespeare to Dante, Keats, and Browning, from Euripides to Mark Twain, from *The Federalist* papers to James Fenimore Cooper, Longfellow, Holmes, Poe and Tennyson.

In an appendix to his *African Game Trails*, Roosevelt said of the books: "They were for use, not ornament. I almost always had some volume with me, either in my saddle-pocket or in the cartridge-bag which one of my gun-bearers carried to hold odds and ends. Often my reading would be done while resting under a tree at noon, perhaps beside the carcass of a beast I had killed, or else while waiting for camp to be pitched; and in either case it might be impossible to get water for washing. In consequence the books were stained with blood, sweat, gun oil, dust and ashes; ordinary bindings either vanished or became loathsome, whereas pigskin merely grew to look as a well-used saddle looks."

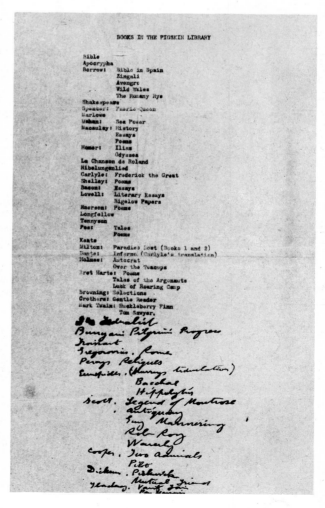

A CAMEL RIDE IN THE DESERT WITH SLATIN PASHA

THE KING OF ITALY delighted Roosevelt. Interested in reading, big-game hunting, history, and social progress, he talked Roosevelt's language. Victor Emmanuel III and Queen Helene "are loving and faithful to each other . . . and it was good to see their relations, together and with the children."

VISITING THE FORUM with Lawrence F. Abbott (left), who acted during the European trip as Roosevelt's secretary, and with Jesse B. Carter, Director of Rome's American School of Classical Studies. At this time Roosevelt had "an elegant row" with Merry del Val, the Papal secretary, about the American Methodist missionaries, one of whom had caused a furor when he called the Pope "the whore of Babylon."

GIFFORD PINCHOT AT PORTO MAURIZIO, where Roosevelt was staying in the villa of his sister-in-law. Pinchot brought with him a sheaf of letters from the progressives Albert J. Beveridge, Jonathan P. Dolliver, and William Allen White, full of complaints against President Taft and his policies.

"MAYBE MR. TAFT'S EAR DIDN'T TINGLE!" read the caption of this Barclay cartoon in the Baltimore *Sun*. The newspapers at home were filled with stories of Gifford Pinchot's meeting with Roosevelt in Europe. Chief Forester Pinchot, who was Roosevelt's planner in the conservation program, was dismissed by Taft when he interfered in the controversy between Secretary of Interior Richard A. Ballinger and Louis Glavis, chief of a field division in Alaska. Pinchot wrote a letter to Senator Dolliver in which he upheld Glavis as the defender of the people's interests and criticized the President for dismissing him. The quarrel grew in intensity, and the issue became conservation versus the spoliation of natural resources. President Taft hesitated to remove Pinchot—well knowing how the action would affect Roosevelt—but finally had to do it. Though Lodge warned against an appearance of enmity toward Taft, Roosevelt would not listen and allowed Pinchot to visit him.

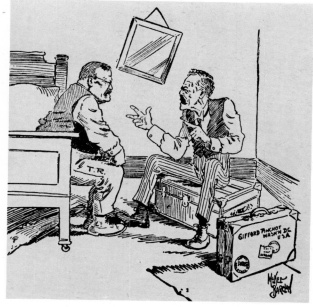

RISK MORNING WALK
imber up after the long ocean voyage. The
tograph was taken in Gibraltar on April 2, 1909.

TOURING THE CAPITALS OF EUROPE

IN PARIS, Roosevelt went sight-seeing, visited Napoleon's tomb, accompanied by the Generals Niox, Feldman, and Dalstein and the Ambassadors Bacon and Jusserand. The following day, on April 23, 1910, he delivered an address at the Sorbonne on "Citizenship in a Republic," making appeal for moral rather than for intellectual or material greatness.

REVIEWING FRENCH TROOPS

Jusserand, the French ambassador to the United States, persuaded Roosevelt to review some troops, otherwise the people might feel that he "did not take her military power seriously, nor deem her soldiers worth seeing." So off he went to Vincennes to see a sham battle "in the usual dreadful dress of the 'visiting statesmen' with frock coat and top hat." When the colonel of the French cavalry regiment suggested that he might like to mount a horse, Roosevelt was delighted at the suggestion. All he asked was to have a pair of leggings, which were duly produced. At the end of the review he was heartily complimented by the troops, who were "very much pleased at my riding."

IN BERLIN, on May 12, the German Emperor, with the Empress and several members of the imperial family, came to the University of Berlin to attend Roosevelt's lecture on "The World Movement," a long and dull discourse on the growth of civilization. The Kaiser seemed to like it, however, "nodding his head or smiling now and then with approval."

ROOSEVELT ARRIVES at the University of Berlin. Until the morning of the lecture it was not certain whether he would be able to deliver the address. For days he had a severe attack of bronchitis, and the physicians were not sure whether he "could use his voice for one hour in safety." Arrangements were made to have someone else read the address if it were found necessary at the last moment. But Roosevelt recovered in time, his vocal cords so well fixed up that when he began to speak, "his eyes directly on the Kaiser," his voice—according to Count Bülow, who was in the audience—sounded "unusually loud and piercing."

Döberitz 11/V 1910
The Armament driven home!
The Germanic & Anglo Saxon Races combined will
Keep the world in order. Wilhelm I.R.

Döberitz 11/V 1910
"A piece of good advice:" Carnegie is an old Peacebore
"send him to d'Estournelles:" Wilhelm I.R.

Döberitz 11/V 1910
On the "Mühlenberg" a grave discussion!
Carnegie look out! Wilhelm I.R.

Döberitz 11/V 1910
Total agreement about the general
Maxims of life & policy between America
& Germany Wilhelm I.R.

FOR FIVE HOURS the Kaiser and Roosevelt conversed. Roosevelt told the Emperor of Andrew Carnegie's suggestion to create a council of nations which could end Europe's dangerous armaments race and assure the settlement of international conflicts by arbitration rather than by guns.

Next day the Kaiser sent Roosevelt the above set of photographs "with really amusing comments of his own pencilled on the back of them." They are published here for the first time in facsimile.

Wilhelm I.R.

The Colonel of the Rough Riders lecturing the Chief of the German Army

KING EDWARD'S FUNERAL

On May 6, 1910, King Edward of England died, and President Taft asked Roosevelt to represent him at the King's funeral.

On May 19—the eve of the funeral—he attended the state banquet at Buckingham Palace with eight monarchs present. Roosevelt enjoyed himself immensely. At one side of the table sat King George of England; at the other, Emperor Wilhelm of Germany. As the dinner began, the face of everyone at the table was "wreathed and distorted with grief," but soon they had forgotten why they had come together. After his return to America, Roosevelt told President Taft: "I have never attended a more hilarious banquet in my life. I never saw quite so many knights." The King of Greece "fairly wept out his troubles to me," and King Alfonso of Spain confided "that he did not like anarchists, but as much as he hated anarchists, he hated the clericals more."

Roosevelt was amused by court etiquette. Caring little where his place was in the procession, he found it funny when the special ambassador from France complained that the Chinese were riding in front of him. Though Roosevelt told him "I did not care where they put me," the Frenchman could not be calmed. "With tears in his eyes, tears of anger," he approached Roosevelt, asking him whether he had noticed "that the other guests had scarlet livery and that ours was black. I told him I had not noticed, but I would not have cared if ours had been yellow and green. My French, while fluent, is never very clear, and it took me another half hour to get it out of his mind that I was not protesting because my livery was not green and yellow."

528

IN LONDON

A CARTOON IN *PUNCH* at the time Roosevelt visited London. In it the lions at Trafalgar Square were wearing signs "Not to be shot," and were guarded by policemen. Roosevelt loved the joke.

SPEAKING AT THE GUILDHALL on May 31 on the occasion of his election as a Freeman of the City of London, he told the distinguished audience that he would not make an "extended address of mere thanks," but that he preferred to speak "on matters of real concern to you."

Taking as his topic "The British Rule in Africa," he told his listeners that "the present condition of affairs is a grave menace to both your Empire and the entire civilized world . . . if you do not wish to establish and keep order there . . . get out of Egypt."

531

AT OXFORD, JUNE 7, 1910, Roosevelt delivered the Romanes Lecture in the Sheldonian Theater on "Biological Analogies in History," one of his most profound and carefully prepared addresses. He showed the draft of it to his friend Henry Fairfield Osborn, who later recalled that he had blue-penciled some sentences. "I have left out certain passages that are likely to bring on war between the United States and the governments referred to."

After Roosevelt's speech the Archbishop of York said: "In the way of grading which we have at Oxford, we agreed to mark the lecture 'Beta Minus,' but the lecturer 'Alpha Plus.' While we felt that the lecture was not a very great contribution to science, we were sure that the lecturer was a very great man."

★

AT CAMBRIDGE, MAY 26, 1910, Roosevelt spoke to the undergraduates—after being elected an honorary member of the literary and debating society—on "The Condition of Success." "If a man lives a decent life," he said, "and does his work fairly and squarely so that those dependent on him and attached to him are better for his having lived, then he is a success . . ."

A CHARMING INCIDENT at Cambridge. Roosevelt said that the students greeted him "as the students of our own colleges would have greeted me." He recalled: "On my arrival they had formed in two long ranks, leaving a pathway for me to walk between them, and at the final turn in this pathway they had

a Teddy Bear seated on the pavement with out-stretched paw to greet me; and when I was given my degree in the chapel the students had rigged a kind of pulley arrangement by which they tried to let down a very large Teddy Bear upon me as I took the degree —I was told that when Kitchener was given his degree they let down a Mahdi upon him, and a monkey on Darwin under similar circumstances. I spoke in the Union to the students, and it was exactly and precisely as if I had been speaking to the Harvard students in the Harvard Union. . . . I was interested to find that there was such exact similarity."

HOME AT LAST. Friends, politicians, newspapermen met the *Kaiserin Augusta Victoria* on a tender to greet Roosevelt as the liner dropped anchor off quarantine on June 18, 1910. It was a rousing welcome he received—the crowd was extremely happy to have him back.

JOURNEY'S END

The Roosevelts descend the gangplank. "I have been away a year and a quarter . . . and I have seen strange and interesting things," he told the press. "I am more glad than I can say to be back in my own country, back among the people I love." He had forgotten that only a few weeks before he had written Cabot Lodge: "Ugh! I do dread getting back to America, and having to plunge into this cauldron of politics."

He further said: "I want to close up like a native oyster. . . . I have nothing to say." This statement only amused the reporters; they were sure they knew better.

UNCLE SAM: "I CAN'T SEE HIM, BUT I THINK I CAN HEAR HIM!"
This Donahey cartoon—especially the caption beneath it—tickled the funnybone of America.
It was "bully" to have him back again; life had not been the same while he was away

RETURN FROM EUROPE. When Roosevelt returned from his European trip, his devotion to Taft was still strong. The President had sent a long and pathetic letter which reached Roosevelt in Southampton. "I do not know," Taft wrote, "that I have had harder luck than other Presidents, but I do know that thus far I have succeeded far less than have others. I have been conscientiously trying to carry out your policies, but my method of doing so has not worked smoothly."

He reviewed his accomplishments. He believed that his tariff bill was a good one, he felt that the tax on corporations was useful, he was pleased that within a short time Arizona and New Mexico would become states of the Union. He proudly reported that the chief conservation measure would become law, as would the postal savings bill.

Roosevelt reassured his friend: "I shall make no speeches or say anything for two months, but I shall keep my mind open as I keep my mouth shut." It was a fine promise—but within days it was forgotten.

★

A YOUNG MAN watches the adulation of his wife's uncle. Nobody cares about him as he leans against the funnel of the boat. He is just one of the many members of the welcoming group. But in the span of a generation he will be the figure in the center of the stage. His name: Franklin Delano Roosevelt.

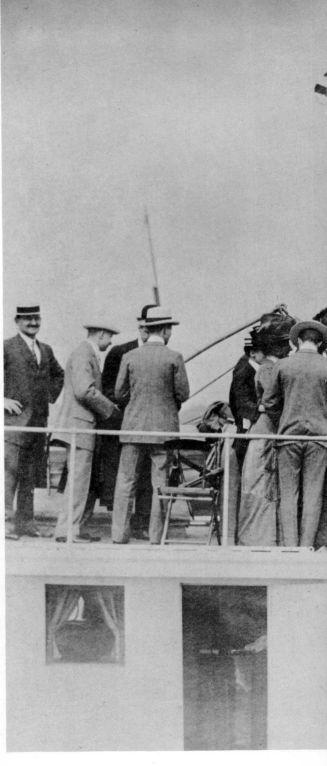

WELCOME HOME! Members of the family and friends gathered around the Roosevelts after they left the ocean liner and made their way on the revenue cutter to the Battery. Mrs. Roosevelt is surrounded

by the group of ladies at the left. In the center, the bearded figure in top hat and with his hand on the railing is Henry Cabot Lodge, faithful friend and adviser. On the right, standing before the funnel, is Franklin D. Roosevelt, the young man whose destiny so closely paralleled that of Theodore, even then being Assistant Secretary of the Navy. On his left is his wife, Eleanor, the niece of Theodore Roosevelt.

FIFTH AVENUE GREETS ITS BELOVED SON

NEW YORK'S WELCOME

"COME TO MY ARMS, MY BEAMISH BOY!"
A cartoon by C. R. Macauley in the New York *World* expressed America's feeling toward the homecomer.

TITLE PAGE OF *HARPER'S WEEKLY*

CHAPTER XXXVIII

FRIENDS
TURN INTO ENEMIES

"It is now a year and three months since I assumed office and I have had a hard time—I do not know that I have had harder luck than other Presidents, but I do know that thus far I have succeeded far less than have others. I have been conscientiously trying to carry out your policies but my method of doing so has not worked smoothly." This was Taft, writing to Roosevelt in London.

Roosevelt was well aware of the stress and strain within the Republican ranks. He had seen Gifford Pinchot in Italy, he had spoken with Elihu Root, and he had received many messages from insurgent Republicans. Their descriptions of the political picture were dark. "Ugh! I do dread getting back to America, and having to plunge into this cauldron of politics," he wrote to Cabot Lodge from Norway. "Our own party leaders did not realize that I was able to hold the Republican party in power only because I insisted on a steady advance, and dragged them along with me. Now the advance has been stopped, and whether we blame the people on the one side, or the leaders on the other, the fact remains that we are in a very uncomfortable position."

Replying to Taft's letter from London, Roosevelt told the President that he was "much concerned about some of the things I see and am told; but what I have felt it best to do was to say absolutely nothing—and indeed to keep my mind as open as I kept my mouth shut!" These same sentiments he repeated after his arrival in New York, promising to "close up like a native oyster."

But how could he remain silent when all he heard was that the party organization was falling apart at the seams? How could he remain silent when he saw that the progressives who had comprised his most devoted supporters were forced into opposition by the President? How could he remain silent when he saw that on the vital political issues of the day—tariff, conservation, railroad regulation—his party was sorely divided?

He was disappointed in Taft, the man whom he had chosen to continue his policies. Only ten days after he set foot in America, he wrote to Gifford Pinchot that "in all probability Taft has passed his nadir. He is evidently a man who takes color from his surroundings. He was an excellent man under me, and close to me. For eighteen months after his election he was a rather pitiful failure, because he had no real strong man on whom to lean, and yielded to the advice of his wife, his brother Charley, the different corporation lawyers who had his ear, and various similar men."

He was aware that Taft's intentions were good, but he also realized that the

President had neither the drive nor the aggressiveness to translate the good intentions into good politics. Amiable, stolid, honest, Taft would have made a passable Chief Executive if only Theodore Roosevelt had not been his predecessor. To follow a flamboyant, colorful man and be successful is always difficult; to follow a Roosevelt in the presidential chair and be successful was impossible. Elihu Root put his finger on it when he said that changing from Roosevelt to Taft was like changing from an automobile back to a horse-cab.

Taft was no master in the art of politics, and he bungled into controversies which another, shrewder man would have avoided. He threw his support behind "Uncle Joe" Cannon, the ultra-conservative Speaker of the House (against whose dictatorial powers the progressives rebelled), though he had no more sympathy for Cannon's autocratic methods than Roosevelt had when he was President. He praised the Payne-Aldrich tariff bill (which the progressives in the party fought violently) as "the best tariff bill that the Republican party has ever passed." And when the storm broke over the remark, he retracted it by saying that "the comparative would have been a better description than the superlative." He appeared to be—especially during the Ballinger-Pinchot controversy—a foe of conservation, which he was not. "Taft, who is such an admirable fellow, has shown himself such an utterly commonplace leader," wrote Roosevelt in August to his English friend Arthur Hamilton Lee, "good natured; feebly well-meaning, but with plenty of small motive, and totally unable to grasp or put into execution any really great policy."

The party was in a turmoil. The progressives were weary of the President and the men around him, and Taft was convinced that the real purpose of the progressives was to wreck his administration and defeat him in 1912. The schism between the two wings grew. In the primaries of 1910 the regular Republicans suffered one defeat after the other with the progressives winning almost every contest.

Roosevelt was in an unhappy mood. It was not hard to see that the fight within the Republican ranks would help the Democrats to victory in the mid-term election. Thus, he felt that he must throw himself into the campaign and unify the two wings that were pulling in opposite directions.

After an unsuccessful attempt in New York State, where he endorsed the direct primary and was compelled to fight the old Republican wheelhorses on the floor of the state convention to win the chairmanship, he left for a speaking tour. His special train covered some 5000 miles in 16 states, and wherever he went, he was greeted with enthusiasm. He would not permit the Republican National Committee to sponsor his trip. "My speeches on the trip will represent myself entirely, nobody else," he told reporters.

As he journeyed through the Middle West his speeches echoed progressive principles; the conservatives got little comfort from them. It was at Osawatomie, Kansas, that he enunciated the doctrine of the New Nationalism and uttered the sentence which chilled the spines of all standpatters. He said, "The man who wrongly holds that every human right is secondary to his profit must now give way to the advocate of human welfare, who rightly maintains that every man holds his property subject to the general right of the community to regulate its use to whatever degree the public welfare may require it." For this the New York *Post* denounced him as "the most radical man in public life in our time."

Having gained the support of the progressives in the West, he returned east, where he sought to convince the regular Republicans that it was in their best interest to work together with the progressives. In speech after speech he came out for moderate regulars and for moderate progressives. But when the election returns were in, they showed that the strategy had not worked—the country repudiated the divided Republican party. The Democrats won with a large majority in the House of Representatives, and they won in New York State, defeating Roosevelt's hand-picked candidate for the governorship.

Never before had Roosevelt suffered such political defeat. Disconsolate in heart and dejected in spirit, he looked toward the future with gloom.

He buried himself in Sagamore Hill, trying to keep out of the limelight. He would not accept any invitations to give speeches. He would not allow himself to be drawn publicly into the increasingly violent controversy between progressives and standpatters. On the surface he was still friendly toward Taft, but the warmth of their relationship was gone. They were not seeing each other, and their correspondence had ceased. Taft could not understand Roosevelt's behavior. "I don't know what he is driving at except to make my way more difficult," he said to Archie Butt after Roosevelt, in *The Outlook,* attacked his arbitration proposals. And he bemoaned the fact of a "devoted friendship going to pieces like a rope of sand." More and more the two former friends drifted apart, their mounting antagonism fostered not only by political but by personal issues. Members of their families, political friends and foes, newspaper writers, Washington gossips, all contributed their part in widening the rift between them until it became an unbridgeable gulf.

The last ties were severed on the very day Roosevelt became fifty-three years old. On that day—October 27, 1911—the Taft administration brought an anti-trust suit against the U. S. Steel Corporation, an action which charged —among other things—that Roosevelt had been misled during the 1907 panic when he allowed U. S. Steel to purchase the Tennessee Coal and Iron Company. Roosevelt was hurt to the quick. He wrote an article in *The Outlook,* castigating the administration and revealing Taft's part in the affair. "The Trust, the People, and the Square Deal," as the article was called, focused the country's attention on him. Rooseveltians of every variety, from ex-Rough Riders to senators, converged on Sagamore Hill, urging him to become a candidate. "I do not want to be President again," said their hero. "I am not a candidate, I have not the slightest idea of becoming a candidate." But to his friend Bishop he confessed: "Taft is utterly hopeless. I think he would be beaten if nominated, but in any event it would be a misfortune to have him in the Presidential chair for another term, for he has shown himself an entirely unfit President."

And as he groped for a decision, all America was asking the same question, the one which the New York *American* put succinctly: "T. R.: R U or R U not?"

STANDPATTERS

NELSON ALDRICH
(1841–1915), son-in-law
of Rockefeller, repre-
sented R. I. in the Sen-
ate from 1881 to 1911.

HENRY C. LODGE
(1850–1924), a close
friend of Roosevelt from
young manhood. Mass.
Senator 1893 to 1924.

REED SMOOT
(1862–1941), prominent
member of the Mormon
sect, was a Senator from
Utah from 1903 to 1933.

EUGENE HALE
(1836–1918) served as
Maine's Senator from
1881 to 1911, for a rec-
ord thirty-year term.

JOHN KEAN
(1852–1914), a Senator
from New Jersey 1899 to
1911, and a personal
friend of President Taft.

WELDON HEYBURN
(1852–1912), a Senator
from Idaho from 1903
until death, helped frame
his state's constitution.

THE PROGRESSIVE REVOLT

Between Abraham Lincoln in 1861 and Theodore
Roosevelt in 1901, the country, with the exception
of the Democrat Grover Cleveland, had elected only
Republicans for the high office. They were weak men
with no ability for leadership. During these forty
years the real power was not in their hands, but in
the hands of big industrialists, big bankers, and big
businessmen. Men like John D. Rockefeller, Andrew
Carnegie, J. Pierpont Morgan, William H. Vanderbilt, James J. Hill wielded more political influence
than any of the Presidents.

It was during these decades that the philosophy
of the Republican party underwent a radical change.
Gone were the days of the reform Republicanism
and idealism of Lincoln; during these years the policies of the party became based on a materialistic
concept. In the Senate the interests of the large industries and combines—of oil, sugar, petroleum, cotton
—were well taken care of. And while a chosen few
amassed fortunes, the people who created the wealth
had to be content with starvation wages.

The greatest sufferers in this era of abundance
were the farmers. Prices for agricultural products

CAUSES FOR THE REPUBLICAN SPLIT:
President Taft praised the conservative Payne-
Aldrich tariff bill, declaring in a speech at Winona,
Minnesota, that it was "the best tariff that has been
passed at all." His remarks caused an uproar in
the Middle West. Progressive Republican Senators
and Representatives from that area, thoroughly
aroused by the high tariff provisions of the bill, bitterly
criticized the President and assailed "Aldrichism."

544

were low, mortgage money was high. The situation cried for a remedy, and when such remedy was not forthcoming, farmers and workers in the Middle West banded together and allied themselves under the Populist banner. The people demanded reform, they cried for justice. But Congress—under the dominant influence of conservative politicians—blocked all reform legislation.

When Roosevelt—who sympathized with many of the progressive proposals—left the White House in 1909, his party was already divided and was growing rapidly toward a schism. President Taft's ineptness hastened this political split. His handling of the tariff issue, his support of Speaker Cannon—who omitted most of the progressives from permanent committees in the House—his dismissal of Gifford Pinchot, enraged the progressives. "Taft is a damn, pig-headed blunderer," said a Middle Western publisher to Roosevelt. The dissatisfaction with the President and his policies grew.

At the time of Roosevelt's return from Europe, the battle lines were already clearly drawn. The conservative standpatters rallied behind Taft, and the progressives looked upon Roosevelt as their man.

R. LA FOLLETTE (1855–1925), twice governor of Wisconsin, entered the Senate in 1906 and served until 1925.

J. DOLLIVER (1858–1910), Iowa Senator from 1900 to 1910, one of the outspoken antagonists of Aldrich.

ALBERT BEVERIDGE (1862–1927), an Indiana Senator 1899–1911 and outstanding biographer of Marshall and Lincoln.

JOSEPH BRISTOW (1861–1944), Kansas Senator 1909 to 1915, newspaper owner, Panama R.R. commissioner.

CAUSES FOR THE REPUBLICAN SPLIT: President Taft sided with the conservative wing of his party, who supported Joseph Cannon, the Speaker of the House, while the progressives were determined to shear "Uncle Joe" of his extraordinary political powers. On March 16, 1910, George W. Norris of Nebraska offered a resolution calling for a Rules Committee on which the Speaker would not sit. After a heated debate the progressives won their case.

ALBERT CUMMINS (1850–1926), Iowa Senator 1908–1926 and delegate to every Republican convention for 46 years.

MOSES E. CLAPP (1851–1931), Senator from Minnesota 1901 to 1917, called by Taft "an unstable light weight."

"THEODORE, THINGS HAVEN'T BEEN THE SAME!" weeps the battered, emaciated
Republican mascot in this Cleveland *Plain Dealer* cartoon, printed the day he returned.

TAFT'S DIFFICULTIES: the tariff. Here he pleads
with Senator Aldrich for a more equitable tariff bill.

TAFT'S ACHIEVEMENTS: his "four little
bills." He points at them with great pride.

"I'VE GOT TO SEE HIM!" After Roosevelt's return, all the insurgent Republicans who were fighting President Taft and his policies flocked to Sagamore Hill to unburden their hearts and ask for advice. Within four days after his arrival Roosevelt had forgotten his promise to keep his ears open but remain silent. In the New York *Times* of June 23 he said that all who were opposed to the direct primary in New York were eligible to the Ananias Club, which "already has a big waiting list." Thus he was back in the "cauldron of politics."

WHAT TO DO? A month after Roosevelt's return from Europe, *Harper's Weekly* published this J. Campbell Cory cartoon, which correctly expressed the feeling of the country and put the finger on Roosevelt's predicament. The lion in the drawing asks: "I wish I knew what you are going to do with me," and Roosevelt replies: "So do I."

Roosevelt was at a crossroads of his life. Fifty-one years old, full of ambition and a driving temperament, he had no office, no political power, and little to do. After eight bully years in the Presidency and after one year of hunting, exploring, lecturing, and mingling with royalty, private life seemed not only tasteless but unbearable. The question was: what next?

TO OYSTER BAY
All those Republicans who were against Taft's policies rushed to see Roosevelt, pouring out their hearts to the attentively listening Colonel. Senator La Follette of Wisconsin, Senator Beveridge of Indiana, two of Taft's staunchest enemies, were among the early visitors. President Taft, seeing Roosevelt's guest list in the newspapers, cried out: "If I only knew what the President wanted!" typically referring to Roosevelt as the President.

JUNE 20, 1910: "I want to close up . . ."

JULY 9, 1910: The Bronco Buster.

SEPTEMBER 24, 1910: The Colonel's baggage.

SEPTEMBER 26, 1910: Personal property.

JUMPING INTO LOCAL POLITICS. In his first speech on American soil Roosevelt promised to remain silent for sixty days and not to take sides in the political battles then raging between President Taft and the Republican insurgents. "I want to close up like a native oyster," he said. But barely four days had passed before the pledge was forgotten. He plunged into the battle over the controversial direct primary bill in New York, which was defeated by the Republican bosses. Undaunted, Roosevelt kept on with his fight. In the Saratoga State Convention he scored a victory by forcing through the gubernatorial nomination for Henry L. Stimson, but in the ensuing election his hand-picked candidate was squarely beaten. Roosevelt said of this repudiation at the polls: "I think that the American people feel a little tired of me, a feeling with which I cordially sympathize."

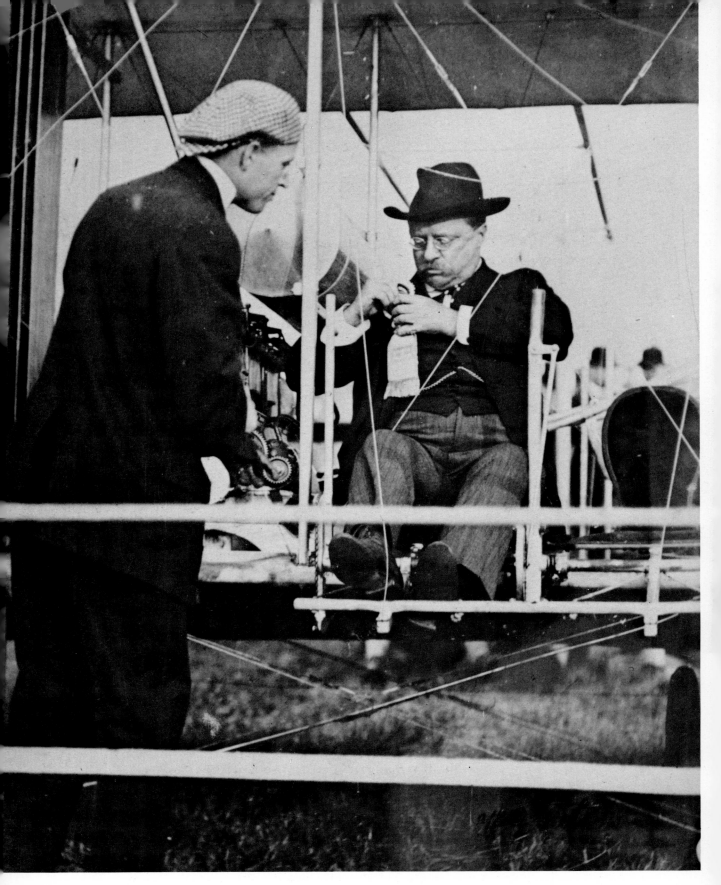

GOING UP

In St. Louis, Roosevelt took his
first airplane ride with aviator
Arch Hoxsey. "It was great."

CAMPAIGNING AGAINST HEAVY ODDS. In August 1910, with a strong tide surging against the Republicans, Roosevelt set out on a tour to turn the voters' sentiments. When asked whether he would speak on behalf of his party, he said: "My speeches on the trip will represent myself entirely, nobody else." He tried to take the middle of the road, trying to influence standpatters and insurgents alike. He went as far as he could in praising Taft's policies. Then—at Osawatomie, Kansas—he made a radical address which at one blow alienated all standpatters. In his speech Roosevelt advocated a New Nationalism, a creed to put "the national need before sectional or personal advantage." He pleaded for freeing the government "from the sinister influence of control of special interests," demanded the supervision of the capitalization of the railroads and other interstate business corporations, asked for an expert tariff commission—free of political influence, for the imposition of graduated income and inheritance taxes, for improved labor conditions, for aid to the farming classes, for conservation of natural resources. It was a revolutionary program indeed, its ideas adopted in part from those of William Jennings Bryan and La Follette.

ON OCTOBER 13, 1910, ROOSEVELT SPOKE IN INDIANAPOLIS ON BEHALF O

"DEE-LIGHTED" says the sorely battered and much patched-up Roosevelt after the decisive Republican defeat in the midterm election of 1910.

"FRAZZLED" says the caption, alluding to Roosevelt's boast before he left for the Saratoga convention that he would beat the bosses to a "frazzle."

THE MIDTERM ELECTION ended disastrously for the Republican party. In the House of Representatives there was an overwhelming Democratic majority, with 228 Democrats facing 162 Republicans. In the Senate the Republicans lost ten seats. Twenty-six states elected Democratic governors. The electorate repudiated both the standpatters and the insurgents. The Republicans were in a bad way. For Roosevelt it was a personal defeat. His candidate for the New York governorship lost the election, even though everyone realized that a vote for Henry L. Stimson was a vote for Theodore Roosevelt as President in 1912. Political observers believed that the crushing defeat would finish his political career.

THE INSURGENT SENATOR ALBERT BEVERIDGE, A FOE OF PRESIDENT TAFT.

THE VICTORIOUS DEMOCRATIC DONKEY: "And don't forget there's another one coming to you two years from now." (Cartoon by Kemble in *Harper's Weekly*, Nov. 19, 1910.)

CHAPTER XXXIX

THE BULL MOOSE CAMPAIGN

As the presidential year of 1912 dawned, the Republican party was in a sad state of disorder—"a house divided against itself." The conservative wing, controlling the party machinery, supported the renomination of President Taft, while the insurgents, rallied in the National Progressive League, were for Senator Robert La Follette of Wisconsin. Though officially behind La Follette, they were eagerly searching for a more popular figure who would be able to command the support of the eastern states and who would be strong enough to beat Taft in the convention. There was only one such person— Theodore Roosevelt.

Roosevelt knew that La Follette had no strong support outside the Middle West. He knew that Taft would have no difficulty to beat La Follette in the convention. But he also knew that with Taft as a candidate, the Republicans would lose the election. Thus, late in 1911 he approved a plan which allowed his progressive supporters to campaign in Ohio against Taft but not for the candidacy of La Follette.

A few weeks later, on February 2, 1912, the La Follette bandwagon came to a final halt in Philadelphia. On that evening the sick La Follette addressed a meeting of periodical publishers. For three hours he ranted, his speech at times incoherent, and when he sat down it was evident that he could no longer be a candidate.

The cry for Roosevelt gained momentum. Most of La Follette's supporters were in his corner. The pressure on him to accept the candidacy was intense, though many of his friends advised caution and suggested waiting until 1916, when the Presidency could certainly be his. Roosevelt, thoroughly bitten by the presidential bug, had no patience. The time to set a setting hen was when the hen wanted to set.

Already before the collapse of La Follette in Philadelphia, he was in the race. On January 12 he hit upon the idea of introducing himself as a candidate in a reply to the progressive governors who had invited him to run. But then he postponed the announcement.

On Washington's Birthday he addressed the Ohio Legislature in Columbus. Most of what he said was moderate in tone, yet the passage about the democratization of the judiciary wrecked all his good intentions, alienating with one stroke the conservative wing and estranging the big business and industrial interests. Republican newspapers referred to the speech, which Roosevelt called "A Charter of Democracy," as "A Charter of Demagogy."

On the way from Columbus, Roosevelt told a newspaperman: "My hat is in the ring. The fight is on and I am stripped to the buff." And within a few days he answered the petition of the seven progressive governors: "I will accept the nomination for President if it is tendered to me and I will adhere to this decision until the convention has expressed its preference." He was now an active candidate, ready to wrest the nomination from Taft.

The President in the White House lost his calm. In his Lincoln Day speech (Roosevelt was not yet a pronounced candidate) he lashed out against the men who "are seeking to pull down the pillars of the temple of freedom and representative government," cast scorn on the doctrine of the recall of the judiciary, and charged that those who urged such changes were "political emotionalists or neurotics." No one could misunderstand such words. They were directed against his former friend, the man who had made him President.

On April 25 the President went to Massachusetts and, goaded by Roosevelt's relentless attacks on the administration, he for the first time struck at his former friend by name. He charged that the ex-President had violated his promise to the American people not to run for the Presidency again. "That promise and his treatment," declared Taft, "only throw an informing light on the value that ought to be attached to any promise of this kind that he may make for the future." He said that his attacks on Roosevelt were made with reluctance. "This wrenches my soul," he declared. But there seemed no other way. "I am here to reply to an old and dear friend of mine, Theodore Roosevelt, who has made many charges against me. I deny those charges. I deny all of them. I do not want to fight Theodore Roosevelt, but then sometimes a man in a corner fights. I am going to fight."

A day after the attack Roosevelt replied in Worcester to Taft's accusation. Urged on by a wildly partisan audience, he put aside his prepared speech and attacked Taft with unprecedented violence. He accused the President of deliberately misrepresenting him, and said that Taft "has not merely in thought, word and deed been disloyal to our past friendship, but has been disloyal to every common or ordinary decency and fair dealings such as should obtain even in dealing with a man's bitterest opponents."

The two men were now enemies. The aroused Taft went onto the stump, vigorously defending his policies. "I don't want to fight," he repeated at meeting after meeting. "But when I do fight I want to hit hard. Even a rat in a corner will fight."

What followed was a titanic battle, a vitriolic verbal brawl between two who had expressed the most unqualified respect and admiration for each other a few years earlier. Across the nation the reverberation of their accusations cut across ties of blood, family, friendship, as well as of party. Republicans turned against Republicans with more feeling than they turned against Democrats. Public passions were running high; accusations flew wildly. It was rumored that Roosevelt had gone mad, and that if he could seize the Presidency, he would make it a hereditary office. "Unless he breaks down under the strain and is taken to a lunatic asylum," warned the Louisville *Courier-Journal*, "there can be in his name and person but one issue, life tenure in the executive office."

556

Roosevelt realized that he could secure the nomination only through direct primaries, in which delegates to the national convention would be chosen by the party rank and file at the polls rather than by the Republican politicians in state conventions. Therefore he launched a vigorous campaign to achieve that end. He won over six state legislatures; and where direct primaries were adopted, he became the favorite by considerable margins. But in all other states which retained the old convention system, Taft had the superiority.

Twelve days before the opening of the convention in Chicago, the Republican National Committee reviewed the credentials of the Roosevelt and the Taft delegates. Roosevelt, from Sagamore Hill, kept in touch with his managers by long-distance telephone and a private telegraph wire. The committee —firmly in the hands of Taft supporters—ruled for the Taft delegates, a ruling which Roosevelt denounced as "a fraud, as vulgar, as brazen, and as cynically open as any ever committed by the Tweed regime in New York forty years ago."

He left for Chicago, and on his arrival declared: "It is a naked fight against theft, and the thieves will not win." Talking to an audience of his supporters the following night, he delivered a most moving address. He told them that the progressive cause should not be allowed to die, despite "the foul victory for which our opponents hope," and appealed to them to fight with him for the right. "We stand at Armageddon, and we battle for the Lord," were his final words.

All such exhortations were of no avail. The Taft men knew what they wanted; they were determined to keep the nomination for their candidate. Of the 254 contested seats, the Credentials Committee of the convention awarded no less than 235 to the President's delegates. Thus Taft won with 561 votes against 107 for Roosevelt and 41 for La Follette. Still, 344 delegates refrained from voting, 344 men would not back the regular candidate of the party. This doomed Republican success in November. "The only question now," said Chauncey Depew as he waited for Roosevelt's candidacy on a third-party ticket, "is which corpse gets the most flowers."

With Taft chosen as the candidate of the convention, the Roosevelt delegates repaired to another hall. There Roosevelt vowed to make the fight and run as a candidate on an independent ticket. The party split which so many thoughtful Republicans feared, became a reality—Taft and the regulars were on one side, Roosevelt and the progressives on the other. It was without doubt that the Democratic candidate, Woodrow Wilson, the reform governor of New Jersey, would benefit by the Republican dissension and be elected President of the United States. On election day Wilson polled 6,286,124 votes against Roosevelt's 4,126,000 and Taft's 3,483,922. The Republican party was in shambles, the progressive hopes broken. Roosevelt, accepting the outcome of the election "with entire good humor and contentment," said: "The fight is over. We are beaten. There is only one thing to do and that is to go back to the Republican party. You can't hold a party like the Progressive party together. . . . There are no loaves and fishes."

BACK TO WORK
AS EDITOR

"RESTING." A cartoon by Phil Porter in the Boston *Traveler* depicts Theodore Roosevelt in 1911, when he was out of the political arena. During this period he did literary work and was contributing editor of *The Outlook*, writing articles for that magazine.

A CHARACTERISTIC GESTURE during his Decoration Day speech at Grant's tomb in New York on May 30, 1911. In his address Roosevelt spoke against "mollycoddles" and "unrighteous peace," meaning the Taft-proposed arbitration treaties with France and England. Taft had suggested that "all questions determinable by the principles of law and equity" were to be submitted to the Hague Tribunal. And though Roosevelt would accept a treaty with England, he would not commit himself with France, giving as the reason that while Britain would never commit an offense which could not be adjudicated, France might. In this way he assailed publicly— and for the first time openly—his successor's policies.

MAY 25, 1912: WHICH WILL WIN?

MARCH 30, 1912: HAVING A BULLY TIM

THE RIFT BETWEEN ROOSEVELT AND TAFT was based not only on political issues, but on the personalities of the two men.

When Roosevelt was President, he was the giver and Taft the receiver. The tables turned when Taft became President, and Roosevelt had not the talent to play the part of a receiver. Mark Sullivan, who knew him well, said: "Only incredible self-restraint and humility, especially on the part of Roosevelt, could have averted a clash." Of this, Roosevelt was incapable.

The growing enmity began with political matters. Roosevelt was hurt that Taft would not keep his appointees—James Garfield, Luke Wright, Henry White—although he had promised to do so. Roosevelt was pained that Taft dismissed Gifford Pinchot, his adviser on conservation. Roosevelt was puzzled that Taft was so pleased with the Payne-Aldrich tariff and that he supported the conservative Speaker Uncle Joe Cannon against the Progressives. Roosevelt was peeved that Taft was under the thumb of the standpatters.

The rift was widened by personal issues. Taft's ambitious wife fanned the flame of discontent against the Roosevelts. In the newspaper of Taft's half-brother, the policies of Roosevelt were frequently criticized. On the other hand, Alice Roosevelt thought it great fun to mimic Mrs. Taft, sending the President's wife into a dither.

In 1911, Roosevelt was at a crossroads of his career. He felt that his political leadership was at an end, and he tried to keep silent—one of the hardest of tasks for a man like him.

UNE 1, 1912: DOWN WITH THE BOSSES

MARCH 23, 1912: THE ISSUE

To Henry Wallace, the father of Franklin D. Roosevelt's Vice President, he wrote that "what is needed for me is to follow the advice given by the New Bedford whaling captain to his mate when he told him that all he wanted from him was silence and damn little of that."

Convinced that the Republicans would lose in the next presidential election, he thought that the best plan would be to renominate Taft, go down in defeat, then reorganize the party under progressive leadership. He would not openly endorse Senator Robert La Follette, the leader of the National Progressive Republican League and an active candidate for the Republican nomination.

Then—on October 27, 1911—Taft's government brought a suit against the U.S. Steel Corporation for violating the Sherman Anti-Trust Act, and this changed the political scene. The implication of the suit was that Roosevelt, under whose administration the steel corporation had bought the Tennessee Coal and Iron Company, was either a tool of big business or a fool, whom bankers and businessmen could deceive at will. Roosevelt was infuriated. In red-hot anger he wrote an article for *The Outlook*. This put the limelight on him; overnight he grew into a presidential candidate, overnight he became the man who was to replace the bungling Taft.

Roosevelt now swam with powerful strokes in the political waters; he was in his element again. The last week of February, after the complete collapse of La Follette's candidacy, he announced: "My hat is in the ring." He was ready to take the nomination away from Taft.

THE BROKEN FRIENDSHIP

On April 25, President Taft told a Massachusetts audience: "I am here to reply to an old and dear friend of mine, Theodore Roosevelt, who made many charges against me. I deny those charges. I deny all of them. I do not want to fight Theodore Roosevelt, but then sometimes a man in a corner fights. I am going to fight." It was the first time that he had attacked Roosevelt openly and by name. Next day Roosevelt replied in Worcester that Taft's attack on him was a "deliberate misrepresentation" of the issues. The voices of the two antagonists grew shrill. On May 4, Taft reiterated at Hyattsville, Maryland: "I'm a man of peace, and I don't want to fight. But when I do fight I want to hit hard. Even a rat in a corner will fight." After that it was a free-for-all.

DEMANDING "POPULAR GOVERNMENT"

"Because I believe in genuine popular rule," said Roosevelt on February 26, 1912, before the Massachusetts Legislature, "I favor direct nominations, direct primaries; including direct preferential Presidential primaries, not only for local but for state delegates. . . ." The New York *Times* wrote that "the radical difference" between Roosevelt's and Taft's political beliefs was over "what the progressives call 'popular government'—the initiative, referendum and recall."

Right:

EVERYWHERE ROOSEVELT WENT he was enthusiastically welcomed. At Easton, Pa., on April 11, 1912, where this picture was taken, his cheering supporters almost dragged him from his automobile.

AN APRIL FOOL CARTOON by Harold T. Webster, published on April 1, 1912, when President Taft was still in a quandary how to fight his former friend. But before the month was out, both men had forgotten their friendship. Taft called his predecessor "a demagogue," a "flatterer of the people," a "dangerous egotist," a man who "could not tell the truth." And Roosevelt shot back that Taft was a "puzzlewit" and a "fathead," with "brains less than those of a guinea pig." It was a deplorable performance. Yet the public loved it.

RUDOLPH M. PATTERSON
REAL ESTATE EXPERT
811 ASHLAND BLOCK

Hon. Franklin MacVeagh,   CHICAGO, May 15, 1912
Sec. of the Treasury,
Washington, D. C.

Dear Sir:-

On December 18, 1910, I offered to give $1000. to an expert Sanity Commission and to the Associated Charities of Chicago and New York, if Col. T. Roosevelt, on examination, was not found to be insane, "non compos mentis" and a dangerous character to be at large among the peaceful citizens of the United States.

I still believe the Colonel is a madman and now raise my offer to $5000., the same to go to an expert Sanity Commission and to the Associated Charities of Chicago, New York, Cleveland, Columbus, Dayton, Washington, Jersey City, Paterson, Pittsburgh, Omaha, Kansas City and St. Louis, if a scientific examination does not develop the fact that Col. Roosevelt is a crazy lunatic and raving maniac whose privilege of freedom is a serious menace to public safety, civilization and progress. Let the writ of "Lunatico inquerendo" issue, directed to a competent and impartial commission, to adjudge the case.

ON BEHALF OF THE SANE AND PLAIN PEOPLE OF AMERICA.

N.B. Enclosed find account of former offer. *R. M. Patterson*

IS HE A MADMAN? A Chicago real estate dealer offered $1,000 to charity (which he later upped to $5,000) if Roosevelt was "not found to be insane." At about the same time Dr. Allen McLane Hamilton in the New York *Times* questioned Roosevelt's sanity, while the psychologist Dr. Morton Price stated that, in his opinion, Roosevelt would "go down in history as one of the most illustrious psychological examples of the distortion of conscious mental processes through the forces of subsconscious wishes." That these doctors who wished to prove insanity were loyal supporters of President Taft goes without saying.

FIGHTING FOR DELEGATES. From April until the opening of the Republican convention in June, Roosevelt campaigned vigorously. He spoke in state after state to secure delegates who would support him. He urged the method of a direct primary, knowing too well that only through the adoption of this method could he be successful. Though the forces of the administration fought the adoption of direct primaries, Massachusetts, Pennsylvania, Illinois, Maryland, Ohio, and South Dakota joined the six states where the direct primary was already in use.

It was a seesaw battle, with hard fighting in every state convention. When words ran out, baseball bats took over. When arguments seemed useless, fists began their reasoning. Taft, as President, started off with a definite advantage. His hold on the Republican organization in the Solid South could not be challenged, and he had in his corner the delegates from New York, Michigan, Kentucky, and Indiana.

But the support for Roosevelt mounted steadily. He won the Illinois direct primary, and he won in Pennsylvania, in California, Minnesota, Nebraska, and South Dakota.

The high point of the contest came in Ohio; both Taft and Roosevelt put all their efforts into winning that state. Within the span of a single week Roosevelt addressed Ohio audiences ninety times, and Taft matched his performance to the letter. The result of the dramatic struggle was a Roosevelt victory; he captured every district delegate of Ohio.

Would that impress the Republican National Committee, which was to decide about the credentials of the delegates? The country waited with bated breath to hear that decision.

THE TAFT-ROOSEVELT FIGHT, AS SEEN BY MACAULEY IN THE NEW YORK *WORLD*

CONTEST FOR DELEGATES. The above cartoons were published the first fortnight of June 1912, at the time the Republican convention assembled in Chicago to name a candidate for the Presidency.

The Roosevelt forces contested 254 seats before the National Committee. This was about one third of the total. Of these contested seats, the committee—more interested in seating the Taft delegates than in handing down impartial judgment—awarded 235 seats to the Taft men and only 19 to those for Roosevelt. Chicago and the country at large were in an emotional turmoil. If the Credentials Committee in the convention was to accept the decision of the Taft-dominated National Committee, Roosevelt could not receive the nomina-

WEBSTER'S CARTOON IN THE NEW YORK *GLOBE* AGAINST CANDIDATE ROOSEVELT

tion. The questions on everybody's lips were: What would be the decision of the Credentials Committee and what would be the decision of the convention? The New York *Times* wrote that the Roosevelt men would stop at nothing short of assault and burglary to see their hero nominated. The celebrated Mr. Dooley predicted that the convention would be "a combynation iv th' Chicago fire, Saint Bartholomew's massacree, the battle iv th' Boyne, th' life iv Jessie James, an' th' night iv th' big wind." And when Hennessey asked him whether he was going, Dooley answered: "Iv course I'm goin'! I haven't missed a riot in this neighborhood in forty years, an' onless I'm deceived by the venal Republican press this wan will rejoice the heart. . . ." It certainly fitted his prediction.

THE REPUBLICAN CONVENTION in Chicago named Taft with 561 votes against 107 for Roosevelt. However, 344 of the delegates abstained from voting.

THE PROGRESSIVE CONVENTION in Chicago nominated Roosevelt, the man who said he stood at Armageddon and would "battle for the Lord."

THE DEMOCRATIC CONVENTION in Baltimore named Woodrow Wilson, the liberal governor of New Jersey, as the party's presidential candidate.

THE CONVENTIONS OF 1912

The Republican convention opened in Chicago on June 18. Passions ran high, and partisanship erupted into fistfights. When Roosevelt's old friend Elihu Root, now a Taft supporter, was chosen as the chairman of the convention, the Roosevelt men shouted: "Liar, thief, swindler"; they accused the Taft organization with steam-rolling the convention. Thus, every time the new chairman rose, they shouted, "Toot-toot!" and rubbed sandpaper sheets together, giving an imitation of a steam roller.

The night before the delegates began to ballot, and when it was already clear that he would be beaten, Roosevelt told his supporters: "What happens to me is not of the slightest consequence; I am to be used, as in a doubtful battle any man is used, to his hurt or not, so long as he is useful and is then cast aside and left to die. I wish you to feel this. I mean it; and I shall need no sympathy when you are through with me." And he ended his eloquent appeal with the memorable words: "We fight in honorable fashion for the good of mankind, unheeding of our individual fates; with unflinching hearts and undimmed eyes, we stand at Armageddon and we battle for the Lord."

Taft was nominated with 561 votes against Roosevelt's 107. But 344 delegates refrained from voting. Their silence meant disapproval of the party's official candidate. That same night Roosevelt said in another meeting: "If you wish me to make the fight, I will make it, even if only one state should support me."

Thus the signal for the third party was hoisted. A few weeks later, on August 5, the Progressives held a convention in Chicago and nominated Roosevelt as their standard-bearer. To twenty thousand cheering supporters Roosevelt delivered his "Confession of Faith," an exceedingly long address. The speech was, in the words of the New York *Sun,* "a manifesto of revolution. It is a program of wild and dangerous changes. It proposes popular nullification of the Constitution. It proposes state socialism." The arch-conservative newspaper was in a doldrum.

The platform of the Progressive party asked for trust regulation and for the development of agricultural credit. It endorsed reform legislation for a direct primary, for woman's suffrage, for a scientific tariff commission, for better working conditions in the factories, for minimum wage standards, for abolition of child labor, for an eight-hour working day.

With the Republicans split in two, there was no doubt that the Democrats would win the election. As their candidate they nominated Woodrow Wilson, the reform-minded governor of New Jersey.

THE FIRST PHOTOGRAPH OF THE PROGRESSIVE PARTY, taken in the Chicago Opera House on June 22, 1912. A few hours before, the Regular Republicans had chosen President Taft as their candidate, and now Roosevelt promised to run on a third-party ticket.

"A PERFECTLY CORKING TIME" read the caption on June 21 under this Macauley cartoon, drawn after the Republicans had convened in Chicago.

"ON TO CHICAGO" read the caption on July 9 under another Macauley cartoon, in which the cartoonist ridiculed Roosevelt and his Bull Moose Party.

THE BULL MOOSE CAMPAIGN

CARTOONISTS ATTACKED ROOSEVELT in the regular Republican press with unprecedented force and violence. Tempers flared; accusations flew freely in this—probably the most emotional campaign in American history. Rollin Kirby drew Roosevelt as Moses. "Follow me, can't you see I'm Moses," read the caption under this cartoon, which *Harper's Weekly* published on September 7, 1912.

"THE REVOLUTIONIST" was the title of this E. W. Kemble *Harper's Weekly* cartoon, printed on June 8, 1912. In it Roosevelt foments the fire of "Class Hatred" and "Discontent" under the chained and suffering figure of "The Republic." In the background Kemble drew a revolutionary mob, with waving flags, knives and rifles, whose dark shadows cheer the deed of the "Revolutionist" Roosevelt.

WILSON ACCEPTED the presidential nomination of the Democratic party at his summer home in Sea Girt, New Jersey. In his acceptance speech he gave a clear outline of his political philosophy, the New Freedom. He promised tariff reform and regulation of the trusts, he pledged to seek adequate laws for the protection of labor, for the conservation of natural resources, and for better education of the nation's youth. And he declared: "We desire to set up a government that cannot be used for private purposes either in the field of business or in the field of politics."

Roosevelt and Johnson

"For there is neither East nor West,
Border nor Breed nor Birth,
When two strong men stand face to face
Though they come from the ends of the earth."
—Kipling

"THE NATIONAL PEST," a Kemble cartoon in the September 28, 1912, issue of *Harper's Weekly*, depicts Roosevelt as an insect which "appears regularly every four years," named "Species Cicada Rooseveltia." On the chest of it the artist drew a big "I," alluding to Roosevelt's egomania. Kemble was one of Roosevelt's most powerful antagonists, scoring savagely as he fought him with his pencil.

THE PROGRESSIVE TICKET. A photographic campaign poster with a Rudyard Kipling quatrain under the pictures of the candidates. Roosevelt had no great hope of winning the election. On August 14 he wrote to his friend Arthur Hamilton Lee that in his judgment Woodrow Wilson, whom he considered to be a good candidate, "will win, and that I will do better than Taft"—a superbly accurate prediction.

WILLIAM H. TAFT, after his nomination by the Republican convention, shied away from the campaign, following the tradition that a President should not stump for his re-election. Though his followers worked hard for him, Taft's hopes were dim long before the voters gave their verdict. "There are so many people in the country who don't like me," he lamented. With Roosevelt and Wilson eloquently expounding their political beliefs, people seemed to have forgotten that there was a third contender in the fray—clumsy, unhappy, well-meaning William Howard Taft.

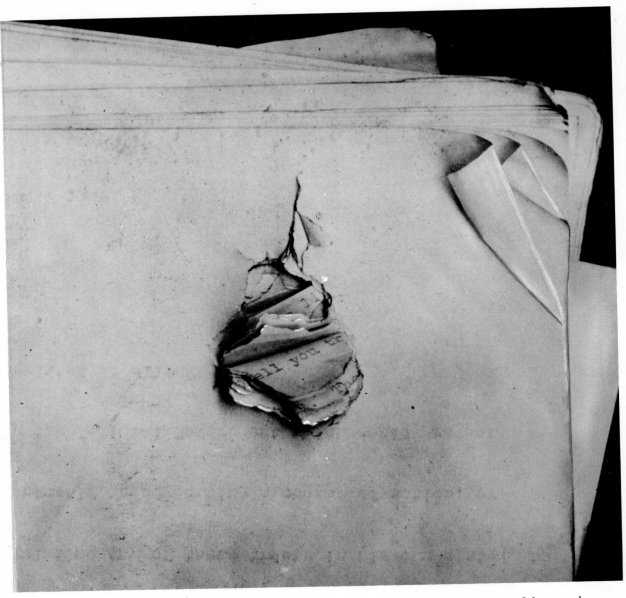

THE BULLET OF THE ASSASSIN pierced through the folded manuscript of the speech and a steel spectacle case which Roosevelt was carrying in his breast pocket. Otherwise it would have killed him.

As the angry crowd jumped upon the assassin, Roosevelt ordered: "Don't hurt the man." Raising his bloody handkerchief, he indicated that he wanted to see his assailant. And as the trembling John Crank stood before him, Roosevelt muttered: "The poor creature."

SHOT IN MILWAUKEE

On October 14 at Milwaukee, as Roosevelt was leaving the Gilpatrick Hotel to make a campaign speech, he was shot by an insane fanatic. The man's name was John Crank, and why he wanted to kill Roosevelt was clear neither to him nor to anyone else.

Though Roosevelt had no knowledge as to the seriousness of his wound, he refused to go to the hospital, but drove on where the people waited for him. "I will make this speech or die. It is one thing or the other."

Reaching the platform, he told the assembly in a whispering voice: "I am going to ask you to be very quiet and please excuse me from making a long speech. I'll do the best I can, but there is a bullet in my body." It was one of the great dramatic moments of his life, and he played it to the full. "I have a message to deliver," he went on, "and will deliver

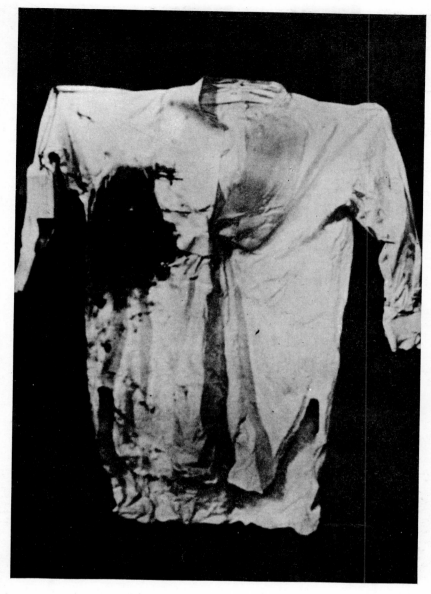

THE BLOODY SHIRT OF ROOSEVELT, which he had later discarded in his railway car. "I shaved and took out the studs and buttons from my bloody shirt and put them in a clean shirt, as I thought I might be stiff next morning. This all tired me a little, and when I lay down in my bunk my heart was again beating fast enough, and my breath was short enough, to make me feel uncomfortable. But after a while I found that I could turn, if I did it very carefully, to my unwounded side, and then I fell asleep."

it as long as there is life in my body."

The audience was under his spell. "I have had an A-1 time in life and I am having it now," he kept on, charging that "it was a very natural thing that weak and vicious minds should be inflamed to acts of violence by the kind of awful mendacity and abuse that have been heaped upon me for the last three months by the papers in the interests of not only Mr. Debs but of Mr. Wilson and Mr. Taft." For an hour and a half he held the platform while the bullet was in his chest.

The X-rays showed that the wound was only superficial. A surgeon commented in awe: "It is largely due to the fact that he is a physical marvel that he was not dangerously wounded. He is one of the most powerful men I have ever seen laid on an operating table. The bullet lodged in the massive muscles of the chest instead of penetrating the lung."

FOR PRESIDENT

BULL & MOOSE

PARTY

Humpty Dumpty sat on the wall,
Humpty Dumpty had a bad fall.
All the ex-bosses
And Bully Moose men,
Can never put Humpty up again.

Kemble

AFTER THE ELECTION Roosevelt said: "The fight is over. We are beaten. There is only one thing to do and that is to go back to the Republican party. You can't hold a party like the Progressive party together. . . . There are no loaves and fishes." He received 4,119,507 votes against Taft's 3,484,956, but Wilson won by a wide margin with 6,293,019 votes.

CHAPTER XL

THE RISE OF WOODROW WILSON

That it was Theodore Roosevelt who opened the gates of the White House for Woodrow Wilson was an irony of fate. Roosevelt came to hate Wilson; he loathed him with an intensity that bordered on the pathological.

Early in the presidential campaign Wilson assessed the fundamental difference between them. "Roosevelt," he said, "is a real vivid person whom the people have seen and shouted themselves hoarse over and voted for, millions strong; I am a vague, conjectural personality, more made up of opinions and academic prepossessions than of human traits and red corpuscles." There was, of course, more to it, but on the whole Wilson's characterization was to the point. The extrovert Roosevelt, with his unparalleled energy, human warmth, and robust animal spirits, was the antithesis of the scholarly and reflective Wilson, a man of quiet tastes who preferred the rapier to the broadsword, and whose closest approach to the "strenuous life" was an occasional game of golf. Roosevelt, spending his adult life in the political cauldron, possessed the common touch to a remarkable degree and was a master in the political art of compromise; Wilson, spending his adult years in the academic groves, was warm with intimate friends but inflexible in his prejudices and unable to accommodate himself to people and ideas he disliked. Yet for all his political inexperience, Wilson proved an amazingly adept politician during the years he was in public office. For all his unaggressive inclination toward the contemplative life, he proved a doughty fighter of unyielding courage when the battle lines were drawn. And for all his aloofness and his tendency to admire the common man from a safe distance, he showed himself to be one of the great leaders of the people.

His life ran on an even keel. Born in Staunton, Virginia, the son and grandson of Presbyterian ministers, he spent his early years in Georgia and the Carolinas amid the devastation and demoralization of the Reconstruction. His family environment imbued him with a respect for learning and a lifelong habit of regarding all public issues in the moral terms of right and wrong. He studied at Davidson College in North Carolina, then at Princeton University, where he read the lives of the great statesmen in order to master the art of public speaking. After his graduation he entered the University of Virginia, where he studied law. A short career as a practicing lawyer followed, but when he realized he could not make a success of it, he went back to more studies at Johns Hopkins University. He decided to become a teacher and taught for four years at Bryn Mawr and Wesleyan. In 1890 he returned to Princeton, joining the faculty as professor of jurisprudence and political economy. Twelve years later—in 1902—he was elected president of that institution. These were the milestones of his career—this was the path of his life.

In 1910, at the instigation of the reform elements within the Democratic party, Wilson became a gubernatorial candidate of New Jersey. In this way— at the age of fifty-four—he started out in politics, the profession he had sought ever since his undergraduate days. "The profession I chose was politics," he later wrote, "the profession I entered, the law. I entered the one because I thought it would lead to the other."

At Princeton, Wilson once said that academic politicians could make party politicians seem like mere amateurs. He now proceeded to demonstrate that the same methods which could win over recalcitrant students or trustees would work also on New Jersey voters. He captivated his audiences by his unassuming candor and his knack for translating complex issues into understandable terms. And when the ballots were counted, they showed that the professor had been elected to the governorship of New Jersey by the biggest majority ever given to a Democrat.

In his new office Governor Wilson proceeded to blast away the preconceptions of the reformers, who had considered him a front for the machine, and the bosses, who had supposed that such an inexperienced theorist would be putty in their hands. Within a few months of his inauguration, he was at the head of the progressive movement. In quick succession, and over the opposition of the bosses, he pushed through a direct primaries law, a corrupt practices act, and an employers' liability act, as well as legislation setting up a public utilities commission and establishing new safeguards against municipal corruption. Before his first year was up, New Jersey had become a virtual laboratory for reform politics and Wilson was thought to be the most probable Democratic candidate for the Presidency in 1912.

And while Wilson was steadily building up his reputation outside his state by extensive speaking tours, his friend Colonel E. M. House, a quiet liberal from Texas, worked behind the scenes on his behalf. Together the two men shared a vision, and together they shared an apprehension. Wilson expressed it in the course of a Western speaking tour: "There is a tremendous undercurrent of protest, which is bound to find expression. Taft will be renominated by the Republicans; unless the Democrats nominate someone whom the people can accept as expressing this protest there will be a radical third party formed and the result of the election may be little short of revolution." Of Roosevelt, whose hat was already in the ring, Wilson said privately: "God save us from him now in his present insane distemper of egotism."

When the Democratic convention met in Baltimore's sweltering Fifth Regiment Armory, the challenge to the party was clear. With the Republican forces split between Taft and Roosevelt, the Democrats were almost certain to win the Presidency. But to be sure of a victory after twenty-four years in the desert, they had to nominate an appealing progressive who could keep the liberal element behind the Democratic candidate and away from the lure of Roosevelt.

William Jennings Bryan, whose Western followers held the balance of power, dramatized this issue by offering a resolution renouncing any candidate under obligation to the "privilege-hunting and favor-seeking class." The Eastern conservatives and Tammany Hall stood firm. They tried to eliminate Wilson by publishing a letter in which Wilson had said—some five years before—that he wished Bryan might be knocked into a cocked hat. Their maneuver failed. Bryan knew better; he would not be swayed by such an obvious political trick. Ballot after ballot was taken, and still no decision. Champ Clark, the Senator of Missouri, commanded the majority of the votes, but he was not able to secure the support of two thirds of the delegates. When after the twelfth ballot Tammany Hall unequivocally came out for him, Bryan declared that he would not support a candidate blessed by Tammany Hall. This was the moment for Woodrow Wilson, who now renounced Tammany in a firm tone. Bryan swung behind Wilson, and the move for the nomination of the New Jersey governor was on. Still, not until the forty-sixth ballot could Wilson become the candidate of his party.

The ensuing campaign was one of the most exciting in American presidential history. Roosevelt battled for the Lord, Taft fought for political survival, and Wilson talked common sense.

As a campaigner, Wilson could not match Roosevelt. He was not a glad-hander; he could not bring himself to slap backs or kiss babies; he admitted that his "Presbyterian face" photographed badly; he disliked the glib generalities implicit in whistle-stop oratory. But what his speeches lacked in bombast they more than made up in sense, and his doctrine of the "New Freedom" held out the hope of an orderly program of reform which would make the government responsible to public opinion and would guarantee freedom from economic exploitation without recourse to radicalism.

Though the election returns gave him only 42 per cent of the popular vote, the victory in the Electoral College was his. He heard the good news after a quiet evening at home, listening to his wife's reading of Browning's poems.

Between his election and his inaugural in March of 1913, the President-elect and his advisers drew up the blueprints for a program that would translate the "New Freedom" into reality—a program which was to include the first real tariff reduction in half a century, a strengthening of anti-trust legislation, establishment of the Federal Trade Commission, a stronger banking system, an eight-hour day for railway labor, and a host of other reforms. "The nation," Wilson declared in his deeply moving inaugural address, "has been deeply stirred by a solemn passion, stirred by the knowledge of wrong, of ideals lost, of government too often debauched and made an instrument of evil. The feelings with which we face this new age of right and opportunity sweep across our heartstrings like some air out of God's own presence, where justice and mercy are reconciled and the judge and the brother are as one."

This was the new voice of the country, this was the new voice of progressivism, this was the new voice which carried on the ideas of Theodore Roosevelt.

THE ANCESTORS OF WOODROW WILSON

GRANDPARENTS. James Wilson set sail from County Down, Ireland, in 1807. He met on the boat Anne Adams from Ulster; the two were married in Philadelphia the next year. A newspaper editor, he later founded the *Pennsylvania Advocate* at Pittsburgh.

PARENTS. Joseph Ruggles Wilson started out as a printer, but because of his interest in the church became a Presbyterian minister. His wife, Janet (familiarly called Jessie), was born in England, her father, Thomas Woodrow, a Presbyterian minister.

WILSON'S BIRTHPLACE, the Manse at Staunton, Virginia, where he was born on December 28, 1856. (He was born twenty-six months before Roosevelt.) Wilson always prided himself on being a Virginian, though his parents came from Ohio, his grandparents from Ireland and England, and his family moved less than a year after his birth to Augusta, Georgia.

WHEN WILSON WAS FOURTEEN his father became a member of the faculty of the Presbyterian theological seminary in Columbia, the capital of South Carolina. Here Wilson (sitting before the pillar) grew up with two sisters and his brother. Three years later his father accepted a pastorate in Wilmington, N. C., and Woodrow Wilson entered Davidson College.

The early life of Woodrow Wilson offered no promise of greatness. His childhood and adolescence were uneventful. Sent by his parents to Davidson College in North Carolina, he spent a year there, then entered Princeton, his father's alma mater. Graduating the year before Theodore Roosevelt received his degree from Harvard, he began the study of law at the University of Virginia, and hung out his shingle in Atlanta, Georgia,

A FAMILY ALBUM OF WILSON'S EARLY LIFE

WILSON AND HIS WIFE. On June 24, 1885, Woodrow Wilson married Ellen Louise Axson, the daughter of a Presbyterian minister at Rome, Georgia. He was then 28; behind him were years of study in Princeton and the University of Virginia Law School.

POSTGRADUATE STUDENT at Johns Hopkins University in the year of 1884. Wilson (standing second from the left) with members of the Glee Club. Though he rebelled against some of the courses required for a doctorate in history, in the seminar led by Professor Herbert Adams his interest was revived, and he wrote *Congressional Government*—his first book.

GRADUATING FROM PRINCETON in 1879, where he was managing editor of the *Princetonian*. His marks were good but not outstanding. On the board of the newspaper were Charles A. Talcott, W. F. Magie, T. D. Warren, G. S. Johns standing; E. O. Roessle, Wilson, and H. B. Fine sitting. After leaving Princeton, he studied law at the University of Virginia.

in 1882. But a year of unremunerative practice convinced him that he was not suited for the career of a lawyer. Wanting to become a teacher, he enrolled at Johns Hopkins University to earn the degree of Ph.D. Two important events—both occurring in 1885—augured well for his future: the writing of a book on *Congressional Government* and his marriage to Ellen Louise Axson, the daughter of a Presbyterian minister in Georgia.

PROFESSOR AT BRYN MAWR

In 1885, the very year that Wilson married Ellen Axson, he became Associate Professor of history at Bryn Mawr. He soon came to the conclusion that the teaching of women was irksome and not to his liking. The following year (June 1886) he earned his Ph.D. degree at Johns Hopkins University. For two more years he stayed at Bryn Mawr, leaving there in September 1888, when he happily accepted a teaching assignment at Wesleyan University in Middletown, Connecticut, delighted to have men students.

PRESIDENT OF PRINCETON

In 1890 Wilson became Professor of jurisprudence and political economy at Princeton. He was content in his post. Besides teaching, he wrote books and articles. Several colleges and universities asked him to become their president, but he declined all offers. In 1902 he was elected president of Princeton, where he introduced the preceptorial system and a plan for departmentalized and co-ordinated study, as well as pressing for a quadrangle plan of housing for the student body, to eliminate the snobbish eating clubs.

THE WILSON FAMILY. The Wilsons with their three daughters: Eleanor Randolph, who later married William Gibbs McAdoo, Margaret, and Jessie Woodrow, later the wife of Francis Bowes Sayre.

GOVERNOR

In the tempestuous 1910 election when the Republican progressives battled against President Taft and the standpatters, the Democrats emerged victorious. With a large majority Woodrow Wilson was elected to the governorship of New Jersey—a stepping stone to the Presidency.

In the photograph Wilson is behind his desk at his Trenton office. Next to him stands his secretary, Joseph P. Tumulty. Sitting on the left is William Bayard Hale, later a Wilson biographer.

TAFT AND HIS SUCCESSOR

Taft was relieved that his troubles were over. He cared little for the Presidency and was not sorry to leave the White House. He loathed the fight and the scramble for political power. He liked peace.

His defeat was complete. Wilson won the election, carrying forty out of the forty-eight states, with 6,293,019 votes. Taft received only 3,484,956, and Roosevelt—who had put him in the Presidency and then opposed him—had 4,119,507 votes. The Republican party was in shambles; the new man of the hour was Woodrow Wilson.

After twenty-four years of Republican rule, Wilson was the first Democratic President, and the first President since Abraham Lincoln to be born in a southern state. He saw "the vision of a new day," and he knew that his work was "a work of restoration."

In his inaugural he indicted the previous administration: "The great government we love has too often been made use of for private and selfish purposes and those who used it have forgotten the people. There has been something crude, heartless and unfeeling in our effort to succeed and be great; our thought has been, let every man look out for himself; let every generation look out for itself."

The new President held out for a better and more abundant life. "This is not a day of triumph," he said in his moving inaugural address, "it is a day of dedication. Here muster not the forces of party but the forces of humanity. Men's hearts must wait upon us; men's lives hang in the balance; men's hopes call upon us to say what we will do. Who shall live up to the great trust? Who dares to try it? I summon all honest men, all patriotic, all forward-looking men to my side. God helping me, I will not fail them if they will but counsel and sustain me."

LEAVING FOR THE INAUGURATION

ONE MORE, PLEASE! asked the photographers as Taft and Wilson faced the battery of cameras before leaving the White House for the inaugural ceremonies on the morning of March 4, 1913.

Taft—in one of his last pictures as President—is his usual jovial self, while Wilson—not yet accustomed to manipulating his face for the public—appears ill at ease. He may have been thinking of the limerick he was so fond of quoting:

For beauty I am not a star,
There are hundreds more handsome by far,
But my face I don't mind it,
For I am behind it,
It's the people in front that I jar.

MARCH 4, 1913: WOODROW WILSON TAKES THE OATH OF OFFICE. In his inaugural address the new President spoke of "the things that ought to be altered." He spoke of the "tariff which cuts us off from our proper part in the commerce of the world . . . and makes the government a facile instrument in the hands of private interests"; he spoke of the banking and currency system, which was in need of overhauling, and he spoke of the "industrial system which . . . holds capital in leading strings, restricts the liberties and limits the opportunities of labor, and exploits without renewing or conserving the natural resources of the country."

Wilson presented an ambitious New Freedom program—to be accomplished within the framework of the existing social system. Based not only on Populist and progressive ideas, but also on Roosevelt's New Nationalism, it was a long-awaited program, a signal program of reform. "We must abolish everything," said Wilson in his first message to Congress, "that bears even the semblance of privilege or any kind of artificial advantage."

CHAPTER XLI

TWILIGHT DAYS

The defeat of 1912 shattered him, but outwardly he acted as if it were of no great consequence that he had lost the fight. To the sympathy notes of his friends he replied with unshaken confidence. "We have fought the good fight, we have kept the faith, and we have nothing to regret," he wrote to James Garfield. "As things were this year, there was no human being who could have made any fight or have saved the whole movement from collapse if I had not been willing to step in and take the hammering," he said to Arthur Hamilton Lee. "It was a phenomenal thing to be able to bring the new party into second place and to beat out the Republicans," he wrote to Henry White.

Still, this was the greatest defeat of his career. Success had now abandoned him and he had to contend with failure. Abused by the regulars for smashing the party, shunned by former friends and assailed by enemies, he was learning the bitter experience of defeat. There was no more surge to shake his hand when he attended a public function. Once when he went with a friend to a meeting of the Harvard Board of Overseers, the atmosphere was so chilly toward them that they felt "like a pair of Airedale pups in a convention of tomcats."

A weaker man would have been crushed under it, but Roosevelt—never a contemplative character—would not moan over the past. For him there was always the tomorrow. He was always full of plans, there was always work ahead of him. He began to work on his *Autobiography,* and he collaborated with Edmund Heller, the naturalist from the Smithsonian Institution, on the *Life Histories of African Game Animals.*

He instituted a libel suit against a small country newspaper editor in Michigan, who charged him with drunkenness. Throughout his political career he was often angered by people accusing him of being a heavy drinker. During the Progressive campaign when rumors again went the rounds about this, he made up his mind to fight them as soon as he had a clear case. Thus, when the Old Guard newspaper editor George A. Newett repeated the charge in print, Roosevelt brought suit, to squelch the lie once and for all.

The case was tried at Marquette, Michigan, the last week of May 1913. For five days, witness after witness testified that they had never seen Roosevelt intoxicated. His former secretary, William Loeb, Jr., told the jury that his chief could not have been drunk during the past fifteen years without his knowing it, yet he never saw him show any effects of alcohol. The Chicago newspaperman O'Laughlin testified: "I not only never have seen Colonel Roosevelt under the influence of liquor but it is an absolutely silly thing to me that anybody should bring such a charge against him."

Roosevelt himself told the court: "I have never drunk a cocktail or highball in my life. . . . I never drank whisky or brandy except under the advice of a physician. I don't care for the taste of either.

"I don't smoke and I don't drink beer. I dislike smoking and dislike the taste of beer. I never have drunk whisky or brandy except when the doctor prescribed it, or possibly on some occasion after great exposure when I was chilled through. But it has been certainly fifteen or twenty years since I have drunk it because of being chilled through."

The newspaper editor, unable to produce a single witness against Roosevelt, retracted his charges and offered an apology. Roosevelt, who had only brought the suit to "deal with these slanders so that never again will they be repeated," requested only nominal damages in the amount of six cents, and these were awarded to him. "I deemed it best not to demand money damages," he said after the trial. "The man is a country editor, and while I thoroughly despise him, I do not care to seem to prosecute him."

It was a few days before he left for Michigan to attend the trial that he wrote to his niece's husband in Washington. Young Franklin Delano Roosevelt, the recipient of the note, had become Assistant Secretary of the Navy two months earlier, and now Theodore Roosevelt sent him a letter of advice. "It is not my place to advise, but there is one matter so vital that I want to call your attention to it. I do not anticipate trouble with Japan, but it may come, and if it does it will come suddenly. In that case we shall be in an unpardonable position if we permit ourselves to be caught with our fleet separated. There ought not to be a battleship or any formidable fighting craft in the Pacific unless our entire fleet is in the Pacific. Russia's fate ought to be a warning for all time as to the criminal folly of dividing the fleet if there is even the remotest chance of war." Franklin agreed wholeheartedly with "Uncle Theodore's" suggestion not to divide the fleet, and asked the elder Roosevelt to write a magazine article about it.

During the summer of 1913, invitations for speeches came from universities in Brazil, Argentina, and Chile. Eager for action, Roosevelt accepted them. He would go to South America, give the requested addresses, then take a trip into the jungle, proving once more that he had not yet become old and that he still had the prowess and the strength as of yore.

On October 5 the New York *Tribune* reported: "Colonel Roosevelt, with his party of six, sailed on his South American trip yesterday by the Lamport & Holt liner *Vandyck,* which left Pier 8, Brooklyn, at 1 P.M.

"There was a crowd to see him sail, but it was not the same sort of throng that congested ship and pier in Hoboken when the colonel started out on his African junket on March 23, 1909."

The party included Mrs. Roosevelt, Kermit, the Reverend John A. Zahn, provincial of the Order of the Holy Cross, and the scientists George K. Cherries and Anthony Fiala.

The lectures taken care of, Mrs. Roosevelt returned to the States, and the expedition—augmented by Colonel Rondon and two Brazilian engineers—was on its way into unexplored territory. On January 16, 1914, Roosevelt wrote to Frank Michler Chapman: "We are now about to go into the real wilderness, where we shall have to travel light, and can hardly collect any big animals. In a month or six weeks we shall reach the headwaters of an unexplored river. If my health continues good, as I expect, I think it possible that I will go down this river to try and find out where it comes out, taking Kermit, Fiala and Cherries with me as well as Colonel Rondon and two of the Brazilians."

His aim was to collect animal and botanical specimens for New York's Museum of Natural History and to map the River of Doubt, an unexplored tributary of the Amazon, flowing for almost a thousand miles from lower Brazil north to that river. It was a perilous voyage, and when it was over, Roosevelt reported: "We have had a hard and somewhat dangerous but very successful trip. No less than six weeks were spent in slowly and with peril and exhausting labor forcing our way down through what seemed a literally endless succession of rapids and cataracts. For forty-eight days we saw no human being. In passing these rapids we lost five of the seven canoes with which we started and had to build others. One of our best men lost his life in the rapids. Under the strain one of the men went completely bad, shirked all his work, stole his comrades' food and when punished by the sergeant he with cold-blooded deliberation murdered the sergeant and fled into the wilderness. Col. Rondon's dog, running ahead of him while hunting, was shot by two Indians; by his death he in all probability saved the life of his master. We have put on the map a river about 1500 kilometers in length running from just south of the 13th degree to north of the 5th degree and the biggest affluent of the Madeira. Until now its upper course has been utterly unknown to everyone, and its lower course although known for years to the rubber-men utterly unknown to all cartographers. Its source is between the 12th and 13th parallels of latitude South, and between longitude 59° and longitude 60° west from Greenwich."

Mile after mile, the unnavigable rapids were mastered by portages through thick jungle growth. Roosevelt was badly hurt when his leg was jammed between a canoe and a rock in the river. Unable to walk, he had to be carried by his companions. And then he contracted jungle fever and could not be moved at all. With the supply of food at a low ebb, he begged the others to leave him behind, a request which fell on deaf ears. As the trip came to its close Roosevelt was 35 pounds thinner.

On May 19, 1914, after seven and a half months in South America, he landed in New York. A newspaper reported that he was "leaning heavily on a cane, and assisted by two men, toiled up the gangway from the landing place. It was a shock to his old friends, to whom his unusual physical vigor had been always a source of wonder, to note the change." Yet ten days later he was on a boat again, sailing to his son Kermit's wedding in Spain.

THE NEWETT LIBEL SUIT

ROOSEVELT SUES FOR LIBEL. During the Progressive campaign rumors spread that the Colonel was a heavy drinker. Exasperated by such accusations, Roosevelt made up his mind that if the charge was repeated in print, he would sue the perpetrator of the slander. Thus, when the *Iron Ore,* a small weekly in Ishpeming, Michigan, printed on October 12, 1912: "Roosevelt lies and curses in a most disgusting way; he gets drunk too, and that not infrequently, and all his intimate friends know about it," the hurt and thoroughly angered victim brought a libel action against the editor of the paper, George S. Newett.

ON THE STAND Roosevelt testified: "I do not drink either whiskey or brandy, except as I shall hereafter say . . .; I do not drink beer; I sometimes drink light wine. . . . I have never drunk a highball or a cocktail in my life. . . . I may have drunk half a dozen mint juleps in a year. . . . At home, at dinner, I may partake of a glass or two glasses of white wine. At a public dinner, or a big dinner, I will take a glass or two glasses of champagne. . . . In Africa the expedition took with it a case of champagne, a case of whiskey and a bottle of brandy."

THE WINNER. A cartoon by Spencer in the Omaha *World Herald* on May 27, 1913, alluding to the publicity value of the suit against a man whose name no one remembered.

Before the court at Marquette, Michigan, scores of witnesses testified that Roosevelt never drank except with moderation. Editor George S. Newett, the defendant in the libel action, was not able to produce a single witness who could testify otherwise; he had to admit that he was not only misinformed, but was wrong and, in effect, offered an apology. Roosevelt asked for but nominal damages, emphasizing that he had brought suit only to deal with the slanders, "so that never again will it be possible for any man, in good faith, to repeat them." He won his case; the court assessed six cents damages against the slandering editor.

IN THE SOUTH AMERICAN JUNGLE

THE SOUTH AMERICAN EXPEDITION WAS UNDER AN EVIL STAR—ENDING ALMOST

"I had to go," said Roosevelt. "It was my last chance to be a boy." So he went. The expedition left New York on October 4, 1913, and returned on May 19, 1914. His son Kermit, who accompanied him on the journey, left a record of these seven and a half dramatic months in his book *The Happy Hunting Grounds.*

At the request of the Brazilian government, the scope of the expedition was enlarged. The party fought their way through the uncharted regions of western Brazil and mapped the River of Doubt, until then an unexplored stream. (Later it was renamed

Rio Téodoro.) From the outset the expedition was under an ill star. One of the men drowned, another went crazy and killed his companion. When the food supply ran out, the men ate what their guns provided and what they could take from the water and from the trees. Tropical downpours drenched them daily, their clothes drying on their backs.

In the first week of April, Roosevelt contracted jungle fever. Still, he kept on. One day, in an attempt to save a pair of canoes, he again injured the leg which had been hurt a dozen years earlier

HIS BIGGEST BAG was a tremendous bull elephant which he shot at Meru. Photograph by Kermit.

TWO OF HIS VICTIMS, a rhinoceros and a bustard, were brought down by him at the same spot.

IN DISASTER FOR THEODORE ROOSEVELT

in the Pittsfield accident. Abscesses developed on the leg, causing him excruciating pain. Believing that his presence only hindered the expedition, he told his son Kermit: "We have reached a point where some of us must stop. I feel I am only a burden to the party," and suggested that he should be left behind and abandoned in the jungle. This was Roosevelt the romantic, Roosevelt the heroic, Roosevelt the dramatic, ready to give up life and die a lonely death to avoid being a burden to his associates. But Kermit and the others brought him down the river to safety.

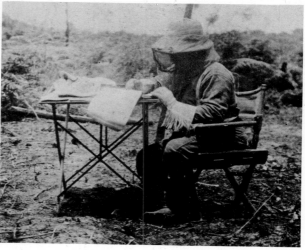

"I DID MY WRITING in headnet and gauntlets." Some of his South American pieces for *Scribner's Magazine* were written when he had a temperature of 105°.

MAY 20, 1914: EMERGING FROM THE JUNGLE.

Roosevelt was given a hero's welcome when he returned from his South American expedition. News photographers caught him smiling, but it was a forced smile. He was worn out, almost too weak to stand on his feet. The fever contracted in the jungle left him tired and exhausted, "a veritable plague of deep abscesses" caused him pain, his leg wound bothered him. He was longing for his home and for a rest. During the period in the jungle he had lost 35 pounds, of which 25 were regained on the homeward trip; but with fever germs still in his body, he was a sick and frail man.

CHAPTER XLII

IN THE WORLD WAR

The very week that Roosevelt returned from his son's wedding in Spain, a Serbian nationalist in Sarajevo, Bosnia, fired a shot that set the world afire. From June 28, 1914, the day of the assassination of the Austrian Archduke Franz Ferdinand, the precarious structure of great-power alliance in Europe tottered in the balance. A month later it erupted in a world cataclysm which Roosevelt had helped to stave off at the Algeciras Conference nine years earlier.

In America the country's opinion was best expressed by Senator John Sharp Williams, who said that he was "mad all over, down to the very bottom of my shoes, at this outbreak of senseless war." Yet the nation's official position remained that of neutrality. President Wilson asked every man and woman to be "impartial in thought as well as in action."

At first Roosevelt shared Wilson's determination to avoid America's entanglement in the European war. "Only the clearest and most urgent national duty," he wrote in *The Outlook,* "would ever justify us in deviating from our rule of neutrality and non-interference." But as the summer waned and Americans became war-minded, so did Roosevelt. Writing his old friend Cecil Spring-Rice, now British Ambassador at Washington, he said: "If I had been President, I should have acted on the thirtieth or thirty-first of July, as head of a signatory power to the Hague treaties, calling attention to the guaranty of Belgium's neutrality and saying that I accepted the treaties as imposing a serious obligation which I expected not only the United States but all other neutral nations to join in enforcing. Of course I would not have made such a statement unless I was willing to back it up." In his articles for the *Metropolitan Magazine* and in his addresses he spoke of America's international duty and its obligation to aid the weak.

Despite the initial revulsion to the war, American "neutrality in thought" proved impossible to maintain. The bonds of language, of temperament, of tradition, and of economics were strong between the United States and the mother country. With the exception of the Germans and the Irish, the sympathies of the country were with Great Britain in the struggle.

The anti-German feeling increased as the atrocities of Germany's unrestricted submarine warfare became publicized. Americans learned with shock and horror that the British liner *Lusitania,* carrying munitions and passengers to England, was torpedoed off the coast of Ireland with the loss of 1100 lives, many of them Americans. President Wilson sent a vigorous protest to the German government—so vigorous indeed that William Jennings Bryan, who held that Americans should be forbidden to travel on the armed ships of belligerents, resigned as Secretary of State rather than associate himself with what he feared would prove an ultimatum.

After the sinking of the *Lusitania,* Roosevelt said that the United States would earn "measureless scorn and contempt if we follow the lead of those who exalt peace above righteousness, if we heed the voice of the feeble folk who bleat to high heaven for peace when there is no peace." Yet Wilson was convinced that the nation as a whole was not ready to go to war. "There is such a thing as a nation being so right that it does not need to convince others by force that it is right," he said in an oft-quoted speech.

For Roosevelt, America's failure to act against Germany was "literally inexcusable and inexplicable." He attacked Wilson: "To treat elocution as a substitute for action, to rely upon high-sounding words unbacked by deeds, is proof of a mind that dwells only in the realm of shadow and shame."

Still, in the summer of 1916 the issue whether America should enter the war or not became a secondary one as the country's attention turned to the nominating conventions. The Democrats renominated President Wilson; the Republicans chose Charles Evans Hughes. Roosevelt, who had previously declined the nomination of the moribund Progressive party, rallied behind the Republican candidate and campaigned for him, though his support of the uninspiring Hughes was not as enthusiastic as it would have been had his party chosen a more effective man.

By an exceedingly slim margin Wilson, who had "kept us out of war," was upheld by the voters. Yet even before he could be inaugurated, Germany informed the United States that all merchant vessels within prescribed zones of the Atlantic and Mediterranean would be sunk without warning. This meant the end of Wilson's neutrality policy.

Diplomatic relations with Germany were severed. Wilson still had some hope that "armed neutrality" might be feasible and that America would not have to enter the conflict. Roosevelt knew better: "There is no question of 'going to war.' Germany is already at war with us. The only question is whether we shall make war nobly or ignobly." In February and March, Germany sank eight American ships, and, as if this were not enough, the British exposed a German plot for bringing Mexico and Japan into war against America. The patience of the United States was exhausted. On April 2 President Wilson asked Congress to put America into the fight "for democracy, for the right of those who submit to authority to have a voice in their own governments, for the rights and liberties of small nations, for a universal dominion of right by such a concert of free peoples as shall bring peace and safety to all nations, and make the world itself at last free." Four days later Congress declared war.

Roosevelt pointed out that Wilson's war message "bears out all I have said for the past two and a half years, and condemns all he has said and done for those two and a half years." With America at war, his consuming desire was to raise a division of his own to take to the front. Since the fall of 1914 he had been making plans for a new edition of the Rough Riders, and he sent to Secretary of War Newton D. Baker an outline of the proposal. Baker replied that it would be considered "should the occasion arise." Now that war had actually come, Roosevelt, putting his pride in his pocket, repaired to Washington to discuss the issue with the President himself. The conversation was amicable; Wilson was charmed with his antagonist. Yet he would not promise Roosevelt what he asked for; he would not send him to Europe at the head of a division. "The business now in hand is undramatic, practical, and of scientific definiteness and precision," he explained later. For Roosevelt, the President's decision of not allowing him to go to the front "was actuated by the basest and most contemptible political reasons," and his hatred for Wilson grew.

Not being able to serve his country on the battlefield, he kept on writing articles, kept on making speeches, throwing himself wholeheartedly into the task of stimulating the country's martial spirit. He urged Americans to action, he denounced the "folly and complacent sloth" of the Wilson administration, which in his opinion had achieved "a miracle of inefficiency" through the lack of an adequate preparedness program. Exasperated that he could only talk or write when "it is only the doers who really count," he wrote to his son Theodore that "the Administration has no conception of war needs, of what war means. . . . If three years ago we had introduced universal military training, if we had begun to build quantities of cannon, machine guns, rifles and airplanes . . . the war would have been over now." He kept on hammering on the issue of preparedness, he kept on urging the speeding up of the war effort and the establishment of universal military training as a permanent policy.

On the floor of the Senate he was described as "the most potent agent the Kaiser has in America." The Hearst newspapers asked for his imprisonment, to which he retaliated that it was Hearst who had helped the German cause, therefore it was the newspaper editor who should be executed.

Though he was sharply criticized by a great segment of the American public, the fact remains that his emotional appeal, his sincerity and deep devotion to his country helped to prepare the United States for the day when she was to enter into the hostilities.

He took profound pride in his four sons, who joined the ranks and served at the front with conspicuous bravery. Theodore, Jr., was wounded and twice cited for gallantry; Kermit won the British Military Cross; Archibald was wounded and won the Croix de Guerre; and Quentin became a combat aviator. He was proud when Finley Peter Dunne told him: "The first thing you know your four sons will put the name of Roosevelt on the map!"

In July 1918 the news came that Quentin, the youngest of the boys, had been shot down behind German lines by two enemy fighter planes.

The death of his youngest son was a crushing blow to him, a blow from which he never recovered. Gone forever was his youthful ebullience, gone forever his vigor and his energy. He was feeble and he was tired; old age knocked at the door. In October of that year, when he became sixty years old, he wrote to his son Kermit that he was "glad to be sixty, for it somehow gives me the right to be titularly as old as I feel."

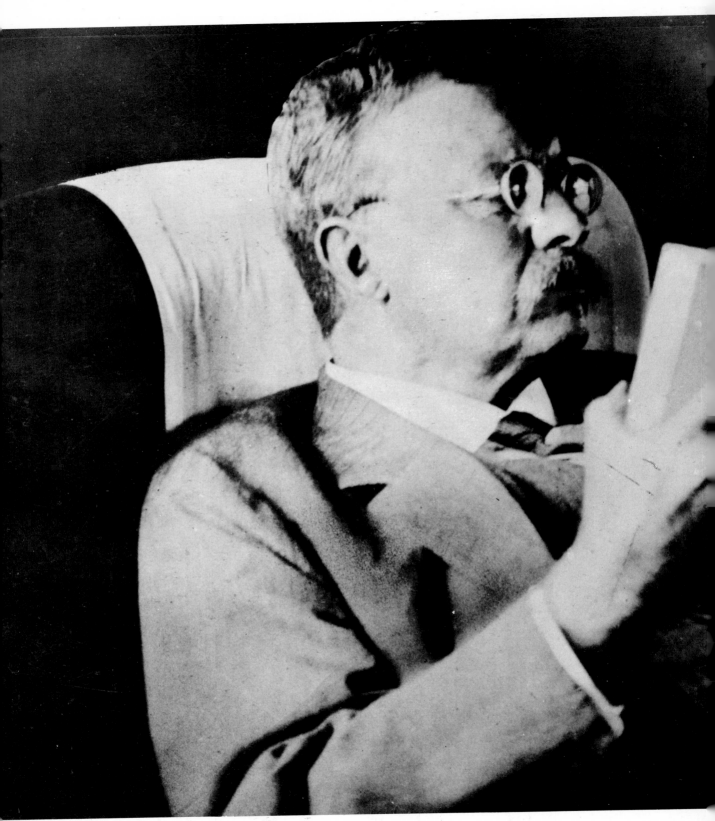

A PRODIGIOUS READER, he was seldom without a book. He read on his travels, he read when he took a break from work, he read amongst a crowd, and he read when he was alone. His literary taste had a wide

THE OUTBREAK OF THE FIRST WORLD WAR

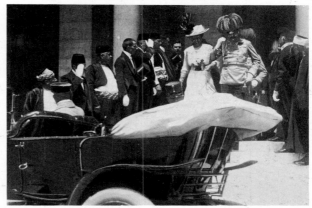

A MOMENTOUS DAY

On June 28, 1914, Archduke Franz Ferdinand, the heir to the throne of the Austro-Hungarian empire, and his wife were shot to death in Sarejevo, Bosnia, by a Pan-Slav nationalist.

A fortnight later the council of Austro-Hungarian ministers—assured by "the complete support of Germany"—was ready to take action against Serbia. On July 23 an ultimatum was sent to Serbia, six days later war was declared. On August 3 Germany began war against France, on August 4 Great Britain took up arms against Germany, on August 5 the Russian army marched into Germany. Within days the great European powers were facing each other on the battlefield in a world holocaust.

★

THE ASSASSIN OF THE ARCHDUKE, Gavrio Princip, is rushed away by the police after his deed.

range. The book he reads here with such concentration is Booth Tarkington's *Penrod.*

AUGUST 1914: BELGIAN VILLAGERS FLEE BEFORE THE GERMAN ADVANCE GUARD.

GERMANY INVADES BELGIUM

The first days in August the German armies invaded Belgium and pressed toward Paris. On August 5 President Wilson announced that the attitude of the United States in the conflict would be that of neutrality.

The German invasion was accepted by official America; it was accepted by Theodore Roosevelt. "When giants are engaged in a death wrestle," he wrote in *The Outlook* on August 22, 1914, "as they reel to and fro they are certain to trample on whomever gets in the way of either of the huge straining combatants." Roosevelt held that the invasion was justified as a strategic necessity. At the outset of the European war Roosevelt referred to the Germans as "a stern, virile and masterful people, a people entitled to hearty respect for their patriotism and far-seeking self-devotion"—for whom one could have nothing but "praise and admiration."

He did not censure the Germans for their destruction of Louvain and the irreplaceable library. He did not raise his voice against the German bombardment of Antwerp. He felt

598

THE GERMAN ARMY MARCHES THROUGH THE DESERTED STREETS OF BRUSSELS.

that Americans had "not the slightest responsibility" for what happened in Belgium, even though the country on the whole sympathized with that state. "Nevertheless this sympathy is compatible with full knowledge of the unwisdom of uttering a single word of official protest unless we are prepared to make the protest effective; and only the clearest and most urgent national duty would ever justify us in deviating from our rule of neutrality and non-interference."

A year later—in 1915—when he published his first war book, Roosevelt altered the above passage. By that time he opposed Wilson's neutrality policy; by that time he was convinced that America must pay the penalty for its "supine inaction" by forfeiting the right to do anything on behalf of peace for the Belgians.

Roosevelt was honest about both passages. He felt strongly about them. His emotions underwent a change as American public opinion changed. With the continuation of the war, Roosevelt—along with his fellow countrymen—was lined up behind the Allied cause.

FIGHTING BOSSISM

THE BARNES TRIAL

Before the elections in 1914, Roosevelt tried to unite the two opposing wings of his party behind an honest gubernatorial candidate for New York. Attacking the state's Republican boss, William Barnes, Roosevelt said that he was as crooked as his Democratic counterpart and asserted that "the two bosses will always be found on the same side openly or covertly, giving one another such support as can with safety be rendered." Barnes initiated a libel suit against Roosevelt next day.

A DEPLORABLE PERFORMANCE.

TWO HOSTILE CARTOONS, drawn by the master craftsman Rollin Kirby for the New York *World*. The top one appeared in the newspaper on April 12, 1915, the bottom one was printed on April 24.

CONGRATULATING THE WITNESS.

IT WAS A SPECTACULAR TRIAL that started in April 1915 in Syracuse, New York, keeping the country spellbound. Roosevelt was on the stand for hours, weathering the attacks and cross-examination of Barnes's attorneys. At times he burst out in tirades and the judge had to stop him. During a cross-examination he firmly asserted that during his presidential years he compromised much less than did President Lincoln.

LEAVING THE COURTHOUSE in Syracuse during the Barnes trial with his counsel, Oliver D. Burden.

The Barnes attorney took this up. "You stand by righteousness, do you not?" he asked.

"I do," answered Roosevelt.

"With due regard to opportunism . . .?"

"No, sir, not when it comes to righteousness."

"Does not your last answer state that?"

"It does not, sir. I say I believe emphatically that you must have a due regard for opportunism in the choice of the time and methods for making the attack. But you must stand for righteousness, whether you are going to be supported or not."

Boss Barnes lost the case. The jury believed Roosevelt's remarks were just, and acquitted him.

THE SINKING OF THE *LUSITANIA* on May 7, 1915, outraged the American people. Theodore Roosevelt demanded firm action, but the country was behind President Wilson, who advocated patience. America had no desire to embark on a war, however strong the provocations were.

The country on the whole sympathized with the Allies, although the large German population and some of the other foreign-borns were for the German cause. Wilson and Congress, sensing the country's attitude, pleaded for time. The President embarked on a lengthy diplomatic correspondence with Germany. On May 13, on June 9, and again on July 21 he dispatched notes demanding from the German government an outspoken disavowal of the *Lusitania's* destruction and a pledge that attacks on unresisting non-combatants would cease. When the answer of the Germans proved "very unsatisfactory," the President warned that the sinking of unarmed merchant vessels would be regarded by the United States as a "deliberately unfriendly" act—an open threat of war. Wilson's diplomatic correspondence brought results. For about a year, while the notes went to and fro between the two nations, Germany refrained from attacking merchant vessels without warning. During that time the horror of unrestricted submarine warfare was lifted and the precarious peace maintained.

HELPING THE PRESIDENT.

WILSON AND HIS HELPERS. A cartoon by Rollin Kirby (July 13, 1915) picturing William Jennings Bryan and Roosevelt "helping the President."

★

AN ENGLISH ADVERTISEMENT
And a German warning in the same column of the New York *Herald* of May 1, 1915.

"MURDER ON THE HIGH SEAS" was Roosevelt's angry comment on the sinking of the British mailship *Lusitania* when German submarines torpedoed her on May 7, 1915, off Kinsdale Head on the Irish coast. Of 1918 persons aboard the liner, only 726 were saved. Among the 114 Americans who lost their lives were sportsman Alfred Gwynne Vanderbilt, theatrical producer Charles Frohman, dramatist Charles Klein, author Elbert Hubbard.

Roosevelt pleaded for strong action, asking for the seizure of all interned German ships and the prohibition of commerce with Germany. "I do not believe that the firm assertion of our rights means war, but, in any event, it is well to remember there are things worse than war."

Three days after the sinking of the *Lusitania,* Wilson spoke in Philadelphia on American ideals. "The example of America must be the example not merely of peace because it will not fight, but of peace because peace is the healing and elevating influence of the world and strife is not," said he. "There is such a thing as a nation being so right that it does not need to convince others by force that it is right . . . There is such a thing as a man being too proud to fight."

Wilson's phrase was taken up by his enemies, who attacked him with renewed vigor. "What a pity Theodore Roosevelt is not President," headlined the New York *Herald.* Roosevelt advocated preparedness, so America should be ready in the event of war, but neither Wilson nor Congress would accept such a policy. It was argued that preparedness would mean the end of neutrality, and the country was not yet ready for war.

Roosevelt denounced Wilson as "the pacifist hero" whose followers were "professional pacifists, the flubdubs and the mollycoddles." Ignoring these exaggerated attacks, Wilson said: "The way to treat an adversary like Roosevelt is to gaze at the stars over his head."

URGING PREPAREDNESS. The leader of the preparedness movement was Roosevelt's old friend General Leonard Wood, under whom he served in the Spanish-American War. The General, supported by private organizations, was the head of a summer training camp at Plattsburg, N. Y., where students, businessmen, and other volunteers received a short military training. All four of Roosevelt's sons were there for instruction. The widely publicized but not too effectual "Plattsburg idea" served well in one respect—it infused the young men of America with the thought that sooner or later they would have to fight.

On August 25, 1915, when the picture below was taken, Roosevelt came to Plattsburg at the invitation of General Wood to address the young men in the camp. He made a restrained speech, without attacking Wilson. But in the evening, as he left the camp, he told the newspapermen that the people of the country should stand behind the President only when he was right, but against him when he was wrong—a dangerous idea which, if followed, could only lead to anarchy.

Roosevelt—much to the amusement of the newspapermen, who reported it next day—pointed to a little dog that ran into him but retreated and remained quiet. "I like him," Roosevelt said with sarcastic intent; "his present attitude is strictly one of neutrality."

604

NOT A CANDIDATE
A photograph taken at Oyster Bay during the 1916 campaign by Conkwright and Winn, N.Y.

ANYTHING TO BEAT WILSON.

HELPING HUGHES.

IN PLACE OF THE ERMINE.

BERLIN'S CANDIDATE.

THE 1916 CAMPAIGN brought the Progressives back into the Republican fold. Roosevelt somewhat reluctantly endorsed Hughes and campaigned against Wilson, the man who "kept us out of war."

In his speeches Roosevelt charged that Wilson would never stand up to the Germans. He said that if he had been President when the *Lusitania* was sunk, he would have seized every German vessel interned in American waters. Reporters questioned Hughes whether he would have done the same, bu

THE LAST HOPE.

HIS OWN BRAND OF AMMUNITION.

SATURDAY'S PARADE EPITOMIZED.

"YOU GUESSED WRONG AGAIN, PAPA."

the gray iceberg" gave an evasive answer.

Roosevelt's last speech was an emotional appeal against Wilson. "There should be shadows now at Shadow Lawn, [the home of Wilson in New Jersey] the shadows of the men, women, and children who have risen from the ooze of the ocean bottom and from graves in foreign lands; the shadows of the helpless whom Mr. Wilson did not dare protect lest he might have to face danger. . . ."

It was of no avail; Wilson won the election.

AMERICA DECLARES WAR

The last day of January 1917 Count von Bernstorff, the German Ambassador, notified the State Department that his country had instituted zones in the Mediterranean and around the British Isles, and that within these zones all neutral shipping would be destroyed if it carried contraband. One clearly marked American vessel would be allowed to sail weekly in each direction. As the United States would not tolerate such restriction, the German Ambassador was handed his passport. On February 3 diplomatic relations between the two countries came to an end.

Three weeks later came the news of an intercepted telegram to Mexico, in which Germany offered the states of Texas, Arizona, and New Mexico if Mexico would invade the United States.

In March, German submarines sank American vessels without warning. This meant war. On April 2 President Wilson told Congress that a state of war existed between the United States and Germany.

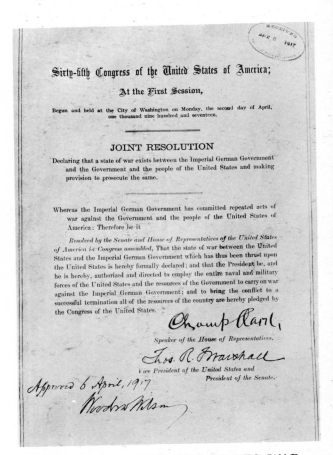

APRIL 6, 1917: CONGRESS VOTES WAR

Right:

★

APRIL 2, 1917: WILSON'S WAR ADDRESS

THREE DAYS AFTER AMERICA ENTERED THE WAR, Roosevelt saw President Wilson in Washington and asked him for permission to recruit a volunteer division. For the Colonel, time seemed to stand still. Nineteen years had gone by since he had led the Rough Riders against the Spaniards in Cuba, and now—nineteen years later—he desired to lead a regiment against the Germans in France.

The interview with Wilson was paved by the young man who had married Roosevelt's niece and who was now Assistant Secretary of the Navy—Franklin Delano Roosevelt. He spoke to Secretary of War Newton D. Baker, and Baker called on Roosevelt at Alice Longworth's Washington home. Roosevelt talked of his hopes to go to war. "I am aware," he said, "that I have not had enough experience to lead a division myself. But I have selected the most experienced officers from the regular army for my staff." All he wanted was to fight.

On April 9 Roosevelt went to the White House and had an hour's talk with Wilson. He complimented the President on his war message, and the two men had a friendly talk. Wilson was charmed. "There is a sweetness about him that is very compelling. You can't resist the man," said he to his secretary, Tumulty, after the visitor left. As to Roosevelt's request the President was noncommittal. Roosevelt, who declared that he would never oppose Wilson if he were allowed to go to Europe, told newspapermen on his leaving the White House that he had great hopes the President would acquiesce to his request.

Yet no word came from Wilson. When the governor of Louisiana interceded on Roosevelt's behalf, the President replied: "Colonel Roosevelt is a splendid man and a patriotic citizen . . . but he is not a military leader. His experience in military life has been extremely short. He and many of the men with him are too old to render effective service, and . . . he as well as others have shown intolerance of discipline."

610

THE YANKS ARE COMING.
American troops marching into Europe
to fight on the side of the Allies.

SPEAKING AT PATRIOTIC MEETINGS. He made speeches under the auspices of the National Security League, he spoke on Americanism, he spoke for the Red Cross, he spoke for everything that helped the war effort. In September 1917 he journeyed west, and spoke at large rallies in Kansas City, Chicago, and St. Paul, urging a determined and speedy offensive. He attacked Wilson and the administration for America's military inadequacy. During this period he often sounded like a demagogue. At times his speeches embraced a political philosophy to which a later generation gave the name "fascism."

His exaggerations at times bordered on intolerance. Thus, he spoke against foreign-born revolutionaries, as against socialists and radicals. His speeches, writes John M. Blum, "fed the spirit that expressed itself in lynchings, amateur witch hunts, intolerance of every kind. And he mixed his hateful talk with his awful cult of purging society by sacrifice in war and his ardent advocacy of compulsory peacetime industrial service for young men and women. . . . He disgraced not just his own but his nation's reputation." It was a sorrowful spectacle.

THE AMERICANS IN FRANCE. On May 18, 1917, President Wilson ordered an expeditionary force of one division under command of General John J. Pershing to proceed to France. On June 13 the first American combat troops sailed from New York, arriving in Europe twelve days later. And while prohibition went into effect in South Dakota, while more than 100 Negroes were killed and wounded in a race riot at St. Louis, while in the shipyards of Hoboken and New York the machinists and boilermakers began a strike for a $4.50 minimum daily wage, General Pershing marched with American troops through the streets of Paris on July 4. Two days later Pershing cabled his superiors in Washington: "Plans should contemplate sending over at least one million men by next May." Yet by January 1, 1918, General Pershing had only one depot division and four combat divisions in France. Again he urged the War Department to send more troops and more equipment. "The Allies are very weak and we must come to their relief in this year, 1918. The year after may be too late." Roosevelt's four sons were with the American Expeditionary Force.

HIS YOUNGEST SON—A WAR CASUALTY

Quentin's death broke his father's spirit. His friend Hermann Hagedorn, who saw him the very day the word came of Quentin's death, noted in his diary that suddenly the boy in Roosevelt had died. From then on until the end of his life—so Roosevelt confessed to another friend—keeping up the fight was a constant effort.

Roosevelt's deeply moving tribute to Quentin contained unforgettable lines: "Only those are fit to live who do not fear to die; and none are fit to die who have shrunk from the joy of life," he wrote. "Both life and death are parts of the same Great Adventure. Never yet was worthy adventure worthily carried through by the man who put his personal safety first." Roosevelt wrote of the duty, service and sacrifice expected of all the American people. "Pride is the portion only of those who know bitter sorrow or the foreboding of bitter sorrow. But all of us who give service, and stand ready for sacrifice, are the torchbearers. We run with the torches until we fall. . . ."

These lines came from his heart. It was his testament. The days of exuberance had gone, life became heavy; his own Great Adventure was closing.

QUENTIN, the youngest of the Roosevelt children, was killed in an aerial battle on July 14, 1918, his plane crashing behind the German lines.

QUENTIN'S GRAVE IN FRANCE, not far from the enemy land where his strafed plane was found.

HONORING QUENTIN'S DEATH—a touching cartoon by John McCutcheon in the Chicago *Tribune*.

THE SUNKEN ROAD AT MISSAYAUX BOIS

Half a century before—in 1862—it was the sunken road at Fredericksburg (see p. 35); now—in 1918— it is a sunken road in France. How little the two photographs differ! They could almost have been taken on the same day, not fifty-six years apart. Two generations had gone by, yet men were still unable to settle their disputes by peaceful means.

WILSON'S FOURTEEN POINTS

On January 8, 1918, Wilson appeared before Congress and delivered his Fourteen Points speech, committing the United States to take responsibility in the affairs of the world, and participate in solving the problems of Europe. Wilson's points reiterated his belief in open diplomacy, freedom of the seas, removal of trade barriers, reduction of armaments, impartial adjustment of colonial claims; his fourteenth point asked for a League of Nations.

In the fall of 1918 when Germany saw that defeat was inevitable, it asked for peace negotiations based on these fourteen points.

THE ROOSEVELT HOME AT OYSTER BAY. If the rooms of his childhood (see page 48) were ornate and elaborate, so were the rooms at Sagamore Hill, where he spent his adult years. The walls of his comfortable study were lined with innumerable books and family photographs, with a large oil painting of his father facing the desk at which he worked.

THE TROPHY ROOM, with antlers, elephant tusks, and other glorious mementoes of his hunting excursions, was added to the main house in 1904.

THERE WERE FIREPLACES in almost every room of Sagamore Hill. Roosevelt loved them, and he liked the feel of the bearskin rugs on the floors.

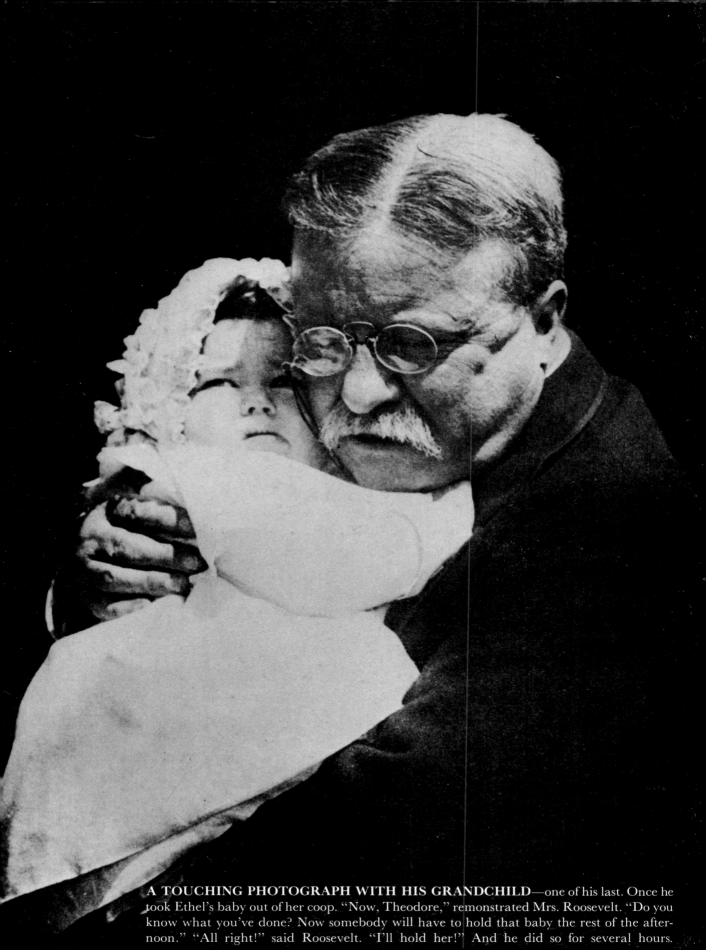

A TOUCHING PHOTOGRAPH WITH HIS GRANDCHILD—one of his last. Once he took Ethel's baby out of her coop. "Now, Theodore," remonstrated Mrs. Roosevelt. "Do you know what you've done? Now somebody will have to hold that baby the rest of the afternoon." "All right!" said Roosevelt. "I'll hold her!" And he did so for several hours.

THE END OF THE ROAD

"We have no selfish ends to serve. We desire no conquest, no dominion. We seek no indemnities for ourselves. We are but one of the champions of the rights of mankind." This was President Wilson, expressing the hope that at the end of the most terrible war in history mankind might expect a new era of peace and international justice. In January of 1918 he translated this aspiration into concrete terms with his Fourteen Points. He called for "open convenants of peace, openly arrived at," for absolute freedom of the seas, for removal of trade barriers and reduction of armaments "to the lowest point consistent with domestic safety," for a policy of self-determination in redrawing national boundaries, and for an association of nations which would guarantee "political independence and territorial integrity to great and small nations alike."

Wilson's idealistic program could not survive in the bitter crucible of hatred and greed that was Europe after four years of devastating war. Still, at the time he proclaimed the Fourteen Points they were accepted as Allied war aims, and it was on their basis that Germany surrendered. To Wilson, to the vanquished Germans, to subject nationalities who found self-determination a magic word, the Fourteen Points were regarded as a solemn compact. To the hard-bitten and vengeance-ridden politicians in Europe they were propaganda weapons.

Roosevelt considered the Fourteen Points nothing more than "fourteen scraps of paper." He told Cabot Lodge that "the language of the fourteen points . . . is neither straightforward nor plain, but if construed in its probable sense many and possibly most of these fourteen points are thoroly mischievous and if made the basis of a peace, such peace would represent not the unconditional surrender of Germany but the conditional surrender of the United States." He wanted to "dictate peace by the hammering guns and not chat about peace to the accompaniment of the clicking of typewriters." On a speaking tour in the fall of 1918 he told a Nebraska audience: "The only way to make a Hun feel friendly is to knock him out. Don't hit the man soft, because he will come back and hit you hard. Put this war through right, so that no nation will look cross-eyed at you." And while he would reluctantly accept the idea of a League of Nations, he would never accept it as a substitute for the preparation of the nation's own defense. "Uncle Sam must, in the last analysis, rely on himself for his safety and not on scraps of paper signed by others," he said, and to Rider Haggard, the well-known English author, he wrote in December: "I don't put much faith in the League of Nations, or any corresponding universal cure-all."

He was urged to run for the governorship of New York, but he refused. "I

NOVEMBER 11, 1918: THE WAR WAS OVER.
And while crowds celebrated the Armistice in New
York, Roosevelt had to return to the hospital.

hate not to do as you, and Henry, and my other friends request," he wrote to William Howard Taft, with whom the old friendly relations again prevailed, "but Will Hays feels as strongly as I do that it is not wise for me under existing conditions to run for Governor of New York."

He threw himself into the campaign of the midterm election with great vigor, violently assailing the President and his policies. For him Wilson was "at heart a pacifist, cold blooded and without a single scruple of conviction." In his Carnegie Hall speech a week before the election Roosevelt said: "We Republicans pledge ourselves to stand by the President as long as he stands by the American people, and to part company from him at any point where in our judgment he does not stand by the people. This is the people's government, this is the people's war, and the peace that follows shall be the people's peace."

But the vigor was only in his voice, not in his body. He was now sick, plagued by recurrent attacks of sciatic rheumatism. The next day he was back in bed and stayed there for weeks except for a few hours on November 5, when he dressed and went to the polling place to cast his vote. The result of the election elated him. "We did an unparalleled thing," he wrote to his friend Rudyard Kipling in England, "and took away the Congress from him [Wilson], on the issue that we stood for forcing the Germans to make an unconditional surrender. I took a certain sardonic amusement in the fact that whereas four years ago, to put it mildly, my attitude was not popular, I was now the one man whom they insisted upon following and whose statements were taken as the platform."

He dictated a letter to his eldest son, but his pains were such that he was not able to sign it. His wife noted in a postscript: "Father is flat on his back with his gout . . . having a horrid, suffering time." For the next seven weeks he was confined in the Roosevelt Hospital in New York. The doctors warned him that he might be confined to a wheel chair for the rest of his life. "All right!" was his answer. "I can work that way, too."

When newspapers speculated about his future and when the New York *Tribune* flatly predicted that he would be "the Republican candidate for President in 1920," he said: "All that is near to me in the male line is in France. If they do not come back what is the Presidency to me?" He was now tired and burdened by his age. "I feel as though I were a hundred years old, and had *never* been young."

Still, he showed a keen interest in political issues. He watched the Communist revolution with alarm. On March 11, 1918, he wrote to his son Kermit: "The Bolshevists seem to have absolutely ruined Russia. Apparently the Russians for the time being lost all national spirit. For centuries they have cruelly persecuted the Jews, and now the Jew leadership in Russia has been a real nemesis for the Russians." Two months later he said to William Allen White: "At the moment I am inclined to think Bolshevism a more serious menace to world democracy than any species of capitalism." And a day before the Armistice he told his son Theodore that "the Republicans must understand that their chance of becoming the successful anti-Bolshevist party depends upon their being sane but thoroughgoing progressives. Mere standpattism, or in other words, the Romanov attitude, ensures disaster."

Early in December, Wilson sailed for France to make sure that his ideals should be written into the peace treaty. The whole basis of his personal leadership of the American delegation was his assumption that he would be able to dictate the terms of peace.

Strangely enough, the same people who came to worship Wilson when he reached European soil were not ready to accept the kind of peace he wanted to bring them, nor were their political leaders ready to accept the magnanimous settlements envisioned in the Fourteen Points. Lloyd George, the British Prime Minister, had recently won a general election by promising to "hang the Kaiser" and to make Germany pay the full cost of the Allied war effort. Georges Clemenceau, the French Premier, desired to grind Germany forever into the dust. He said: "Mr. Wilson bores me with his Fourteen Points. Why, God Almighty has only ten!" And Orlando, the Prime Minister of Italy, was interested mainly in territorial loot.

It was cynicism, bitterness, and a desire for "peace with a vengeance" which prevailed when the peace conference began in January. By then Roosevelt was back at Sagamore Hill, exhausted and in pain, spending the better part of each day in bed. Mrs. Roosevelt wrote to her eldest son that at dusk "he watched the dancing flames and spoke of the happiness of being home. . . . I think he had made up his mind that he would have to suffer for some time to come and with his high courage had adjusted himself to bear it." Once when she was leaving the room he looked up and said to her: "I wonder if you will ever know how I love Sagamore Hill."

On January 6, 1919—while President Wilson was traveling toward Versailles —Theodore Roosevelt died. Death came to him quietly. Until the last he worked, dictated letters, reviewed an ornithological book, wrote editorials for the Kansas City *Star*. To his bedridden sister, Mrs. Cowles, he sent the message: "I feel like a faker because my troubles are not to be mentioned in the same breath with yours." To editor Ogden Reid of the New York *Tribune* he protested against an editorial: "For Heaven's sake never allude to Wilson as an idealist or militaire or altruist. He is a doctrinaire when he can be so with safety to his personal ambition and he is always utterly and coldly selfish. He hasn't a touch of idealism in him."

An hour before midnight on January 5, after laying aside the proofs of an editorial he had corrected, he said to his valet: "James, please put out the light." They were his last words. Shortly after four the next morning he died in his sleep. "Death," said Vice-President Marshall, "had to take him sleeping. For if Roosevelt had been awake, there would have been a fight."

His son Archibald cabled to his brothers, who were serving with the Army in France:

"THE OLD LION IS DEAD."

WILSON, THE PEACEMAKER

JULY 20, 1917: The blindfolded President draws a draft number meaning military service for 4557 Americans, one man from each registration district.

OCTOBER 12, 1918: The President marches in New York's Liberty Loan parade. On Wilson's right are Dr. Grayson and his secretary, Tumulty.

DECEMBER 25, 1918: Wilson, accompanied by General Pershing, visited the American Expeditionary Force and received a rousing welcome.

DECEMBER 26, 1918: Wilson recrossed the Channel to pay a visit to England. At London's Charing Cross station he was met by King George V.

THE PRESIDENT SAILS TO EUROPE

Woodrow Wilson wanted to make certain that the ideals embodied in his Fourteen Points would become part of the peace treaty. In December 1918 he sailed to France to be present at Versailles, where the peace negotiations were to begin.

Roosevelt was angry, his hatred against Wilson without bounds. Only a few weeks earlier the country had elected a Republican Congress. To Roosevelt this meant a clear repudiation of the President's policies. Immobilized in a New York hospital, where he was being treated for his rheumatic condition, he issued a statement. "Mr. Wilson," said Roosevelt,

DECEMBER 4, 1918: Wilson, with the American delegates to the Peace Conference in Paris, crosses the ocean on the S. S. *George Washington.*

DECEMBER 13, 1918: Arriving at Brest, where President Poincaré met him. The French President accompanied Wilson on the ensuing journey to Paris.

DECEMBER 26, 1918: A tremendous crowd filled the square before London's Buckingham Palace and cheered lustily for the American President.

DECEMBER 31, 1918: King George V, Queen Mary, and their daughter, pose with the Wilsons before they leave England to return to France.

"has no authority whatever to speak for the American people at this time. His leadership has just been emphatically repudiated by them. Mr. Wilson and his Fourteen Points and his four supplementary points and all his utterances every which way have ceased to have any shadow of right to be accepted as expressive of the will of the American people."

Still, when Wilson reached the shores of Europe, he was greeted by the long-suffering people as no American had been greeted before him. He was the bearer of glad tidings of a better life. "The mass of European peasantry," said an observer, "looked forward to his arrival as men looked in medieval times to the second coming of Christ."

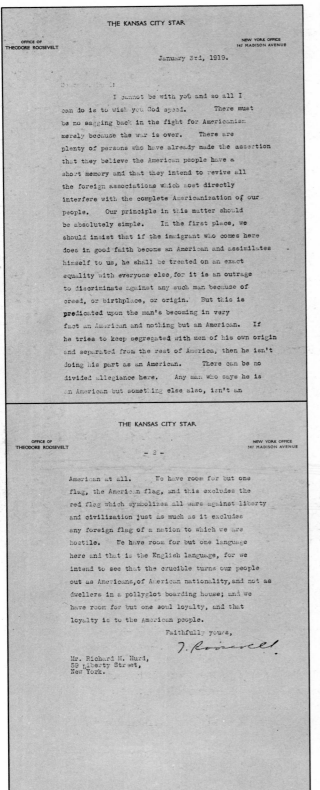

THE KANSAS CITY STAR

OFFICE OF
THEODORE ROOSEVELT

NEW YORK OFFICE
347 MADISON AVENUE

January 3rd, 1919.

Dear Mr. Hurd:

I cannot be with you and so all I can do is to wish you God speed. There must be no sagging back in the fight for Americanism merely because the war is over. There are plenty of persons who have already made the assertion that they believe the American people have a short memory and that they intend to revive all the foreign associations which most directly interfere with the complete Americanization of our people. Our principle in this matter should be absolutely simple. In the first place, we should insist that if the immigrant who comes here does in good faith become an American and assimilates himself to us, he shall be treated on an exact equality with everyone else, for it is an outrage to discriminate against any such man because of creed, or birthplace, or origin. But this is predicated upon the man's becoming in very fact an American and nothing but an American. If he tries to keep segregated with men of his own origin and separated from the rest of America, then he isn't doing his part as an American. There can be no divided allegiance here. Any man who says he is an American but something else also, isn't an

THE KANSAS CITY STAR

OFFICE OF
THEODORE ROOSEVELT

NEW YORK OFFICE
347 MADISON AVENUE

- 2 -

American at all. We have room for but one flag, the American flag, and this excludes the red flag which symbolizes all wars against liberty and civilization just as much as it excludes any foreign flag of a nation to which we are hostile. We have room for but one language here and that is the English language, for we intend to see that the crucible turns our people out as Americans, of American nationality, and not as dwellers in a polyglot boarding house; and we have room for but one soul loyalty, and that loyalty is to the American people.

Faithfully yours,

T. Roosevelt.

Mr. Richard M. Hurd,
59 Liberty Street,
New York.

HIS LAST MESSAGE to Richard Hurd was read at an all-American benefit concert a day before his death.

HE WORKED UNTIL THE END. His mind was clear, his thinking powers unimpaired. He wrote articles, he wrote letters, he kept in touch with his friends. He was occupied with political matters; he fought Wilson till the last.

Three days before his death he wrote to Carroll E. Armstrong in Clinton, Iowa, "that unlike Mr. Wilson I have never erred in intellectual honesty and moral straightforwardness" and "that as regards Mr. Wilson I never erred but once and that was on the occasion in question, when for the first sixty days after the outbreak of the World War I, I heartily supported him." Republicans once more began to look upon him as their next presidential candidate.

If Roosevelt had lived, he would most probably have been nominated in 1920 and would then certainly have been elected. How different the course of history would have run with him as President!

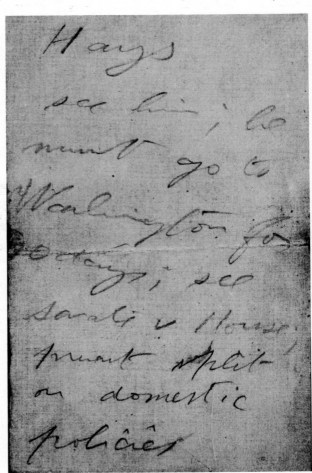

HIS LAST WRITTEN WORDS, found at his table: a memo to see Will Hays, the Chairman of the Republican National Committee, and tell him that "he must go to Washington for 10 days; see Senate & House; prevent split on domestic policies."

THE ROOM WHERE THEODORE ROOSEVELT DIED

The bedroom at Oyster Bay where, in the early hours of January 6, 1919, he breathed his last. The night before, the local doctor was called to treat his inflamed joints. Roosevelt told him: "I feel as though my heart was going to stop beating."

Ever since the early part of 1918 he had been ill. An abscess on his thigh and abscesses in his ears caused him severe pains, and he had to go to the hospital. "My old Brazilian trouble, both the fever and abscesses recurred and I had to go under the knife," he wrote to his son Kermit, then with the American Army in France. The operation left his balance impaired, he had to learn to walk anew, and he lost the hearing in his left ear. He suffered, but he took the pains without complaint. "The Doctors think I will be all right in the end," he said. "I hope so; but I am ahead of the game anyhow. Nobody ever packed more varieties of fun and interest in the sixty years."

On October 27, 1918, he was sixty years old. Two weeks later, the day of the signing of the Armistice, once more he had to return to the hospital. This time it was inflammatory rheumatism. For Christmas he returned home. On January 5 he wrote his regular editorial for the Kansas City *Star*. At eleven he asked his valet, "Please put out the light." They were his last words. Soon after four the following morning he died in his sleep. The immediate cause of death was "malignant endocarditis and embolism in the coronary arteries."

THE NEW YORK *WORLD*'S FRONT PAGE JANUARY 7, 1919

FAREWELL!
"The long, long trail," Jay N. ("Ding") Darling's moving tribute to Roosevelt, printed in the Des Moines *Register* on the day after his death.

Right:

HIS LAST LIKENESS
A bust by James Earle Fraser, completed from a mask which the sculptor took the day following Roosevelt's death.

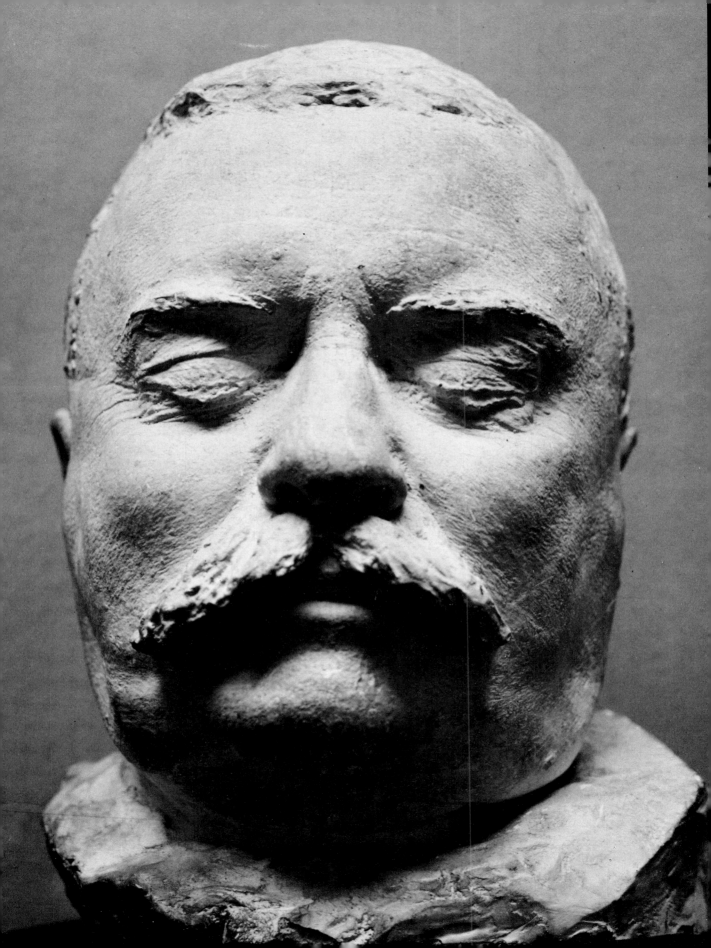

THEODORE ROOSEVELT'S COFFIN IS CARRIED TO ITS FINAL RESTING PLACE.

TAFT AT THE FUNERAL

He had written to Roosevelt when he heard of his sickness, and friendly letters were exchanged. One day in 1918 Taft entered Chicago's Blackstone Hotel and, seeing Roosevelt in the dining room, he opened his arms. "Theodore, I am glad to see you." Roosevelt asked Taft to dine with him, and within minutes antagonism had faded away.

THE END OF THE ROAD. The coffin was lowered into the earth and covered; the minister had said his prayers; the family and friends had gone. In the cold winter air a solitary soldier stayed behind and stood guard over the remains of Theodore Roosevelt.

Once, Roosevelt wrote to the poet Robinson: "There is not one among us, in whom a devil does not dwell; at some time, on some point, that devil masters each of us; he who has never failed has not been tempted; but the man who does in the end conquer, who does painfully retrace the steps of his slipping, why he shows that he has been tried in the fire and not found wanting. It is not having been in the Dark House, but having left it, that counts. . . ." The Dark House was behind him now, as was life.

A VIEW OF THE CITY OF NEW YORK IN THE YEAR OF 1919—AT THE TIME

In 1919 about five and a half million people lived in New York, four and three quarter millions more than in 1858 (see p. 20), the year Theodore Roosevelt was born. In the sixty years that spanned his life, the city had made phenomenal progress; it was now the largest in the world—larger even than London. Thirty-eight per cent of the population was foreign-born, coming from Russia, Italy, Germany, Ireland, Austria, England, and Hungary, in that order. Only two per cent of the city's inhabitants were Negroes. In the description of the English journalist W. L. George: "There is so much in the streets;

WHEN THEODORE ROOSEVELT DIED AT SAGAMORE HILL, OYSTER BAY

everything hurries—motor cars, street cars, railway cars. In the restaurants endless vistas of napery and crystal extend away. One goes up Broadway at night to see the crowded colored signs of the movie shows and the theatres twinkle and eddy, inviting, clamorous, Babylonian! . . . New York is all the cities. It is the giant city grouped about its colossal forest of parallelepipeds of concrete and steel."

No less than 33,000 factories produced three billion dollars' worth of goods yearly; there were 1,500 hotels and just as many churches, over a hundred hospitals, and 850 theaters, movies, and music halls.

PARK AVENUE, north from 84th Street. Six decades before—when Theodore Roosevelt was born—this section was not yet developed; it was filled with shanties inhabited by the poorest of the poor. By 1919, however—the year of Roosevelt's death—it had become one of the most fashionable residential areas of the city. As New York expanded, the wealthy people moved uptown; it added to social prestige to have a luxurious apartment on Park Avenue.

MADISON SQUARE, with the world's largest structure at the time of Theodore Roosevelt's death—the Metropolitan Life Insurance Building. The 52-story tower, reminiscent of the Campanile in Venice, was 700 feet high. The building's assessed value of $15,550,000 was the greatest in the city.

The tower on the left, piercing dark into the sky, ornamented Madison Square Garden. Next to it is the Appellate Court and Dr. Parkhurst's church.

SIXTH AVENUE AND BROADWAY, north from the 33rd Street platform of the elevated railway, had some of the heaviest traffic in the busy city.

FIFTH AVENUE AND 42ND STREET. In the middle of the street was New York's first traffic tower, with a policeman directing the flow of cars.

PARK ROW, the home of the city's great newspapers—the *World,* the *Sun,* the *Tribune,* the *Times.* Running from Ann Street northeast to Chatham Square, it skirted City Hall Park on the east. The dome on the left was over the main post office; west of it was Printing House Square, with the statue of Benjamin Franklin. "This is Brobdingnag, the land of giants," exclaimed a foreign visitor in awe. "Gigantic chaos, that is the first feeling I had in New York."

GREENWICH AVENUE from 8th Street station in winter dress, a photograph taken by Arthur D. Chapman, whose pictures of New York during the teens belong to the best records of the city's life. This street is like one in Berlin, Budapest, or Vienna, with leisurely traffic and people not in a hurry. So idyllic, it is hard to believe that this is New York, "the wonderful, cruel, enchanting, bewildering, fatal, great city"—a description by O. Henry.

SEVENTH AVENUE AT 50TH STREET
The huge car barn was situated where today stands the Roxy Theater, with the Hotel Taft to the left.

FIFTH AVENUE AT 48TH STREET
On the left is the Collegiate Church of St. Nicholas and throngs of strolling worshipers on Easter Sunday.

THE LEADER OF THE FREE WORLD. President Woodrow Wilson at Versailles, acknowledging the cheers of the crowds the very week that Theodore Roosevelt died in America.

TWELVE DAYS AFTER THEODORE ROOSEVELT'S DEATH the Peace Conference met in Paris. On January 18, 1919, delegates of twenty-seven nations filed into the Clock Room of the French Foreign Office for the opening session. Electing Georges Clemenceau, the Prime Minister of France, as their president, the making of a new world was begun.

A SHORT SELECTED BIBLIOGRAPHY

ROOSEVELT'S OWN WRITINGS

The Works of Theodore Roosevelt (National Edition, ed. Hermann Hagedorn, New York, 1926), in 20 volumes, includes his literary output: his books, and some of his addresses and articles.

Presidential Addresses (Review of Reviews Co., 1910), in 8 volumes, contains his important political pronouncements.

His magazine articles are in *The Outlook*, the *Metropolitan Magazine*, and other publications.

His *An Autobiography* (1926) is an attempt to recount the events of his life.

The Letters of Theodore Roosevelt, in 8 volumes, a superbly edited work (ed. Elting E. Morrison, John M. Blum, and John J. Buckley, Cambridge, 1951), contains most of his important letters. His correspondence of some 100,000 pieces is in the Theodore Roosevelt Collection of the Library of Congress. It was microfilmed for the Theodore Roosevelt Collection of the Harvard College Library.

Other letter collections which preceded the definitive edition are: *Letters from Theodore Roosevelt to Anna Roosevelt Cowles* (1924), *Theodore Roosevelt's Letters to His Children* (1919), *Letters to Kermit from Theodore Roosevelt* (1946), and *Selections from the Correspondence of Theodore Roosevelt and Henry Cabot Lodge* (2 vols., 1925).

REMINISCENCES OF THE FAMILY

His daughter, Alice Longworth, wrote *Crowded Hours* (1933). His son Kermit published an excellent account of the South American expedition, *The Happy Hunting Grounds* (1920). His sister Corinne Robinson penned *My Brother Theodore Roosevelt* (New York, 1921). His daughter-in-law, Eleanor Roosevelt, wrote *Day Before Yesterday* (New York, 1959), a biography of Theodore, Jr., with many amusing sidelights on her father-in-law.

BIOGRAPHIES AND OTHER WORKS

The official biography, *Theodore Roosevelt and His Time*, by Joseph J. Bishop (2 vols. New York, 1920), is what one expects of it. Lord Charnwood's *Theodore Roosevelt* (1923) leaves much to be desired. Hermann Hagedorn's *Roosevelt in the Bad Lands* (Boston, 1921) is the best work on that period of Roosevelt's life. *Theodore Roosevelt, A Biography*, by Henry F. Pringle (1931), is entertaining, but not always fair.

During the last few years a number of books have come out which have great merit.

Carleton Putnam's projected four-volume work will be—when completed—without question the outstanding Roosevelt biography. So far only one volume, *The Formative Years 1858–1886* (New York, 1958), has appeared.

Edward Wagenknecht's *The Seven Worlds of Theodore Roosevelt* (1958) is eminently readable.

George E. Mowry's *The Era of Theodore Roosevelt 1900–1912* (New York, 1958) is a scholarly account in the best tradition of Roosevelt's political life. Professor Mowry's previous book, *Theodore Roosevelt and the Progressive Movement* (Wisconsin, 1946), is a superb thesis on the subject.

Howard K. Beale's *Theodore Roosevelt and the Rise of America to World Power* (1956) is excellent.

Hermann Hagedorn's *The Roosevelt Family of Sagamore Hill* (New York, 1954) draws a warm and vivid picture of the Roosevelts' home life.

John Morton Blum's slim volume, *The Republican Roosevelt* (Cambridge, 1954), is a brilliant study. The same author's essays in *The Letters of Theodore Roosevelt* are the best of their kind.

BOOKS BY THOSE WHO KNEW HIM

Everyone who was near Roosevelt wrote about him. Reminiscences of politicians and writers are legion.

Mark Sullivan pictured him amusingly in chapters of his five-volume social history, *Our Times* (1926–1935). Archibald W. Butt, in *Taft and Roosevelt: The Intimate Letters of Archie Butt, Military Aide* (1930), reveals the relation of the two Presidents.

Some of the other notable memoirs: Richard Harding Davis, *Notes of a War Correspondent* (1910); Chauncey M. Depew, *My Memories of Eighty Years* (1922); Joseph B. Foraker, *Notes of a Busy Life* (1916); John Hay, *Letters and Diaries* (1908); Herman Henry Kohlsaat, *From McKinley to Harding* (1923); Robert M. La Follette, *Autobiography* (1911); Thomas C. Platt, *The Autobiography of Thomas Collier Platt* (1910); George Haven Putnam, *Memories of a Publisher* (1915); Henry L. Stoddard, *As I Knew Them* (1927); Oscar Straus, *Under Four Administrations* (1922); Mrs. William Howard Taft, *Recollections of Full Years* (1914); William Allen White, *Marks in a Pageant* (1928); Owen Wister, *The Story of a Friendship* (1930).

7918

DATE DUE

6515

B
Roosevelt

Lorant, Stefan
Life and Times of
Theodore Roosevelt